W9-BDH-909

TIME *and* ETERNITY

The fusion of the material and the spiritual into the organic, living unity called civilization is beautifully propounded by Christopher Dawson in this bold pilgrimage into metahistory.

Dawson examines the four vital essences of society—biology, geography, economy, and religion—and shows how they interact. He analyzes concepts of world history as diverse as those of Toynbee and St. Augustine. Most important, he harmonizes all these insights into a system that renders each meaningful today.

Dawson's unique ability to interpret the human record in the light of spiritual achievement, and his unparalleled skill in harmonizing all those disciplines through which man studies man, make *The Dynamics of World History* a superb adventure into human self-knowledge. A synthesis of some thirty-five years of scholarly writing, *Dynamics* finds in Christianity the historical apex of human knowledge and action . . . and in the fusion of time and eternity the touchstone of all progress.

•

"A master of understatement while uttering the most explosive ideas . . . the vastly erudite Christopher Dawson grows in stature with the years."

—*The Sign*

Other MENTOR OMEGA Books

A Preface to Metaphysics *by Jacques Maritain*

Seven lectures on metaphysics by the distinguished French Neo-Thomist. (#MP403—60¢)

American Catholic Dilemma *by Thomas F. O'Dea*

The Catholic contribution to American intellectual life, discussed by a well-known sociologist of Fordham University. (#MP404—60¢)

The Dead Sea Scrolls and Primitive Christianity
by Jean Danielou

A Jesuit Professor at the Catholic Institute of Paris discusses and analyzes the relations between the Essenes and the beginnings of Christianity.

(#MP405—60¢)

To Our Readers

We welcome your request for our free catalog of SIGNET and MENTOR books. If your dealer does not have the books you want, you may order them by mail, enclosing the list price plus 5¢ a copy to cover mailing. The New American Library of World Literature, Inc., P. O. Box 2310, Grand Central Station, New York 17, New York.

The
DYNAMICS
of
WORLD HISTORY

by

CHRISTOPHER DAWSON

Edited by John J. Mulloy

A MENTOR OMEGA BOOK
Published by the New American Library

From twenty centuries of literature and scholarship, Mentor Omega Books present a treasury of Catholic thought for the modern reader.

© Copyright Sheed & Ward Inc. 1956

All rights reserved. No part of this book may be reproduced without permission from the publisher. For information address Sheed & Ward Inc., 64 University Place, New York 3, New York.

Published as a MENTOR OMEGA BOOK
By Arrangement with Sheed & Ward Inc.

FIRST PRINTING, MARCH, 1962

MENTOR TRADEMARK REG. U.S. PAT. OFF. AND FOREIGN COUNTRIES
REGISTERED TRADEMARK—MARCA REGISTRADA
HECHO EN CHICAGO, U.S.A.

MENTOR OMEGA BOOKS are published by
The New American Library of World Literature, Inc.
501 Madison Avenue, New York 22, New York

PRINTED IN THE UNITED STATES OF AMERICA

INTRODUCTION

Two hundred years is a relatively brief space in the history of mankind upon the globe. But in that time a greater change has taken place in man's ways of living than in all the preceding centuries of recorded human existence. The inventions introduced by the scientific revolution of the past two centuries have transformed the face of nature and of human society, and in all the five continents people are being moulded by the standardizing influences of a technological civilization. Nor is it likely that the present movement of rapid social change will in any degree abate its speed. It is this fact which imparts a unique character to the social situation of the present moment.

But it has not been simply the scientific revolution which has shattered the patterns men have inherited from the past. Equally destructive have been the social and political upheavals of the past forty years. The impact of two world wars in one generation of the twentieth century and the development of totalitarian ideologies in Central and Eastern Europe have radically changed the structure of European society and fundamentally altered the balance of power on which European world hegemony rested. No longer is it possible for Western man to view the rest of the world from the eminence of a privileged position of superior power and wealth. Within Europe itself the hurricanes of war and revolution have levelled to the ground many of Europe's most historic institutions; while from without, the rising tide of Oriental nationalism and xenophobia has all but erased the islands of European culture and political power which previously existed in the East.

It is little wonder that such a situation has increasingly turned the attention of the educated layman and even the general public to questions concerning man's historical destiny and the meaning of the present moment in world history. If it no longer seems valid to accept the Progress theory of history which assured the man of the nineteenth century of the happy outcome of the changes he saw taking place around him, in what new light shall the man of the twentieth century view the revolutionary developments of the present era?

It is in reply to this question that contemporary philosophers of history have obtained an ever widening audience for their views: whether the idea be that of the inevitable decline of each historic civilization described with such compelling imagery by Oswald Spengler, or the view of Arnold Toynbee that each civilization achieves its individual character by overcoming the obstacles that confront it, or the thesis of F. S. C. Northrop that East and West are by their nature meant to complement each other in the formation of a future world civilization. And these, of course, are but a few of the interpreters of history and culture who have attempted to explain the meaning of the changes taking place in the rapidly expanding universe of modern civilization.

How does the work of Christopher Dawson fit into this picture? By what particular features may his approach to the interpretation of history be defined? What does he believe to be the elements most important for cultural progress, or does he consider progress on the broad scale to be possible in history? How does his thought compare with that of other "metahistorians" [1] and philosophers of culture?

It is to provide an adequate answer to these and other questions of a similar nature that the present volume has been assembled. Selected from Mr. Dawson's writings over the last thirty-five years, beginning with his earliest published article in *The Sociological Review* in 1921 ("Sociology and the Theory of Progress") and concluding with his critique of Arnold Toynbee's *Study of History* in the April 1955 issue of *International Affairs,* the book aims to present a representative cross section of his thought on world history.

Between these two dates practically the whole of Christopher Dawson's career as a writer lies; during this period, in books and magazine articles, he has formulated a conception of world history that, in scope and in vision, ranks with the work of Spengler, Northrop and Toynbee. However, the significance of his thought as a philosopher of history and culture has been obscured by the fact that the majority of his books have been devoted specifically to two major tasks: (1) tracing the historical development of Western culture, and (2) analyzing the causes of the contemporary world crisis. In several of his earlier works, however, and in many uncollected articles, Mr. Dawson has dealt with other sub-

[1] See below, "The Problem of Metahistory," pp. 281–87.

jects that are of vital interest to students of comparative culture. It is with the purpose of bringing into focus these neglected aspects of Mr. Dawson's thought, and calling them particularly to the attention of anthropologists and sociologists, that the present selection has been made.

First in these fields of Christopher Dawson's thought on comparative culture is what we may call "The Movement of World History," his investigation of the cross-fertilizing contacts between different civilizations and cultures, and the enlargement in the area of cultural communication which these contacts bring about. His first volume, *The Age of the Gods* (1928), subtitled "A Study in the Origins of Culture in Prehistoric Europe and the Ancient East," which narrates the development of civilization down to about 1000 B.C., is the largest work he has devoted to this subject. However, *Progress and Religion,* published in the following year (1929), treats in more condensed form the intermingling of sociological with intellectual factors in the development of civilization, providing an account from primitive times down to the modern period; and it is in this volume that Mr. Dawson has afforded us the best synthetic view of his conception of world history. *Progress and Religion* has served as a seed bed for several of his later works, for the ideas presented there in spare but impressive outline are in these other volumes elaborated and developed. Possibly the most important of these later books for the present topic is *Enquiries* (1933). In addition to three or four longer papers illustrating the main points in his conception of world history, it contains several penetrating studies of social and religious movements.

The second area of Christopher Dawson's thought which the present volume is intended to illustrate may be called "The Dynamics of Culture." Since it is upon his philosophy of culture that Mr. Dawson draws for the principles that govern his approach to history, we shall provide an extended analysis of this philosophy in a later part of the present book. For an understanding of Dawson's view of the dynamics of culture, the three volumes we have mentioned above and also the first series of his Gifford Lectures, *Religion and Culture* (1948), are indispensable. Both the first and third sections of the present selection—"The Sociological Foundations of History" and "Urbanism and the Organic Nature of Culture"—contain articles of great significance for this topic.

Then, of course, there is the area of Dawson's work concerned with evaluation and criticism of various conceptions of world history. Previously his contributions to this subject have been so scattered through different books and magazines that we believe that a most valuable feature of the present work lies in the fact they are now brought together under one cover. The last two sections of the present volume —grouped under the heading "Conceptions of World History"—contain all of Dawson's articles in this area, we believe, with the exception of one on Hegel's philosophy of history, which has very recently been published in *Understanding Europe* and thus is readily available to the reader.

A fourth general topic dealt with rather extensively in Christopher Dawson's writings on world history is what is usually termed Comparative Religion. From the viewpoint of Mr. Dawson's approach, however, it might more accurately be called the Meaning of Mankind's Religious Experience. Two volumes are particularly rich with his insights into this problem: *Progress and Religion,* which devotes a third of its pages to this topic, and *Religion and Culture,* where the whole book is devoted in one way or another to its consideration. For our purposes we have chosen a more condensed form of his interpretation of this subject, taken from a small book published in 1931 under the title *Christianity and the New Age.* In this essay, which gives special attention to primitive religion and the Oriental world religions, he shows the unity which lies behind man's developing understanding of religious reality and traces the basic needs in human nature which all religions attempt to satisfy. In some ways this essay of Dawson's suggests the goal which Etienne Gilson set himself in the field of philosophy in such a volume as *The Unity of Philosophical Experience* or, even closer to the subject of comparative religion, in *God and Philosophy.*

Organization of the Book

In organizing this volume to present the main ideas of Christopher Dawson's thought in these four areas, we have preferred to bring together articles dealing with the same general subject matter rather than to present the selections in the chronological order of their publication.[2] The gen-

[2] See below, "Sources," for the original date and place of publication of each article.

eral plan of the book is to illustrate how Christopher Dawson's view of history is built upon his conception of the sociological factors that are the dynamics for historical events and movements. We therefore devote the first section of the book to Dawson's discussion of the nature of sociology and the elements in culture and society which he finds most significant; this is followed by a presentation of certain aspects of world history as influenced by factors of a sociological nature. The third section considers a topic of central importance in Dawson's sociology and one which he believes has had far-reaching influence on the course of history: the nature of urban development, and the need for a highly developed civilization, if it is not to become abstract and formless, to retain its roots in the regional environment from which it has sprung.

These three sections constitute the first major division of this work, called "Toward a Sociology of History." Of the articles it contains, the one entitled "Religion and the Life of Civilization" comes closest to giving us (although in an abbreviated form) Dawson's own conception of world history. It thus may be used for comparison with those articles in Part II which provide a critique of the views of other contemporary interpreters of world history.

This second major division of the volume—"Conceptions of World History"—approaches history from the viewpoint of ideas men have held concerning its significance rather than from the standpoint of actual human societies in contact with their environment. It illustrates the manner in which the history of mankind is affected as much by intellectual forces as by realities of a more material nature. But it also shows that a purely philosophical approach to history is likely to result, as it did in Greece and India, in the denial that history has any ultimate significance and in the acceptance of the principle of recurrence rather than progress as the key to historical events. Only when a conception of history is based upon a regard for sociological facts can it avoid the explaining away of history which is the pitfall of the philosopher.

It was precisely because the Christian view of history was rooted in the social tradition of the Hebrew Law and the Prophets and had developed from the historical experience of a particular people, the Jews, that it was able to break through the closed circle of the ancient world's "recurrence" conception of history. Because its ideas were not mere philosophic abstractions, but grounded in social and historical realities, Christianity laid the foundations for a view of history which is both universal and progressive: that is, it embraced the whole of humankind in its vision and it saw history as moving toward an ultimate goal of unique and transcendent significance.

This new attitude toward history introduced by the Judaeo-Christian tradition has become the source of the intense interest in the meaning of history which distinguishes Western culture from the civilizations of the Orient and has resulted in an increasingly rich development in Western philosophies of history from St. Augustine down to Karl Marx and Arnold Toynbee. (It will be noted that two of the articles devoted to the Christian interpretation of history in Part II of this volume are at the same time discussions of the influence of the Christian view of history upon social and historical thought in the West.) As a result of its universal and progressive view of history, and the social activity and historical dynamism which this view has engendered, Western culture has had a more revolutionary impact upon mankind than any other civilization and has gradually brought the other world cultures into a single area of communication with itself.

Thus the link between the two major divisions of the present volume is to be found in the emphasis they both place on sociological factors in history, whether those factors are manifested directly in historical developments or are mediated through the support they provide to world-transforming historical ideas. This emphasis on culture and sociological factors does not mean that the intellectual life of man is merely determined by material conditions, as Marx would claim, but it does signify that ideas do not grow and develop as social forces or exercise their full influence unless they are supported by a social tradition and possess some vital communion with the life of the particular society they seek to influence.

Regarded as a whole, there is a progress from sociology to world history in the general plan of the present volume, and a linking up of material factors in cultural development with those of a more intellectual nature.[3]

JOHN J. MULLOY

[3] For the interrelation between sociology and history in Christopher Dawson's thought, see below, pages 403–57.

CONTENTS

Part One: Towards a Sociology of History

PART I : Towards a Sociology of History

SECTION I: THE SOCIOLOGICAL
FOUNDATIONS OF HISTORY

1
The Sources of Culture Change

AFTER a century and more of historical specialism and archaeological research, of the minute criticism of documents and sources, the time has come when it is becoming possible to reap the fruits of this intensive labour, and to undertake some general synthesis of the new knowledge of man's past that we have acquired. It is a truism that we cannot understand the present without a knowledge of the past or the part without the whole, but previous to our own age it has been difficult to realize this. Men were forced to rest content with the history of a few favoured peoples and exceptional periods—like classical Greece and Rome or our own immediate past—that were islands of light in a sea of darkness. But now, thanks not only to the sensational discoveries of the great civilizations of the Ancient East, but even more to the patient investigation of the dry bones of archaeology—literal bones and fragments of pottery and rude implements—a general vision of the whole past of our civilization has become possible. There is still no lack of gaps in our knowledge, there is an infinity of problems that still await solution, but at least the broad outlines are there, and no educated person need any longer be ignorant of the primary foundations on which our civilization has been built up.

The practical importance of this knowledge is obvious. If we have not a general framework into which to fit our knowledge of history, we are forced to fall back on some lesser unity in relation to which we order our ideas, and this lesser unity will of course be the national state. During the last two centuries the history of Europe has been given an almost exclusively national interpretation. And since the unit is a political one, the method of interpretation has tended to be political also, so that history has often sunk to the level of political propaganda and even some of the greatest of nineteenth century historians—such as Macaulay, Froude, Treitschke, even Mommsen himself—have been unashamed political partisans.

This state of things was one of the great predisposing causes of the late War,[1] and it is certain that the peoples of Europe will never be able to co-operate in peace, so long as they have no knowledge of their common cultural tradition and no revelation of the unity of European civilization. Now the alternative to the nationalist conception of history is the cultural or sociological one, which goes behind the political unit and studies that fundamental social unity which we term a culture.

I. *The Nature of Culture.* What is a culture? A culture is a common way of life—a particular adjustment of man to his natural surroundings and his economic needs. In its use and modification it resembles the development of a biological species, which, as Dr. Regan pointed out in his address to the British Association in 1925, is primarily due, not to change in structure, but to the formation of a community, either with new habits, or in a new and restricted environment. And just as every natural region tends to possess its characteristic forms of animal and vegetable life, so too will it possess its own type of human society. Not that man is merely plastic under the influence of his material environment. He moulds it, as well as being moulded by it. The lower the culture the more passive it is. But the higher culture will express itself through its material circumstance, as masterfully and triumphantly as the artist through the medium of his material.

It is true that three of the main influences which form and modify human culture are the same as in the case of the formation of an animal species. They are (1) race, i.e. the

---

[1] World War I.

genetic factor; (2) environment, i.e. the geographical factor; (3) function or occupation, i.e. the economic factor. But in addition to these there is a fourth element—thought or the psychological factor—which is peculiar to the human species and the existence of which frees man from the blind dependence on material environment which characterizes the lower forms of life. It is this factor which renders possible the acquisition of a growing capital of social tradition, so that the gains of one generation can be transmitted to the next, and the discoveries or new ideas of an individual can become the common property of the whole society. In this way a human culture is able to modify itself more rapidly and adapt itself more successfully to a new environment by an inheritance of acquired characteristics, such as does not seem to exist under the purely biological law of development which governs animal species. The formation of a culture is due to the interaction of all these factors: it is a fourfold community—for it involves in varying degrees a community of work and a community of thought as well as a community of place and a community of blood. Any attempt to explain social development in terms of one of these to the exclusion of the rest leads to the error of racial or geographical or economic determinism or to no less false theories of abstract intellectual progress.

At present the dominant fashion is to look to the racial factor as the *deus ex machina* of the human drama. Yet race is itself but the product of the process of interaction that we have mentioned. In the address to the British Association to which I have already referred, Dr. Tate Regan shows how various species and subspecies of fishes have been differentiated owing to their segregation in particular areas and the corresponding variation of their habits. Thus the plaice of the Baltic have become differentiated from those of the North Sea, and the colonies of freshwater char in the lakes of Great Britain and Ireland, which have been segregated since the glacial period, have acquired each their special group characteristics.

Now the same process occurs in the formation of human races. A particular way of life in a particular environment produces a specialized human type if it is continued over a long enough course of time. Thus the Mongol is the result of a uniform way of life on the steppes of Eastern Central Asia, a totally different way of life in the tropical forest has produced the Negro, and so on. In other words, the primitive cultures of the nature peoples have endured for such vast periods that their human products have become stabilized as fixed types, which have remained the raw material, as it were, of all the later developments. And every subsequent culture, in so far as it involves a way of life peculiar to itself, tends to produce a new racial type, even though it does not enjoy uniform conditions long enough to be fixed. It may be that the unscientific habit of talking about "the Latin race" or "the Anglo-Saxon race," instead of the Latin or "Anglo-Saxon" culture, is due to a half-conscious popular realization of this fact.

It must of course be admitted that many racial characteristics, such as skin color, and probably nose form, are due to a purely passive reception of climate and geographical influences. Nevertheless, in the formation of any culture even of the lowest type, such as the ways of living of the prehistoric ancestors of the Negroid or Mongoloid peoples, human activity and spontaneous co-operation with nature take a leading part. Perhaps no culture is more completely controlled by, and in harmony with, its environment than that of the Esquimaux. He belongs to the Arctic no less than the animals on whom he is a parasite—the seal and the reindeer. At every point—in his use of skin for boats and tents and clothing, of bone for weapons and tools, of blubber for warmth and light—he is bound down to an absolute dependence on the little that nature has given him. Yet his culture is not a necessary result of climatic and economic determinism, it is a work of art, a triumph of human inventiveness and endurance, and it is the fruit of an age-long cultural tradition, which may well stretch back as far in time and space as the Magdalenian culture of the European glacial age.

And here, too, we see that a culture may be no less a fixed type than is a race. When once a new way of life has been discovered, when man has attained some permanent state of equilibrium with the external world, he will preserve it indefinitely from age to age, and any change will come, not from within, but from the foreign pressure of some external culture. Today the Esquimaux are learning a new manner of life, they are becoming civilized, but at the same time and for the same reason they are a dying race.

II. *The Problem of the Change and Progress of Cultures.*

In spite of this tendency towards the fixation of culture in unchanging social types, it is impossible to deny the reality and importance of cultural progress. This progress is not, however, as the philosophers of the eighteenth century believed, a continuous and uniform movement, common to the whole race, and as universal and necessary as a law of nature. It is rather an exceptional condition, due to a number of distinct causes, which often operate irregularly and spasmodically. Just as civilization itself is not a single whole, but a generalization from a number of historic cultures each with its own limited life, so Progress is an abstract idea derived from a simplification of the multiple and heterogeneous changes through which the historic societies have passed.

Hence in place of a single uniform law of Progress it is necessary to distinguish the following main types of social change:

(A) The simple case of a people that develops its way of life in its original environment without the intrusion of human factors from outside. This is exemplified in those primitive race-forming "precultures," of which we have spoken above.

(B) The case of a people which comes into a new geographical environment and re-adapts its culture in consequence. This is the simplest type of cultural change, but it is of great importance. There is a constant process of steppe peoples entering the forest, and vice versa, of mountaineers descending into the plains, and inland peoples coming into contact with the sea. The consequences are most striking when the climatic differences of the two regions are widely different, as in the case of the invasion of India by peoples from the steppes and plateaux of Central Asia.

(C) The case of two different peoples, each with its own way of life and social organization, which mix with one another usually as a result of conquest, occasionally as a result of peaceful contact. In any case, this involves the preceding factor (B) also, for at least one of the two peoples.

This is the most typical and important of all the causes of culture change, since it sets up an organic process of fusion and change, which transforms both the people and the culture, and produces a new cultural entity in a comparatively short space of time. It is the origin of practically all those sudden flowerings of new civilization, which impress us as almost miraculous (e.g. *le miracle Grec*). It is possible to compare this process of fusion of peoples and cultures in very numerous instances in different ages and in different parts of the world, and everywhere we see the cycle of change passing through the same phases and lasting for an approximately similar time. First there comes a period of several centuries of silent growth during which a people lives on the tradition of the older culture, either that which they have brought with them, or that which they found in the land. Secondly there comes a period of intense cultural activity, when the new forms of life created by the vital union of two different peoples and cultures burst into flower; when we see the reawakening of the forms of the old culture fertilized by contact with a new people, or the creative activity of a new people stimulated by contact with the old autochthonous culture. It is a time of great achievement, of abounding vitality, but also of violent conflicts and revolts, of spasmodic action and brilliant promise that has no fulfillment. Finally the culture reaches maturity, either by the absorption of the new elements by the original people and its culture, or by the attainment of a permanent balance between the two, the stabilization of a new cultural variation.

(D) The case of a people that adopts some element of material culture which has been developed by another people elsewhere. This is a comparatively superficial change compared with the last one, but it is of great importance as showing the close interdependence of cultures. We see how in the past the use of metals, agriculture and irrigation, a new weapon or the use of the horse in war, have spread from one end of the Old World to the other with amazing rapidity. Moreover, such material changes bring with them profound social changes, since they may alter the whole system of social organization. We have seen instances of such change almost in our own times; in the case of the adoption of the horse by the Indians of the Plains, and the spread of the use of firearms and of European clothing among primitive peoples. But it is remarkable how often such external change leads not to social progress, but to social decay. As a rule, to be progressive change must come from within.

(E) The case of a people which modifies its way of life owing to the adoption of new knowledge or beliefs, or to some change in its view of life and its conception of reality. Up to this point it may seem that the process of culture change is a rigidly deterministic one, and leaves no room for any free moral or intellectual progress.

For it might be thought that if the highest products of a culture are the flowers of a social organism that has had its roots in particular geographical and ethnological circumstances, no permanent and objective progress will be achieved and the greatest works of art and thought will simply reproduce in a more sophisticated form the results of the past experience of the organism. Certainly we must admit that every past condition will express itself in the life-impulses and life-concepts of a society, and that thus the cultural achievements of a people are largely determined by the past. But this does not occur mechanically. The existence of Reason increases the range of possibilities in the fulfillment of instinctive purpose. An old impulse acting in a new environment, different from that to which it was originally adapted, may be not merely a decadent survival, but a stepping-stone to the acquisition of new powers and to some new conception of reality. Thus there is a continual enlargement of the field of experience, and, thanks to Reason, the new does not simply replace the old, but is compared and combined with it. The history of mankind, and still more of civilized mankind, shows a continuous process of integration, which, even though it seems to work irregularly, never ceases. For Reason is itself a creative power which is ever organizing the raw material of life and sensible experience into the ordered cosmos of an intelligible world—a world which is not a mere subjective image, but corresponds in a certain measure to the objective reality. A modern writer has said: "The mind of man seems to be of a nature to assimilate itself to the universe; we belong to the world; the whole is mirrored in us. Therefore, when we bend our thoughts on a limited object, we concentrate faculties which are naturally endowed with infinite correspondences." [2]

We cannot shut our eyes to the significance of this steadily growing vision of Reality, which is at once the condition and the result of the life-purpose of human society.

It is easy for us to see how in the case of modern science or Greek philosophy a culture has been directly moulded by the influence of thought. But the importance of the psychological factor is not confined to purely intellectual knowledge,

[2] *Times Literary Supplement,* 1923, p. 330.

it is manifested equally in the religious outlook, which dominates even the most primitive cultures. Every religion embodies an attitude to life and a conception of reality, and any change in these brings with it a change in the whole character of the culture, as we see in the case of the transformation of ancient civilization by Christianity, or the transformation of the society of Pagan Arabia by Islam. Thus the prophet and the religious reformer, in whom a new view of life—a new *revelation*—becomes explicit, is perhaps the greatest of all agents of social change, even though he is himself the product of social causes and the vehicle of an ancient cultural tradition.

And thus the great stages of world-culture are linked with changes in man's vision of Reality. The primitive condition of food-gathering and hunting peoples does not necessarily imply reasonable purpose or any reflective vision of Reality; consequently it does not imply civilization. The dawn of true civilization came only with the discovery of natural laws, or rather of the possibility of man's fruitful co-operation with the powers of Nature. This was the foundation of the primitive cultures of Elam and Babylonia and Egypt. To it belongs the discovery of the higher agriculture, the working of metals and the invention of writing and the calendar, together with the institutions of kingship and priesthood and an organized state.

It governed the progress of civilization for thousands of years and only passed away with the coming of the new vision of Reality which began to transform the ancient world in the fifth and sixth centuries B.C.—the age of the Hebrew Prophets and the Greek Philosophers, of Buddha and Confucius, an age which marks the dawn of a new world.

—1928.

2

Sociology as a Science

SOCIOLOGY is the youngest of the sciences, and there are still many who question its right to be considered as a science at all. It is but a century since Auguste Comte announced the advent of the new science that was to be the keystone of the scientific edifice and the crown of man's intellectual achievement, and though the last hundred years have seen a great increase of interest in social questions and an enormous production of sociological and semi-sociological literature, there is still little prospect of the realization of his ideal. In fact, there has been, in some respects, a distinct retrogression from the position that had been reached in the middle of the last century. Sociology no longer possesses a clearly defined programme and method; it has become a vague term which covers a variety of separate subjects. Sociologists have abandoned the attempt to create a pure science of society and have directed themselves to the study of practical social questions.

Sociology seems in danger of becoming a scrap-heap on which are thrown any items that cannot otherwise be disposed. Nor is this the only danger. Even the writers who do deal with genuinely sociological problems frequently do so in an entirely unscientific way.

This is most unsatisfactory, not only from the point of view of the sociologist, but in relation to the scientific outlook in general. The problem of sociology is probably the most vital scientific issue of our time, for if we admit the impossibility of creating a scientific sociology we are confessing the failure of science to comprehend society and human culture. It is impossible to create a scientific civilization from outside by a development of the material resources and the external mechanism of society. There can be no scientific civilization without a science of society. You cannot plan the future of a society if you have no knowledge of the true nature of the society in question. Moreover, at the present day the plans of the economists are at the mercy of the policies of the politicians, and the politicians themselves are the instruments of a public opinion which is swayed by obscure and nonrational forces. The statesman who fails to understand these forces is a failure, but his failure is often less dangerous to society than the success of the "practical politician" who understands how to use these forces for his personal advancement without understanding their social significance.

The crisis of so-called scientific modern civilization is due to its combination of an elaborate technical and mechanical equipment with an almost complete lack of social direction. The societies of the past possessed their own organs of social direction and their formal principles of order, which were not indeed scientific, but were based on social tradition. Modern society has abandoned this social traditionalism in the name of rational principles, but it has done little to create the foundation of scientific sociology that these principles seem to demand. Instead of this our social order is still based on the political and moral dogmas of the philosophers of the eighteenth century. The doctrines of modern democracy are not a scientific theory, but a moral and semireligious creed which owes more than we generally realize to the personal inspiration of Rousseau and is hardly separable from the mystical Deism with which it was originally associated. This doctrine is, in reality, much further from scientific sociology than was the old Aristotelian political philosophy, which was, within its limits, firmly grounded on a basis of observed facts and a rational theory of social life and development. Moreover, the new movements that have arisen in opposition to the dominant theories of liberal democracy are also deficient in a pure sociological foundation, and are derived either from the economic theories of the nineteenth century or from the political philosophy of nationalism.

Thus we are faced by the contrast of a highly specialized development of scientific technique in the external conduct of life with an almost complete absence of scientific direction in regard to the life of society itself. And yet there can be no question of the vast resources of social knowledge that have been accumulated during the last century and more. The modern development of history and anthropology, of economics and the comparative study of religion is hardly less remarkable than that of the physical sciences. A new world has been opened to us in the past, and our resources for the understanding of human development and its social processes have been immeasurably increased. There is no *a priori* reason for excluding all this new knowledge from the field of science. It is genuine scientific knowledge, as reliable and as systematic in its own sphere as that of the physical sciences. It is no mere collection of scattered facts and subjective opinions, but an organized department of knowledge, or rather a number of such departments.

Why, then, need we despair of the science of society when the available resources of knowledge are so great and the need is so obvious? But the fact is that these conditions, that are at first sight so favourable, have actually been a hindrance rather than a help to the development of sociology. The most successful sciences are those, like physics and mechanics, which found their method before they were involved in a mass of detailed observation and before there was any question of using them for a practical or utilitarian purpose.

The development of sociology has followed the opposite course and has suffered accordingly. It started with an embarrassing wealth of material and a desire for premature practical results, but with no assured method. The besetting sin of the sociologist has been the attempt to play the part of a social reformer, whether, like Comte, he embarked on grandiose schemes for the reconstitution of society or, with the modern sociologist, he plunges into the practical work of civic reform.

The early sociologists were great systematizers with a gift for generalization that carried them far beyond the limits of sociology proper into the deep waters of ethics and metaphysics. They improvised a whole philosophy as a basis to their real work as sociologists, with the result that they came to think more of their philosophy than of sociology itself. Thus the efforts of the Encyclopaedists, the St. Simonians and the Positivists result in the creation of a theory of society which was at the same time a philosophy of history, a system of moral philosophy and a nontheological substitute for religion.

This identification of sociology with philosophy tended to bring the whole subject into discredit and caused a considerable body of opinion in the later nineteenth century to despair of the scientific possibilities of sociology, and to look instead to the new science of anthropology as an alternative. It caused sociologists themselves to react against the speculative tendencies of the earlier sociology, which they condemned as "armchair sociology," and to immerse themselves in detailed statistical and practical enquiries which alone seemed to offer a prospect of concrete results. But the new movement avoided rather than solved the real problem of scientific method, and it often involved a substitution of the study of social machinery for that of society itself. Nor did it even escape the old danger of abstract philosophical generalization. Modern English and American sociology remains to a great extent dependent on the old tradition of eighteenth-century moral philosophy. In America, especially, the ideal of the last generation even went so far on one occasion as to define sociology as "a moral philosophy conscious of its task." It is easy to understand how, under the existing circumstances, the sociologist was forced to look to an ethical ideal for guidance and help. But nothing could in fact be further from the ideal of scientific sociology and it led merely to the creation of a pragmatic system of social ethics that embodied all the impurities and confusions of thought that it is the purpose both of philosophy and science to eliminate.

The continental schools of sociology, on the other hand, have been far more conscious of the need for a strict definition of scientific method and for the delimitation of the province of sociology from both that of philosophy and that of the other social sciences. Hitherto, however, they have not been altogether successful, although they have accomplished much valuable work. Their efforts have been handicapped by the confusion that has characterized the development alike of modern philosophy and that of the social sciences. In the case of the latter there has been an overlapping, due in part to the riches of the available material, in part to uncertainty of method, and also in part to a non-scientific rivalry between the different sciences.

This has been most serious in the case of the two new sciences of sociology and anthropology, which have been, from the beginning, competitors in the same field. They started out, like rival prospectors, to establish as large a claim as possible in the unoccupied territories of the new world of knowledge; and consequently they both developed far more territory than they had the means to develop. Both of them take as their motto *"Nihil humani a me alienum puto."* The sociologist claims all social phenomena as his province, and there are few human phenomena that are not social. The anthropologist claims that his science is the science of man and of human development, and consequently includes everything from human palaeontology to the comparative study of religions.

It is obvious that if these claims are taken at their face value, neither science leaves any room for the other, except in so far as the sociologist does admit the existence of physical anthropology as an independent discipline. We may almost say that both sciences deal with the same subject, and that they differ only in the manner of their approach. In practice, however, a certain *modus vivendi* has been reached, although it is neither logical nor final. The anthropologist deals with primitive man and his society and culture, the sociologist with the more advanced cultures and with the phenomena of contemporary social life. The anthropologist has had somewhat the better of the bargain, since his material lends itself more easily to objective scientific study, and consequently he has done as much in recent years for sociological studies as the sociologist himself. This is particularly the case in America, where anthropologists, such as Kroeber, Wissler, Lowie and Goldenweiser, have produced works which are admirable introductions to sociological study and are far superior in scientific method to the average textbook of sociology.

This superiority is largely due to the fact that, in dealing with primitive culture, the anthropologist is not embarrassed by the rival claims of the historian and the archaeologist. The archaeologist and the anthropologist co-operate with one another in the study of primitive culture, and there is no attempt on the part of the one to dispense with the help of the other. The case of the sociologist is very different, through no fault of his own. It was hardly to be expected that the historian would welcome the co-operation of the sociologist, in the same way as the archaeologist and the prehistorian have welcomed that of the anthropologist.

The advent of sociology found history already in posses-sion of an established position and enjoying a well-earned prestige. It was regarded, not as a science, but as literature; it was a branch of the humanities, and as such must be judged by artistic rather than scientific standards. This con-ception goes back in origin to the historiography of the ancient world from which our own historical tradition is ultimately derived. To the Greeks history was a form of rhetoric and had nothing in common with science, which finds its true pattern in mathematics and geometry. Science is concerned with the universal; history with the particular. Science belongs to the world of absolute and eternal reality; history to the world of time and change. Science is Truth; history is Opinion. In this respect every Greek was a Platonist at heart and shared Plato's belief that the less a science has to do with facts which are inevitably subject to perturbation and change, the more perfect it is, and the more it immerses itself in the sensible world, the less right has it to be con-sidered scientific. Now this ideal, stripped of its metaphysical connotations, has been passed down by the scholars and scientists of the Renaissance to modern times, and has had a profound influence on current conceptions of history. Right down to our own days scholars have continued to repeat that history is not science, because there can be no science of the particular, and history is concerned with the study of particular events.

Consequently the historian is driven either to fall back on the old literary-rhetorical idea, which still possesses a distinguished champion in Professor Trevelyan at Cam-bridge,[1] or to return to the ethical ideal and like Acton to attribute to history the office of a moral censor, or, finally, with Croce to identify history with philosophical intuition.[2]

But none of these alternatives is really satisfactory to the

[1] *Clio, a Muse.*

[2] *Theory and History of Historiography* (Eng. trans., 1921).

modern historian, and the prevailing tendency is to maintain the independence of history at all costs by treating history as an end in itself.

The most distinguished representative of this tendency was the late Eduard Meyer.[3] His attitude to history was, indeed, that of the scientist rather than the man of letters, and has nothing in common with the literary-rhetorical ideal. But on the other hand he maintains the absolute dissimilarity of history from the other social sciences, and bases its claim to independence precisely on the old argument of its particular and individual character. Sociology and anthropology seek, no less than the sciences of nature, to submit human development to general laws and to order the multiplicity of social facts according to universal concepts. But in history there is no room for general laws or causal principles; its world is the world of chance and free human actions, and it cannot pass beyond this. That is why, he says, "the modern attempts to transform the essence of history, and to set before it other and 'higher' tasks, leave the historian unmoved; history exists once for all, such as it is, and will always maintain itself in this form, and the business of the historian is with things as they are and not with abstract theories. Whether history is valued more or less is a matter of no concern to him." [4]

But in reality, as J. B. Bury has pointed out, it is impossible to dismiss the question of the significance of history as a matter of no importance. If history has no end except the collection of facts for their own sake, it becomes merely an intellectual pastime, like stamp collecting. If it is to receive the respect that it has always claimed, it must mean something in terms of reason and have some relation to the social sciences. The fact is that this opposition of history and science ignores the whole change that has passed over the world of knowledge since modern science and modern history made their appearance. Modern science does not aim, like that of the Greeks, at the contemplation of unchanging truth. It is essentially inductive and experimental, and surveys the whole world of nature as it lives and moves. It is not satisfied with the establishment of a few abstract laws;

[3] See the Introduction to the third edition of his *History of Antiquity* (1910), especially ch. iii.

[4] *Ibid.*, p. 739.

it seeks to know all the facts about the world and to control the forces of nature. Moreover, it has been profoundly affected by the development of modern biology and the influence of the concept of evolution. The new sciences of living matter such as botany and zoology, and even non-biological sciences like astronomy and geology, are profoundly historical in spirit. They do not contemplate a static universe, but an evolving process in which the time factor is of primary importance.

And, on the other hand, modern history is no longer satisfied with rhetorical narrative or moral criticism. It seeks to understand the past rather as an organic process than as a mosaic of isolated facts. It tends to pay less attention than in the past to the superficial activity of politicians and diplomatists and more to the action of the permanent social and economic forces that determine the life of peoples. Above all, it is coming to accept the new concept of Culture which has been brought into currency by the anthropologists. It recognizes that the state is not, as the nineteenth-century historians believed, the ultimate social unit and the final end of historical study. The cultural unity is both wider and deeper than that of the state. It is not an intellectual abstraction or a by-product of the political process. It is itself the fundamental social reality on which all the other social phenomena are dependent.

History is, in fact, whether consciously or unconsciously, becoming the science of social development; not merely the science of the past, but the science of the whole human culture-process in so far as it can be studied by documentary evidence. Thus the old opposition between science and history is being done away and history is being brought into increasingly intimate relations with the other social sciences, and above all with sociology. History and sociology are, in fact, indispensable to one another. History without sociology is "literary" and unscientific, while sociology without history is apt to become mere abstract theorizing. Hitherto the greatest weakness of sociology has been its indifference to the facts of history. It has tended to manufacture a history of its own which will be the obedient servant of any theory it happens to propound. It is hardly possible to open a modern sociological treatise without coming across historical "facts" that are unknown to the historians and dogmatic solutions of historical problems which the historians themselves approach with the utmost diffidence.

This is the inevitable result of the mutual distrust between history and sociology and the attempt of each of them to assert its own independence and self-sufficiency. In reality sociology and history are two complementary parts of a single science—the science of social life. They differ, not in their subject matter, but in their method, one attempting a general systematic analysis of the social process, while the other gives a genetic description of the same process in detail. In other words, sociology deals with the structure of society, and history with its evolution, so that they are related to one another in the same way as general biology is related to the study of organic evolution.

Thus a sociological study of Greek culture would concern itself primarily with the organic structure of Greek society —with the city-state and its organization, the Greek family and its economic foundation, the functional differentiation of Greek society, the place of slavery in the social order, and so forth; but all these elements must be studied genetically and in relation to the general development of Greek culture on the basis of the material provided by the historian; while the latter, on his side, requires the help of the social analysis of the sociologist in order to interpret the facts that he discovers and to relate them to the organic whole of Greek culture, which is the final object of his study. It is for the sociologist to define the form of a culture and for the historian to describe its content.

Actually, however, the sociologists have accomplished very little in this direction. As we have seen, the discovery and the systematic analysis of the cultural unit have been due to the work of the anthropologists rather than of the sociologists. The latter have been apt to despise such comparatively modest tasks and have aimed at something much more ambitious. From the beginning sociology has been haunted by the dream of explaining social phenomena by the mathematical and quantitative methods of the physical sciences and thus creating a science of society which will be completely mechanistic and determinist. The path of sociology is strewn with the corpses of defunct systems of "social physics," "social energetics" and "social mechanics," and their failure does little to discourage fresh adventures. Such systems have little use for history or for social reality; they content themselves with generalizations that have no significance and with "laws" which are nothing but false analogies. Thus one writer maintains that social association is a variety of "the law of molecular gravitation" (Carey), another that culture is nothing but an apparatus for the transformation of solar energy into human energy (Carver and Ostwald), while Winiarsky argued that social change proceeds according to the laws of thermodynamics. Such extravagances explain the distrust shown towards sociology by the historians, for their experience of the complex reality of the social process makes them naturally hostile to the crude simplicity of pseudo-scientific generalizations.

Yet, on the other hand, it is equally impossible to understand the life of man and society without the help of the natural sciences. In a thousand ways human life is conditioned and determined by material factors, and there is a legitimate materialism which consists in the definition and analysis of these relations. History by itself is not enough, for it is impossible to understand a society or a culture in purely historical terms. Underlying the historical process and the higher activities of civilized life there are the primary relations of a society to its natural environment and its functional adaptation to economic ends. The sociologist has to study not only the inter-social relations of man with man, but also that primary relation of human life to its natural environment which is the root and beginning of all culture. Here sociology approaches the standpoint of the natural sciences and comes closer to the biologist than to the historian, for the study of a society in its mutual relation with its geographical environment and its economic activity has a real analogy with the biologist's study of an organism in relation to its environment and its function.

The application of this "biological" method to the phenomena of society was the work of Frederic Le Play, who more than any other sociologist may be regarded as the discoverer of a scientific method of social study. In this respect he compares very favourably with his more famous contemporaries such as Marx, Spencer and Buckle. He succeeded in giving an economic interpretation of society which avoids the one-sided determinism of the Marxian hypothesis; he showed the influence of geographical factors in social life in a far more exact and scientific way than Buckle or Ratzel, and he provided a biological interpretation of society which had nothing in common with the semi-scientific, semi-philosophical generalizations of writers such as Herbert Spencer. Le Play took as his unit the study of the family in its concrete geographical and economic circumstances and analyzed its social life and structure in terms of Place and Work. His great work, *Les Ouvrièrs Européens,* which appeared in 1855, contains a detailed study of thirty-six typical workers' families chosen from every part of Europe from Eastern Russia to the North of England and from every stage of culture from the Tartar herdsmen of the Steppes to the artisans and factory workers of Western Europe.[5] He studied these, not at second hand, through statistics and blue-books, but by the direct observation of their way of life and by a meticulous study of their family budgets, which he used as a basis for the quantitative analysis of the facts of family life. Le Play's method of social analysis affords an insight into just those fundamental social realities which so often escape the notice of the historian and the student of politics.

But although Le Play's method provides a genuinely scientific means for the study of society, it is not an exhaustive one. It required to be completed by a similar study and analysis of the other social units besides the family —the rural community, the city with its region, and the people and the state, and finally by an historical analysis of the social development and the cultural traditions of the society as a whole. Owing to his concentration on the family, Le Play and his school tended to overestimate the importance of the economic and geographical factors and to neglect the contribution of history. Not that Le Play was in any sense a materialist. He avoided the pitfall of natural-istic determinism which has been the downfall of so many sociologists, and fully realized the autonomous character of the moral and religious element in social life. But he conceived this in a static form, as an invariable which governs social life from outside without entering into it.

But a culture is not merely a community of work and a community of place; it is also, and above all, a community

---

[5] These were selections from the three hundred monographs that he had actually prepared.

of thought, and it is seen and known best in its higher spiritual activities, to which alone the name of Culture was first applied. It is impossible to understand or explain society by its material factors alone without considering the religious, intellectual and artistic influences which determine the form of its inner cultural life.

Even if we consider society in its simplest form—the family —we still find these factors intervening in a decisive way. Not only do the religious and moral beliefs of a society always affect the structure and life of the family, but in some cases, as in China and in classical antiquity, the family was itself a religious unit and its whole life was consecrated by religious rites and based on religious sanctions.

It may be said that it is not the business of a sociologist to concern himself with religious beliefs or philosophical theories or literary and artistic traditions, since they lie outside his province and are incapable of scientific definition or quantitative analysis; yet, on the other hand, it seems absurd for him to study the physical environment of a society and to neglect the spiritual forces that condition its psychic life. The primary task of sociology is, no doubt, the study of the social structure, but this structure, on the one hand, rests on the material foundation of geographical environment and economic function, and, on the other, is itself the foundation of a spiritual superstructure which embodies the higher cultural values. If we isolate society from its material body and its cultural soul, we have nothing left but an abstraction. To see the Greek city, for example, in its social reality we must view it at once as a product of the earth and as an embodiment of Hellenism, like Erectheus, the hero-king of Athens, who was the child of the Earth Goddess and the foster-son of Pallas Athene.

The intrusion of these qualitatively distinct categories or orders of being into the sociological field is a great stumbling-block in the social sciences. The natural scientist has a completely homogeneous material in the material phenomena that he investigates; so also has the philosopher in the region of ideas; but the sociologist has to deal impartially with material and spiritual factors, with things and ideas, with moral and economic values, with all the multifarious experience of the two-sided nature of man.

Sociologists have always been conscious of this problem, and the spectacle of the brilliant results attained by physical science in its uniform field of study has often tempted them to find a way out of their difficulties by an arbitrary or one-sided simplification of their data. There is something very attractive about a "simple" explanation of the social process which treats the relation of the different factors as one of simple causal dependence and regards one of them as absolute and the rest as secondary derivations from it.

The most popular type of "simple" explanation is, of course, the materialist one, which attempts to deduce the whole social process from economic or geographical or racial factors, and relegates the cultural superstructure to a lower plane of reality as a subjective reflection of material conditions. The classical example of this is the Marxian theory, which reduces both history and society to their economic elements and regards the spiritual element in culture as secondary and derivative. In the words of Marx, "the mode of production in material life determines the character of the social, political and spiritual processes of life. It is not the consciousness of men that determines their existence, but their existence that determines their consciousness . . . with the change of the economic foundation the entire immense superstructure is more or less rapidly transformed." [6]

Now the error of this method of interpretation does not consist in the view that the ideological aspects of culture have a material basis in the economic life of society, but in the assertion of an absolute causal dependence which denies the independent significance of the spiritual factor in society. On the one hand, the concept of culture is arbitrarily impoverished by being emptied of all the values that are not explicable in economic terms, and on the other the economic category is arbitrarily expanded in order to include a whole series of non-economic elements.

This fallacy is not peculiar to the Marxists; we find it equally in the theories that profess to explain the whole development of culture on racial grounds and which use the Aryan race or the Nordic type as the *deus ex machina* of the historical process. Such theories explain everything, but also they explain nothing; they are like the conjuror's hat, which is equally capable of producing a cabbage or a white rabbit, as the occasion demands.

[6] *Zur Kritik der Politischen Oekonomie* (Introduction).

At the opposite pole of these materialistic simplifications is the idealist simplification which deduces the social process from the spiritual element in culture. To Hegel and his followers History is the progressive self-manifestation of absolute Mind. Each culture or people is a successive proposition in the process of a cosmic dialectic, and the material aspects of culture are merely the embodiment of the immanent idea. Such theories are now almost entirely discredited; nevertheless, we must remember that they played an essential part in the development of their apparent opposite—the dialectical materialism of Marx. Moreover, although the historical panlogism of the Hegelians is looked on by sociologists today merely as an historical curiosity, its elder rival, the rationalist idealism of the Liberal Enlightenment, still preserves its prestige in spite of all the ridicule and argument that have been directed against it from the time of Burke and de Maistre to our own days. This Liberal idealism is marked by a belief in an absolute Law of Progress and an unlimited faith in the power of reason to transform society. Concepts such as Liberty, Science, Reason and Justice are conceived, not as abstract ideas, but as real forces which determine the movement of culture; and social progress itself, instead of being regarded as a phenomenon that requires explanation, is treated as itself the efficient cause of social change. Beliefs of this kind are religious rather than sociological, as Pareto has shown in the incisive criticism of *Trattato di sociologia generale*. Nevertheless, they still exercise a powerful influence on popular sociology, and they are not altogether absent from the theories of such distinguished modern writers as the late Professors L. T. Hobhouse and Lester Ward.

There remains yet a third type of explanation, which seems at first sight to offer a more satisfactory way of approach than either the materialistic or the idealist theories, since it professes to explain social phenomena in purely social terms. Nevertheless, this "sociologism" suffers from precisely the same defect as the other "simple" theories. For if, on the one hand, we attempt to study social relations apart from their material foundations and their cultural value, as the "formal" school of sociologists represented by Simmel and von Wiese wish to do, we empty sociology of its content and are left with a series of logical abstractions. If, on the other hand, we reduce both the material and spiritual element in culture to purely social sources, we are guilty of just the same unscientific simplification as the adherents of economic determinism or Hegelian panlogism. No doubt the exponents of this theory, such as Emile Durkheim, give a much wider analysis of the spiritual element in culture than do the materialists, and, in particular, they do full justice to the importance of the social function of religion, but they do this only by hypostatizing society into an independent spiritual power: not only is the social the cause of the religious, but the two are identical, and the Divine is the social sublimated to an ideal plane. This is not a scientific explanation, but an amalgamation of religion and society by means of an illegitimate substitution of one category for another.

The fact is that all "simple" explanations are unsatisfactory and irreconcilable with scientific sociology. It is impossible either to make society its own cause or to deduce social phenomena exclusively from material or spiritual ones. As Pareto has shown, the essential requirement of sociological method is to abandon the idea of a one-sided relation of causal dependence between the different factors and view the social process as the result of a complex series of interdependent factors. Material environment, social organization and spiritual culture all help to condition social phenomena, and we cannot explain the social process by one of them alone, and still less explain one of the three as the cause and origin of the other two.

Although the sociologist must take account of the geographical, economic and intellectual or religious conditions of a social culture, he has no more right to lay down the law on philosophy or theology than on geography or economics. But though this is generally recognized in the case of the science of nature and even the other social sciences, sociology has been far less scrupulous in dealing with the sphere of the higher spiritual values. It is often argued that these are a product of the social process, since there can be no spiritual culture apart from society, and therefore "spiritual sciences" (*Geisteswissenschaften*) can claim no scientific autonomy.

This, however, is the result of a naive confusion of thought. All the spiritual activities that appear in culture—religion, philosophy and science—possess their own formal principle. They are not mere functions of society, but have their own ends, which in a real sense transcend the social category. The sociologist, no doubt, is justified in studying a religious belief in its influence on society, but the theologian does not judge his belief or theory in terms of social value, but in terms of religious truth.

So, too, with scientific ideas, Durkheim has given a most ingenious explanation of the way in which man's ideas of time and space have a subjective basis in the rhythm and order of social life. But the scientist himself aims at transcending all such social subjectivism and attaining some absolutely objective standard of measurement. In other words, the more "anthropomorphic" a scientific idea is, the more interesting it is to the sociologist, and the more worthless it is to the practitioner of the particular science in question.

Actually, however, there is little danger—at least, outside Russia—of the sociologist dictating to the naturalist or attempting to "sociologize" science as a whole. But there is, as we have seen, a real danger of the sociologist trespassing on the territory of the other *Geisteswissenschaften* and attempting to play the part of a theologian or a philosopher.

A sociologist is, of course, quite within his rights in arguing that religion is necessary to society, or the reverse, or that a particular religion is beneficial or harmful to a particular society. For example, he might conclude from the study of ancient civilization that the introduction of Christianity was fatal to the institutions of the city-state and the tradition of Hellenic culture. But this would not justify him in drawing conclusions about paganism or Christianity *qua* religion. That is a matter for the theologian.

When Professor Ellwood, in his well-known book *The Reconstruction of Religion,* argues that religion is necessary to society and performs important social functions, he is reasoning as a sociologist, but when he goes on to "reconstruct" religion and to propound a new form of socialized Christianity, he is exchanging the role of a sociologist for that of a theologian.

It is no matter whether the religious theories that we propound are materialist or supernaturalist, rationalist or mystical, theistic or humanitarian. The point is that when we once begin to make a religion or to discuss purely religious values, we enter the theological region and speak as theologians, not as sociologists.

Ever since the time of Comte, there has been a constant

succession of theological sociologies which aim, not at the study of actual societies or actual social phenomena, but at the reformation of society on the basis of a new religious ideal. These attempts have been almost uniformly unsuccessful, for they are vitiated by an inherent confusion of method. They try to produce a synthesis between religion and sociology, and they succeed only in creating a hybrid monstrosity that is equally obnoxious to scientific sociology and to genuine religious thought.

I do not say that it is impossible for a sociologist-philosopher-king to plan the organization of society deliberately on the basis of general philosophical principles. Something of the kind was, indeed, accomplished by the Tokugawa Shoguns, who gave Japanese culture a conscious unity like that of a work of art. But they could appeal to the prestige of the Confucian tradition—that is to say, to an inspired sociology that had a genuine religion and a divinized sage behind it. If Iyeyasu had manufactured a new religion of his own to meet a purely social need, it is very unlikely that he would have been as successful as he was.

The sociologist who creates a religion of his own for sociological purposes is just as unscientific as if he were to invent new anthropological or geographical facts to suit his theories.

As sociologists we have to accept the existence of this independent order of spiritual truths and values and to study their influence on social action. Whether society requires a religious foundation; what is the actual working religion of our particular society; how far material and social factors affect religious beliefs and philosophical points of view;—all these are questions for our study. But the objective intellectual validity or spiritual value of religious doctrines and philosophical theories lies entirely outside our province.

It does not, of course, follow that these questions are in themselves insoluble or otiose. There is no reason for the sociologist who observes the limits of his science to write off everything beyond it as unreal or as matters of arbitrary speculation. No doubt the study of social phenomena in their complex irrationality has often led sociologists to prefer the despairing scepticism of a Machiavelli or a Pareto to the self-confident dogmatism of the idealists. Nevertheless, if such an attitude is justifiable it must be justified on philosophical grounds. The sociologist as such does not possess the necessary data for making a universal judgment of this kind. Here again he must follow the example of the historian, who no longer seeks to use history in order to justify his political or religious opinions, but who seeks to understand the beliefs of the past as a means to understanding its history.

This method of sociological analysis can be applied to practically every social phenomenon, even to those which seem at first sight to be entirely non-spiritual in character. For example, Max Weber, one of the first modern exponents of "a sociology that understands" (*verstehende Soziologie*), has shown how the development of Capitalism is not to be explained as a purely economic process, but has its spiritual roots in a new religious attitude towards industry and saving that grew up in Protestant Europe after the Reformation. On the other hand, there are other phenomena which seem at first sight to be purely religious and yet have their basis in economic or social causes.

Thus every social type or institution is the result of the complex interaction of a number of factors that are qualitatively distinct and can never be reduced to simple unity. Take for example the social type of the Samurai in Japan, a type which seems sociologically simple enough, since it represents an obvious social function in Japanese society. Nevertheless, in order to understand it, it is not enough to study the historical evolution of Japanese feudalism and the economic structure of Japanese society. The Samurai type is also the embodiment of a whole complex of moral ideas and religious beliefs—native, Confucian and Buddhist—some of which have a very remote relation both to Japan and to the military tradition. And the ethical code or cultural ideal that is the outcome of all this is not merely a matter of historical interest; it is an abiding element in the Japanese social tradition, and without it it is impossible fully to understand either Japanese politics or Japanese thought.

But if sociology needs the help of philosophy and theology in order to understand the spiritual elements in the social process, it also renders services to them in return. We cannot understand an idea unless we understand its historical and social foundations. We cannot understand the Greek institution of citizenship unless we study its spiritual foundations in the religion of the city and family. But on the other hand we cannot understand the Greek philosophical ideal of political liberty and its ethical ideal of "magnanimity" without a knowledge of the political life and the social structure of the Greek state. And even our modern ideas of liberty and democracy are not unaffected. The philosophers of the eighteenth century interpreted the classical ideas of liberty, democracy, etc., in an abstract and unsociological way, and consequently they misinterpreted them, and this misinterpretation was not without its influence on their philosophical thought.

In the same way the theologians have often failed to recognize the social and economic elements in religious phenomena, with the result that they have confused religious and sociological values and have allowed a racial or economic opposition to translate itself into a religious conflict. Most of the great schisms and heresies in the history of the Christian church have their roots in social or national antipathies, and if this had been clearly recognized by the theologians the history of Christianity would have been a very different one.

A scientific method of sociological analysis may serve the same purpose for society as a psychic analysis may accomplish for the individual by unveiling the cause of latent conflicts and repressions and by making society conscious of its real ends and motives of action. The actual tendency of practical politics, especially in democratic countries, is unfortunately just the opposite, since they invest such conflicts with a halo of idealism and thrive on sociological misunderstandings.

This is the more regrettable because the modern state is daily extending its control over a wider area of social life and is taking over functions that were formerly regarded as the province of independent social units such as the family and the church, or as a sphere for the voluntary activities of private individuals. It is not merely the state that is becoming more centralized, but that society and culture are becoming *politicized*. In the old days the statesman was responsible for the preservation of internal order and the defense of the state against its enemies. Today he is called on to deal more and more with questions of a purely sociological character, and he may even be expected to transform the whole structure of society and refashion the cultural traditions of the people. The abolition of war, the destruction of poverty, the control of the birth-rate, the elimination of the unfit— these are questions which the statesmen of the past would no more have dared to meddle with than the course of the seasons or the movements of the stars; yet they are all vital issues today, and some of them figure on the agenda of our political parties. It is obvious that the solution of these problems calls for all the resources of sociological science—even supposing that science was in a much more advanced state than it actually is; yet the unfortunate politician is expected to provide a solution by his common sense enlightened by a cloudy mixture of economic materialism and moral idealism. We can hardly wonder at the popularity of Marxian Socialism, for that at least has a sociology of a kind, though it is elementary and one-sided.

A sociology which disregards its proper limits may create Utopias, but it cannot help the statesman in his practical tasks. What we need is a scientific sociology which will transform the art of politics in the same way that the modern sciences of biology and physiology have transformed the art of medicine. In the task of restoring spiritual order and social health to our distracted civilization sociology has, as Comte realized, an essential part to fulfill. But it is to be achieved, not by usurping the functions of philosophy and theology, as in the Positivist synthesis, nor by ignoring moral and spiritual values, as with Marx. It must recognize at once the determination of natural conditions and the freedom of spiritual forces, and must show how the social process embraces both these factors in a vital union like that of the human organism.

Such a sociology alone can prepare the way for the coming of a new applied science of politics which would plan the City of Man, not by the rule of abstract ideas and visionary theories, nor in terms of material size and wealth, but as a true community.

—1934.

3

Sociology and the Theory of Progress

As the modern world gradually lost touch with the organized Christianity which had been the governing spirit of European civilization in the past, it began to find new inspiration for itself in the ideal of Progress. From the second quarter of the eighteenth century onwards through the nineteenth, faith in human progress became more and more the effective working "religion" of our civilization; a religion fundamentally the same under the more or less philosophic or scientific disguise of the Encyclopaedists or of Herbert Spencer as in the Messianic rhapsodies of the *Légende des Siècles*.

It is true that, alongside of this religious current and intermingling confusedly with it, there has been a genuine attempt to study the laws of social change and the positive development of civilizations, but this scientific theory of progress has naturally been slower in developing and less fertile in results than its more emotional companion. The latter, which we may call the Gospel of Progress to distinguish it from the scientific theory of social development, had the advantage of finding for its apostles a series of great men of letters. From the time of the Abbé St. Pierre and Voltaire down to that of Victor Hugo, it was the dominant inspiration of the great literary movements of the age, most of all in

France, but to a considerable degree in Germany and England also. Nor is this surprising: for it was the culmination of a literary tradition; its roots lie deep in the Renaissance culture, and if the Gospel of Progress itself was not explicitly held by the men of the sixteenth century, that was because the Renaissance as a whole only came to complete fulfillment in the eighteenth-century Enlightenment.

The dominant characteristic of the culture of the eighteenth century, and one that it had received as a direct heritage from the earlier Renaissance, was a conception of Civilization as something absolute and unique—a complete whole standing out in symmetrical perfection, like a temple by Poussin or Claude, against a background of Gothic confusion and Oriental barbarism.

It was the old dualism of Hellenism and barbarism rendered abstract by generations of Renaissance culture; but whereas the sixteenth-century scholar still looked back to the classical past as to a golden age, the eighteenth-century philosopher had ceased to despise the present. He looked forward to the immediate advent of a civilization which should be no less "polite" (urbane) than that of Greece or Rome, while it would be far richer in knowledge and in material resources. This ideal was well suited to the temper of the age, but it tended to diverge from and even stand in antagonism to the dispositions of a scientific sociology. It introduced a cleavage between the facts of social development and the ideals of the cultured world. The same spirit that Molière expressed regarding mediaeval art

> Le fade goût des monuments gothiques
> Ces monstres odieux des siècles ignorants

was shown towards all the social institutions of the immediate past, and the offspring of the historic life of Europe was mercilessly hacked about on the Procrustean bed of eighteenth-century reason and "good sense." When Condorcet sets himself to write a complete history of the progress of humanity, he condemns almost every institution which the societies of the past had evolved, and attaches supreme importance to the progress of intellectual enlightenment in the mind of the individual. As pure taste could create the perfect work of art, so pure reason would construct a perfect society. The history of the past was little more than a dismal catalogue of absurdities and crimes against humanity, all of which would have been avoided if man had been content to follow his innate good sense. When once he had learned that simple lesson, an Apocalypse of Reason would usher in the true Millennium.

This absolutism of method was as characteristic of the nature-worship of Rousseau, as it was of the rationalism of the champions of progress, and both these currents united in the French Revolution in an attempt to make a clean sweep of the past and to construct a perfect society on the foundations of pure doctrine.

In spite of the failure of these hopes and the powerful re-action that the experiment aroused, in spite of the work of Burke and de Maistre and the German thinkers of the period of national awakening, the temper of the eighteenth-century Enlightenment did nevertheless survive into the nineteenth century, and provided the main doctrinal foundation for the creed of Liberalism. The scientific temper of the new age could not, however, rest very contented with the purely abstract conception of progress which had satisfied the eighteenth century. The need was felt for a scientific law of progress which should be deducible from the observation of material phenomena, and numerous attempts were made to discuss the external forces which were responsible for social change. Hence the characteristic nineteenth-century Theories of Progress elaborated by Buckle in 1856, by Karl Marx in 1867, and by Herbert Spencer between 1851 and 1876. It was the latter who brought the idea of social progress systematically into relation with a general theory of evolution (that of Lamarck rather than Darwin), and treated it as the culminating branch of a universal development, physical, organic, social. But all these theories, we now see, were biassed by a certain "materialism," that is to say a more or less one-sided externalism in their attitude to history; hence their failure to attain a truly vital conception of society. It is true that Spencer insists at length on the idea of society as an organism, yet his prevailing externalism and individualism is seen in that he had no difficulty in reconciling the idea with his mechanical, utilitarian and individualistic views of the State.

To Buckle and Spencer civilization was primarily a state of material well-being such as they saw around them in the successful members of the community; and the greater spiritual currents that historically have moulded the higher civilizations were either neglected by them, or else were treated as forces which more or less retarded and distorted the normal development of society. Thus they regarded the civilization of their own age and country not as the result of the psychical development of a single, highly peculiar period, but as an absolute thing which was susceptible of improvement, but yet was in the main lines final and immutable. More than half a century before Spencer wrote, Herder (doubtless not a little influenced by Montesquieu) had given a far deeper and richer analysis of the movement of social development. He had shown "that the happiness of man is in all places an Individual good; that it is everywhere climatic and organic, the offspring of tradition and custom," [1] but his thought was unsystematic and confused. Like Vico, he founded no school, and he stands by himself as the inspired precursor rather than the creator of a true theory of social evolution.

It was in fact during the second and third quarters of the nineteenth century in France that the foundations of a genuinely sociological science were laid for the first time. The post-Revolution period was a time of intense intellectual activity. Social thought had been stimulated not only by the catastrophes of the Revolution itself but also by the new movement which had rediscussed the Middle Ages and shaken the complacency of the eighteenth-century attitude towards the past. Moreover, new foreign influences—Lessing and Herder, Fichte and Hegel, and even the long unrecognized Vico—were being felt for the first time.

Thus it was that men like St. Simon and Comte while retaining all the eighteenth-century enthusiasm for Humanity and Progress, were able at the same time to combine with it a sense of the past at once realistic and appreciative and a recognition of the relativity of contemporary civilization, as one phase in the secular evolution of humanity.

The whole philosophy of Comte hinges on a Theory of Progress, but it was no longer Progress conceived in the external eighteenth-century fashion. He had made the discovery that all social development is the expression of a spiritual *consensus* and it is this which creates the vital unity of society. Consequently the emphasis of Progress is neither on an

[1] Herder's *Ideas towards the Philosophy of the History of Mankind*, Bk. viii, ch. 5.

improvement in material well-being as the Abbé St. Pierre believed nor an increase in the freedom and enlightenment of the individual such as Condorcet had traced in his *Tableau Historique;* the accent now is on the formation and growth of a living community which embraces every aspect of human life and thought, and in which every age has a living and internal connection with the past and the future. In other words, in order to construct a genuine sociology, the study of social institutions must go hand in hand with the study of the intellectual and spiritual forces which give unity to the particular age and society in question.

Unfortunately, in his own attempt to give scientific form to a general theory of Progress, Comte failed to free himself altogether from the vices of the older method. His survey of the whole field of social phenomena was made in the light of a brilliant generalization based on the history of Europe, and indeed of Western Europe alone, which is after all but one term of the social development of the human race. But though his actual interpretation of history was, as it were, pre-sociological, he had at least defined the true nature of social science, and had shown what were the tasks that it had to accomplish in the coming age. An adequate analysis of social life was only possible when the way had been prepared by the progress of the new sciences of anthropology, social geography and social economics, in the second half of the nineteenth century.

Frederic Le Play, the man who, more than any other, first brought social science into touch with the concrete bases of human life, was a striking contrast to the earlier sociologists, or rather social philosophers. He was not concerned with theories of progress, and he had no general philosophy to serve. He was at once a man of faith, and a man of facts, a traditionalist, who loved his Europe, and desired to bring it back to the ancient foundations of its prosperity. In his patriarchalism, he came closer to Confucius and the classical teachers of China than to any modern Western thinker.

His method is well expressed in that saying of Fontenelle's which he chose as the motto of his great work: "He enquired with care into the value of soils, and their yield, into the aptitude of the peasants, their common fare and their daily earnings—details which, though they appear contemptible and abject, nevertheless belong to the great art of government."

It was by these enquiries, by the observation of the simplest forms of life in their natural economic relations, that Le Play and his school arrived at a clear conception of the natural region, as the mother and nurse of every primary social type. And this discovery was of capital importance for the future development of sociology since it supplied that concrete basis, the lack of which had vitiated all earlier social thinking. Without a true grasp of regional life and regional individuality, history becomes a literary exercise and sociology a theorizing in the void. For we have to study not Man in the abstract, nor "the Aryan race," nor even the national type, but men in their fundamental local relations to the earth and the life of Nature.

This does not, of course, mean that social science must envisage man as the passive product of geographical and economic factors. Le Play himself would have been the first to deny it. Social progress and the very existence of society itself are the results of the creative force of human personality. The vital principle of society is spiritual, and the causes of progress must be sought, as Comte sought them, in man's physical development rather than in the play of external circumstance. True social science must synthesize not only social geography and economics but also social psychology and ethics.

Nor can we limit ourselves to studying the psychology and ethics of the regional society alone. That is only adequate in the case of the Nature Peoples; as soon as the beginnings of culture are reached it is necessary to consider not only the relation of the regional society to its environment, but also the actions and reactions that take place between the regional society and the individualities of the wider social units—the nation and the civilization.

It is, of course, highly necessary to give a regional interpretation to the history of even the most advanced peoples, if it is to be properly understood. For example the change which transformed the Spain of the twelfth and thirteenth centuries into the Spain of the sixteenth century is much more than a political change from separatism to absolutism, it is above all the transformation of a culture which was based on the regional life of the Guadalquivir valley and the Valencian coast, into one based on the Castilian plateau and the

Galician and Biscayan coasts. In each age both these elements were present, but the one dominated, and gave its character to the Spain of the early Middle Ages, the other to the Spain of the sixteenth century.

Nevertheless this interpretation of Spanish civilization is not exhaustive. If we take two typical artistic products of the two regions, such as the Great Mosque at Cordova and the Cathedral of Burgos, we find that while each of them could only have been produced in that particular region, yet neither of them is explicable from the life of the region itself. They are both of them local variants of world types. Behind one stands the world movement of mediaeval Christendom, behind the other the faith and culture of Islam.

Or take the case of the local men of genius. In Averroes of Cordova we see the final flowering of an intellectual movement which goes back to Avicenna of Bokhara and to the Syriac scholars of Mesopotamia, while his Castilian contemporary, St. Dominic, worked side by side with Italians and Frenchmen and Germans in a common task of spiritual reconstruction which affected all Western and Central Europe. Here again then we have spiritual world forces expressing themselves in local forms, and what is true of the works of art and the men of genius is equally true of the societies which gave them birth.

This brings us near to the famous generalization of Ibn Khaldun, the historian of the Berbers, according to which the Tribe which is the product of the region, and the Religion, which is a world force, are the two main factors in history. Under the breath of a common religious inspiration the tribes are bound together into a civilization, and when the inspiration passes the tribes fall back into their natural separatism. They live on, but the civilization dies.

Civilization is essentially the co-operation of regional societies under a common spiritual influence. This influence need not be religious in the ordinary sense of the word, for the Hellenic world and the civilization of modern Western Europe, as well as Islam and mediaeval Christendom, form genuine spiritual unities.

But on the other hand a true civilization is much more than a mere piecing together of the different cultural elements, supplied by different regions. It has an individuality of its own, which is capable of moulding, as well as being moulded by, the life of its component parts.

In the case of primitive civilizations, like that of Egypt, the expression of this individuality takes a symbolic religious form which it is difficult for the modern mind to comprehend; but as soon as these closed local civilizations had been brought into close contact with one another, and had begun to be united into more composite cultural wholes, we find behind every such unity a common view of life and a common conception of human destiny which give psychological unity to the whole social complex.

Behind every civilization there is a vision—a vision which may be the result of the joint labour of many minds, but which sometimes springs from the sudden flash of inspiration of a great prophet or philosopher. The faith in Progress and in human perfectibility which inspired the thinkers of the eighteenth and nineteenth centuries in Europe, was essentially of this order, just as much as was that great vision of the vanity of human achievement which Mohammed saw in the cave of Mount Hira and which made civilization and all temporal concerns as meaningless as "the beat of a gnat's wing," in comparison with the splendour of Eternal Power, burning alone like the sun over the desert. Nor can we doubt that the material progress of modern Europe as opposed to the material stagnation of Islam is, at least to some extent, the result of the different psychological effects produced by these two different visions.

Of course it may be argued with considerable truth that the inspiration of Mohammed was itself the product of his environment—of the desert caravan routes and the close juxtaposition of civilization and emptiness which is characteristic of the life of the oasis, but we must also remember that, only a century or two after its appearance, this vision had become the dominant spiritual power in Syria, Babylonia and Egypt, the three richest and most populous regions of the Middle East. For a vision to be so universal in its effects there must be also something universal in its causes, and we cannot suppose it to be a merely fortuitous product of local circumstance. It is a world phenomenon that, in spite of its individuality, is in some sense governed by general laws which are susceptible of scientific investigation.

This is one of the main tasks in front of the social sciences, for while, thanks to the school of Le Play and to the anthropologists, great progress has already been made in the study of the evolution of regional life, little has been done to study, in the method of Science, the problem of the formation of the higher social unities. Hitherto historical science has concerned itself not with the spiritual unities, *i.e.*, the Civilizations, but with the political unities, the State and the Empire, and these moreover it has sought to interpret in terms either of race or of politics instead of in terms of world culture or of regional life. If once we begin to consider Race apart from Region and Civilization, it becomes a pernicious abstraction which falsifies the whole view of history. Witness the false generalizations of the mid-nineteenth-century historians of England and Germany, and still more the curious race-mysticism of such writers as Houston Stewart Chamberlain. And even commoner and more dangerous than this is the political or imperialist misreading of history, which justifies whatever is successful and measures social values in terms of material power. This is the error that lies at the root of most of our current misconceptions of progress, by substituting a false idea of social unification for the true one. Unlike civilization which is a spiritual co-operation of regional societies, Imperialism is an external forced unification, which may injure or destroy the delicate organisms of local life. It can only be of real value to culture, if it acts as the servant of a cultural unity or a spiritual force which is already existent, as the Roman Empire was the servant of Hellenism, the Byzantine of Christianity and the Chinese of Confucianism. During the last fifty years Imperialism, whether military or economic, has tended to predominate over the spiritual element in the European world-society. The economic organization of the world has far outstripped its spiritual unity, and the natural development of regional life has been repressed or forced away by a less vital, but mechanically stronger world-power. Thus it is that the great modern city, instead of fulfilling the true vocation of the city, which is to be the meeting and the marriage of region and civilization, is neither regional nor cultural, but is merely the misshapen product of world industry and economic imperialism.

These forces are in fact part of a movement of degeneration as well as of growth, yet they have been hailed all over the world as the bringers of civilization and progress. True progress, however, does not consist in a quantitative advance in wealth and numbers, nor even in a qualitative advance in technology and the control of matter, though all these play their subsidiary parts in the movement. The essential fact of Progress is a process of integration, an increasingly close union between the spirit of the whole civilization and the personality of the local society. This evolution of a richer and fuller group-consciousness we can trace through the history of all the ages that are known to us. Partial lines of progress, continuous improvement in the arts for instance, are obscure and often impossible to trace, but this great movement of integration which has proceeded almost without a break from the dawn of civilization in the river valleys down to the present day is real and incontestable. Nor can we set aside as merely Utopian the idea that this process is likely to continue until humanity as a whole finds social expression—not necessarily in one State—but in a common civilization and a common consciousness—a synthesis in which every region can bring its contribution to the whole, without losing its own soul under the pressure of the dead hand of world imperialism.

This progressive realization of the unity of mankind was indeed Comte's interpretation of the historical process, and in this at least he was not simply misled by an abstract theory. Where he failed was in his attempt to determine the exact form of this final unification, in his ambition to draw up a constitution for the human race, and to create the spirit that was to animate it. But the laws by which a further synthesis may be reached are not to be determined by abstract theory, they are discoverable only by the study of the formation and disintegration of similar syntheses in the past —unities such as Hellenism and Islam, or China and India, which were but partial syntheses, it is true, but were universal in their aim.

In the militant world-state of Islam, and in the pacific social culture of China, in the free communion of the Hellenic cities, and in the life of mediaeval Christendom with its common spiritual unity and its infinite diversity of local and civic forms, we may find not only more instruction, but more inspiration for the future of our civilization than in all the Utopias that philosophers and poets have ever dreamed.

—1921.

4
Civilization and Morals

IF we make a survey of human history and culture, we see clearly that every society has possessed a moral code, which is often clearly thought out and exactly defined. In practically every society in the past there has been an intimate relation between this moral code and the dominant religion. Often the code of ethics is conceived as the utterance of a divine law-giver, as in Judaism and Islam. In non-theistic religions, it may be viewed as a "discipline of salvation," a harmonizing of human action with the cosmic process as in Taoism (and to some extent Confucianism) or else as the method by which the individual mind is freed from illusion, and led to Reality (Buddhism and Vedantism).

But it may be asked is it not possible to go behind these historic world-religions, and find a simpler, purely social ethic? Certainly primitive morality is entirely customary, but it is also closely bound up with primitive religion or magic (if the two can be distinguished). A moral offence is not so much an offence against a man's fellow tribesmen, as doing something which provokes the mysterious powers that surround man; the primitive "moralist" is the man who understands how to placate these powers and render them friendly. But if there is not much evidence for the existence of a pre-religious morality, there is no doubt about the existence of

53

a post-religious one. In every advanced civilization, as men become critical of the dominant religion, they tend to elaborate systems of philosophy, new interpretations of reality and corresponding codes of ethics. In every case, the metaphysic and the ethic are inseparably connected, and in theory it is the metaphysic which is the foundation of the ethic. In reality, however, it may be questioned whether the reverse is not often the case, whether the ethical attitude is not taken over from the formerly dominant religion, and then justified by a philosophical construction.

Thus I believe Kant's ethic may be explained as a direct survival of the intensive moral culture of Protestantism, and many similar instances could be adduced. But apart from these cases of direct inspiration, it is only to be expected there should be some relation between the dominant religion and the characteristic philosophies in the case of each particular culture.

The situation with regard to ethical codes, in a society in which a religion is no longer completely dominant, is somewhat as follows:

A. There is a minority which still adheres completely to the old faith and corresponding ethical system.

B. There is a still smaller minority which adheres consciously to a new rational interpretation of reality, and adopts new ideals of conduct and standards of moral behaviour.

C. The great majority follow a mixed "pragmatic" code of morality made up of (1) the striving for individual wealth and enjoyment, (2) an "actual" social ethic of group-egotism or "tribal" patriotism, (3) certain tabus left over from the old religion-culture. These are usually the great precepts of social morality, e.g., against murder, theft, adultery, etc., but they may be purely ritual restrictions (e.g., the survival of the Scotch Sunday in spite of the disappearance of the religious substructure); (4) to a slight extent a top-dressing of the new moral ideals from B.

This situation is to a great extent characteristic of the modern world, but we must also take account of a great movement, neither a religion nor a philosophy in the ordinary sense of the words, which may be regarded as a kind of reflection of the old religion-culture or else as the first stage of a new one. This is the Democratic or Liberal movement, which grew up in England and France in the eighteenth century, and which found classic expression in the Declaration of Independence, 1776, and the Declaration of the Rights of Men, 1789. It was based on the new naturalist philosophy and theology of the English Deists and the French philosophers, and it owed much to the political and economic teaching of the Physiocrats and Adam Smith, but its great prophet and true founder was Rousseau. This movement continued to grow with the expansion of European civilization in the nineteenth century. It is at present the established religion of the U.S.A. and Latin America, any deviation from it being regarded as heretical, and it is by no means a negligible force in Europe. It is doubtful, however, whether it can be regarded as a new culture-religion, since it seems simply to carry on, in a generalized and abstract form, the religious and ethical teaching of the previously dominant religion.

Supposing that we have correctly outlined above the general course of the development of moral conceptions, the chief problems to be solved are the following—

(1) Is the development of moral conceptions progressive, and if so, in what direction does this progress tend?

(2) What is the cause of the changes in the dominant conception of Reality, on which the change of moral systems seems to depend?

(3) Is it possible to elaborate a rational system of ethics based on a modern scientific interpretation of Reality?

Now it seems clear that it is impossible to have a purely "practical" morality divorced from an interpretation of Reality. Such a morality would be mere social custom and essentially unprogressive. Progress springs very largely from the attempt to bring actual conditions and social habits into harmony with what are conceived as the laws or conditions of real life. The very conception of morality involves a duality or opposition between what "is" and what "ought to be." Moreover from the very earliest conditions of primitive savagery up to the highest degree of intellectual culture, the ethical standard can be shown to be closely connected with some kind of world-view or conception of reality, whether that is embodied in a mythology, or a philosophy, or is merely vaguely implicit in the customs and beliefs of the society.

Now the great obstacle to the attainment of a purely rational system of ethics is simply our lack of knowledge of Reality. If we can accept some metaphysic of Absolute Being, then we shall quickly possess an absolute morality, as the Platonists did. But if we limit ourselves to positive and scientific knowledge of Reality, it is at once evident that we are limited to a little island of light in the middle of an ocean of darkness. Unfortunately, Herbert Spencer's attitude towards the Unknowable will not help us here, for the *machina mundi* is a dynamic unity, and the part of it that we know shares in the movement of the unknown whole. Most philosophies and religions have supposed that there is some kind of meaning or reason in the world process; though there are thinkers like Lucretius (and perhaps Bertrand Russell) who deny this, and yet try to fashion a kind of "island" morality for reasonable humanity shipwrecked amidst the chaos of an irrational universe. Nevertheless the great majority of modern thinkers, and in fact modern men, believe profoundly in the existence of progress, and not merely a progress of succession but a progress of improvement. "Life moves on to ever higher and richer forms. Here is an adequate goal for moral effort! Here is a justification of moral values! Here is the true foundation for a modern system of ethics!"

But from the purely rational point of view what does all this amount to? So far from explaining the problems of human existence, it adds fresh difficulties. There is continual movement from the Known to the Unknown. Something that was not before, has come to be. Granted that the true morality is that which subserves Progress, how can we know what it is that will best serve the Unknown? Could Aurignacian man divine the coming of civilization? Could the men of the Mycenean age foresee Hellenism? When the people of Israel came raiding into Canaan, could they look forward to the future of Judaism? And yet all these achievements were in some degree implicit in the beginnings of these peoples. They created what they could not understand. If they had limited themselves to the observance of a purely rational social ethic based on the immediate advantage of the community, they might have been more prosperous, but they would not have been culturally creative. They would have had no importance for the future. The highest moral ideal either for a people or for an individual is to be true to its destiny, to sacrifice the bird in the hand for the vision in the bush, to leave the known for the unknown, like Abram going out from Harran and from his own people, obedient to the call of Yahweh, or the Aeneas of Virgil's great religious epic.

This of course seems mere mysticism and the very contradiction of a reasonable ethical system. Nevertheless it seems to be the fact that a new way of life or a new view of Reality is felt intuitively before it is comprehended intellectually, that a philosophy is the last product of a mature culture, the crown of a long process of social development, not its foundation. It is in Religion and Art that we can best see the vital intention of the living culture.

Ananda Coomaraswamy, writing of Indian art, says:—"The gods are the dreams of the race in whom its intentions are most perfectly fulfilled. From them we come to know its innermost desires and purposes. . . . He is no longer an Indian, whatever his birth, who can stand before the Trimurti at Elephanta, not saying 'but so did I will it. So shall I will it.' " [1]

The modern psychologist of Art will probably object that this view of the meaning of Art is purely subjective and fanciful. A work of Art, he will say, represents simply the solution of a psychic tension, the satisfaction of a rather recondite and complicated impulse, which is of importance only for the psychic life of the individual. From the point of view of the psychologist this is no doubt justified, but then from the same point of view all cultural activities, nay the life process itself, may be explained in terms of psychic tensions and their solution. Yet this is merely an analysis of the psychic mechanism, and it takes little or no account of the underlying physical realities. For instance, when one eats one's dinner, one satisfies an impulse, and solves a psychic tension, viz., the hunger tension, but at the same time one builds up the physical organism, and the results of a persistent neglect to take food cannot be assessed simply in terms of a repression psychosis.

Consequently, in the case of Art, it is not enough to look at the psychic impulse of the individual artist. It is only in times of cultural decadence and social dissolution that Art is a "refuge from reality" for the individual mind. Normally it is an expression of mastery over life. The same purposeful fashioning of plastic material which is the very essence of a culture, expresses itself also in art. The Greek statue must be first conceived, then lived, then made, and last of all

[1] A. Coomaraswamy, *The Arts and Crafts of India and Ceylon*, p. 59.

thought. There you have the whole cycle of creative Hellenic culture. First, Religion, then Society, then Art, and finally Philosophy. Not that one of these is cause and the others effects. They are all different aspects or functions of one life.

Now it is obvious that if such a central purpose or life-intention exists in a society, the adhesion to it or the defection from it of the individual becomes the central fact in social morality. There remain, of course, a certain number of obvious moral duties without which social life is hardly conceivable and which must be much the same in every age and society. But even these acquire very different meaning according to the ruling principle to which they are related. The offence of murder, for example, cannot have the same meaning in a society such as ancient Assyria, where religion and morality were essentially warlike, as among the Jains to whom taking of life, under any circumstances and in respect to any creature, is the one unpardonable sin. Again to the modern European or American, social justice necessarily involves an increasing measure of equality and fraternity; to the ancient Indian on the other hand, justice involves the strictest preservation of every barrier between classes and occupations, to him the very type of lawlessness is the man who oversteps the boundaries of his caste. If morality was purely social, and concerned entirely with the relation of the individual to the group in which he lives, this difference of moral standards would no doubt be less, though it would not be eliminated. But actually men's views of social reality form but a part of their conception of cosmic reality and morality involves a constant process of adjustment not only between individual impulse and social reality, but also between the actual life of society and the life of the whole, whether that is conceived cosmically or is limited to humanity. There is a tendency in every organism, whether individual or social, to stop at itself, to turn in on itself, to make itself a goal instead of a bridge. Just as the individual tends to follow his antisocial impulses so the society also tends to assert itself against the larger interests of humanity or the laws of universal life. We see clearly enough that a dominant class is only too apt to make society serve its own ends, instead of subordinating itself to the functional service of society, and the same thing happens with every actual society, in its relations towards other societies and towards humanity at large.

This is why moral systems in the past have (except in China) so often shown a tendency of hostility to the actual social group, and have established themselves in a super-social sphere. Certainly the great moral reformers have usually found the greatest opposition not in the "immoral" and impulsive individual, but in the regularly constituted organs of social authority and law. And it is one of the greatest difficulties in the democratic system that the force of this actual social authority is so enormously strengthened by its identification with public opinion that the position of the individual whose moral standards and whose grasp of reality are in advance of his society is increasingly hard to maintain: instead of the triangle Government, People, Reformers, we have the sharp dualism Governing people, Reformers.

At first sight there may seem to be a contradiction between the idea of individuals being in advance of the morality of their society and the conception of the existence of a central life-purpose in every civilization. But it must be remembered that there is a great distinction between the age-long racial and spiritual communion which is a civilization and the association for practical ends which is an actual political society. Not for thousands of years—perhaps not since the earliest kingdoms of Egypt and again excepting China—have the two coincided. There is always a dualism between the Hellenic state and Hellenism, the Christian state and Christendom, the Moslem state and Islam, the "modern" state and "Modern civilization," and the individual man has a double citizenship and a double allegiance. Certainly every actual society is moulded by the civilization to which it belongs, and to which it always professes a certain loyalty, but the whole emphasis of its activity is on the present, the actual, the practical, and it tends to regard the civilization as something fixed and achieved, as a static background to its own activities. Consequently there are frequent conflicts between the spirit of the culture, and that of the actual society, which become manifest in the opposition to the actual social will of those individuals whose minds are in closer contact with the wider movement of the whole civilization. For a man's social contacts vary with the richness of his psychic life, and it is only in the mind of the man whom we call a genius that the creative movement in the living culture becomes explicit. The ordinary man is only conscious of the past, he may belong to the cultural present by his acts, by the part that he plays in the social life of his time, but his view of reality, his power of sight is limited to what has been already perceived and formulated by others.

About 2,500 years ago civilization underwent a great revolution owing to a change in men's conceptions of Reality. Throughout the ancient world from the Mediterranean to India and China, men came to realize the existence of a universal cosmic law to which both humanity and the powers of nature are subject. This was the foundation of the great religious civilizations whether theistic or non-theistic, which have controlled the world for some 2,000 years. In some cases, especially in India and China, the old worship of the nature powers was carried over into the new culture, but even there, and still more in Islam and Christendom, there was a neglect of the material side of civilization due to a concentration on ideal values and absolute existence, which in some cases, especially in Greece and Mesopotamia, led to a decline in material culture.

Since the Renaissance there has been first in the West, and then increasingly throughout the world, a new comprehension of Reality, due to the turning of man's attention once more to the powers and processes of nature and resulting in the elaboration of scientific laws. On this new knowledge, and on the new power of control over nature that it gives, our modern Western Civilization is being built up. Thus it is in a sense a reaction against the second stage described above, and since European and still more Oriental culture has been based traditionally upon that stage, there is at present a conflict and a dualism existing within the culture itself. Moreover, the new third stage of culture while far superior to the second in knowledge and power with regard to particulars, is far less unified and less morally sure of itself. It arose either as an expansion or as a criticism of the second stage, and not as an independent self-sufficient culture. As the recent history of Europe has shown, it may easily end in a suicidal process of exploitation and social self-aggrandizement, or it may lose itself in the particular. Therefore, the great problem, both moral and intellectual, of the present age lies in securing the fruits of the new knowledge of nature without sacrificing the achievements of the previous stage of culture, in reconciling the sovereignty of universal cosmic law with man's detailed knowledge of himself and the powers and processes of nature.

—1925.

5

Progress and Decay in Ancient and Modern Civilization

OF all the changes that the twentieth century has brought, none goes deeper than the disappearance of that unquestioning faith in the future and the absolute value of our civilization which was the dominant note of the nineteenth century. That age was as full of wars and revolution as any century has ever been, but reformers and rebels alike, from the time of the French Revolution to the days of Mazzini and Garibaldi, all had a robust faith in the inevitable victory of the forces of enlightenment and in the coming reign of the great abstractions—Humanity, Liberty and Progress. They were all of them good Europeans with an immense belief in the European idea. To their contemporaries they may have seemed dangerous and disquieting, but their ideas were of the same fundamental optimism as those of the bourgeois Liberals.

The reaction from this optimism and security that we are now experiencing is not, as is often thought, simply a product of the Great War. It was preparing during that period of material prosperity and spiritual disillusionment that followed 1870. It was then that the new industrialism and finance became truly international. Men became conscious that they had destroyed the shackles of the old traditional local despotism only to be faced by an infinitely more formidable power, world-wide in extent and strong enough to use any government as its instrument. The last twenty years of the nineteenth century was an age of imperialism not only on the Continent of Europe, but across the seas. The spirit of the age was shown alike in the scramble for Africa, and in the vast expansion of American industrialism.

Hence a growing disaffection both among the subject classes and the subject nationalities, and outside the organized socialist and anti-imperialist movements, there was an even deeper human revolt against the harshness and ugliness of a machine-made civilization. Not only the Ruskins and the William Morrises but even more the Tolstois and the Dostoievskis preached a radical turning away from the victorious material civilization of the West, and a return to the past or a flight to the desert. Even these who fully accepted the scientific and material progress of the nineteenth century came to realize the dangers and instability of the new order. They felt the dangers of social parasitism and physical degeneration in the enormous and growing agglomeration of badly-housed humanity, which everywhere accompanied industrialism. They saw everywhere the destruction of the finer forms of local life and popular arts and crafts before a standardized mechanical culture, and the havoc that was wrought among the primitive peoples through their exploitation by Western capital. A few even realized the destructiveness of an order which was recklessly exhausting the resources of nature for immediate gain, which destroys forests to produce its newspapers and wastes in smoke irreplaceable coal.

But undoubtedly until the European War nineteenth-century optimism and faith in progress was still generally dominant—it was at least the orthodox dogma.

It was the War, and still more the subsequent period of confusion and disillusionment, which made the average man realize how fragile a thing our civilization is, and how insecure are the foundations on which the elaborate edifice of the modern world-order rests. The delicate mechanism of cosmopolitan industrialism needs peace more than any previous order. If modern civilization has increased enormously in wealth and power, it has also become more vulnerable. Our civilization is in danger just because of the amazing progress that it has accomplished during the last century and a half. Because it is more universal, more highly centralized, more mechanically elaborate, it is exposed to perils of which a more rudimentary culture is hardly conscious. Under the old order it was possible for a country like France to engage in almost continuous wars throughout the seventeenth and eighteenth century without causing much disturbance in the general life of the communities under modern conditions war between great nations affects every detail of public and private life. The new system owed everything to the forty years of peace—1870–1910—but it did nothing to ensure their continuance. National rivalries grow more intense, and in modern war the nations do not simply fight against one another: they tear to pieces the nerves and arteries of their common life.

We have seen enough of this process already to admit that the men of the nineteenth century were altogether too naive and optimistic in their conception of progress. They concentrated all their attention on Progress, and neglected the equally important social factor of Degeneration. All change was progress, and they conceived this not as the growth of a living organism, but as a number of additions to a fixed sum of knowledge and wealth and political liberty. Thus whatever was the fate of particular societies it was always possible to follow the progress of humanity in the converging lines of individual progress—economic, intellectual and political.

This was the creed of Condorcet and many more of the great minds of the eighteenth century, but in the course of time it was cheapened and vulgarized into a practical apology for the late nineteenth-century industrial civilization—a world that was growing larger and louder and richer and more self-confident, but which was at the same time decreasing in vitality and losing its hold on its true cultural traditions.

In reality any sound science of social progress must concern itself first and last with the concrete historical and individual cultures and not with the achievements of civilization in the abstract. For a culture is essentially a growth, and it is a whole. It cannot be constructed artificially, nor can it be divided. It is a living body from the simple and instinctive life of the shepherd, the fisherman and the tiller of the soil up to the highest achievements of the artist and the philosopher. The man of genius is not an absolute and unrelated phenomenon in society, a kind of celestial visitant. He is, in an even more intimate sense than the ordinary man, the product of a society and a culture. Science and philosophy are social products just as much as language is, and Aristotle or Euclid could no more have appeared in China, than could Confucius in Greece. A great culture sets its seal on a man, on all that he is, and all that he does, from his speech and gesture to his vision of reality and his ideals of conduct; and the more living it is, the deeper is the imprint, and the more highly developed is the element of *form* in Society. Hence every culture develops its own types of man, and norms of existence and conduct, and we can trace the curve of the growth and decline of cultural life by the vitality of these characteristic types and institutions as well as by the art and literature in which the soul of the culture finds expression. In certain periods—for instance, the Elizabethan age or the reign of Queen Anne in England—this element of form is strongly marked, and the characteristic types are numerous and full of vitality:—in others—for instance the third century A.D. in the Roman Empire—society seems amorphous and formless. The traditional types have become shadowy and unreal, and the types that are most living (such as the barbarian mercenary, or the Oriental diviner) are alien to the traditional spirit of the culture. Moreover there is a close union between the primary creativeness of the culture in life, and its secondary creativeness in literature and art. Falstaff is as true and characteristic a product of the Elizabethan culture as was Drake, and there is a vital link between the style of Addison and the polity of eighteenth-century England. Thus a parallelism may be traced between the rise and decline of the great literary and artistic styles, and that of the life of the society—or the particular phase of its life—which produced them. The Gothic Cathedral rises, comes to its perfect flowering and fades in unison with the rise and fall of the mediaeval communal development. Baroque architecture and sculpture is equally closely connected with the growth and decay of the Counter-Reformation monarchies.

A style lives not by its abstract beauty or suitability but by its communion in the living culture. When the social tradition is broken, when there is a deliberate choice of styles, as in a modern building contract, true style ceases—there is death. That is why mediaeval building has the same relation to modern Gothic, that a live lion has to a wooden one. The same principle holds good in the case of social and political institutions. Just as an artistic or literary fashion can be adopted in an external and artificial way, as was the case with French taste in the eighteenth century, or with the modern Oriental imitations of Western trade goods, so too can a people adopt the political and social forms of a different culture without having vitally incorporated them. If this process is carried far enough it may involve the end of the living culture, and that is why it is possible for an abstract and superficial progress to be the mark of a vital decline. When the successors of Alexander covered Asia with municipalities, theatres, gymnasia and schools of rhetoric, they did not turn the Asiatics into Greeks, but they did put an end to the native culture traditions, which lingered on only among poor men and country folk. The great network of municipal institutions with which the Hellenistic princes, and afterwards Rome, covered the subject countries were a mechanical and external creation, as compared with the vital and internal impulse that created the Greek City-State. The same thing may be true of representative institutions, universal education, a daily press and all the other insignia of modern civilization. We have to consider not merely whether an institution is reasonable or good, but first and foremost whether it is alive. There can be no question, for example, but that the modern representative system as it exists in Germany or Austria or Italy, with its elaborate proportional representation and its universal suffrage is, in the abstract, highly superior to the English Parliamentary system of the eighteenth century, with its rotten boroughs, its absurd anomalies of suffrage, and its corruption. Yet the latter was the living expression of an age and a people of creative political genius; it was one of the great forces that shaped the modern world; while the former is without a living relation to its society, and is liable to be set aside, as recently in Italy, in favour of a more primitive system which is more deeply rooted in the political traditions of the people. Only so long as change is the spontaneous expression of the society itself does it involve the progress of civilization; as soon as the internal vital development of a culture ceases, change means death.

Anyone looking at the Mediterranean world in the age of Pericles might have thought that the future of humanity was assured. Man seemed at last to have come of age and to have entered into his inheritance. Art, Science and Democracy were all coming to a magnificent flowering in a hundred free cities; and the promise of the future seemed even greater than the achievements of the present. Yet at the very moment when the whole Mediterranean world was ready to embrace the new knowledge and the new ideals of life and art, when the barbarians everywhere were turning to the Hellenic cities as the centre of power and light, all this promise was blighted. Hellenism withered from within. The free cities were torn asunder by mutual hatred and by class wars. They found no place for the greatest minds of the age—perhaps the greatest minds of any age—who were forced to take service with tyrants and kings. So that at last Hellenic science became domesticated at the court of the Macedonian Pharaohs at Alexandria, and the free cities became the spoil of every successful *condottiere*.

What was the reason of this sudden blighting of Hellenic civilization? Not, I think, any of the external causes that have been invoked—the Peloponnesian War, the introduction of malaria, the exhaustion of the soil. These were at most secondary causes. Nor was it, as Professor Gilbert Murray says in his interesting book on Greek religion, due to a "loss of nerve." It goes deeper than that. Hellenic civilization collapsed not by a failure of nerve but by the failure of life. When Hellenic Science was in full flower, the life of the Hellenic world withered from below, and underneath the surface brilliance of philosophy and literature the sources of the life of the people were drying up.

As the life passed out of Hellenic civilization, we see the gradual disappearance of those vital characteristic types in which the spirit of the culture had embodied itself, the passing away of the traditional institutions and the fading of the vivid and highly differentiated life of the regional city-state into a formless, cosmopolitan society, with no roots in the past and no contact with a particular region, a society which was common to the great cities everywhere from Mesopotamia to the Bay of Naples. Hence the degradation of the Greek type. The people is no longer represented by the citizen-soldier, who brought down the power of Persia, but by the "Starveling Greek" of Juvenal's satire, the Jack of all trades from rhetoric to rope-dancing. Instead of the Hellene being by nature the master and the barbarian the slave, we get Persius' centurion, "big Vulfenius," who, "with a guffaw, offers a bad halfpenny for a hundred Greeks."

Yet throughout the period of this vital decline, the intellectual achievements of Hellenic civilization remained, and Greek culture, in an abstract and standardized form, was spreading East and West far more than it had done in the days of its living strength.

If intellectual progress—or at least a high degree of scientific achievement—can co-exist with vital decline, if a civilization can fall to pieces from within—then the optimistic assumptions of the last two centuries concerning the future of our modern civilization lose their validity. The fate of the Hellenic world is a warning to us that the higher and the more intellectually advanced civilizations of the West may be inferior in point of survival value to the more rudimentary Oriental cultures.

Yet we need not necessarily assume that our civilization is fatally bound to go the same way as that of ancient Greece. If we accept Herr Spengler's theory of isolated cultures, each with a fixed life-cycle which it cannot survive, this would indeed follow. But his philosophy, powerful as it is in its realization of the vital unity of the individual culture movement, fails to take account of the enormous importance of cultural interaction in producing development and change. It was to this factor that the late Dr. Rivers, in consequence of his researches into the history of Melanesian society, came to attribute the whole process of social evolution. "I was led," he says, "to the view that the current concept of independent evolution, which I had accepted so blindly, was a fiction. The evidence from Melanesia suggests that an isolated people does not invent or advance, but that the introduction (by an immigrant people) of new ideas, new instruments and new techniques leads to a definite process of evolution, the products of which may differ greatly from either the indigenous or the immigrant constituents, the result of the interaction thus resembling a chemical compound rather than a physical mixture. The study of Melanesian culture suggests that when this newly set-up process of evolution has reached a certain pitch it comes to an end, and is followed by a period of stagnation which endures until some fresh incoming of external influence starts anew a period of progress." [1]

[1] *Psychology and Politics*, p. 118.

Now in the great majority of cases a change of culture is due to the presence of an immigrant people, and the rise of a new civilization is the result of the coming of a new people into an old culture-field, for instance the coming of the Dorians and Achaeans into the Aegean region, of the Aryans into Northern India, and of the Germanic people into the Roman Empire. Consequently the process of fusion and change to which Dr. Rivers refers, extends not only to the culture but to the people itself. We must take account (1) of the action of the new geographical environment on the man and the society that have grown up in another region; (2) of the actions and reactions of the culture of the conquered on that of the conquerors, and (3) finally of the gradual physical mixture of the two peoples. All these factors go to produce the new culture which is neither that of the immigrants nor that of the indigenes, nor a mere juxtaposition of the two, but a new creation.

Of course culture change is not exclusively racial in origin. As Dr. Rivers suggested, any new cultural element may set up a process of evolution in the society into which it is introduced. We have the case of the introduction of Indian Buddhism into China, which was one of the main factors in producing the Chinese culture of the Tang and Sung periods, but even here it is only fair to point out that some writers explain the new element in Chinese culture as due to the region and people of the Yangtse valley as against those of the Yellow River, where Classical Chinese civilizations originated. In cases such as these, of culture drift, or merely intellectual influence, it is not a new culture that is evolved, but it is the old culture that is developed and enriched. A new and original culture invariably requires new human elements in the society. Moreover, even in the most autochthonous and continuous of culture traditions the element of new blood counts for much. Even in Egypt it may prove to be the case that while the enduring culture tradition is always native, the two great culture cycles, which culminated respectively in the age of the Pyramid Builders and in that of the Eighteenth Dynasty, were set up by the intrusion and assimilation of new racial elements, first in the Delta, and in the second case (from 1700 B.C.) in upper Egypt.

The whole cycle of assimilation and change that goes to build up a new culture appears in most cases to occupy a period of about ten centuries, and it is possible that this remarkable similarity in the duration of culture cycles which has struck so many thinkers, both in the present and in the past, may be due to the process of racial fusion and change requiring a fixed number of generations in which to work itself out. The formation of a new culture is like that of a race or even of a new species. If it is adapted to the region in which it is placed and to the needs of life, it may persist indefinitely as a stable type; if, on the other hand, it fails to secure this adaptation, it will fade away or collapse. In many cases the passing of a civilization is connected with the alteration or disappearance of an immigrant stock— its complete assimilation by the conquered people and the new environment. We may trace this process clearly in the history of India. The change from the simple Homeric existence of the warriors and herdsmen of the Vedic age to the world of Buddha, and yet more of Kalidasa, was also a change of peoples. We can see the gradual weakening of the northern stock before malaria and the countless ailments of the tropics; their powerlessness to preserve purity of physical type in spite of the multiple elaboration of caste restrictions. We can see their healthy straightforward polytheism being gradually overclouded by the teeming mystery of the tropics, until the men from the North lose their zest for life and turn away with the Buddha from the disheartening endless round of birth and death. Finally, the process ends in the victory of the gods of the land, the Northerners are completely assimilated and their culture tradition is fused with that of the indigenes in the great and characteristically Hindu civilization of the Gupta period, the mature fruit of the whole Aryo-Indian culture cycle.

The same process of racial or ethnical change is observable in the case of Hellenic civilization. There is the same gradual adaptation of an immigrant society to a new environment, and the growing preponderance of Mediterranean influence, alike in culture and in blood. But this process is not sufficient by itself to account for the sudden and almost catastrophic enfeeblement of Hellenism in the fourth century B.C. Its premature decline would seem to be due to something analogous to disease in the individual organism. For there is a vital difference between the fixation or stagnation of a civilization like that of China or Egypt, after the close of its formative and progressive culture cycle, and the organic dissolution of a culture, such as we see in the case of ancient Greece and Asia Minor. The cultures of China and Egypt survived for thousands of years because they preserved their foundations intact. By their fixed and hieratic ordering of social relations they gave to the simplest and humblest functions all the consecration of religion and tradition. But other civilizations have neglected the roots of their life in a premature concentration on power or wealth, so that their temporary conquest of the world is paid for by the degeneration and perhaps the destruction of their own social organs. The most striking instance of this morbid and catastrophic decline— and that which most closely resembles our own condition—is that of ancient Rome in the first and second centuries B.C. Here there was no question of senescence. Society came near to dissolution while at the very height of its cultural activity, when its human types were more vigorous than ever before. The danger to civilization came not from the decline of vitality, but from a sudden change of conditions—a material revolution, which broke down the organic constitution of the society.

Rome, more than any other city-state of antiquity, was essentially an agrarian state. The foundation of her power and of her very existence was the peasant-soldier-citizen. The lands of the Latin farmers grouped in strategic positions all over Italy, and those of the Roman citizens concentrated in the best land of central Italy, gave the Roman power a broader basis than any other ancient state possessed and differentiated profoundly the Roman legion from the mercenary armies of the Hellenistic states. The peasant religion, the peasant economy and the peasant morale underlie all the characteristic achievements of the republican epoch. But with the conquest of the Mediterranean all this was changed. The peasant-soldier could not be used to garrison Spain or Asia, and his place was taken by a new type of soldier, not as yet mercenary, but at any rate professional. Vast masses of land and slaves were thrown on the market. A new type of agriculture based on the plantation system as it had been worked out in Carthage and the East, gradually took the place of the small yeoman holding. The tribute of Sicily and Asia caused an influx of cheap wheat into Italy which drove home-grown corn out of the market. Finally, there were even greater opportunities for Roman citizens to make great fortunes by speculation, by the exploitation of the conquered peoples and by engaging in the slave and corn trades.

Hence there arose a progressive degeneration and transformation of the characteristic Roman types.

The fundamental peasant-soldier-citizen gave place—as farmer to the slave—as soldier to the professional—as citizen to a vast urban proletariat living on Government doles and the bribes of politicians. So, too, the noble began to give place to the millionaire, and the magistrate to the military adventurer. Rome became more and more a predatory state that lived by war and plunder, and exhausted her own strength with that of her victims.

Faced by this situation, political circles in Rome were divided between two opposing policies. The conservatives—the men like the Elder Cato—hoped to carry the state through by keeping alive the old Roman tradition and adhering in everything to social and political precedent. The reformers, inspired by the tradition of Greek Radical Democracy, aimed at restoring the citizen class by a drastic redistribution of property among the landless proletariat. Both policies were tried and both ended in disaster. The republic slowly foundered amidst massacres and counter massacres, slave wars and a continual growth of political and financial corruption. It was only by the genius and persistence of Augustus that Rome regained some hold on her traditions. And even Augustus failed to cure the fundamental malady of the Roman state, though he well realized its importance. He could not restore the citizen-farmer in the place of the slave, nor could he cope with the cosmopolitan urban development of the city of Rome itself. For it was literally Rome that killed Rome. The great cosmopolitan city of gold and marble, the successor of Alexandria and Antioch, had nothing in common with the old capital of the rural Latin state. It served no social function, it was an end in itself, and its population drawn from every nation under heaven existed mainly to draw their Government doles, and to attend the free spectacles with which the Government provided them. It was a vast useless burden on the back of the empire which broke at last under the increasing strain.

This is an extreme example of the perils that result from the urbanization of a society, but a similar morbid process can be traced in many other cases of cultural decline.

First comes the concentration of culture in the city with

a great resultant heightening of cultural activity. But this is followed by the lowering of the level of culture in the country and the widening of the gulf between townsman and peasant. In some cases, as in ancient Greece, this amounts to a gradual but thorough rebarbarization of the country, in others—as in Russia since Peter the Great, and in the Hellenistic East since Alexander—the peasants still cling to the traditions of a native culture, while the towns adopt a ready-made urban civilization from abroad.

In the last stage the cities lose all economic and vital contact with the region in which they are placed. They have become parasitic; less dependent on nature and more dependent on the maintenance of an artificial political and economic system.

It is this process of urban degeneration and not Industrialism or Capitalism or Racial Deterioration or Militarism that is also at the root of the weakness of modern European Culture. Our civilization is becoming formless and moribund because it has lost its roots and no longer possesses vital rhythm and balance.

The rawness and ugliness of modern European life is the sign of biological inferiority, of an insufficient or false relation to environment, which produces strain, wasted effort, revolt or failure. Just as a mechanistic industrial civilization will seek to eliminate all waste movements in work, so as to make the operative the perfect complement of his machine, so a vital civilization will cause every function and every act to partake of vital grace and beauty. To a great extent this is entirely instinctive, as in the grace of the old agricultural operations, ploughing, sowing and reaping, but it is also the goal of conscious effort in the great Oriental cultures—as in the caligraphy of the Moslem scribe, and the elaboration of Oriental social etiquette. Why is a stockbroker less beautiful than a Homeric warrior or an Egyptian priest? Because he is less incorporated with life, he is not inevitable, but accidental, almost parasitic. When a culture has proved its real needs, and organized its vital functions, every office becomes beautiful. So too with dress, the full Victorian panoply of top hat and frock coat undoubtedly expressed something essential in the nineteenth-century culture, and hence it has spread with that culture all over the world as no fashion of clothing has ever done before. It is possible that our descendants will recognize in it a kind of grim and Assyrian beauty, fit emblem of the ruthless and great age that created it; but, however that may be, it misses the direct and inevitable beauty that all clothing should have, because, like its parent culture, it was out of touch with the life of nature and of human nature as well.

The essential need of our civilization is a recovery of these lost contacts—a return to the sources of life. A hundred years ago Comte realized the dangers of European disintegration and the need for the re-creation of a positive social order, based on the European Culture-tradition. Comte's view of civilization was, however, strongly intellectualist. It was left for Le Play to analyze the ultimate human and natural bases of a society in the life of the region. Yet the two methods supplement one another since every society has two kinds of roots in place and time—in the natural life of the Region, and in the tradition of the Culture. However far the process of degeneration has gone, there is always a possibility of regeneration, if a society is conscious of this double bond through which it enters into communion, on the one hand with the life of nature, on the other with the life of humanity.

—1924.

6

Art and Society

NOTHING is more difficult for the natural man than to understand a culture or social tradition different from his own, for it involves an almost superhuman detachment from inherited ways of thought and education and the unconscious influence of his social environment. Indeed the more highly educated he is in his own tradition the less will he be able to appreciate all that diverges from it. It is the old contrast between Hellene and Barbarian, Jew and Gentile which reappears today in the mutual incomprehension of American and European, or Latin and Teuton, or Occidental and Oriental. We cannot bridge the gulf by a purely scientific study of social facts, by the statistical and documentary methods that have been so much used by modern sociologists, for these can never grasp the essential difference of quality that makes a culture what it is. No amount of detailed and accurate external knowledge will compensate for the lack of that immediate vision which springs from the comprehension of a social tradition as a living unity, a vision which is the natural birthright of those who share in the common experience of the society, but which members of other cultures can only obtain by an immense effort of sympathetic imagination.

It is here that Art comes to our help, for Art, in the widest sense of the word, is the great bridge which crosses the gulf of mutual incomprehension that separates cultures. To understand the art of a society is to understand the vital activity of that society in its most intimate and creative moments. We can learn more about mediaeval culture from a cathedral than from the most exhaustive study of constitutional law, and the churches of Ravenna are a better introduction to the Byzantine world than all the volumes of Gibbon. Hence an appreciation of art is of the first importance to the historian and the sociologist, and it is only by viewing social life itself as an artistic activity that we can understand its full meaning.

It is true that this point of view is not an obvious one for men of our age and civilization. In modern Europe Art has become a highly specialized activity entirely divorced from the practical needs of ordinary life. We are accustomed to look for Art not in the workshop and the market place, but in the galleries and private collections where the artistic achievements of different ages and cultures are collected like the bones of extinct animals in a museum. The sight-seer goes to gaze on a Madonna by Rafael or a Greek statue in the same spirit that he visits the lions at the Zoo. They are something outside our daily life and they owe their value to their strangeness. Modern artistic production has been almost entirely parasitic on wealth, and the little world of the artists, the collectors, the dealers and the critics lives its own life apart from the main current of our modern civilization.

It would be a mistake to suppose, however, that this state of affairs is normal: it is the peculiar product of an exceptional society. Throughout the greater part of history the art gallery, the critic, and the collector have been unknown, though artistic production has been continuous and universal. It is in fact one of the most fundamental of human activities. It is common to the savage and the civilized man. It goes back to palaeolithic times, and it is from the artistic record of the human race that almost all that we know regarding the cultures of prehistoric times has been derived. It is indeed difficult to separate the beginnings of Art from the beginnings of human culture, for as I have said, social activity is of its very nature artistic; it is the shaping of the rough material of man's environment by human skill and creativeness. Man has been defined as a tool-using animal, and the tool is from the beginning that of the artist no less than that of the labourer. Like other forms of life, man is subject to the control of geographical and climatic factors, but he differs from the lower animals in the independence and creativeness of his response to the stimulus of natural conditions. He is not limited to a single type of climate or vegetation; to a large extent he is even the creator of his environment.

We can scarcely imagine a more complete dependence on natural conditions than that which governs, for example, the life of the Esquimaux. Man is here a parasite upon the Arctic fauna, the reindeer, the seal and the whale. Everything he has—food, light, warmth, clothing, tents and means of transport—comes from them. And yet his culture is not a necessary result of climatic and economic determinism. It is a triumph of human inventiveness and skill, a work of art not without its own perfection and beauty, the result of an age-long process of social co-operation and creative endeavour.

If we study any actual community, whether it be an Esquimaux or an English village, we shall find that every function of the social organism expresses itself in some significant material form. To every way of life, there corresponds a whole cycle of the arts of life. In the case of a simple village economy there is the craft of the mason and the carpenter, the blacksmith and the wheelwright, the potter and the weaver, the thatcher and the hurdler, and many more; and each of them has its value and significance from the artistic as well as the economic point of view. Even the village settlement as a whole with its church and manor house, its outlying farms and its core of inn and cottages centring in the village green or street, has the form and unity of a work of art. In the past this was all so much a part of men's common experience that it was not consciously realized. It is only now when the English countryside is being submerged by the stereotyped uniformity of the modern house manufacturer and when the local tradition of craftsmanship is dying or dead, that we have come to recognize the inexhaustible richness and variety of the old rural tradition. We see how every region of England produced its peculiar and characteristic types, so that the stone houses of the Cotswolds, the timber work of Cheshire and the cot and thatch of Devonshire or the Down lands are as intimate a part of the landscape in which they have grown up as the trees and the crops.

But popular art does not only mirror the diversities of regional life, it also expresses the differences of functional type. There is an art of the Peasant, and an art of the Hunter, an art of the Warrior and an art of the Priest, so that it is possible to judge merely from the cursory examination of an artistic style what is the dominant social or economic element in the civilization that produced it. Indeed the greatest authority in prehistoric art, the late Professor Hoernes, used this criterion as the main basis of scientific classification in dealing with primitive styles.

But is this also the case when we come to a more advanced stage of culture? Hitherto it has been the tendency of writers on art to admit social control in the domain of primitive art and craftsmanship, but to deny it in the case of the more advanced types of art. The Fine Arts, to use the aristocratic Renaissance expression, are looked upon as something absolute, standing on a plane far removed from social and economic categories. Artistic creation is essentially the work of an individual genius, who is independent of the milieu in which he works. He is a kind of Melchizedech appearing out of the void, "without father, without mother, without descent, having neither beginning of days nor end of life."

This view has been handed down from the days of the Renaissance, and it has its roots in the individualism of fifteenth-century Italy, when the artist and the Humanist, like the successful tyrant, transcended the bounds of the narrow world of the mediaeval city-state. It is itself the product of an exceptional and highly specialized type of society, which has few parallels in the history of the world. It would never suggest itself to a critic who was familiar only with the art of India, or Persia or Byzantium. But this idea has a special attraction in our modern industrial societies where Art is usually thought of either as a refuge from life, or as the privilege of a cultural minority. Of late years, however, there has been a marked reaction against this aristocratic individualism.

In reality a great art is always the expression of a great culture, whether it be manifested through the work of an individual genius or embodied in a great impersonal tradition. For society rests not only on the community of place, the community of work, and the community of race, it is also and before all a community of thought. We see this in the case of language, which is fundamental to any kind of social life. Here ages of thinking and acting in common have produced a terminology, a system of classification and even a scale of values which in turn impose themselves on the minds of all who come under its influence, so as to justify the old saying that a new language is a new soul. There is also a common conception of reality, a view of life, which even in the most primitive societies expresses itself through magical practices and religious beliefs, and which in the higher cultures appears in a fuller and more conscious form in religion, science and philosophy. And this common view of life will also tend to embody itself in external forms and symbols, no less than do the more material and utilitarian activities of the society. As a matter of fact we know from the magnificent cave paintings of palaeolithic times that man already possessed a religious or magical art of no mean order long before he had learnt to build houses, to cultivate the ground or to domesticate animals.

Thus side by side with these simple arts of life which spring from man's relation to his environment and the labour by which he lives—the domain of craftsmanship—there also exists from the beginnings another type of art which is the direct expression of man's psychic life, and of his relation to those hidden powers which he believes to control his destinies. It is in the religious life of primitive peoples that we must look for the origins of conscious artistic endeavour and indeed of human culture itself.

The social character of art is of course most obvious in the case of a simple unified state of society, such as we find in modern Islam or our own Middle Ages, but it is essentially true of all art. A great art is the expression of a great society, as much as of a great individual, or rather it is the expression of a great society *through* a great individual. It has been said that a committee has never painted a great picture, but it is surely undeniable that great works of art are often the expression of a corporate tradition. Take the Homeric poems, or the Gothic cathedrals. Of the latter Professor Lethaby writes: "The work of a man, a man may understand; but these are the work of ages, of nations . . . They are serene, masterly, like the non-personal life work of nature"; and the same may be said of the great achievements of religious art all over the world—in ancient India and Ceylon, in Buddhist China and Java, in the Byzantine churches and the early Syrian mosques—where the personal element is merged in an ancient and impersonal tradition.

Nor is it difficult to correlate, for example, the artistic outburst of the Gothic period with the other manifestations of mediaeval genius, whether in thought or action. The rise of Gothic architecture corresponds both in time and place with that of the communal movement in northwestern Europe, so that it is hardly an exaggeration to speak of it as the art of the French communes. So too with the development of mediaeval philosophy. This—like mediaeval architecture—falls naturally into two periods, the second of which, like Gothic, attains its full development in the middle of the thirteenth century and in the north of France. It is true that we cannot trace that any one of these movements is the cause of the others. Each of them is autonomous and follows its own law of life. Yet each is but an aspect of a real unity—that common social effort which we call mediaeval civilization.

After the Renaissance when European civilization becomes increasingly complex, and art is dominated by individualism on the one hand and the rules of formal criticism on the other, its social character naturally becomes less obvious. Yet even the spirit of individualism itself is a characteristic social trait of the period, and the attempt to regulate life according to abstract rational canons obtains in politics and thought no less than in art. In this as in other things art is the faithful mirror of society.

Moreover, under the cosmopolitan veneer of this conformity to the canons of criticism, society continues to exercise a deep subconscious influence on the mind of the artist and the poet. The great individual artist, Leonardo da Vinci or Velasquez, is essentially the great Italian and the great Spaniard; each expresses that which is deepest and most characteristic in the mind of the people and the age from which he springs. When a man seems to escape from all such categories and to be a stranger in his age, it is usually because he is a stranger in literal fact—one who brings his social past with him into an alien environment; like Theotocopuli the Cretan who learned his craft from the great Venetians, and developed his individual genius in the theocratic and mystical atmosphere of Philip II's Spain, yet remained to the last essentially "El Greco," the Byzantine Greek. So too with the typical *déracinés* of nineteenth-century literature (e.g. Heine, half German, half Parisian, but at bottom a Jew). These were in their time powerful influences of fermentation and change, just because they were able to see life with eyes alien to those of the society in which they lived, and thus fertilized the mind of one people by a perhaps unrealized contact with the soul of another. They talked the language of the people among whom they dwelt, but their deeper thoughts and instincts were those of the people from whom they had come.

—1954.

7

Vitality or Standardization in Culture

IF we accept the principle of social planning from the bottom upwards without regard for spiritual values we are left with a machine-made culture which differs from one country to another only in so far as the process of mechanization is more or less perfected. To most people this is rather an appalling prospect, for the ordinary man does not regard the rationalization of life as the only good. On the contrary, men are often more attracted by the variety of life than by its rationality. Even if it were possible to solve all the material problems of life—poverty, unemployment and war—and to construct a uniform scientifically-organized world order, neither the strongest nor the highest elements in human nature would find satisfaction in it.

These views are usually dismissed by the progressive as reactionary. They are in fact the arguments of the conservative, the traditionalist and the romantic. They were first developed by Burke and the romantics against the social rationalism of the Enlightenment and the French Revolution. But their criticism was based on a real sense of historical realities and they had, above all, a much clearer and deeper sense of the nature of culture than the philosophers whom they criticized.

They saw the immense richness and vitality of European

culture in its manifold development in the different nations through the ages, and, in comparison, the philosophic ideal of a society founded on abstract rational principles seemed lifeless and empty.

And today, even in spite of all the achievements of scientific technique and the increased possibilities of social control, the problem still remains whether it is possible to produce by scientific planning a culture that will be as rich and varied and vital as one that has grown up unconsciously or half-consciously in the course of ages.

Comparing the modern planned society with the unplanned historical societies which it has succeeded we see that it is enormously superior in power and wealth, but it has two great weaknesses: (a) it seems to leave little or no room for personal freedom, and (b) it disregards spiritual values.

We see these twin defects most strongly marked in the totalitarian states, which have been absolutely ruthless in their treatment of personal rights. But wherever modern mechanized mass culture obtains, even in countries of liberal tradition, we find the freedom of the personality threatened by the pressure of economic forces, and the higher cultural values sacrificed to the lower standards of mass civilization. This is not simply a question of class conflict, for it is not only the life of the proletariat that is standardized. On the contrary, the most extreme forms of cultural standardization are to be found in the higher economic levels. The luxury hotel is the same all over the world and represents a thoroughly materialistic type of culture, while the inn which caters to the poorer classes has preserved its cultural individuality and national or local character to an exceptional degree.

The older type of culture was characterized by a great inequality in regard to individual freedom. Freedom was a manifold thing. There were all kinds of different freedoms. The noble, the bourgeois and the peasant each had his own freedom and his own constraints. On the whole there was a lot of freedom and no equality, while today there is a lot of equality and hardly any freedom.

Similarly the older type of culture had very little power over its environment, natural or social. But it had very clearly defined spiritual standards and was rich in cultural values. These were of course primarily religious, for religion was the supreme unifying force in the old type of society, but they were also cultural in the narrower sense, so that these societies had a much greater sense of style than our own.

Today we have made incalculable progress in the scientific control of our environment, but at the same time our culture has lost any clearly defined spiritual standards and aims, and our cultural values have become impoverished.

In fact at the present time it looks as though we were beginning to witness a sort of persecution of culture, corresponding to the anti-clerical and anti-religious movement of the last century. Of course the culture that is being attacked is by no means the same thing as the religious or humanist culture of the past. It is a sort of devitalized intellectualism which no longer possesses a social function or a sense of social responsibility.

A culture of this kind is a decadent and dying form of culture, and it is bound to disappear. But that does not mean that society can exist without culture at all. It is all very well saying "To Hell with Culture," but that is just what has happened, and see where it has landed us! During the last thirty years the natural leaders of Western culture have been liquidated pretty thoroughly—on the battlefield, by firing squads, in concentration camps and in exile. A tough may be better than a highbrow, but a society that is dominated by toughs is not necessarily a tough society: it is more likely to be a disintegrated and disordered one. It is a phenomenon that is common enough in history, a typical phenomenon of periods of transition, and it is often followed by a sharp reaction which prepares the way for a spiritual renaissance.

Sooner or later, there must be a revival of culture and a reorganization of the spiritual life of Western society.

The more successful and complete is the process of economic organization the greater will be the need for a super-economic objective of social action. If man's increased control over his environment and his greater material resources were simply devoted to the quantitative multiplication of his material needs and satisfactions, civilization would end in a morass of collective self-indulgence. But the more natural and rational solution would be to devote the increased power and wealth and leisure that would emerge in a planned society towards cultural ends or, in other words, to the creation of a "good life" in the Aristotelian sense. For the higher culture is, after all, essentially the fruit of the surplus energy and resources of society. Cathedrals and theatres, universities and palaces—such things flower naturally from a healthy society as soon as it has acquired a bare margin of freedom and leisure.

It is obvious that the new planned society should be more and not less culturally creative than the societies of the past which accomplished such great things in spite of their poverty and weakness. The reason it has not been so hitherto has been due to our intense and one-sided preoccupation with the economic issue, which led to the starvation of all the non-economic functions and which also created the unemployment problem in the form in which we know it. But a planned culture which is the necessary complement to a planned economy would restore the balance of society, since it would devote no less a degree of organized social effort and thought to the development of the non-economic functions. In this respect it would mark a return to the traditions of the pre-industrial age, which put a much higher social value on the non-economic functions than we have done in the West for the last century and more.

But if we admit the creative powers of reason and the primacy of the spirit, we shall have to leave room in our planned world for the intervention of a power which transcends planning. And the only place for this power in a planned society is at the summit as the source of spiritual energy and the guiding principle of the whole development. For as economic planning is impossible unless a society possesses a certain amount of physical vitality—a will to live which provides the motive power for work—so cultural planning requires an analogous principle of spiritual life without which "culture" becomes a pale abstraction.

The only way to desecularize culture is by giving a spiritual aim to the whole system of organization, so that the machine becomes the servant of the spirit and not its enemy or its master. Obviously this is a tremendous task, but it is one that we cannot avoid facing in the near future. And while the present situation in many respects seems more difficult than any in past history, it is at the same time also more unstable, less fixed in custom and less emotionally attached. In fact the mechanization of human life renders it more sensitive to spiritual influence, in some respects, than the old unorganized type of culture; at the present time this response is most evident where the forces in question are most evil, but clearly this cannot be the only possibility, and the great problem that we have to face is how to discover the means that are necessary to open this new world of apparently soulless and soul-destroying mechanism to the spiritual world which stands so near to it.

—1942.

8

Cultural Polarity and Religious Schism: An Analysis of the Causes of Schism

IT may be said that the collaboration of Christians on the basis of fundamental principles is impossible, because it ignores the real nature of our disagreement. Granted that Catholics, Anglicans, Orthodox, Lutherans and Free Churchmen all believe in the Church of the Living God as the pillar and ground of the truth, the fact remains that it is not the same Church in an objective, institutional sense that is the object of this faith. We see this most clearly in the case of Catholics and Orthodox. Here are two perfectly concrete and definite, organized spiritual societies which agree to a remarkable extent in their conception of their nature and office, but which are mutually exclusive, so that it would seem that the more profound is their belief in "the Church," the more complete is their separation from one another. In the case of the Protestant denominations and especially the Free Churches, the situation is of course far less clearly defined, owing to the complete disappearance of structural and intellectual unity. Nevertheless it is conceivable that reaction against the fissiparous tendency of Protestantism, of which reaction the Ecumenical Movement is the most striking example, might result in the creation of a reunited Protestant Christendom, which would stand over against the Catholic Church, in the same way that Eastern Orthodoxy has done in the past.

Thus we are brought up once more against the fundamental problem of Christian disunity which is the problem of schism. In practice this problem is so closely associated with that of heresy, i.e. difference of religious belief, that they are apt to be confused with one another. But it is nevertheless important to distinguish them carefully, and to consider the nature of schism in itself, for I believe that it is in the question of schism rather than that of heresy that the key to the problem of the disunity of Christendom is to be found. For heresy as a rule is not the cause of schism but an excuse for it, or rather a rationalization of it. Behind every heresy lies some kind of social conflict, and it is only by the resolution of this conflict that unity can be restored.

In order to illustrate what I mean I would take as an example the schism between the Byzantine and the Armenian churches, for that controversy is sufficiently remote for us to treat it in a completely impartial spirit. Here the theological issues at stake were the Monophysite heresy and the decrees of the council of Chalcedon; matters of the highest importance which involved the most profound and subtle problems of theological science. Yet even from the beginning it is obvious that the passions which filled the streets of Alexandria with tumult and bloodshed and set bishops fighting like wild animals were not inspired by a pure desire for theological truth or even by purely religious motives of any kind. It was a spirit of faction which used theological slogans, but which drew its real force from the same kind of motive which causes political strife or even war and revolution.

And when we leave the primary conflict at Alexandria and Ephesus and come to its secondary results in Armenia or Abyssinia, it is obvious that the theological element has become practically negligible, and the real conflict is one of national feeling. Take as an example the rubric, which used to appear in the Greek liturgy for the week before Septuagesima Sunday and which I quoted in *The Making of Europe:* "On this day the thrice cursed Armenians begin their blasphemous fast which they call artziburion, but we eat cheese and eggs in order to refute their heresy." Here, it seems to me, we can see in an almost pure state the spirit which causes religious dissension. To put it crudely, it means that the Greeks thought the Armenians beastly people, who were sure to be wrong whatever they did. And where such a spirit reigns, what could be hoped for from theological discussions? The same spirit which made the eating of cheese a confutation of Armenian depravity would never have any difficulty in finding some theological expression, and if it had not been the doctrine of the Incarnation, then something else would have served just as well.

Now it is easy for us to condemn the Greeks and the Armenians, because we belong to a different world, and if we fast at all, we find it difficult to understand how people can attach such enormous importance to the questions of exactly when and how the fast is made. But can we be sure that the same spirit is not just as strong today, though it takes quite different forms? I remember, years ago, reading a story of an eminent Nonconformist divine whose name I have forgotten, which struck me as an example of this. He had been on a visit to Assisi and was immensely impressed with the story of Saint Francis and the mediaeval art in which it is expressed. But one evening, as he was visiting the lower church, he happened to come across a friar and a group of peasant women making the Stations of the Cross and singing one of those mournful traditional chants which are so different from our English hymn tunes, and strike one as half Oriental. And suddenly he experienced a violent revulsion of feeling and said to himself: "This religion is not my religion and this God is not the God that I worship."

This seems to me a perfect instance of what I have in mind because the intellectual or theological motive is entirely absent. It is not as though he jibbed at Mariolatry or the pomp of a High Mass. He was revolted by the very thing in Italy for which Evangelical Nonconformity has stood in England, a spontaneous manifestation of popular Christocentric devotion. And what upset him was not any divergence of theological views but merely the alien setting and the different cultural tradition which separate the world of the Italian peasant from that of the well-to-do, middle-class Englishman.

There is no need to labour the point. It was realized only too forcibly by the writers and thinkers of the Enlightenment from Bayle to Gibbon and Thomas Paine, and it was largely responsible for the reaction against orthodoxy in the eighteenth century. But, unfortunately, its use as a weapon against revealed religion has tended to blind orthodox apologetics to its real significance. History has shown that no true solution is to be found in the direction which the eighteenth-century Enlightenment took, i.e., by constructing a purely rational philosophy of religion based on the abstract generalities that are common to all forms of religion. For deism is nothing but the ghost of religion which haunts the grave of dead faith and lost hope. Any real religion must recognize, on the one hand, the objective character of religious truth—and hence the necessity of a theology—and on the other, the need for religion to embody itself in concrete forms appropriate to the national character and the cultural tradition of the people. It is right that Italian peasants and the English shopkeepers should express their feelings in different forms; what is wrong is that they should worship different gods or should regard each other as separated from the mind of Christ and the body of the Church because they speak a different language and respond to different emotional stimuli. In other words: difference of rite ought not to involve differences of faith.

Now it is hardly necessary to point out the bearing that this has on the problem of the reunion of Catholic and Protestant Europe. To the average Protestant, Catholicism is not the religion of Saint Thomas and Saint Francis de Sales and Bossuet; it is the religion of Wops and Dagoes who worship the images of the Madonna and do whatever their priests tell them. And the same is true of the average Catholic, *mutatis mutandis*.

Underlying the theological issues that divide Catholicism and Protestantism there is the great cultural schism between Northern and Southern Europe which would still have existed if Christianity never had existed, but which, when it exists, inevitably translates itself into religious terms.

Yet this division is a natural one which cannot be condemned as necessarily evil since it is part of the historical process. If it had been possible to keep life to a dead level of uniformity, in which Englishmen and Spaniards, Frenchmen and Germans, were all alike, conditions might be more favourable to religious unity, but European civilization would have been immensely poorer and less vital, and its religious life would probably have been impoverished and devitalized as well. It is the besetting sin of the idealist to sacrifice reality to his ideals; to reject life because it fails to

come up to his ideal; and this vice is just as prevalent among religious idealists as secular ones. If we condemn the principle of diversity or polarity in history, and
demand an abstract uniform civilization which will obviate
the risk of wars and religious schisms, we are offending
against life in the same way as though we condemned the
difference of the sexes, as many heretics actually have done,
because it leads to immorality. And this is not a bad parallel,
because the polarity or duality of culture of which I have
spoken is but an example of the universal rhythm of life
which finds its most striking expression in the division of
the sexes. Of course I do not mean to say that the duality
of culture is an absolute, fixed, unalterable law; it is rather
a tendency which acts differently in different societies and
in different stages of the development of a single society.
But this is a tendency which is always present and which
seems to become more clearly defined when social life and
culture is most vital and creative, as, for example, at the
time of the Renaissance.

Any vital point in the life of society may become the
centre of such a polarization, and where a culture has an
exceptionally rigid organization, as in the Byzantine Empire,
the principle of duality may find expression in an apparently
arbitrary division, like those of the Circus factions—the Blues
and the Greens—which played so important a part in the
social life of Constantinople. As a rule, however, race and
religion are the vital points around which the opposing forces
in society coalesce. Thus we see how the Ionian and Dorian
strains form the two opposite poles of Greek civilization
and finally become defined in the conflict between Athens and
Sparta which tore Greece asunder in the fifth century B.C.

Sometimes the two types of motive coalesce and reinforce
one another, as in Ireland, where the cause of religion and
race became identified, so that the opposition between Celt
and Anglo-Saxon finds religious expression in the opposition of Catholic and Protestant. We find a similar state of
things in Poland, where it was twofold, and showed itself
in the conflict of Catholic Pole and Orthodox Russian in
the East, while in the South, where the conflict was a purely
national one between Catholic Pole and Catholic Austrian,
feeling was less intense and the cultural opposition less
strongly marked. On the other hand in Bohemia at an earlier

period, where the opposition of Czech and German also manifested itself in a religious form, Slav nationalism took an heretical form and the German ascendancy was identified with the cause of the Church.

But, in addition to these cases, where the principle of social polarity is exemplified in its crudest form, we have a more subtle kind of socio-religious polarity which develops inside the unified national society and within the boundaries of a common religious tradition. A most striking example of this is to be found in England, where the tension of opposing social forces found expression in the religious opposition between the Established and the Nonconformist Churches. At first sight it may seem as though the diversity and disunity of Nonconformity are inconsistent with what I have said about religious schism as an expression of duality of culture and the tendency of social forces to converge round two opposite poles. But if we leave aside the theological aspect of Nonconformity and concentrate our attention on its social character, we shall see that the opposition of Church and Chapel, of conformity and dissent has an importance in the life of the eighteenth- and nineteenth-century English village or small town which far outweighs the differences between the various Nonconformist sects. And to some extent at least this religious opposition forms a spiritual background or foundation for the political division between the great English parties, so that in many parts of England it was taken for granted that a Nonconformist would be a good Liberal and a Churchman would be a good Conservative. It is true that this does not hold good of the early period of Methodism, but Methodism arose at a time when the Whigs represented the established social order, and it owes its importance to the fact that it made its chief appeal to the disenfranchised classes to whom the political parties of the day made no direct appeal.

But whatever view we may take of the causes of any particular schism and the social significance of particular religious movements, there can, I think, be no question but that in the history of Christendom from the Patristic period down to modern times, heresy and schism have derived their main impulse from sociological causes, so that a statesman who found a way to satisfy the national aspirations of the Czechs in the fifteenth century, or those of the Egyptians in the fifth, would have done more to reduce the centrifugal force of the Hussite or the Monophysite movements than a theologian who made the most brilliant and convincing defense of Communion in One Kind or of the doctrine of the two natures of Christ. Whereas it is very doubtful if the converse is true, for even if the Egyptians had accepted the doctrine of Chalcedon, they would have found some other ground of division so long as the sociological motive for division remained unaltered.

What bearing has all this on the problem of Reunion as it exists today? It would be a profound mistake to conclude that because religious disunion in the past has been based on social and political causes, we must accept it in a spirit of fatalism, as an evil which cannot be remedied except by political or economic means. The cause of Christian unity can best be served neither by religious controversy nor by political action, but by the theological virtues: faith, hope and charity. And these virtues must be applied both in the intellectual and religious spheres. It is, above all, necessary to free the religious issue of all the extraneous motives that take their rise in unconscious social conflicts, for if we can do this we shall deprive the spirit of schism of its dynamic force. If we can understand the reason of our instinctive antipathy to other religious bodies, we shall find that the purely religious and theological obstacles to reunion become less formidable and more easy to remove. But so long as the unconscious element of social conflict remains unresolved, religion is at the mercy of the blind forces of hatred and suspicion which may assume really pathological forms. If it seems that this is an exaggeration, you have only to look back at our own past and consider the history of the Gordon Riots or the Popish Plot.

Hence the first and greatest step toward religious unity is an internal and spiritual one: the purging of the mind from the lower motives which may contaminate our faith. For in the vast majority of cases the sin of schism does not arise from a conscious intention to separate oneself from the true Church, but from allowing the mind to become so occupied and clouded by instinctive enmities or oppositions that we can no longer see spiritual issues clearly, and our religious attitude becomes determined by forces that are not religious at all.

It is easy enough to see, in the fifteenth century, for example, how vested interests and material motives caused the leaders both of Church and State to oppose necessary reforms, but it is no less evident that the passion of revolt that drove a great religious leader like Martin Luther into schism and heresy was not purely religious in origin, but was the outcome of a spiritual conflict in which religious motives were hopelessly confused, so that if Luther had not been such a "psychic" person, to use the word in Saint Paul's sense as well as the modern one, he would have been able to judge the deep things of God as a spiritual man: he would still have been a reformer without becoming an heresiarch.

When we turn to the English Reformation, the influence of the non-religious factors in the schism is so obvious that there is no need to insist on it. It was to a great extent a movement of the State *against* the Church, and the driving force behind it was the awakening of national consciousness and the self-assertion of national culture. Hence the religious issue became so identified with the national cause that Catholicism became the representative of all the forces that were hostile to nationality, and every Catholic was regarded as a bad Englishman and a disloyal subject. To the average Englishman the typical Catholic was not Thomas More but Guy Fawkes, and the celebration of the Gunpowder Treason became a kind of primitive ritual expression of the popular detestation of the hereditary enemy of the tribe.

This identification of religion and nationality endured for more than two hundred years, and even today it remains as a subconscious prejudice at the back of men's minds. But it has inevitably tended to diminish with the growth of modern secular civilization. There is no longer any need for nationalism or class feeling or economic motives to disguise themselves in the dress of religion, for they have become the conscious and dominant forces in social life. The ideologies which today form the opposite poles of social tension are not religious, but political, national and economic ones, which have cut across and largely obliterated the older socio-religious divisions which separated Catholic and Protestant Europe.

Here it seems to me that the present age is more favourable to the cause of unity than any time since the Middle Ages. For, if Christianity becomes a minority religion, if it is threatened by hostility and persecution, then the common cause of Christianity becomes a reality and not merely a phrase, and there is a centre round which the scattered forces of Christendom can rally and reorganize. We must remember that behind the natural process of social conflict and tension which runs through history there is a deeper law of spiritual duality and polarization which is expressed in the teaching of the Gospel on the opposition of the World and the Kingdom of God and in Saint Augustine's doctrine of the two cities Babylon and Jerusalem whose conflict runs through all history and gives it its ultimate significance.

Thus when Christians allow the conflicts and divisions of the natural man to transgress their bounds and permeate the religious sphere, the cause of God becomes obscured by doubts and divisions, and schism and heresies arise. But when the Church is faithful to its mission, it becomes the visible embodiment of this positive divine principle standing over against the eternal negative of evil.

I believe that the age of schism is passing and that the time has come when the divine principle of the Church's life will assert its attractive power, drawing all the living elements of Christian life and thought into organic unity. For since Christ is the Head of the Church and the Holy Spirit is the life of the Church, wherever there is faith in Christ and the Spirit of Christ there is the spirit of unity and the means of reunion. Therefore it is not necessary to talk much about the ways and means, for the ways of the Spirit are essentially mysterious and transcend human understanding. It may even be that the very strength of the forces that are gathering against the Church and against religion will make for unity by forcing Christians together, as it were, in spite of themslves; or it may be that the Church will react positively to the situation by a fresh outpouring of the apostolic spirit, as Blessed Grignon de Montfort prophesied two centuries ago.

—1942.

9

Prevision in Religion

THERE is no sphere of human activity in which prevision has had a wider scope than in that of religion. Indeed, religious prevision has always been one of the chief conditions and causes of religious change. The function of the religious prophet has been far more creative than that of the political prophet and possesses, as the latter does not, an organic relation to the process of development with which it is concerned. Nevertheless, this religious prevision is entirely different from the sociological prevision which is the subject of our discussion. It is not merely unscientific, it is essentially hostile to any prevision of religious development that is based on purely rational data. It asserts the word of God against the word of man, the invasion of the known by the unknown, the reversal of the human logic of history and its human values by the abrupt interposition of a transcendent principle.

Now, there is no doubt that of all forms of change, religious changes are apparently the most arbitrary and the most unpredictable. A political revolution, however sudden and catastrophic it may be, has a firm basis in the past, and all its elements are to be found existing in the previous state of society. But there is an unknown quantity in religious change which defeats the most careful historic analysis. The state of the Near East, in the sixth century, for example, certainly suggested the possibility of a religious change. But judging by the available historical evidence, one might have foretold the religious revolt of the eastern provinces of the Byzantine Empire and the constitution of a homogeneous Christian Monophysite culture. No one could have foreseen the sudden apparition of Islam and the lightning speed with which it swept over the world from the frontiers of India and China to the Atlantic.

In the same way a contemporary observer might have foreseen the development of a new religious unity in the soil of the Roman Empire. He might have envisaged the rise of a philosophic syncretism of the type of Neoplatonism or the spread of an Oriental mystery religion like Mithraism. But he could not have foreseen the birth of Christianity in Palestine or its triumphant progress in the face of the hostility of the secular power and the competition of its rivals or its final acceptance by Constantine and his successors as the official religion of the Roman Empire itself.

It would seem that the possibilities of sociological prevision in regard to religion are even more limited than in other departments of life. Indeed, the word *prevision* is somewhat misleading, since the most that can be attempted is to study the permanent factors in the religious situation, to determine how far religion exerts a constant influence on social life and what are the forms through which that influence manifests itself. It is true that in the past sociologists have conceived their task in a much more ambitious way. A detailed prevision of the future development of religion was the characteristic feature of the earlier nineteenth-century sociology. Not only did men believe that they had discovered the general sociological laws that governed religious change, they also believed that it was possible to foretell the actual form and content of the religion of the future. This tendency reached its extreme point of development with Comte, who assumed the role of a sociological Moses, at once prophet and legislator of the new religious dispensation; but it was by no means confined to him and to his followers, for there are few sociologists before the time of Pareto who did not follow the same direction. Thus sociology transgressed its proper limits and aspired to become at once a philosophy of history, a system of ethics, and a non-theological substitute for religion, with the result that the whole subject was brought into discredit and sociology became regarded as unscientific and speculative.

The attempt of Comte to abolish metaphysics and theology by absorbing them into sociology was, in fact, even more fatal to sociology than to theology. For in so far as he "sociologized" theology, he "theologized" sociology and thus produced an impure amalgamation of the two which was equally unsatisfactory from the standpoint of the sociologist and of the theologian.

The sociologist cannot study religion fruitfully unless he recognizes that religion is an autonomous activity which has its own independent principles and laws. It is impossible to understand religion simply as a function of society, or to identify the social and the religious categories, as Durkheim attempted to do. It is his business to study religion as a factor in the social process, but this is only one aspect of religion and by no means exhausts its content. The other aspects of religion—the trans-social ones, if I may use the expression, have also to be taken account of, though here the sociologist is incompetent to make final conclusions. Here the sociologist is dependent on the data furnished by theology or the science of religion, which alone can attempt to define the nature and scope of religion comprehensively.

Thus the sociology of religion is a borderland subject which demands the co-operation of two different sciences—two sciences, moreover, which are apt to regard one another with a certain amount of distrust. Nor is this surprising when we consider how widely the two sciences differ in their angle of vision and method of approach. From the theological point of view, religion is essentially concerned with the transcendent and the absolute, with absolute values and eternal truths. But in so far as religion answers to this definition, it has little meaning or value for the sociologist. The figure of Buddha under the bo tree, absorbed in the contemplation of Nirvana, is of the highest interest to the student of religion, but to the sociologist it must appear as the apotheosis of the non-sociological aspect of human life. On the other hand, the type of religion that interests the sociologist—that which is entirely bound with social customs and institutions—is despised by the theologian, who regards it as hardly worthy of the name of religion.

Actually, however, every historic religion contains both elements. Even Confucianism, the most sociological and the least theological of religions, rests on the conception of an absolute principle to which all human action must conform itself, while Buddhism, which seems at first sight to leave no room for the social and the institutional, expresses itself in social institutions like other religions and has a formative influence on culture. Granted that the highest religious act is a going out of the soul from the temporal and the sensible towards the absolute and the eternal, there is a movement in the inverse direction which is equally essential to religion—the movement of return which aims at the consecration of social life and at bringing human action into conformity with the divine order. This second movement takes a different form in every different religion and culture, but it is everywhere present, from the lowest forms of fetishism and animism up to the highest types of theism. A living religion always aspires to be the centre round which the whole culture revolves, so that whatever is most vital in social institutions and activities is brought into relation with religion and receives a religious function.

Consequently, in so far as sociological prevision is possible with regard to the organic development of society in general, it will be possible to foresee the social form that religion will tend to acquire in any given culture.

Thus if we take the Geddes-Le Play formula, which interprets social life in terms of the mutual interaction of Place, Work, and Folk, we shall find that each of these factors plays a corresponding part in the religious development, so that the sociological form of any given religion can be analyzed in terms of these factors. In other words, the sociological form of a religion is determined by the way in which it supplies a religious sanction or consecration to Place, to Work, and to the Social Bond itself.

1. In every form of social organization from the totemic group of the Australian aboriginal to the patriarchal family of the Greeks and the Romans, and from the barbaric Negroid kingdoms of West Africa to the great theocratic monarchies of Egypt and Babylonia and China, we find that the social bond is everywhere *sacred* in the technical religious sense and that social authority rests on religious sanctions. It is here that the possibilities of sociological prevision in regard to religion are to be seen most clearly. For if a society adopts a new form of organization owing to political causes we may expect to find a corresponding change

in its religion. But here again the possibilities of prevision are strictly limited. For example, in the ancient world we can see how the passing of the classical civic polity was accompanied by a corresponding decline in the civic religion. And we should expect to find that the transformation of the Roman Empire into an absolute monarchy of a semi-Oriental type would have been accompanied by the introduction of a theocratic state religion like that of the Sassanian monarchy. Now the actual course of events largely fulfils this prevision. We see the appearance in the West of a cult of the solar monarchy under Aurelian and his successors, while the Byzantine Empire has many of the characteristics of a sacred theocratic monarchy. Nevertheless the development is not complete. For it was not the solar monarchy of Aurelian and Julian that triumphed, but Christianity— a religion which in some respects was actually hostile to the divinization of the monarchy and the imperial state, since it favoured the independence of the spiritual authority and the emancipation of one side of social life from state control.

2. It is, however, by the consecration of work and economic activity that religion enters most profoundly into the sociological process. Nothing determines the form of religion, at least in primitive society, so much as the functional activity of the society in question. Each of the primary nature occupations produces its characteristic type of religion: there is a religion of the hunter, a religion of the peasant, and a religion of the pastoralist. Of these the first is characterized by the cult of animal guardian spirits and by the magical rites for the multiplication of game of which we seem to find traces even in palaeolithic culture. The second is marked by the worship of the Mother Goddess and by the fertility rites which exist almost universally among the peasant cultures, while the third finds its typical expression in the worship of the Sky god and in the religious practices connected with domestic animals, above all the cow. Nor is this all. Each of these types of religion possesses its own religious ethos and its own spiritual ideal. The religion of the hunter finds its highest expression in the individualistic visionary experience of the Shaman and shows a marked tendency to asceticism. That of the peasant is of a mystical and sacramental character. It finds its centre in a communal act of sacrifice and tends to develop an elaborate system of

ritual. Finally the pastoral religion is marked by a high standard of social morality and is accompanied by a more ethical conception of divinity than is to be found among the peasant cultures. These primitive occupational types of religion continue to persist in the higher cultures. Indeed, the development of the higher culture in the Near East seems to be largely based on the higher religious development of the peasant culture. The ritual cycle of the agricultural year becomes the basis of the sacred calendar which holds such an important place in the life of ancient civilization, as we see above all in China and in the Maya culture of Central America; while the development of a priestly class, which is responsible for the correct carrying out of the elaborate ceremonial of the fertility cult, favours the formation of a learned élite like that which played so essential a part in the higher culture of Mesopotamia and Egypt. In the same way the pastoral culture, with its virile ethos and its patriarchal organization, provides the basis for the development of the religion and culture of the warrior peoples such as the Aryans, who take a leading part in the development of civilization from the close of the Bronze Age and even earlier.

Moreover, as these social types come into contact and conflict with one another and give rise to new composite forms of social organization, so is it with the corresponding religious types. The most familiar example of this process is to be found in the case of a settled peasant culture that is conquered and dominated by a warrior people. This gives rise not only to a dualism of culture, but to a religious dualism, in which the gods of the conquerors exist side by side with those of the subject population, and each religious tradition influences the other, until the whole society possesses a common religion of composite type. In ancient Greece, for example, we find the old chthonic cults of the Aegean world subsisting alongside of the worship of the Olympian gods until the two are blended in a composite pantheon. Still more remarkable is the interaction between the religion of the warlike pastoral Hebrew tribes and the fertility cults of the conquered Canaanite population, for here the conflict was exceptionally sharp and the "gods of the land" never succeeded in coming to terms with the deity of the immigrants. The religious development of the Jewish people owed its characteristic form to a series of reactions on the part of the religious tradition of the conquerors *against* the process of assimilation which was the normal condition elsewhere. But whether the process of religious change takes the form of co-operation or of conflict, it is conditioned, in one case as in the other, by the co-existence of two social and religious traditions, so that the existence of this spiritual dualism was just as essential to the monotheistic development of Judaism as it was to the polytheistic syncretism of Greek or Indian religion.

3. The influence of the Place-factor on religious development seems at first sight more external and superficial than that of the two others which we have discussed. Nevertheless, its importance is obvious enough, especially in primitive religion. Even in the lowest type of culture—among the food gatherers, and in the mixed hunting and food-gathering culture of Australia—the Holy Place already holds an important place in the social and religious life of the community, and its importance tends to increase rather than to diminish with the advance of culture. In the archaic civilizations of the Near East, above all in Mesopotamia, the Holy Place develops into the Sacred City and plays a decisive part in the new civic development. Moreover, at this stage of culture, if not earlier, we find the consecration of place extending from the local sanctuary to the whole territory, so that we may have not merely a Holy Place, but a Holy Land. In other cases, as in ancient Greece, we find the Holy Place becoming the centre of a federal union or, as in the case of Delphi, the common sanctuary of the Hellenic peoples and exercising a wide influence on colonization and international intercourse. A remarkable example of this kind of development is to be found in West Africa in modern times, where the famous sanctuary of Aro-Chuko in the Cross River district became the centre of an extensive network of intertribal commercial relations, among peoples who possessed no common social unity or political organization.

We might expect this factor to lose its significance with the coming of the world religions which no longer deify the powers of nature and which transcend the frontier of country and race. Actually, however, it is not so. Alike in Buddhism, in Islam, and in mediaeval Christendom the Holy Place and the practice of pilgrimage that is associated with it, take a very prominent place and supply an element of social cohesion which might otherwise be lacking.

These three forms of activity—the consecration of place, the consecration of work, and the consecration of the social *bond* itself—are the main channels through which religion finds social expression and acquires a sociological form, and the greater their share in the religious development, the greater is the possibility of sociological prevision. Where religion transcends the categories of Place, Work, Folk, as it does in its most profound manifestations (e.g. in the essential religious experience of the mystic), the role of sociological prevision is almost negligible. In other words, the more completely a religion is identified with a particular culture and the more closely the religious and social life of a people is unified, the more room there will be for sociological prevision. But where a religion is divorced from social life, as with a new religion that has not yet achieved social acceptance, or with an old religion that has lost it, the possibilities of prevision are proportionately restricted.

Now this is the situation with regard to our own culture, which has been growing progressively more secular during the last five or six centuries, and which now seems to be without any organic relation to any definite form of religion. In such a case, however, the old channels of socioreligious activity are not entirely closed. They have lost their primary religious character, but they continue to exert a secondary influence of a quasi-religious kind: Place, Work, and Folk are no longer consecrated by being brought into relation with a transcendent religious principle, as in the case of a living religion, but they retain a kind of inherent sacredness which they have acquired from ages of religious association. The transition of social institutions and ideas from the sphere of the sacred to that of the profane is neither instantaneous nor complete. There is an intermediate region of quasi-religious ideas through which a culture in process of secularization must pass. For example, when in the seventeenth and eighteenth centuries the societies of Western Europe abandoned the old monarchical forms which were consecrated by religious tradition and by the doctrine of divine right, they did not by any means abolish the sacred character of the social bond. On the contrary, they transferred all the sacred associations of the past to the new form of popular sovereignty. The representatives of the old regime, such as Kaunitz or Frederick II, were rationalists who treated politics in a completely secular spirit, while the revolutionaries, from the time of Robespierre to that of Mazzini, were political mystics who regarded the rights of the People as essentially sacred, and who dedicated their lives to the cause of Democracy in a thoroughly religious spirit. And the same too is true of the consecration of work and the consecration of place. The three main substitutes for religion in the modern age, Democracy, Socialism, and Nationalism, which are typical of the age of transition from a religious to a secular society, are each of them based on one of these fundamental factors. Democracy bases its appeal on the sacredness of the People—the consecration of Folk; socialism on the sacredness of Labour—the consecration of Work; and Nationalism on the sacredness of the Fatherland—the consecration of Place. These concepts still arouse a genuinely religious emotion, though the emotion has no basis in transcendent religious values or sanctions. It is religious emotion divorced from religious belief. Social activities are no longer consecrated by being brought into relation with the transcendent realities and values which are the proper objects of religion. They are, as it were, consecrated to themselves and elevated into substitutes for the ends to which they were formerly subjected.

This, however, is an anomalous and temporary state of things. It is due to the existence of an inherited social capital of religious feeling, which has been created by objective religious beliefs and by the influence of living historic religions. But if the old religious beliefs disappear and if no new creative religious power arises to take their place, the inherited stock of religious emotion must inevitably become exhausted and the quasi-religious social idealisms of the intermediate type will themselves disappear like the true social religions of which they are the reflection.

This brings us to the fundamental problem of sociological prevision as applied to religion. How far is it possible to foresee the ultimate culmination of this process of cultural secularization? Is the society that abandons its historic religion capable of persisting indefinitely in a purely secular atmosphere, or is this state of secularization simply the transitional phase through which society passes in its progress from one form of religion to another? Now, there have been many attempts to provide a theory of the civilization-cycle, in all of which the study of religious change has occupied an important place. In recent years we had Herr Spengler's theory, which is universally known, and the less well-known theory of Sir Flinders Petrie, which appeared a few years earlier. And in addition to these theories, which are based on the study of self-contained cultural units, we have the older theories of Vico, St. Simon, Ballanche, and Comte, which involve even wider generalizations, based on universal historical data.

None of these theories is entirely satisfactory from a scientific point of view. Yet they possess common elements which point to the existence of a certain uniformity in cultural development and at least to the possibility of discovering general laws of cultural change. Thus, I believe it is necessary to admit the existence of an organic cultural unity which goes through a process of growth and decay, although the uniformity and regularity of this process have been much exaggerated. This cultural unity is always closely associated with a religious unity to which it owes its inner cohesion and form. In some cases, indeed, it is hardly possible to differentiate the two, as with Islam, which is at once a culture and a religion, and in which the culture can hardly be conceived of as existing apart from religion. Consequently a society that loses its religion loses at the same time its principle of inner cohesion, and it seems justifiable to suppose in normal cases that the loss of the historic religion of a society is a sign that it is undergoing a process of social dissolution. The process is a slow one, for, as we have seen, a religion may be replaced by a quasi-religious form of idealism which temporarily fulfils the sociological function of a genuine religion. Moreover, we must distinguish between a society that becomes partially secularized by the extension of its activities without losing its religious form, and the genuine secularization which destroys the religious form itself. We cannot, however, assume the possibility of a culture continuing to preserve its unity and to persist indefinitely without any religious form whatsoever. When the process of secularization is completed, the process of social dissolution is consummated and the culture comes to an end.

If this is so, a culture like our own, which is approaching the final stage of secularization, is faced with two alternatives:

(A) The complete secularization of Western culture may

be followed by its gradual dissolution and by the reassertion of the traditional religion-cultures of Asia which have been temporarily overshadowed by the European world-hegemony. The modern European predominance has a certain resemblance to that of Rome in the ancient world. It is based on a true culture, but it is also an imperialism which owes its extension to its superiority in military science and in mechanical organization. Hence its material development is disproportionate to its vital human resources, and the external uniformity that it is able to impress on the subject peoples veils a real diversity of culture. The weakening or dissolution of the original social nucleus on which the imperial organization is built is at once followed by the reassertion of submerged cultural traditions which seemed to have disappeared, but which were in reality only dormant. In this way a very rapid transformation of the whole cultural situation may take place without the intervention of any positively new factors. The plaster façade of civilization has crumbled and revealed the diversities of the structure behind.

(B) On the other hand, it is possible that the process of secularization may be checked or reversed either by the coming of a new religion or by a revival of the old religion with which the culture was formerly associated. This latter alternative is usually regarded as incompatible with the law of progress which so many sociological theorists have taken for granted. It is, however, by no means impossible, as we see, for example, from the history of China, which owed its apparent stability to a series of deliberate revivals of the Confucian tradition.

A development of this kind is hardly to be expected in the case of so untraditional a civilization as that of Western Europe. On the other hand, the historic religion of Europe —Christianity—has shown itself to be peculiarly adaptable to different cultural situations. Nothing could be more dissimilar than the Byzantine culture of the ninth century and the Baroque culture of the seventeenth. Both, however, were Christian cultures, and though their religion expressed itself in very different social and aesthetic forms there can be no question of its theological identity. Consequently we cannot rule out the possibility of Christianity finding further social expression in some future development of the European cultural tradition.

Nothing, however, is more difficult for the sociologist to

foresee than the particular form of religion which will dominate the mind of society, for in these matters his judgment is likely to be affected by his private religious and philosophic beliefs. The sociologist is apt to judge religious issues not merely as a sociologist, but as a theologian—and an amateur theologian at that, in the same way that the theologian who writes on social subjects is tempted to construct an amateur sociology. And as a rule the sociologist is peculiarly ill-fitted to pronounce on theological matters, since the natural bias of his own studies tends to make him emphasize those aspects of religion which are secondary and unessential from the purely religious point of view. It is necessary to remember that the successful type of religion is not that which commends itself to the politician, or the sociologist or the philosopher, but that which appeals to the religious man. For example, in eighteenth-century England, Deism, the religion which seemed to conform itself to the mentality of the age, was from the religious point of view a complete failure, and proved unable to compete successfully with the Wesleyan revival, a movement which made no appeal except to the purely religious consciousness. Thus the decisive question for the sociologist to consider will be not what type of religion is most capable of coming to terms with the secular elements in our culture, with modern secular thought, or even with modern science, but rather what is the type of religion which is strongest on its own ground, which makes the greatest appeal to the religious consciousness and possesses the most authentically religious character. Thus the sociologist of nineteen centuries ago would have had to direct his attention not to the obvious phenomenon of the Augustan revival, with its official propaganda and its admirable literary expression, nor to the fashionable religious philosophy of Stoicism, but to the obscure religious movements that were taking place among the populace in the Oriental provinces of the Empire. Such awareness is, of course, inconceivable in the circumstances of that age, but we may well doubt if it would be possible even today, and this example may afford some measure of the extent of the task that lies before sociology in the religious field.

—1934.

10

T. S. Eliot on the Meaning
of Culture [1]

IT is eighty years ago since Matthew Arnold first took up the
cudgels in defence of culture against the Philistines as represented by John Bright and Frederic Harrison and the *Daily
Telegraph*. At that date the very word was unfamiliar, and
when John Bright described it as "a smattering of two dead
languages" he was probably expressing the views of the average Englishman. Today the situation has entirely changed.
The word is not only accepted; it has been adopted by the
planners and the politicians, and has become part of the
international language or jargon of propaganda and ideological controversy. Consequently when Mr. Eliot comes forward in defence of culture, his first task is to rescue the
word from the bad company into which it has fallen, to
define its proper limits and to restore its intellectual respecta-
bility and integrity. In this he stands nearer to Matthew
Arnold than he would perhaps be willing to admit. For,
like Arnold, he is defending what are commonly termed the
"spiritual values" of our Western tradition against degradation
and debasement; and Matthew Arnold's Philistines who

[1] T. S. Eliot, *Notes towards the Definition of Culture* (London, Faber & Faber, 1948; New York, Harcourt, 1949).

denied the value of culture are represented today by Mr. Eliot's antagonists who use the word "culture" as a convenient omnibus expression to cover all the subordinate non-economic social activities which have to be included in their organization of a planned society.

It is true that Mr. Eliot is no longer using the word in Matthew Arnold's sense. For while the latter was concerned only to maintain and extend its traditional classical sense as the harmonious development of human nature by the cultivation of the mind, the former has adopted the modern sociological concept of culture as a way of life common to a particular people and based on a social tradition which is embodied in its institutions, its literature and its art. Now I entirely agree with Mr. Eliot in this definition, which is in fact my own, and I believe that this use of the word has become indispensable to the historian and the sociologist. Nevertheless our acceptance of this definition should not blind us to the fact that the older classical and humanist conception of culture still prevails in English usage. In fact, the modern degradation of the word by politicians and publicists of which Mr. Eliot rightly complains is a degradation of the old aristocratic and individualist ideal of literary culture, and has little or nothing to do with the modern sociological concept of culture as the principle of social unity and continuity which has not yet established its place in current usage.

The resultant confusion is to be seen in the most unlikely quarters, for instance among the communists who one might have expected to be among the first to abandon the individualist conception of culture which is so profoundly steeped in bourgeois associations. Yet when a Soviet representative to U.N.O. recently [2] objected to the return of Russian wives to Western husbands on the ground that the married woman in England was debarred from cultural activities, he did not mean that the bourgeois housewife could not influence the common way of life owing to her low social status; he merely meant that she was so overworked that she had no time to go to the theatre or the cinema. No doubt theatre-going may be a cultural activity, just as dancing or dress-making or attending lectures may be, but how superficial and insignificant

[2] Professor Alexei Pavlov in the legal committee of the United Nations, at Paris, December 8, 1948.

are such activities in comparison with the work of making a new family; for this is not only the life-cell of the social organism, but also the vital organ of the transmission of culture in the wider sense of the word!

The value of Mr. Eliot's approach may be seen by the way in which it directs our attention to those great primary elements of culture—family, region and religion—which tend to be ignored equally by the socialist advocates of a planned society, on the one hand, and by the surviving champions of the liberal ideal of free individual culture on the other.

He does not, however, deal as fully wih the social function of the family as we might have expected, since his chapter on the organic structure of culture is almost entirely concerned with the question of classes and élites. Unfortunately contemporary opinion on this subject has been so deeply affected by the economic individualism of the nineteenth century and by the Marxian ideology of class war that it is now almost impossible to restore the sociological concept of class as Mr. Eliot sees it and as it existed in the past. For even the nineteenth-century terminology of "upper," "middle" and "lower" was already economic rather than sociological in character. (It is nearly thirty years since I heard the traditional Christian English class words—"gentle and simple" —actually used by a countryman, and even then it seemed like a voice from the remote past.) It was the need for some new terminology which would do justice to the vital non-economic sociological factors that led the late Professor Karl Mannheim [3] to introduce Pareto's term "the élites" to describe the culture-creating groups, which in his view were not necessarily identical with the dominant economic class. I do not think that Mr. Eliot is altogether justified in his criticism of this descriptive method on the ground that it posits an atomic view of society. The question as Mannheim saw it is how we can make people who are actually living in an atomic state of society understand those fundamental factors of social change which are ignored by the dominant Marxian philosophy because they have a non-economic character.

But while Mannheim is primarily interested in the mechanism of social change, Mr. Eliot is concerned above all with

---

[3] Cf. *Ideology and Utopia* (1936) and, above all, *Man and Society in an Age of Reconstruction* (1940).

the problem of social tradition—i.e. the maintenance and transmission of the standards of culture. This, he argues, is the function of the class, rather than the élite, for "it is the function of the class as a whole to preserve and communicate standards of *manners*—which are a vital element in group culture." At this point Mr. Eliot comes into sharp collision with the dominant ideologies not only of Marxian socialism but of his own democratic world. For the equalitarian traditions of the American and the French Revolutions have always been profoundly hostile to the idea of an organic class structure; and though American society has travelled a long way from the agrarian democracy of the early nineteenth century, it has always accepted the atomic conception of society which Mr. Eliot condemns; so that the millionaires, at any rate in theory, represent an economic élite with no uniform social background rather than a governing class or an economic aristocracy. Hence when Mr. Eliot asserts his belief in a society with a class structure and a continuous gradation of cultural levels, he is stating what would have been a truism to Burke and Fitzjames Stephen, but is now dismissed without discussion as a reactionary prejudice by both the political camps into which the modern world is divided.

Nevertheless the problem is a serious one which at least deserves serious discussion. We are too apt to believe that everything would go well with the world if only we could enforce common standards by universal economic planning and some form of political world organization, and we ignore the tremendous dangers which threaten man's spiritual freedom under the impersonal tyranny of a mechanized order in which the individual is considered merely as one among the hundred million or five hundred million units which compose the modern promiscuous mass society. But no class system or stratified social structure can save us from the horrors of total planning. On the contrary, I am sure that the mechanization of society would inevitably produce a new and more exclusive system of specialized classes or castes, such as was developed in a more primitive form by the collectivism of the later Roman Empire.

Religion, not social differentiation, is the real safeguard of spiritual freedom, since it alone brings man into relation with a higher order of reality than the world of politics or even of culture and establishes the human soul on eternal foundations. This, however, does not mean that religion is alien from or indifferent to culture. No one could put the case for the unity of religion and culture more strongly than Mr. Eliot does. In fact he argues that if a culture is the way of life of a whole people, then a Christian people, which seeks to be wholly Christian and Christian all the time, must inevitably aspire to the identification of religion and culture. In other words, a culture is the incarnation of a religion: they are not two different things which may be related to one another, but different aspects of the same thing: one common life, viewed at different levels or in reference to different ends.

If this view is carried to its logical conclusion, it leads us into considerable difficulties, as Mr. Eliot himself admits. "To reflect that from one point of view religion is culture," he writes, "and from another point of view culture is religion, can be very disturbing. To ask whether the people have not a religion already, in which Derby Day and the dog-track play their parts, is embarrassing: so is the suggestion that part of the religion of the higher ecclesiastic is gaiters and the Athenæum. It is inconvenient for Christians to find that as Christians they do not believe enough, and that on the other hand they, with everyone else, believe in too many things: yet this is a consequence of reflecting that bishops are a part of English culture, and that horses and dogs are a part of English religion."

Yet, in spite of these paradoxical consequences Mr. Eliot remains convinced that religion and culture are inseparable and that the traditional conception of a *relation* between religion and culture as two distinct realities is fundamentally erroneous and inacceptable. Yet I believe that the idea of such a relation is inseparable from the traditional Christian conception of religion and that the paradoxes that are inherent in his view are gratuitous difficulties which are due to ignoring the necessary transcendence of the religious factor. No doubt there are religions, like those of ancient Greece and Rome, which are inseparably bound up with their respective culture and are in a sense cultural products. But the higher religions, and especially Christianity, involve a certain dualism from the nature of their spiritual claims. Here the relation of religion and culture is simply the social corollary of the relation between *Faith* and *Life*.

When St. Augustine came to Kent the Jutes already possessed their common way of life and their national or tribal culture. Their conversion to Christianity certainly affected their way of life in some respects, but it did not abolish it in order to create a Christian culture *de novo*. Religion and culture were in fact two distinct traditions which were *related* to one another but never wholly identified. And the same holds good of modern society. Our religion, if we are Christians, is founded on a conscious act of faith, which may or may not be a transforming influence in our lives. But our culture is a way of life which already exists without any deliberate choice on our part, and which depends on external circumstances of place and work and language and social institutions.

Certainly religion is the great creative force in culture and almost every historic culture has been inspired and informed by some great religion. Nevertheless Religion and Culture remain essentially distinct from one another in idea, and the more religious a religion is the more does it tend to assert its *"otherness"* and its transcendence of the limits of culture. This ultimate dualism is most strongly marked in Christianity which has always placed its centre of gravity outside the present world, so that the Christian way of life is seen as that of a stranger and an exile who looks home towards the eternal city in which alone his true citizenship is to be found. This "otherworldliness" has often been a cause of offence to modern critics of religion who regard Christianity as a reactionary force and an obstacle to the progress of civilization. It is true that if we regard culture as the fruit of a natural process of adaptation by which society finds a way of life perfectly fitted to its natural environment, any higher religion is bound to exert a disturbing influence. Christianity brings a sword of division into human life, and closes the gate which leads back to the dream of a social Utopia and a state of natural perfection.

Nevertheless this introduction of a higher spiritual principle into man's life—this denial of the self-sufficiency and self-centredness of human life—is no more opposed to the development of culture than it is to the freedom of the personality. On the contrary, the widening of man's spiritual horizon, which results from the Christian view of the world, also widens the field of culture, just as the personality of the individual is deepened and exalted by the consciousness of his spiritual destiny.

No one understands this better than Mr. Eliot, who has done so much to restore to our generation a consciousness of the high tradition of Christian culture. Indeed, his own poetic achievement is a most striking example of the way in which the Christian view of reality has enriched and deepened the inner life of our own contemporary culture. And what is here achieved in the unique personal form of poetic creation may be realized also at every level of the social process in the common life of the people as a whole. Everywhere man's way of life is capable of being guided and informed by the spirit of religious faith. But, however completely a culture may seem to be dominated by religion, there remains a fundamental dualism between the order of culture which is part of the order of nature and the principle of faith which transcends the natural order and finds its centre outside the world of man.

It is this conception of the intervention of a transcendent divine principle in the life of man which none the less retains its roots in the earth and in the order of nature that renders the history of Christian culture so difficult to investigate and the ideal of Christian culture so hard to realize. But it is a problem that we cannot afford to ignore. In the past the problem was simplified by the existence of a common religious tradition and a common standard of literary culture which were generally accepted by Christians and educationalists. Today these common traditions have been abandoned by the rulers of the modern State and the planners of modern society, while at the same time the latter have come to exercise a more complete control over the thought and life of the whole population than the most autocratic and authoritarian powers of the past ever possessed. In this situation the work of men like Mr. T. S. Eliot who are able to meet the planners and sociologists on their own ground without losing sight of the real spiritual issues may be of decisive importance for the future of our culture.

—1949.

SECTION II: THE MOVEMENT OF WORLD HISTORY

1

Religion and the Life of Civilization

EVER since the rise of the modern scientific movement in the eighteenth century there has been a tendency among sociologists and historians of culture to neglect the study of religion in its fundamental social aspects. The apostles of the eighteenth-century Enlightenment were, above all, intent on deducing the laws of social life and progress from a small number of simple rational principles. They hacked through the luxuriant and deep-rooted growth of traditional belief with the ruthlessness of pioneers in a tropical jungle. They felt no need to understand the development of the historic religions and their influence on the course of human history; for, to them, historic religion was essentially negative, it was the clogging and obscurantist power ever dragging back the human spirit in its path towards progress and enlightenment. With Condorcet, they traced religious origins no further than to the duplicity of the first knave and the simplicity of the first fool.

And in the nineteenth century, apart from the St. Simonian circle, the same attitude, expressed with less frankness and brutality, it is true, still dominated scientific thought, and found classical expression in England in the culture-history of Buckle and in the sociology of Herbert Spencer. Indeed, today, in spite of the reaction of the last thirty years, it has largely become a part of our intellectual heritage, and is taken for granted in much current sociology and anthropology. Religion was conceived of as a complex of ideas and speculations concerning the Unknowable, and thus belonged to a different world to that which was the province of sociology. The social progress which the latter science studies is the result of the direct response of man to his material environment and to the growth of positive knowledge concerning the material world. Thus social evolution is a unity which can be studied without reference to the numerous changing systems of religious belief and practice that have risen and fallen during its course. The latter may reflect, in some degree, the cultural circumstances under which they have arisen, but they are secondary, and in no sense a formative element in the production of culture.

And undoubtedly these ideas held good for the age in which they were formed. During the eighteenth and nineteenth centuries the world of secular culture was an autonomous kingdom, whose progress owed nothing to the beliefs and sanctions of the existing authoritative religion. But it is dangerous to argue back from the highly specialized conditions of an advanced and complicated civilization to the elementary principles of social development. Indeed, it needs but a moment's thought to realize that that extraordinary age of intellectual, political and economic revolutions is comparable to no other period in the history of the world. It was at once creative and destructive, but essentially transitional and impermanent, and this instability was due to no other cause than to that very separation and dislocation of the inner and outer worlds of human experience, which the thinkers of the age accepted as a normal condition of existence.

Religion and the Rise of Ancient Civilization

For a social culture, even of the most primitive kind, is never simply a material unity. It involves not only a certain uniformity in social organization and in the way of life, but also a continuous and conscious psychic discipline. Even a common language, one of the first requirements of civilized life, can only be produced by ages of co-operative effort—common thinking as well as common action. From the very dawn of primitive culture men have attempted, in however crude and symbolic a form, to understand the laws of life, and to adapt their social activity to their workings. Primitive man never looked on the world in the modern way, as a passive or, at most, mechanistic system, a background for human energies, mere matter for the human mind to mould. He saw the world as a living world of mysterious forces, greater than his own, in the placation and service of which his life consisted. And the first need for a people, no less vital than food or weapons, was the psychic equipment or armament by which they fortified themselves against the powerful and mysterious forces that surrounded them. It is impossible for us to draw the line between religion and magic, between law and morals, so intimately is the whole social life of a primitive people bound up with its religion. And the same is true of the earliest civilization. The first development of a higher culture in the Near East, the beginnings of agriculture and irrigation, and the rise of city life were profoundly religious in their conception. Men did not learn to control the forces of nature, to make the earth fruitful, and to raise flocks and herds as a practical task of economic organization in which they relied on their own enterprise and hard work. They viewed it rather as a religious rite by which they co-operated as priests or hierophants in the great cosmic mystery of the fertilization and growth of nature. The mystical drama, annually renewed, of the Mother-Goddess and her dying and reviving son and spouse, was, at the same time, the economic cycle of ploughing and seed time and harvest by which the people lived. And the king was not so much the organizing ruler of a political community, as the priest and religious head of his people, who represented the god himself and stood between the goddess and her people, interpreting to them the divine will, and sometimes even offering up his own life for them in a solemn ritual ceremony.

Thus there was a profound sense that man lived not by his own strength and knowledge, but by his acting in harmony with the divine cosmic powers, and this harmony could only be attained by sacrifice and at the price of blood; whether the sacrifice of virility, as in Asia Minor, of the first-born children, as in Syria, or of the life of the king himself, as we seem to see dimly in the very dawn of history throughout the Near East.

It is even possible that agriculture and the domestication

of animals were exclusively religious in their beginnings, and had their origin in the ritual observation and imitation of the processes of nature which is so characteristic of this type of religion. Certainly the mimicry of nature was carried to very great lengths, as we can see in the religion of Asia Minor in historic times. Sir William Ramsay has even suggested that the whole organization of the shrine of the great goddess at Ephesus and at other places in Lydia and Phrygia was an elaborate imitation of the life of the bees and the hive; the priestesses being named "mellissae"—the working bees; the priests, or "essenes," representing the drones; while the goddess herself was the queen-bee, whose behaviour to her temporary partner certainly bears a striking analogy to that of the goddess to Attis in the Phrygian legend.

But it is only in highly conservative regions like Asia Minor that we can see this primitive religion in comparative simplicity. In Babylonia at the very dawn of history, in the fourth millennium B.C., it had already developed a highly specialized theology and temple ritual. The god and goddess of each city had acquired special characteristics and personalities, and had taken their place in a Sumerian pantheon. But Sumerian civilization still remained entirely religious in character. The god and the goddess were the acknowledged rulers of their city, the king was but their high-priest and steward. The temple, the house of the god, was the centre of the life of the community, for the god was the chief landowner, trader and banker, and kept a great staff of servants and administrators. The whole city territory was, moreover, the territory of the god, and the Sumerians spoke not of the boundaries of the city of Kish or the city of Lagash, but of the boundaries of the god Enlil or the god Ningirsu. All that the king did for his city was undertaken at the command of the god and for the god. Thus we read how Entemena, of Lagash, "made the mighty canal at the boundary of Enlil for Ningirsu, the king whom he loved." At the command of Enlil, Nina and Ningirsu he cut the great canal from the Tigris to the Euphrates— the Shatt el Hai—which was one of the greatest feats of ancient engineering. And the remains of the ancient literature that have come down to us prove that this is not merely the phraseology of the State religion; it represented a profound popular belief in the interdependence and communion of the city and its divinity.

And if we turn to Egypt, we find a no less intensely religious spirit impregnating the archaic culture.

Never, perhaps, before or since, has a high civilization attained to the centralization and unification that characterized the Egyptian state in the age of the pyramid-builders. It was more than state socialism, for it meant the entire absorption of the whole life of the individual, in a cause outside himself. The whole vast bureaucratic and economic organization of the empire was directed to a single end, the glorification of the Sun-God and his child, the God-King.

> It is he (the sun-god) who has adorned thee (Egypt).
> It is he who has built thee.
> It is he who has founded thee
> Thou dost for him everything that he says to thee
> In every place where he goes.
> Thou carriest to him every tree that is in thee.
> Thou carriest to him all food that is in thee.
> Thou carriest to him the gifts that are in thee.
> Thou carriest to him everything that is in thee.
> Thou carriest to him everything that shall be in thee.
> Thou bringest them to him
> To every place where his heart desires to be.[1]

It is indeed one of the most remarkable spectacles in history to see all the resources of a great culture and a powerful state organized, not for war and conquest, not for the enrichment of a dominant class, but simply to provide the sepulchre and to endow the chantries and tomb-temples of the dead kings. And yet it was this very concentration on death and the after-life that gave Egyptian civilization its amazing stability. The sun and the Nile, Re and Osiris, the pyramid and the mummy, as long as these remained, it seemed that Egypt must stand fast, her life bound up in the unending round of prayer and ritual observance. All the great development of Egyptian art and learning—astronomy and mathematics and engineering—grew up in the service of this central religious idea, and when, in the age of final decadence, foreign powers took possession of the

[1] Breasted, *Development of Religion and Thought in Ancient Egypt*, pp. 13–14.

sacred kingdom, Libyans and Persians, Greeks and Romans all found it necessary to "take the gifts of Horus" and to disguise their upstart imperialism under the forms of the ancient solar theocracy, in order that the machinery of Egyptian civilization should continue to function.

The Decline of the Archaic Religion-Culture

Yet, both in Egypt and in Western Asia, the primitive theocratic culture had begun to decline by the second half of the third millennium B.C. The rise of the great states of Egypt and Babylonia had, on the one hand, made man less dependent on the forces of nature, and, on the other hand, had brought him face to face with a new series of problems —moral and intellectual—which appear in a striking form in the early Egyptian literature of the Middle Kingdom. The Song of King Intef, the Admonition of Ipuwer, the Complaint of Khekheperre-Sonbu, and, above all, the so-called Dialogue of One Weary of Life with his own Soul, all bear witness to a profound criticism of life, and an intense spiritual ferment. And at the same period in Babylonia we find a similar attitude expressed in the poem of the Righteous Sufferer, the so-called Babylonian Job. Man no longer accepted the world and the state as they were, as the manifestation of the divine powers. They compared the world they knew with the social and moral order that they believed in, and condemned the former. Consequently, for the first time we get a sense of dualism between what is and what ought to be, between the way of men and the way of the gods. The state and the kingship are no longer entirely religious in the kings of the new type—those Twelfth-Dynasty monarchs who are among the greatest and most virile rulers that have ever reigned. We are conscious of a clear realization of human, personal power and responsibility, and at the same time of a profound disillusionment. We see this in the famous inscription which Senusret III set up at the southern boundary of Egypt, bidding his subjects not to worship his statue, but to fight for it; and yet more intimately in the warning that the founder of the dynasty, Amenemhet I, gave to his son and successor: "Fill not thy heart with a brother, know not a friend, make not for thyself intimates wherein there is no end, harden thyself against subordinates, that thou mayest be king of the earth, that thou mayest be ruler of the lands, that thou mayest increase good." [2]

The same spirit of pride and self-reliance breathes in the fierce leonine faces of Senusret III and Amenemhet III, and distinguishes the sculpture of the Twelfth Dynasty from that of the Old Kingdom, which, for all its realism, was interpenetrated by a profoundly religious spirit. Hence, perhaps, the premature ending of this brilliant epoch, and the return, after the Hyksos invasions, to the traditional religiosity of the past, which was inseparable from the survival of the Egyptian state. That the new spirit of criticism and thought continued to be active is, however, proved by the appearance under the Eighteenth Dynasty, in the fourteenth century B.C., of Akhnaten's bold attempt to institute a new solar monotheism as the state religion of Egypt and Syria. Here already, in the fourteenth century B.C., we find the essentials of a world religion—a religion that is universal in its claims, and which attempts to find the source and first principle which lies behind all the changing phenomena of nature. But the traditional theocratic religion-culture of the Nile Valley was too strong for any such innovation, and the author of the reform went down to history as "the criminal of Akhetaton."

The Coming of the World-Religions

But, in the course of the following millennium B.C., a spiritual change of the most profound significance passed over the world, a change which was not confined to any one people or culture, but which made itself felt from India to the Mediterranean and from China to Persia. And it brought with it a complete revolution in culture, since it involved the destruction of the old religious civilization that was based on a co-operation with the divinized forces of nature, and the discovery of a new world of absolute and unchanging reality beside which the natural world—the world of appearances and of earthly life—paled into a shadow and became dream-like and illusory.

Alike in India and in Greece we can trace a striving towards the conception of an invisible underlying cosmic cause

[2] *Cambridge Ancient History*, I, 303; Breasted, *op. cit.*, p. 303, A.R.E., I, 474–83.

or essence—Atman, Logos, the One—and of the unreality of the continual flux which makes up the phenomenal world, but it was in India that the decisive step was first taken, and it was in India that the new view of reality was followed out unwaveringly in all its practical implications.

"He who, dwelling in the earth," says Yâjnavalkya, "is other than the earth, whom the earth knows not, whose body the earth is, who inwardly rules the earth, is thy Self (Atman), the Inward Ruler, the deathless. He who, dwelling in all beings, is other than all beings, whom all beings know not, whose body all beings are, who inwardly rules all beings, is thy Self, the Inward Ruler, the deathless. He who, dwelling in the mind, is other than the mind, whom the mind knows not, whose body the mind is, who inwardly rules the mind, is thy Self, the Inward Ruler, the deathless. He, unseen, sees; unheard, hears; unthought, thinks; uncomprehended, comprehends. There is no other than he who sees—hears—thinks—comprehends. He is thy Self, the Inward Ruler, the deathless. All else is fraught with sorrow." [3]

Hence the one end of life, the one task for the wise man, is deliverance—to cross the bridge, to pass the ford from death to life, from appearance to reality, from time to eternity—all the goods of human life in the family or the state are vanity compared with this. "Possessed by delusion, a man toils for wife and child; but, whether he fulfills his purpose or not, he must surrender the enjoyment thereof. When one is blessed with children and flocks and his heart is clinging to them, Death carries him away as doth a tiger a sleeping deer." [4]

How far removed is this attitude from the simple acquiescence in the good things of this world that is shown by the nature-religions and by the archaic culture that was founded on them! The whole spirit of the new teaching is ascetic, whether it is the intellectual asceticism of the Brahman purging his soul by a kind of Socratic discipline, or the bodily asceticism of the "sannyasi," who seeks deliverance by the gate of "tapas"—bodily penance. And so there arose

[3] Brihadaranyaka Upanishad, III, vii, trans. L. D. Barnett.
[4] Mahabharata, XII, chap. 175 and chap. 174, trans. L. D. Barnett.

in India, especially in the fifth and sixth centuries B.C., a series of "disciplines of salvation"; that of the Jains, that of the Yoga and many more, culminating in the greatest of them all, the Way of Buddha. Buddhism is perhaps the most characteristic of all the religions of the new universalist and absolute type, since it seems to make the fewest metaphysical and theological assumptions, and yet to present the anti-natural, world-denying conception of life in its extremest form. Life is evil, the body is evil, matter is evil. All existence is bound to the wheel of birth and death, of suffering and desire. Not only is this human life an illusion, but the life of the gods is an illusion, too, and behind the whole cosmic process there is no underlying reality—neither Brahman nor Atman nor the Gunas. There is only the torture-wheel of sentient existence and the path of deliverance, the *"via negativa"* of the extinction of desire which leads to Nirvana—the Eternal Beatific Silence.

At first sight nothing could be further removed from the world-refusal of the Indian ascetic than the Hellenic attitude to life. Yet the Greeks of Ionia and Italy, during the sixth and fifth centuries B.C., were bent, no less than the Indians, on piercing the veil of appearances and reaching the underlying reality. It is true that the Greeks set out in their quest for the ultimate cosmic principle in a spirit of youthful curiosity and free rational inquiry, and thereby became the creators of natural science. But there was also the purely religious current of Orphic mysticism, with its doctrines of rebirth and immortality, and the progressive enlightenment of the soul and its emancipation from the defilements of corporeal existence, which had a powerful influence on the Greek mind and even on Greek philosophy, until at last the vision of eternity, which had so long absorbed the mind of India, burst on the Greek world with dazzling power.

It was through the golden mouth of Plato that the vision of the two worlds—the world of appearance and shadows, and the world of timeless, changeless reality—found classic expression in the West. The Greek mind turned, with Plato, away from the many-coloured, changing world of appearance and unreality to that other world of the eternal Forms, "where abides the very Being with which true knowledge is concerned, the colourless, formless, intangible essence, visible only to the mind, the pilot of the soul"; [5] "a nature which is everlasting, not growing or decaying or waxing or waning, but Beauty only, absolute, separate, simple and everlasting, which, without diminution and without increase or any change in itself, is imparted to the ever-growing and perishing beauties of all other things." [6] "What if man had eyes to see this true Beauty—pure and unalloyed, not clogged with the pollutions of mortality and all the colours and vanities of human life," [7] would not all human and terrestrial things become mean and unimportant to such a one? And is not the true end of life to return whence we came, "to fly away from earth to heaven," to recover the divine and deific vision which once "we beheld shining in pure light, pure ourselves and not yet enshrined in that living tomb which we carry about, now that we are imprisoned in the body, like the oyster in his shell." [8] This note, so characteristic and so unforgettable, is never afterwards wholly lost in the ancient world, and it is renewed with redoubled emphasis in that final harvest of the Hellenic tradition, which is Neo-Platonism.

The World-Religions and Material Progress

It is easy for us to understand a few exceptional men, philosophers and mystics, adopting this attitude to life, but it is harder to realize how it could become the common possession of a whole society or civilization. Yet, in the course of a few centuries, it became the common possession of practically all the great cultures of the ancient world. It is true that Confucian China was a partial exception, but even China was almost submerged, for a time, by the invasion of Indian mysticism and monasticism, for which the way had already been prepared by the native Taoist tradition.

And each of the cultures had to deal with essentially the same problem—how to reconcile the new attitude to life with the old civilization that they had inherited, a civilization that had been built up so laboriously by the worship

[5] *Phaedrus*, 247.

[6] *Symposium*, 211.

[7] *Ibid.*, 211.

[8] *Phaedrus*, 250.

and cultivation of the powers of nature. It is obvious that the new religions were not themselves productive of a new material civilization; their whole tendency was away from the material and economic side of life towards the life of pure spirit. It is indeed difficult to see how the most extreme examples of this type of religion, such as Manichaeanism, were reconcilable with any material social culture whatever. In other cases, however, especially in India, the archaic culture was able to maintain itself almost intact, in spite of the dominance of the new religions. As Professor Slater has well said, it is in the great temple cities of Dravidian India that we can still see before us today the vanished civilizations of Egypt and Babylonia.[9]

To the teacher or ascetic of the new religion the ancient rites have acquired an esoteric and symbolic significance, while the common people still find in them their ancient meaning, and seek contact through them with the beneficent or destructive powers of nature that rule the peasant's life. In yet other cases, above all in Islam, this dualism is impossible, and the whole of life is brought into direct relation with the new religious conception. Terrestrial life loses its intrinsic importance, it is but as "the beat of a gnat's wing" in comparison with the eternal. But it acquires importance as a preparation, a time of training and warfare, of which the discipline and suffering are repaid by the eternal joys of Paradise.

Thus the new religions in these three main types are, on the whole, not favourable to material progress. In some cases they are even retrograde. Sir William Ramsay has shown, in the case of Asia Minor, how the passing of the old nature-religions had a depressing effect on agriculture, on economic prosperity and even perhaps on hygiene; and the same thing is no doubt true, in some degree, of many different regions. The great achievements of the new culture lie in the domain of literature and art. But, from the material point of view, there is expansion rather than progress.

---

[9] "In other parts of India, one feels oneself sometimes carried back into the Middle Ages . . . in such a temple as that of Menakshi and Siva in Madura one can only dream of having revisited some great shrine of Isis and Osiris in Egypt, or of Marduk in Babylon."—Slater, *The Dravidian Element in Indian Culture*, p. 167.

The new culture simply gave a new form and a new spirit to the materials that it had received from the archaic civilization. In all essentials Babylonia, in the time of Hammurabi, and even earlier, had reached a pitch of material civilization which has never since been surpassed in Asia. After the artistic flowering of the early Middle Ages the great religion-cultures became stationary and even decadent. Eternity was changeless, and why should man, who lived for eternity, change?

This is the secret of the "Unchanging East," which has impressed so many Western observers, and which gives to a civilization such as that of Burma its remarkable attractiveness and charm. But such societies are living on the past; they do not advance in power and knowledge, it even seems as though they are retreating step by step before the powers of primitive nature until at last they disappear, as the marvellous achievements of Ankhor and Anuradapura have been swallowed up by the jungle.

The Rise of the Modern Scientific Culture

But a ferment of change, a new principle of movement and progress, has entered the world with the civilization of modern Europe.

The development of the European culture was, of course, largely conditioned by religious traditions the consideration of which lies outside the limits of this enquiry. It was, however, not until the fifteenth and sixteenth centuries that the new principle, which characterized the rise of modern civilization, made its appearance. It was then that there arose—first in Italy and afterwards throughout Western Europe—the new attitude to life that has been well named Humanism. It was, in fact, a reaction against the whole transcendent spiritualist view of existence, a return from the divine and the absolute to the human and the finite. Man turned away from the pure white light of eternity to the warmth and colour of the earth. He rediscovered nature, not, indeed, as the divine and mysterious power that men had served and worshipped in the first stages of civilization, but as a reasonable order which he could know by science and art, and which he could use to serve his own purpose.

"Experiment," says Leonardo da Vinci, the great precursor,

"is the true interpreter between nature and man." Experience is never at fault. What is at fault is man's laziness and ignorance. "Thou, O God, dost sell us all good things for the price of work."

This is the essential note of the new European movement; it was applied science, not abstract, speculative knowledge, as with the Greeks. "Mechanics," says Leonardo again, "are the Paradise of the mathematical sciences, for in them the fruits of the latter are reaped." And the same principles of realism and practical reason are applied in political life.

The State was no longer an ideal hierarchy that symbolized and reflected the order of the spiritual world. It was the embodiment of human power, whose only law was Necessity.

Yet no complete break was made with the past. The people remained faithful to the religious tradition. Here and there a Giordano Bruno in philosophy or a Machiavelli in statecraft gave their whole-hearted adhesion to Naturalism, but for the most part both statesmen and philosophers endeavoured to serve two masters, like Descartes or Richelieu. They remained fervent Christians, but at the same time they separated the sphere of religion from the sphere of reason, and made the latter an independent autonomous kingdom in which the greater part of their lives was spent.

It was only in the eighteenth century that this compromise, which so long dominated European culture, broke down before the assaults of the new humanists, the Encyclopaedists and the men of the Enlightenment in France, England and Germany. We have already described the attitude of that age to religion—its attempt to sweep away the old accumulation of tradition and to refound civilization on a rational and naturalistic basis. And the negative side of this programme was, indeed, successfully carried out. European civilization was thoroughly secularized. The traditional European polity, with its semi-divine royalty, its state Churches and its hereditary aristocratic hierarchy, was swept away and its place was taken by the liberal bourgeois state of the nineteenth century, which aimed, above all, at industrial prosperity and commercial expansion. But the positive side of the achievement was much less secure. It is true that Western Europe and the United States of America advanced enormously in wealth and population, and in control over the forces of nature; while the type of culture that they had developed spread itself victoriously over the old world of Asia and the new world of Africa and Oceania, first by material conquest, and later by its intellectual and scientific prestige, so that the great Oriental religion-cultures began to lose their age-long, unquestioned dominance over the daily life and thought of the peoples of the East, at least, among the educated classes.

Progress and Disillusionment the Meaning of Modern Social Unrest

But there was not a corresponding progress in spiritual things. As Comte had foreseen, the progressive civilization of the West, without any unifying spiritual force, and without an intellectual synthesis, tended to fall back into social anarchy. The abandonment of the old religious traditions did not bring humanity together in a natural and moral unity, as the eighteenth-century philosophers had hoped. On the contrary, it allowed the fundamental differences of race and nationality, of class and private interest, to appear in their naked antagonism. The progress in wealth and power did nothing to appease these rivalries; rather it added fuel to them, by accentuating the contrasts of wealth and poverty, and widening the field of international competition. The new economic imperialism, as it developed in the last generation of the nineteenth century, was as grasping, as unmoral, and as full of dangers of war, as any of the imperialisms of the old order. And, while under the old order the state had recognized its limits as against a spiritual power, and had only extended its claims over a part of human life, the modern state admitted no limitations, and embraced the whole life of the individual citizen in its economic and military organization.

Hence the rise of a new type of social unrest. Political disturbances are as old as human nature; in every age misgovernment and oppression have been met by violence and disorder, but it is a new thing, and perhaps a phenomenon peculiar to our modern Western civilization, that men should work and think and agitate for the complete remodelling of society according to some ideal of social perfection. It belongs to the order of religion, rather than to that of politics, as politics were formerly understood. It finds its only parallel in the past in movements of the most extreme religious type, like that of the Anabaptists in sixteenth-century Germany, and the Levellers and Fifth-Monarchy Men of Puritan England. And when we study the lives of the founders of modern Socialism, the great Anarchists and even some of the apostles of nationalist Liberalism like Mazzini, we feel at once that we are in the presence of religious leaders, whether prophets or heresiarchs, saints or fanatics. Behind the hard rational surface of Karl Marx's materialist and socialist interpretation of history there burns the flame of an apocalyptic vision. For what was that social revolution in which he put his hope but a nineteenth-century version of the Day of the Lord, in which the rich and the powerful of the earth should be consumed, and the princes of the Gentiles brought low, and the poor and disinherited should reign in a regenerated universe? So, too, Marx, in spite of his professed atheism, looked for the realization of this hope, not, like St. Simon and his fellow-idealist Socialists, to the conversion of the individual and to human efforts towards the attainment of a new social ideal, but to "the arm of the Lord," the necessary, ineluctable working-out of the Eternal Law, which human will and human effort are alike powerless to change or stay.

But the religious impulse behind these social movements is not a constructive one. It is as absolute in its demands as that of the old religions, and it admits of no compromise with reality. As soon as the victory is gained, and the phase of destruction and revolution is ended, the inspiration fades away before the tasks of practical realization. We look in vain in the history of United Italy for the religious enthusiasm that sustained Mazzini and his fellows, and it took very few years to transform the Rousseauan idealism of revolutionary France, the Religion of Humanity, into Napoleonic and even Machiavellian realism.

The revolutionary attitude—and it is perhaps the characteristic religious attitude of modern Europe—is, in fact, but another symptom of the divorce between religion and social life. The nineteenth-century revolutionaries—the Anarchists, the Socialists and, to some extent, the Liberals—were driven to their destructive activities by the sense that actual European society was a mere embodiment of material force and fraud—*"magnum latrocinium,"* as St. Augustine says—that it was based on no principle of justice, and organized for no spiritual or ideal end; and the more the simpler and more obvious remedies—republicanism, universal suffrage, national self-determination—proved disappointing to the reformers, the deeper became their dissatisfaction with the whole structure of existing society. And, finally, when the process of disillusionment is complete, this religious impulse that lies behind the revolutionary attitude may turn itself against social life altogether, or at least against the whole system of civilization that has been built up in the last two centuries. This attitude of mind seems endemic in Russia, partly, perhaps, as an inheritance of the Byzantine religious tradition. We see it appearing in different forms in Tolstoi, in Dostoievski and in the Nihilists, and it is present as a psychic undercurrent in most of the Russian revolutionary movements. It is the spirit which seeks not political reform, not the improvement of social conditions, but escape, liberation—Nirvana. In the words of a modern poet (Francis Adams), it is

> To wreck the great guilty temple,
> And give us Rest.

And in the years since the War, when the failure of the vast machinery of modern civilization has seemed so imminent, this view of life has become more common even in the West. It has inspired the poetry of Albert Ehrenstein and many others.[10]

Mr. D. H. Lawrence has well expressed it in Count Psanek's profession of faith, in *The Ladybird* (pp. 43–4):

I have found my God. The god of destruction. The god of anger, who throws down the steeples and factory chimneys.

Not the trees, these chestnuts, for example—not these— nor the chattering sorcerers, the squirrels—nor the hawk that comes. Not those.

What grudge have I against a world where even the hedges are full of berries, branches of black berries that hang down and red berries that thrust up? Never would I hate the world. But the world of man—I hate it.

I believe in the power of my dark red heart. God has put the hammer in my breast—the little eternal hammer. Hit— hit—hit. It hits on the world of man. It hits, it hits. And it hears the thin sound of cracking.

[10] For instance, the following verse:
Ich beschwöre euch, zerstampfet die Stadt.
Ich beschwöre euch, zertrümmert die Städte.
Ich beschwöre euch, zerstört die Maschine.
Ich beschwöre euch, zerstöret den Staat.

Oh, may I live long. May I live long, so that my hammer may strike and strike, and the cracks go deeper, deeper. Ah, the world of man. Ah, the joy, the passion in every heartbeat. Strike home, strike true, strike sure. Strike to destroy it. Strike, Strike. To destroy the world of man. Ah, God. Ah, God, prisoner of peace.

It may seem to some that these instances are negligible, mere morbid extravagances, but it is impossible to exaggerate the dangers that must inevitably arise when once social life has become separated from the religious impulse.

We have only to look at the history of the ancient world and we shall see how tremendous are these consequences. The Roman Empire, and the Hellenistic civilization of which it was the vehicle, became separated in this way from any living religious basis, which all the efforts of Augustus and his helpers were powerless to restore; and thereby, in spite of its high material and intellectual culture, the dominant civilization became hateful in the eyes of the subject Oriental world. Rome was to them not the ideal world-city of Virgil's dream, but the incarnation of all that was anti-spiritual— Babylon the great, the Mother of Abominations, who bewitched and enslaved all the peoples of the earth, and on whom, at last, the slaughter of the saints and the oppression of the poor would be terribly avenged. And so all that was strongest and most living in the moral life of the time separated itself from the life of society and from the service of the state, as from something unworthy and even morally evil. And we see in Egypt in the fourth century, over against the great Hellenistic city of Alexandria, filled with art and learning and all that made life delightful, a new power growing up, the power of the men of the desert, the naked, fasting monks and ascetics, in whom, however, the new world recognized its masters. When, in the fifth century, the greatest of the late Latin writers summed up the history of the great Roman tradition, it is in a spirit of profound hostility and disillusionment: *"Acceperunt mercedem suam,"* says he, in an unforgettable sentence, *"vani vanam."*

This spiritual alienation of its own greatest minds is the price that every civilization has to pay when it loses its religious foundations, and is contented with a purely material success. We are only just beginning to understand how intimately and profoundly the vitality of a society is bound up with its religion. It is the religious impulse which supplies the cohesive force which unifies a society and a culture. The great civilizations of the world do not produce the great religions as a kind of cultural by-product; in a very real sense, the great religions are the foundations on which the great civilizations rest. A society which has lost its religion becomes sooner or later a society which has lost its culture.

What then is to be the fate of this great modern civilization of ours? A civilization which has gained an extension and a wealth of power and knowledge which the world has never known before. Is it to waste its forces in the pursuit of selfish and mutually destructive aims, and to perish for lack of vision? Or can we hope that society will once again become animated by a common faith and hope, which will have the power to order our material and intellectual achievements in an enduring spiritual unity?

—1925.

2

The Warrior Peoples and the Decline of the Archaic Civilization

The Pacific Character of Primitive Culture

THE Archaic Civilization reached its full development in the third millennium B.C. Thereafter the note of the civilizations of the Near East was conservation rather than progress. In many respects the general level of material culture stood higher in that age than in any subsequent period. All the great achievements on which the life of civilization rests had been reached, and there was no important addition to its material equipment until the rise of the great scientific and industrial movement in Western Europe in modern times. The most important inventions which characterize the higher culture, such as agriculture and the domestication of animals, the plough and the wheeled vehicle, irrigation and the construction of canals, the working of metals and stone architecture, navigation and sailing ships, writing and the calendar, the city-state and the institution of kingship, had been already achieved by the fourth millennium, and by the third we find organized bureaucratic states, written codes of laws, a highly developed commerce and industry, and the beginnings of astronomy and mathematics. At first sight it is difficult to understand why a civilizing movement that had gone

133

so far should go no further, and why the creative power of the Archaic Civilization should have deserted it when it was still almost in its prime. To some extent, indeed, it was due to the obscure laws that govern the life of peoples and civilizations, above all to the rigidity which seems to characterize a form of culture that has attained a complete equilibrium with its environment. But it also finds an external explanation in the rise of a new type of warlike society, which put an end to the autonomous development of the Archaic Culture, and for a time imperilled its very existence. The close of the neolithic age in Europe and corresponding period in the Near East was marked by far-reaching movements of peoples and warlike invasions which broke down the frontiers of the old culture-provinces and produced new social forms and a new distribution of peoples and cultures. It may be compared to the ages of barbarian invasion, which so often in later history marked the end of one civilization and the beginning of a new age. Indeed, it is the earliest example of this process, the first occasion in which we can trace the appearance of organized warfare as a factor in historical development. The earlier changes in culture in Europe had been predominantly peaceful. There is no sign that the transition from the palaeolithic to the neolithic age of the expansion of peasant culture in Eastern and Central Europe, or even the beginnings of the age of metal in the Mediterranean, were due in any degree to warlike invasions. In fact, from their open settlements and the lack of weapons, war can have played little part in the life of the neolithic peasant peoples. And the same is true, though to a lesser extent, of the Archaic civilizations of the Near East. There, certainly, war was not unknown, either between the city states of Sumer, or in the early states of the Nile Valley, but it was exceptional and of a rudimentary type. Society was not organized for war as in later times. There was no military caste. As Professor Breasted points out, the Egyptians of the Old Kingdom were essentially unwarlike. Their army consisted of an untrained levy of peasants, such as was used equally for the quarrying and transportation of stone for the great monuments, and its command was entrusted by the Pharaoh to some leading official who was himself not a professional soldier.

It may seem paradoxical to suggest, as Mr. Perry has

done,[1] that war is a comparatively late development in the history of humanity. It has been commonly assumed that the savage is essentially a fighter, and that the early stages of social development were marked by continual warfare. Indeed, many writers have gone further and supposed that man was by nature a beast of prey, and that his progress has been due to a ruthless struggle for existence, in which the weaker were constantly being killed off and possibly eaten by the stronger—*Homo homini lupus*, as the Romans said—regardless of the fact that even beasts of prey do not usually prey upon each other.

The error has arisen largely from the fact that civilized man, both in antiquity and in modern times, has been continuously brought into contact with warlike tribes less civilized than himself—Huns and Tartars, Caribs and Iroquois, Zulus and Maori—and has regarded these as the typical savages. Whereas in reality they are advanced and specialized types, even further removed from the really primitive peoples than they are from the civilized. Even in modern times, in spite of the ages during which men have had to adapt themselves to warlike conditions or perish, the most primitive peoples—the food-gatherers—are predominantly peaceful. Thus in America, while the most warlike peoples, such as the Aztecs and the Iroquois, were comparatively civilized, the least warlike were the exceedingly backward peoples of California and Tierra del Fuego. In Oceania there is the same contrast between the more advanced Polynesians and Fijians and the primitive natives of Australia and Tasmania. Most remarkable of all is the case of the aborigines of New Zealand and the Chatham Islands, the Moriori, who, in their relation to the warlike Maori invaders, adhered to the strict pacifist principle of non-resistance and allowed themselves to be slaughtered without resistance, like sheep.

The unwarlike character of the most primitive peoples depends mainly on the conditions of their life. War is not a paying proposition for them, since it can yield no booty, for hunters and food-gatherers possess no stored-up wealth of goods or cattle. They may fight to defend their hunting-grounds, but unless they are driven to seek new lands by some natural calamity, such as drought, each tribe tends to

[1] Cf. W. J. Perry, *An Ethnological Study of Warfare* (1917), and *War and Civilization* (1918).

keep to its own territory, and not to interfere with its neighbours. An attack on the civilized agriculturalists and cattle-keepers would, of course, be profitable, but primitive food-gatherers and hunters are too few and weak to be a serious danger to a settled population. Their relations are like those of gypsies to villagers—a danger to the henroosts, but nothing more. On the whole it is the primitive peoples who are the sufferers and the civilized who are the aggressors, as we have seen in modern times in the extinction of so many defenceless peoples, such as the Tasmanians or the natives of the West Indies at the hands of European colonists.

The Pastoral Society and the Rise of the Warrior Peoples

But when the hunters have begun to acquire some elements of the higher culture from their more civilized neighbours, the case is altered. When once they possess flocks and herds, or begin to cultivate the ground, their sparse population increases, and they become numerous enough to be formidable. Originally, as we have pointed out before, the domestication of animals went hand in hand with agriculture, and was probably the discovery of the higher settled culture. But it was an invention, which in the nature of things spread quickly and widely. Tame animals which had strayed or been stolen must sooner or later come into the possession of the hunters, just as the horses of the Spaniards were acquired by the Indians of the plains; and natural increase would suffice to do the rest. Thus, there grew up a new type of society—that of the nomadic pastoral tribe—based on the combination of the life of the hunter with that of the shepherd, as the ancient agricultural civilization had been based on the combination of agriculture and the domestication of animals.

In this way there tends to grow up round every centre of the higher civilization a zone of lower culture which is to some extent dependent or parasitic upon its civilized neighbours, while at the same time possessing a higher degree of mobility and a greater aptitude for war. Thus to the settled Semitic civilizations of Mesopotamia and Syria and South Arabia there corresponds the predatory nomad culture of the Bedouin, and to Egypt the pastoral culture of the Libyans and the other Hamitic peoples of North Africa. So, too, in Eastern Asia we find a similar zone of nomad Mongolian peoples on the north-western frontiers of China, and in Central Asia the peoples of the steppes have owed their culture to the settled civilization of Persia and Turkestan; while in prehistoric Europe the same relation existed between the peasant cultures of the Danube and the Dnieper and the warlike peoples to the north and east.

But in spite of their original relation of cultural dependence, the social organization of the pastoral peoples was in almost every respect a complete contrast to that of the sedentary agriculturalist. Whereas the latter rested on the basis of a fixed territorial settlement and on common labour, the former was characterized by the development of the institutions of property and kinship. The importance of a tribe or a family depended on their wealth in flocks and herds, an ever-varying factor which at once introduced an element of inequality, whereas the amount of land held by a primitive agriculturalist is strictly limited by his powers of cultivation. Any man can take as much land as he wants, by clearing a patch of jungle, but it is not the land itself that is valuable, but the labour which renders it fruitful. Thus the woman who cultivates the ground is, as has been noticed before, as important as or even more important than the man, and the primitive agricultural community often possesses a matrilinear or matriarchal organization.

On the other hand, the pastoral tribe is patriarchal and aristocratic, and the masculine element everywhere predominates. The shepherd requires no less daring and hardihood than the hunter. He has to defend his flock against the attacks of wild beasts, and the raids of other nomads. The choice of new pastures and the conduct of tribal forays constantly call for the exercise of qualities of leadership and decision.

The pastoral society produces types like Abraham, men rich in flocks and herds, with many wives and children, wise in counsel, and resolute in war. The peasant has only to follow the traditional routine of custom and labour, and he is sure to gain his bare subsistence, but the pastoralist is always an adventurer, and if he fails he is faced in a moment with the loss of his wealth and the scattering of his tribe, like Lot, or Job who lost in a single day his 7,000 sheep and 3,000 camels and all the rest of his flocks and herds.

This contrast between the agricultural and the pastoral societies finds a counterpart in their religions.

Both of them are Nature Religions, and have their origin

in the vague undifferentiated religion of primitive peoples that we have described earlier, but each has concentrated its worship on a different aspect of nature. The Religion of the Peasant is concerned above all with the mystery of life, and he sees the divine power embodied in the Earth Mother and the Vegetation God who is her consort or son. The Religion of the Shepherd, on the other hand, is concerned not so much with the Earth as with the Heavens, and it is the powers of Heaven—the Sky, the Sun, and the Storm, that take the first place in his worship.

Among the pastoral peoples all over the world, from Siberia to Africa, we find the Sky God as a vague and often impersonal power which is yet conceived as the creator and supreme ruler of the universe. It is characteristic alike of the ancient Aryans, the Turks, the Mongols, the Hamites, and many of the Negro people of Africa,[2] and even among peoples of the higher culture such as the Sumerians and the Chinese it appears as one of the earliest elements in their religion, inherited perhaps from an older phase of barbarism. Even the lower peoples of the hunting culture are not entirely devoid of the conception, and it has a good claim to be considered the oldest and most universal religion of the world.[3]

With the advance of the pastoral culture and the development of the warrior tribe, the Sky God tends to become personified as a celestial hero and chieftain, but at the very end of the development, in classical times, men could still speak of the Sky God in the old undifferentiated way, as in the Roman expression *"sub Jove"* for "under the open sky."

The Sky God of the warrior people is, however, above all the god of the thunderbolt and the storm. He is the Adad and Amor of the Semites, the Teshub of Asia Minor, the Aryan Indra, and the Scandinavian Thor. These are incalculable and formidable powers, whom man cannot control or co-operate with, jealous and arbitrary rulers after the image of their own chieftains who must be feared and obeyed implicitly and blindly. Nevertheless, they have the virtues as well as the defects of the warlike pastoral psychology.

[2] E.g. Engai among the Masai, Juok among the Shilluk, Leza among the Ba-ila, Nyami among the Ashanti, and many more.

[3] Cf. especially Pettazzoni, *Dio. I, l'Essere Celeste nel Credenze dei Popoli Primitivi.*

They are the guardians of the masculine tribal morality—righteous gods who hate lies and uncleanness and disobedience. While the religions of the settled agricultural peoples were idolatrous and immoral, or at least non-moral, it was the pastoral peoples who developed such high conceptions of the divinity as Varuna, the guardian of righteousness, and Ahura Mazda, the Wise Lord. Above all the Jewish people could never have developed their ethical and monotheist religion amidst the idolatrous and voluptuous cults of the agricultural peoples of Syria, had it not been for their pastoral and tribal tradition, and it was to the desert that the prophets and reformers turned for inspiration in the great crises of national history.

It is in fact characteristic of the pastoral peoples that their intellectual and moral development should be far more advanced than one would expect from their material civilization. The pastoral life alone frees men from the grinding necessity of continual labour, while stimulating the activity of mind and body, so that the Highland or Montenegrin shepherd is often a man of higher spiritual culture than the wealthy farmer or trader of the plains.[4] And even in primitive times, poetry and reflection on the problems of existence have been common features among pastoral peoples of a comparatively rudimentary culture.

The Social Crisis of the Third Millennium in Egypt and Mesopotamia

It is clear that the existence of these pastoral societies, with their intensely masculine and warlike ethics, their mobility, and the high degree of physical efficiency which their wandering life entailed, was a great potential danger to the civilization of the settled agriculturalists. The actual materialization of the danger was delayed by a number of causes, such as their geographical segregation in the outer steppes, their inferiority in material equipment, and the prestige of the older and higher civilization, as well as the mere influence of tradition and routine. It is indeed probable that it was the civilized peoples who were the first aggressors, and that

---

[4] Cf. the remarkable description of the characteristics of the warlike pastoral culture of the Dinaric tribesmen in the Balkans today in Cvijic's *La Peninsule Balkanique*.

it was from them that the barbarians first learnt the possibilities of organized warfare, as well, no doubt, as the use of weapons of metal. Certainly the great wave of invasion of the men of Gutium from the north which overwhelmed Mesopotamia in the twenty-sixth century B.C. followed close upon the period of Sargon and Naram Sin, who were the first to lead Mesopotamian armies into the uncivilized mountainous regions to the north and east of Tigris, and in the same way in Egypt the later days of the Old Kingdom had been marked by expeditions of conquest against "the Sanddwellers" of the north and the Nubians of the south, which may have helped to provoke the subsequent movement of invasion.

However this may be, the ultimate advantage was all on the side of the barbarians, for every fresh invasion increased their warlike efficiency, whereas the destructive effects of warfare on the higher civilization were cumulative. Peace and security were essential to the life of the Archaic Culture, and a few years of disorder might cause irreparable damage to the highly organized system of irrigation and canalization on which the prosperity of Egypt and Mesopotamia rested. Moreover, the psychology of the archaic cultures was essentially unwarlike. Its mainspring was the spirit of unquestioning loyalty and submission to the will of the gods, as incarnated in the divine monarchy or the temple priesthood. The initiative rested with a small ruling class on whom the mass of the peasant population was entirely dependent, so that when, as in the Spanish conquest of Peru, the centre of the government fell into the hands of an enemy, the rest of the people were left as defenceless and unresisting as a flock of sheep.

Hence the age of invasions in the third millennium B.C. shook the foundations of the Archaic Culture, and produced a wave of pessimism and moral confusion. Men lost faith in the immutable divine order on which the old theocratic state was based. The gods had shown themselves unable to protect their people, or even themselves, from violence and outrage. The temple liturgies which make up so large a part of the later Sumerian and Accadian literature are full of lamentations over the destruction of the holy places of Sumer and the carrying away of the gods into captivity—lamentations which recall those written nearly 2,000 years later on the fall of the Holy City of Jerusalem and the destruction of the Temple.

They describe the deluge of invasion passing over the land. "Order was destroyed. The sacred dynasty was exiled from the temple. They demolished the city, they demolished the temple. The rulership of the land they seized. The divine prince was carried away to a strange land." But above all they depict the evil plight of the Mother Goddess, ravished by unclean hands, chased forth from her shrine, like a bird from its nest, and carried away to a strange land, while the splendid festivals and the solemn rituals cease in the great temple of Eanna.

The Egyptian documents of this period give an even more vivid impression of the social disorder and moral confusion that followed the collapse of the divine order of the Old Kingdom. One of these, known as the Admonitions of Ipuwer, is of especial interest, not only on account of the picturesque detail with which it describes the conditions in Egypt during the period of foreign invasion, but also because it shows that the breakdown of the Archaic Civilization was marked by the same phenomena of social revolution and class war which have so often accompanied the decline of wealthy and advanced societies in later times.

The document is too long and too fragmentary to quote in full, but it may be condensed as follows:

I. The Ruin of Egypt

"Behold, strangers have come into the land. The men of Egypt are no longer found anywhere. The people of the desert take their place.

"The land is desolate, the homes are laid waste. Bowmen from a strange country have come up into Egypt.

"The vessel of Upper Egypt goes adrift. The towns are destroyed. Men flee into the open country; they dwell in tents.

"The roads are watched. Men lie in ambush by the wayside to put the wayfarer to a shameful death, and spoil him of his goods.

"The cattle are left to stray. There is no man to herd them. When the Nile overflows, none ploughs, for they say, 'We know not what hath come to pass in the land.'

"Blood is on every side. Death ceases not. Men are few, and he who lays his brother in the earth is everywhere. Women become barren, for the Creator fashions not men by reason of the state of the land."

II. The Social Revolution

"The nobles are in afflication and the base rejoice. Every city saith, 'Come and let us put down those who are in authority amongst us.'

"The land turns like a potter's wheel. Thieves become men of substance, and the wealthy are plundered. The great are hungry and in distress, while those who served now have servants. He who bore messages for others now hath messengers to do his bidding.

"The poor possess riches. He who was wont to go barefoot now hath precious things. He who had not a yoke of oxen possesseth flocks and herds. Luxury is spread abroad among the people. Gold and jewels adorn the necks of slaves; but the mistresses say, 'Ah! that we had something to eat!' The honourable ladies suffer like servants. Their slaves are the mistresses of their mouth. Hardly will they suffer them to speak.

"Those who built for themselves tombs are become hirelings; those who rowed in the boat of the God are under the yoke. Men sail not to Byblus today. What shall we do for cedars for our mummies, with the products of which the Pure are buried, and with the oil of which princes are embalmed, as far as the land of Keftiu (Crete)? They return no more. The gold and the precious things are found no more. Men throw their dead into the river. The Nile becomes a burying-place."

III. The Destruction of the Divine Order

"Behold! that which has never been aforetime has come to pass. The king is taken away by men of naught. Men without faith or understanding have deprived the land of its royalty. They have revolted against the Holy Crown, the defender of Re, which causeth the Two Lands to be at peace. The Serpent is taken from its place, and the secret of the Kings of the Upper and the Lower Land is laid bare.

"As for the sublime Judgment Hall, its writings are carried away, its inner places are exposed. The government offices are opened and their writings carried away, so that serfs become lords of serfs. Woe is me for the evil of this generation! The writings of the clerks of the census are carried away. The grain of Egypt is for whoever will come and take it.

"The laws of the Judgment Hall are cast forth. The poor break them open in the public streets. The poor man attains to the greatness of the Divine Ennead, while the children of the princes are thrown into the street.

"The things that were seen of old have perished. The land is exhausted like uprooted flax. Would that there might be an end of men, that conception and birth should fail! Would that the cry of the land might cease and that strife should be no more!

"Wherefore when Re first created Man, did he not separate the righteous from the ungodly? It is said that he is the Shepherd of Men. When his flock is scattered, he watches over them and gathers them together.

"Would that he had perceived their nature in the beginning. Then he would have stretched forth his arm and destroyed the evil seed. But in this age, there is no longer any pilot. Where is he? Does he sleep? His power is not seen." [5]

This spirit of pessimism finds an even more poignant expression in "The Dialogue of a Man with his Own Soul," which is one of the masterpieces of ancient Egyptian literature. The just man, in despair at the victory of the forces of evil and at his own abandonment by men, turns to death as the one haven of rest.

> "Death is before me today (he says)
> Like the recovery of a sick man,
> Like going forth into a garden after sickness.

> "Death is before me today
> Like the odor of myrrh,
> Like sitting under the sail on a windy day.

[5] The whole document has been edited and translated by A. H. Gardiner, *The Admonitions of an Egyptian Sage* (Leipzig, 1909). The text is full of difficulties and lacunae, but I have attempted to convey the general sense, using so far as possible the words of the original as interpreted in the above translation and in the partial extracts given by Breasted in *The Development of Religion and Thought in Ancient Egypt*, pp. 204–15, and by Moret in *Le Nil et La Civilisation Egyptienne*, pp. 261–8.

> "Death is before me today
>   As a man longs to see his house
>   When he has spent years in captivity." [6]

But the writer's conception of the after-life is far more spiritual than that of the earlier literature of the Old Kingdom, which is non-moral, and sometimes even utterly barbaric, as in the famous Pyramid Text which describes the dead King Unis as "eating the gods," "the great ones for his breakfast, the middle ones for his dinner, the little ones for his supper"; "their charms are in his belly, he has eaten the knowledge of every god."

It owes nothing to the belief in the efficacy of the machinery which under the Old Kingdom secured the welfare of the deceased in his tomb. For the writer recognizes that this also is vanity; that the lot of those who built for themselves the great Pyramid tombs, who adorned their sepulchres like the dwellings of the gods, is no better than that of "those weary ones who die on the dyke," their bodies a prey to fish and crocodiles. It is an intensely personal utterance, the earliest emergence of an independent criticism of life on the part of the individual, and the first appeal to the life to come as a deliverance from the injustice and misery of terrestrial existence. There is no sign of this in the contemporary literature of Babylonia, though that also is marked by the same atmosphere of gloom and disillusionment. For the Babylonians had no hope of a celestial hereafter. Their religious outlook was limited to the present life, and when the decline of the Archaic Civilization threatened the existence of the divine state on earth, they took refuge in a fatalism which was even darker than that of the Egyptian pessimist. The great epic of Gilgamesh, of which the Babylonian version dates from this period (c. twenty-first century B.C.), is dominated by a sense of bitter frustration. The gods have cheated man of the gift of life. "When the gods first made man, they allotted to him death, and life they held in their own keeping." In spite of all the labours of the hero, fate robs him of the one reward he asks, "that mine eyes may continue to see the light of the sun." When at last his friend returns from the grave, it is only to tell him that there is no escape from

---

[6] Breasted, *op. cit.*, p. 195.

the dismal underworld, the House of Hades. The lot of the hero is even worse than that of other men, for dying in battle or in the desert, he fails to receive the rites of burial or the funeral offerings, and his soul like a dog must lick up "the leavings of the pot, the refuse that is thrown into the street."

In this age of ruin and disillusionment the civilization of the ancient world came very near to complete destruction—how near we can never know. It was saved by the work of the great rulers and organizers who appeared at the close of the third millennium, men like Hammurabi in Babylonia and the Twelfth-Dynasty monarchs of Egypt, as was predicted (after the event, it is true) in the almost Messianic utterance of Neferre Hu: "A king shall come from the South. He shall take the White Crown and the Red, and the Two Gods who love him shall take pleasure in him. The Right shall be restored and Injustice shall be cast forth. Blessed is he who shall see these things and who shall serve this King." But the spirit of the new monarchy was different from that of the old theocracy. Indeed these kings, in whose veins perhaps ran the blood of foreign invaders, were warriors rather than priests, and the ideal of kingship loses the exclusively religious character that it had possessed under the Old Kingdom. "I have set up my statue on the frontier," says Senusret III in his Nubian inscription, "not that ye should worship it, but that ye should fight for it. I am the King and what I say I do." And this clear realization of personal power and human responsibility is no less clearly expressed in the admonition to his successor that is attributed to Amenemhet I, the founder of the dynasty. "Fill not thy heart with a brother, know not a friend, make not thyself intimates wherein there is no end, harden thyself against subordinates, that thou mayest be King of the Earth, that thou mayest be Ruler of the Lands, that thou mayest increase good."

And the same ideal of kingship finds expression in a hymn of gratitude and loyalty to Senusret III:

How great is the Lord towards his City. He alone is millions, other men are but small.

He has come to us: he has seized Upper Egypt and placed the White Crown upon his head.

He has united the two countries and joined the Reed (the symbol of Upper Egypt) with the Bee (the symbol of the Delta).

He has conquered the Black Land (the Nile Valley) and has subjected the Red (the desert).

He has protected the Two Lands and given peace to the two
banks.

He has given life to Egypt, and abolished her sufferings.

He has given life to men, and made the throat of the dead to
breathe.

He has trodden down the strangers and smitten the Troglodytes
that feared him not.

He has fought for his frontier and driven back the spoilers.

He has granted us to rear our children and to bury our aged (in
peace). [7]

The spirit of heroic energy and lonely power which inspired
these Twelfth-Dynasty rulers still lives for us in the magnificent
art of the Middle Kingdom—in the fierce and virile faces of
Senusret III and Amenemhet III, so different from the placid
majesty of the God Kings of the Old Kingdom. But in the
Middle Kingdom, no less than in the age of the Pyramid
Builders, everything depended on the person of the King. The
Archaic Civilization remained fundamentally pacific and was
incapable of adapting itself to warlike conditions. When the
next wave of invasion from the north reached Egypt, there
was no longer a royal superman like Senusret III to guard the
frontiers, and the short-lived prosperity of the Middle Kingdom ended in darkness and confusion. About the beginning
of the seventeenth century, Egypt fell into the hands of Asiatic conquerors—the so-called Hyksos or Shepherd Kings.
These were probably Semites from Northern Syria, but their
invasion of Egypt was not an isolated fact. It forms part of a
great movement of peoples which was convulsing the whole of
the Near East in the first centuries of the second millennium.
The power of Babylon had fallen before a Hittite raid, perhaps as early as 1870 B.C., and a whole series of new peoples
was making its appearance in the highland regions to the
north.

The Indo-European Invaders of the Second Millennium and Their Origin

This marks the first appearance of the Indo-European
peoples who were subsequently to play so great a part in
history, for there is no reason to believe that the earlier north-

[7] Erman, *Literatur der Ägypter*, pp. 179–82.

ern invaders of Mesopotamia in the middle of the third millennium—the men of Gutium—were of Indo-European stock. Indeed their racial origin is a mystery, for their rulers bear strange names—Irarum, Ibranum, Igesaus, etc., which it is not easy to connect with any known group of languages. However, it is possible that even at that date the period of the Indo-European migrations had already begun, and that the people of the hills were being driven forward on Mesopotamia by the coming of new peoples from the north and west.

The origin of this great movement of peoples may have been due in part to natural causes, such as the growing aridity of Central Asia which may have forced the population to seek new homes, but it was undoubtedly facilitated by another fact which gave a great impetus to the mobility and aggressiveness of the pastoral peoples. This was the taming of the horse and its utilization as a draught animal, an invention that was to revolutionize the art of warfare in the second millennium. It was probably the peoples of the Painted Pottery Culture of Susa and Anau who were the first to domesticate the horse, for horses' bones are common in their settlements as well as in those of the Painted Pottery Culture of Eastern Europe, and the hunting people of the steppe probably acquired it later, by the process of cultural expansion that has been described, and turned the invention to warlike uses. On the other hand, the horse was unknown to the higher civilizations of the Near East. In Mesopotamia it makes its first appearance on the eve of the northern invasions, and its Babylonian name—"the ass from the East"—shows that it was introduced across the mountains from Persia. So, too, in Egypt the horse and chariot were first introduced by the Hyksos invaders, but they were certainly not of Syrian origin, and the Hyksos themselves must have acquired them from the invading peoples from farther north. In fact the appearance of the horse seems to be closely associated with that of the Indo-European peoples, so that the early Aryans, like the Homeric heroes, were above all "tamers of horses" and chariot fighters. It is remarkable that the earliest known treatise on chariot driving, a document found at Boghaz Keui, and written by a certain Kikulli of Mitanni, uses Indo-European words as part of the technical vocabulary of the charioteer.

The actual period of the invasions is naturally an age of

darkness in which historical evidence is almost completely lacking, but in the following period we find traces of Indo-European influence all over the Near East. The Kassites, who established themselves in Babylonia in the eighteenth century B.C., were not themselves Indo-Europeans, but some of their rulers possessed Indo-European names, and they seem to have worshipped Aryan divinities such as Suryash the Sun God. Farther west, in the land of Mitanni in North Mesopotamia, the Aryan element is much stronger, and one of the most remarkable discoveries of modern times—a document discovered at Boghaz Keui, the Hittite capital—has shown that some of the gods of the rulers of Mitanni were practically identical with the early Aryan divinities of India —Indara (= Indra), Aruna (= Varuna), Mitra and the two Nashatiya (= the Ashvins), while the rulers themselves bear Aryan names such as Shutarna and Artatama. Farther south the Egyptian documents of the period of the Eighteenth Dynasty show the existence of Indo-European princes in Palestine in the fourteenth or fifteenth century—Shuwadata of Keilah near Hebron, Yashdata of Taanach, Artamanya of Zir Bashan, Rusmanya of Sharon and Biridashwa of Yenoam, and the occurrence of these names so far south suggests that Indo-Europeans may have played a part in the Hyksos invasion of Egypt. All these names, together with those of the Kassite and Mitannian divinities, belong to the Eastern Indo-Iranian branch of the Aryan linguistic group, but the decipherment of the Hittite archives of Boghaz Keui has shown that the ruling element among the Hittites spoke a language which has remarkable affinities with the western group and especially with Latin. Hence it is clear that the movement of peoples that we are discussing was a very complex one. The old theory of a common "Aryan Cradle" in the steppes of Transcaspia or Turkestan would explain the appearance of Indo-European elements in Western Asia at this time well enough, but the divergence between "Hittite" and the Indo-Iranian language spoken by the ruling element in the land of Mitanni is much too deep to have had a recent origin.

Of course a resemblance between languages does not prove a community of race any more than a similarity of racial type implies a community of speech. Many of the peoples of Indo-European speech, in the West as well as in the East, only acquired their present languages at a comparatively recent date, and these facts have tended to throw discredit on all theorizing concerning "the Aryans" as a racial entity. Nevertheless, sometime and somewhere there must have existed an original centre or cradle-land in which the earliest form of Indo-European speech was developed, and from which it spread throughout Europe and through a large part of Asia. Many attempts have been made to locate this original centre, and every kind of argument based on philology, archaeology, and anthropology has been employed. The latter is perhaps the least conclusive, owing to the paucity and uncertainty of the evidence, but there is some reason to think that the early Indo-European peoples, or at least the dominant element among them, were Nordic in type, and that their original home must be looked for within the Nordic racial area. The philological evidence, based on the vocabulary common to all branches of Indo-European speech, is, however, more enlightening. It suggests that the original Indo-Europeans before their dispersion were a pastoral people of patrilinear social organization, who possessed the horse and wagon, the ox and the sheep, and worshipped a Sky God (Jupiter, Dyaus, etc., and also perhaps Ouranos, Varuna). The common words for metal, as well as other important objects, seem to have been borrowed from the higher culture of Mesopotamia or Asia Minor, but on the whole the main features of their common culture point to a neolithic stage of development. The common words for flora and fauna suggest a region of forest and steppe, and the occurrence of common words for the beech, the birch and the hazel in the European members of the group point more definitely to Central or Northwestern Europe.

It is, however, the archaeological evidence that is the most conclusive. We have seen that the Aryans appear in Western Asia early in the second millennium, as an invading people of warriors and horsemen. Now a similar expansion of peoples of warlike culture occurred in Europe at an earlier period in late neolithic times, overrunning the old peasant cultures of Central and Eastern Europe, and the course of this movement coincides so fully with the distribution of the chief families of Indo-European speech in later times, that it is difficult to avoid the conclusion that the invading peoples were themselves Aryans, and that we must look to Europe for the source of the great movement of peoples which afterwards affected the whole of Western Asia, and even extended as far as India and Eastern Turkestan. Thus the expansion of the Aryans was not a slow and painful movement of peasant colonization, but the swift advance of victorious warriors, and this explains not only their rapid diffusion over the vast continental region between Northern Europe and India, but also the remarkably homogeneous character of their languages, which offers so complete a contrast to the heterogeneity of speech found among peoples of sedentary peasant culture, such as those of Asia Minor. We find a somewhat similar contrast in Africa between the homogeneous group of Bantu languages which likewise owe their diffusion to the comparatively recent expansion of a warlike pastoral stock, and the settled peasant peoples of West Africa, where almost every district has its own distinct language.

The influence of the Indo-European invasions was not, however, wholly destructive, it was in fact far less so than that of the Turkish and Mongol conquerors of the Middle Ages. They possessed a natural aptitude for assimilating the higher culture of the peoples that they conquered, and the vigorous life of the warrior tribes fertilized the ancient civilizations and gave birth in time to a new and brilliant development of culture. Nevertheless, the civilization of the warrior was always in a sense parasitic upon that of the Mother Goddess. Even in Europe, it was the influence of the Archaic Civilization which supplied the initial impetus to the native development of culture, and the warrior peoples of the north were not independent of it. First comes the Age of the Gods, to use Vico's phrase, then the Age of the Heroes.

—1928.

3

The Origins of Classical Civilization

The Society of the Heroic Age

THE fourteenth and thirteenth centuries B.C. represent a gradual transition from the rich and brilliant civilization of the Late Minoan Period to the chivalrous but semi-barbarized world of the Homeric epic. The accumulated resources of the peaceful Aegean Culture were gradually dissipated by rulers who lived for plunder and war. For the Mycenaean Culture was, to an even greater extent than the Hittite Empire, or the New Kingdom in Egypt, that of a thoroughly warlike society. Its centres were not peaceful cities, like those of Minoan Crete, but royal burgs whose great walls of Cyclopean masonry remain to this day as a witness to the power of the princes who once bore rule there.

When Schliemann opened the shaft graves at Mycenae they were still lying there, crowned and covered with gold, with their long swords by their sides and their gold death-masks on their faces—grim, bearded faces of warrior kings, very different from the effeminate beauty of the Priest King of Crete who stands unarmed and almost naked among the flowers in the great painted relief of the Palace of Cnossus.

Thus, though their culture, their art, and their way of living were modelled upon those of Crete, it was in the same way as that in which the Ostrogothic kingdom of Italy entered into the tradition of the later Roman civilization. The society was not the society of a sacred city-state, but that of a military aristocracy. It is the heroic society of the Homeric epic, and in Homer's world there is no room for citizen or priest or merchant, but only for the knight and his retainers, for the nobles and the Zeus-born kings, "the sackers of cities." It is a society of princes and pirates.

It is true that the Homeric poems, at least in their present form, date from a much later period, long after the passing of the Mycenaean Age. Nevertheless, they faithfully preserve the tradition of the older civilization. The map of the Homeric world is that of Mycenaean Greece and the Aegean before the age of the Dorian invasion. The heroes of the epic are the Mycenaean princes of Pylos and "rich Mycenae" and "Tiryns of the great walls." They use bronze weapons and armour, they fight from chariots, and their dwellings are true Mycenaean palaces. The tradition of the old civilization and its political organization still survived, and prevented the development of a true tribal society like that of the early Dorian States. In the Homeric Age the leading element in society is the war leaders and their bands of retainers who carve out new kingdoms at the point of their swords, and who succeed to the position of the rulers of the older civilization, like Theodorich or Stilicho at the fall of the Roman Empire, who were at once leaders of barbarian war bands and Roman consuls and patricians. The tendency for a renowned war-leader to attract adventurers from every quarter to his standard naturally interferes with the strict tribal organization, and so we find an intertribal or supertribal society of warrior princes and pirates, living on the plunder of the older civilized societies, and welcoming at their courts roving adventurers like Odysseus and wandering minstrels like the rhapsodists who first composed the lays of the Trojan War. Professor Chadwick [1] has pointed out the remarkable parallels that exist between this Heroic Age of Ancient Greece and that of the Germanic peoples in the fifth and sixth centuries A.D. as we see it in the fragments of the great Teutonic epic cycle of the Age of the Invasions.

In each case the contact of a primitive warlike society

[1] *The Heroic Age.*

with an ancient settled civilization had set up a process of change which affected alike the culture of the conquered and that of the conquerors and produced a transitional type of society which prepared the way for a new age. It is true that the culture of the Homeric period was relatively higher and in closer contact with the older civilization than was that of the Teutonic people, but nevertheless the changes that were taking place in the Mediterranean world during the twelfth and thirteenth centuries were no less destructive in their effects on the ancient civilizations of the Levant than were the barbarian invasions of the fifth century A.D. in the Roman world. The Homeric poems only lift the curtain on a corner of the stage; a far greater drama was taking place, of the details of which we know practically nothing.

About the close of the thirteenth century the whole of the Eastern Mediterranean was in turmoil. A great movement of peoples was taking place which entirely destroyed the Hittite Empire and almost proved fatal to Egypt. With this wave of unrest the Trojan War, which Greek tradition usually assigned to the years 1192–1182, was also probably connected.

There is no reason to suppose that the fall of the Hittite Empire was due to a new migration of peoples from Thrace at the beginning of the Iron Age. The great movement of invasion seems to have come not from the land but from the sea, and to have been due to the Mediterranean peoples who were known to the Egyptians as "the Peoples of the Sea." These consisted of a large number of different peoples, whose names appear on the Egyptian monuments.

The fact that the Peoples of the Sea were associated with the Libyans rather than with the Hittites in their invasion of Egypt is on the whole more favourable to the theory of their Western origins. Moreover, Greek tradition preserved a vague memory of a great invasion from the west. According to Myrsillus of Lesbos,[2] the "Pelasgian Tyrrheni" owing to disturbances in Italy returned eastwards to Greece and other lands in the second generation before the Trojan War, and Plato's story of the great expedition of the empire of Atlantis, at the head of all the peoples of the West as far as Libya and Tyrrhenia, against Egypt and Greece, seems to represent a similar tradition.

[2] In *Dionysius Halic*, i, 68.

The Birth of Hellenism

These great invasions of Syria and Egypt at the close of the Bronze Age may have been due to the fall of the old thalassocracy of the Anatolian Peoples of the Sea who had dominated the Mediterranean and western trade routes since the third millennium. But whatever the source of the movement of the Sea Peoples, there can be no doubt that it marks an epoch in the history of the Near East. From this moment the Hittite Empire vanishes for ever, and though it is extremely improbable that the Sea Peoples actually penetrated into the Hittite homelands, their defeat of the Hittite armies at Carchemish or elsewhere in northern Syria may well have led to the collapse of the kingdom, and its replacement by the Phrygians as the leading power in Asia Minor. The victories of Merneptah and Rameses III saved Egypt herself for a time, but her control over southern Syria gradually lapsed. The Israelite tribes established themselves in the interior of Palestine, while the coasts fell into the hands of the remnants of the Philistine and Zakaray invaders, whose "fenced cities" became the chief centres of civilization in southern Palestine.

At the same time a similar process was taking place in Western Asia Minor and the neighbouring islands. As we have seen, the Trojan War probably formed part of the same great movement of the Peoples of the Sea which caused the Philistine invasion of Syria and Egypt, and the subsequent Hellenic colonization of Aeolis and Ionia is a parallel phenomenon to the settlement of the Philistines in Palestine.

These events seem to have prepared the way for the final decline of the Mycenaean Culture and the Dorian invasion of Greece and Crete. The newcomers were closely related to the other Hellenic peoples in race and language, and it is improbable that they originated farther north than Macedonia or Epirus. Nevertheless they came from outside the limits of the Mycenaean culture-province, and consequently their occupation of the centres of Aegean civilization in the Argolis, Sparta, and Crete, involved the destruction of the older culture. Their relation to the Achaeans was like that of the Lombards to the Ostrogoths, or that of the Allemanni to the Burgundians, and, as with the second wave of Germanic invasion in the Roman Empire, their coming marked the complete victory of the warlike tribal society and the temporary disappearance of the higher city culture. The Aegean world was only saved from complete barbarization by the survival of the tradition of the older culture on the coast of Asia Minor, in Aeolia, and above all in Ionia, where the Asiatic element in Greek culture was strongest.

It was on the coasts and islands of Asia Minor that the Hellenic civilization of classical times had its origins, gradually returning westward to European Greece with the revival of trade and economic prosperity in the seventh and eighth centuries. Thus the rise of classical civilization was to a great extent the renaissance of the old Aegean culture. It did not proceed in equal measure from all Greek-speaking peoples. On the contrary, it was practically confined to those regions which had already taken part in the Mycenaean development. Outside this area—in North-west Greece, for example, the Greeks remained a semi-barbarous population of warlike tribesmen and peasants, without literature, without science, and without the city-state. For the Greek city was the heir of the immemorial tradition of the Archaic culture of Western Asia. Like the old Oriental sacred city, it had its centre in the shrine of the city goddess—the temple of Artemis at Ephesus, the temple of Aphrodite at Corinth, or the temple of Athene at Athens—and, at least in the case of Ephesus, there is a direct continuity between the Greek temple and the pre-Greek sanctuary of the great goddess of Anatolia.

Nevertheless it would be a mistake to look upon the Greeks as mere barbarians who owed all their culture to the higher civilization that they had conquered, like the Kassites in Babylonia, or the Mongols in China. They brought with them not only new blood, but new institutions, new ideals, and a new spirit. If the Greek city was ancient and Oriental, Greek citizenship was new and European. The city-state, the greatest and most original creation of the Greek genius, owes its existence to the marriage of the Oriental sacred city with the Indo-European warrior tribe. From the one parent came the religious feeling that inspired such intense devotion to the Hellenic city with its splendid buildings, its great temples, and its wealth of statuary; from the other the strict discipline, the sense of civic solidarity and common kinship which made every city a kind of large family, and gave birth to a tribal loyalty very different from the passive obedience of an Oriental people to its god, and his human representative, the priest king. The latter attitude eventually triumphed even in the Greek world, but the greatest achievements of both Greece and Rome were made when the tribal spirit was yet strong. The culture-tradition of the Mediterranean world remained largely Oriental, and retained its contact with Western Asia, but there came into it as a new leaven the tribal society from the north, and the consequent process of fermentation resulted in the production of the classical culture of the ancient world, and the rise of a true European civilization.

The Origins of Rome

The Roman state and its culture was due to the fusion of two distinct elements—the Etruscan city-state and the Italic peasant community. As in the Aegean, the union of the Oriental city with the tribal society of Bronze Age Europe gave birth to a new type of civilization. From the one side came the city itself and all the institutions of city life—the magistracy with its insignia, such as the curule chair, the purple toga, the ivory sceptre, and the rods and axes of the lictors. Etruscan also were the triumphal procession and the public games which played so large a part in the life of the Etruscans, and also of the Veneti. No less important was the influence of Etruria in the sphere of religion and art, for it was from the Etruscans that the Romans learned their science of augury and probably much of their religious ritual, as well as the plan of their temples and the knowledge of statuary. Finally, not only the Romans, but all the Italic peoples, were indebted to the Etruscans for their knowledge of the alphabet and the art of writing—the most decisive mark of the attainment of true civilization.

On the other hand, the Latin stock contributed its peasant solidity and virility, its courage and laboriousness, qualities which were possessed in equal measure by other Italic peoples, such as the Samnites, but which were lacking in the more highly civilized cities of Etruria. If the Roman and Praenestine nobles of the earlier period had shared in the personal luxury of the Etruscan culture, the prevailing ideal during the age of the early Republic was one of peasant simplicity and military severity and discipline. Indeed, the Latin reaction against

Etruscan culture may be compared to the somewhat earlier Dorian reaction against the luxurious Ionian culture in Greece. Alike in Greece and Italy, we can trace the conflict between a relatively advanced city culture and a simple tribal culture, out of which there arose a new type of society unlike anything that had existed before. Nevertheless, in both cases the rise of the classical city-state was due, not to a spontaneous development of the European tribal society, but to a direct inheritance from the old West Asiatic and Aegean culture of the Bronze Age, the tradition of which had survived in Asia Minor whence it was transmitted to Europe, on the one hand by the Ionian Greeks, and on the other by the Etruscans.

Thus the Early Iron Age witnessed a complete fusion between the culture of the warrior peoples and that of the ancient city. In Asia, the Assyrian Empire represents the complete militarization of the Archaic sacred monarchy, while in Europe the union of the sacred city and the warrior tribe gave birth to the new city-state of classical times. But this new Iron Age type of culture did not possess the stability which is so impressive a feature of the Archaic culture as we see it in Egypt or Babylonia, perhaps because it was a hybrid form which failed to achieve internal equilibrium, or because the predominance of the military element produced a premature exhaustion of the class of citizen soldiers which was the foundation of this type of society. Thus the Etruscan culture, and the Assyrian and Persian Empires were all notably short-lived, and even the Greek city and the Latin peasant republic, in spite of their immense achievements, experienced an almost equally rapid decline. The new cultures, in fact, represent an intermediate transitional stage between the two more permanent forms of religion-culture—between the Archaic Civilization of the ancient East, and the new World-Religions which were already coming into existence during this period. Throughout the pre-Christian Iron Age from the Assyrian to the Roman Empires, the military element was predominant, but the following period witnessed a return to the purely religious conception of life and to a theocratic ideal of the state, such as we find in Sassanian Persia and in the Byzantine Empire, and above all in Islam and in mediaeval Christendom.

—1928.

4

The Patriarchal Family in History

THE traditional view of the family was founded on a somewhat naive and one-sided conception of history. The knowledge of the past was confined to the history of classical civilization and to that of the Jews, in both of which the patriarchal family reigned supreme. But when the European horizon was widened by the geographical discoveries of modern times, men suddenly realized the existence of societies whose social organization was utterly different to anything that they had imagined. The discovery of totemism and exogamy, of matrilinear institutions, of polyandry, and of customs of organized sexual licence gave rise to a whole host of new theories concerning the origins of marriage and the family. Under the influence of the prevalent evolutionary philosophy, scholars like Lewis Morgan elaborated the theory of the gradual evolution of the family from a condition of primitive sexual promiscuity through various forms of group-marriage and temporary pairing up to the higher forms of patriarchal and monogamous marriage as they exist in developed civilizations. This theory naturally commended itself to socialists. It received the official imprimatur of the leaders of German Socialism in the later nineteenth century, and has become as much a part of orthodox socialist thought as the Marxian interpretation of history. It was, however, never fully accepted by the scientific world, and is today generally abandoned, although it still finds a few supporters among anthropologists. In England it is still maintained by Mr. E. S. Hartland and by Dr. Briffault, whose vast work *The Mothers* (3 vols., 1927) is entirely devoted to the subject. According to Briffault, primitive society was purely matriarchal in organization, and the primitive family group consisted only of a woman and her offspring. A prolonged sexual association, such as we find in all existing forms of marriage, except in Russia, is neither natural nor primitive, and has no place in matriarchal society. The original social unit was not the family, but the clan which was based on matrilinear kinship and was entirely communistic in its sexual and economic relations. The family, as we understand it, owes nothing to biological or sexual causes, but is an economic institution arising from the development of private property and the consequent domination of women by men. It is "but a euphemism for the individualistic male with his subordinate dependents."

But in spite of its logical coherence, and the undoubted existence of matrilinear institutions in primitive society, this theory has not been borne out by recent investigations. The whole tendency of modern anthropology has been to discredit the old views regarding primitive promiscuity and sexual communism, and to emphasize the importance and universality of marriage. Whether the social organization is matrilinear or patrilinear, whether morality is strict or loose, it is the universal rule of every known society that a woman before she bears a child must be married to an individual male partner. The importance of this rule has been clearly shown by Dr. Malinowski. "The universal postulate of legitimacy," he writes, "has a great sociological significance which is not yet sufficiently acknowledged. It means that in all human societies moral tradition and law decree that the group consisting of a woman and her offspring is not a sociologically complete unit. The ruling of culture runs here again on entirely the same lines as natural endowment; it declares that the human family must consist of the male as well as the female." [1]

It is impossible to go back behind the family and find a

---

[1] B. Malinowski, *Sex and Repression in Savage Society* (1927), p. 213.

state of society in which the sexual relations are in a pre-social stage, for the regulation of sexual relations is an essential pre-requisite of any kind of culture. The family is not a product of culture; it is, as Malinowski shows, "the starting point of all human organization" and "the cradle of nascent culture." Neither the sexual nor the parental instinct is distinctively human. They exist equally among the animals, and they only acquire cultural significance when their purely biological function is transcended by the attainment of a permanent social relation. Marriage is the social consecration of the biological functions, by which the instinctive activities of sex and parenthood are socialized and a new synthesis of cultural and natural elements is created in the shape of the family. This synthesis differs from anything that exists in the animal world in that it no longer leaves man free to follow his own sexual instincts; he is forced to conform them to a certain social pattern. The complete freedom from restraint which was formerly supposed to be characteristic of savage life is a romantic myth. In all primitive societies sexual relations are regulated by a complex and meticulous system of restrictions, any breach of which is regarded not merely as an offence against tribal law, but as morally sinful. These rules mostly have their origin in the fear of incest, which is the fundamental crime against the family, since it leads to the disorganization of family sentiment and the destruction of family authority. It is unnecessary to insist upon the importance of the consequences of this fear of incest in both individual and social psychology, since it is the fundamental thesis of Freud and his school. Unfortunately, in his historical treatment of the subject, in *Totem and Tabu*, he inverts the true relation, and derives the sociological structure from a pre-existent psychological complex instead of vice versa. In reality, as Dr. Malinowski has shown, the fundamental repression which lies at the root of social life is not the suppressed memory of an instinctive crime—Freud's prehistoric Oedipus tragedy—but a deliberate constructive repression of anti-social impulses. "The beginning of culture implies the repression of instincts, and all the essentials of the Oedipus complex or any other complex are necessary by-products in the gradual formation of culture." [2]

The institution of the family inevitably creates a vital ten-

[2] Malinowski, *op. cit.*, p. 182.

sion which is creative as well as painful. For human culture is not instinctive. It has to be conquered by a continuous moral effort, which involves the repression of natural instinct and the subordination and sacrifice of the individual impulse to the social purpose. It is the fundamental error of the modern hedonist to believe that man can abandon moral effort and throw off every repression and spiritual discipline and yet preserve all the achievements of culture. It is the lesson of history that the higher the achievement of a culture the greater is the moral effort and the stricter is the social discipline that it demands. The old type of matrilinear society, though it is by no means devoid of moral discipline, involves considerably less repression and is consistent with a much laxer standard of sexual behaviour than is usual in patriarchal societies. But at the same time it is not capable of any high cultural achievement or of adapting itself to changed circumstances. It remains bound to its elaborate and cumbrous mechanism of tribal custom.

The patriarchal family, on the other hand, makes much greater demands on human nature. It requires chastity and self-sacrifice on the part of the wife and obedience and discipline on the part of the children, while even the father himself has to assume a heavy burden of responsibility and submit his personal feelings to the interests of the family tradition. But for these very reasons the patriarchal family is a much more efficient organ of cultural life. It is no longer limited to its primary sexual and reproductive functions. It becomes the dynamic principle of society and the source of social continuity. Hence, too, it acquires a distinctively religious character, which was absent in matrilinear societies, and which is now expressed in the worship of the family hearth or the sacred fire and the ceremonies of the ancestral cult. The fundamental idea in marriage is no longer the satisfaction of the sexual appetite, but, as Plato says: "the need that every man feels of clinging to the eternal life of nature by leaving behind him children's children who may minister to the gods in his stead." [3]

This religious exaltation of the family profoundly affects men's attitude to marriage and the sexual aspects of life in general. It is not limited, as is often supposed, to the idealization of the possessive male as father and head of the house-

[3] *Laws,* 773 F.

hold; it equally transforms the conception of womanhood. It was the patriarchal family which created those spiritual ideals of motherhood and virginity which have had so deep an influence on the moral development of culture. No doubt the deification of womanhood through the worship of the Mother Goddess had its origin in the ancient matrilinear societies. But the primitive Mother Goddess is a barbaric and formidable deity who embodies the ruthless fecundity of nature, and her rites are usually marked by licentiousness and cruelty. It was the patriarchal culture which transformed this sinister goddess into the gracious figures of Demeter and Persephone and Aphrodite, and which created those higher types of divine virginity which we see in Athene, the giver of good counsel, and Artemis, the guardian of youth.

The patriarchal society was in fact the creator of those moral ideas which have entered so deeply into the texture of civilization that they have become a part of our thought. Not only the names of piety and chastity, honour and modesty, but the values for which they stand are derived from this source, so that even where the patriarchal family has passed away we are still dependent on the moral tradition that it created.[4] Consequently, we find that the existing world civilizations from Europe to China are all founded on the tradition of the patriarchal family. It is to this that they owed the social strength which enabled them to prevail over the old cultures of matrilinear type which, alike in Europe and in Western Asia, in China and in India, had preceded the coming of the great classical cultures. Moreover, the stability of the latter has proved to be closely dependent on the preservation of the patriarchal ideal. A civilization like that of China, in which the patriarchal family remained the corner-stone of society and the foundation of religion and ethics, has preserved its cultural traditions for more than 2,000 years without losing its vitality. In the classical cultures of the Mediterranean world, however, this was not the case.

[4] For this reason the Catholic Church has always associated its teaching on marriage with the patriarchal tradition, and even today she still concludes the marriage service with the ancient patriarchal benediction: "May the God of Abraham, the God of Isaac, and the God of Jacob, be with you and may he fulfill his blessing upon you that you may see your children's children even to the third and fourth generation."

Here the patriarchal family failed to adapt itself to the urban conditions of the Hellenistic civilization, and consequently the whole culture lost its stability. Conditions of life both in the Greek city-state and in the Roman Empire favoured the man without a family who could devote his whole energies to the duties and pleasures of public life. Late marriages and small families became the rule, and men satisfied their sexual instincts by homosexuality or by relations with slaves and prostitutes. This aversion to marriage and the deliberate restriction of the family by the practice of infanticide and abortion was undoubtedly the main cause of the decline of ancient Greece, as Polybius pointed out in the second century B.C.[5] And the same factors were equally powerful in the society of the Empire, where the citizen class even in the provinces was extraordinarily sterile and was recruited not by natural increase, but by the constant introduction of alien elements, above all from the servile class. Thus the ancient world lost its roots alike in the family and in the land and became prematurely withered.

The reconstitution of Western civilization was due to the coming of Christianity and the re-establishment of the family on a new basis. Though the Christian ideal of the family owes much to the patriarchal tradition which finds such a complete expression in the Old Testament, it was in several respects a new creation that differed essentially from anything that had previously existed. While the patriarchal family in its original form was an aristocratic institution which was the privilege of a ruling race or a patrician class, the Christian family was common to every class, even to the slaves.[6] Still more important was the fact that the Church

[5] He writes that in his days the diminution of population in Greece was so great that the towns were becoming deserted and the fields untilled. The reason of this is neither war nor pestilence, but because men "owing to vanity, avarice or cowardice, no longer wish to marry or to bring up children." In Boeotia especially he notes a tendency for men to leave their property to clubs for public benefactions instead of leaving it to their heirs, "so that the Boeotians often have more free dinners than there are days in the month."—*Polyb., Books* XXXVI, 17, and XX, 6.

[6] The same change, however, has taken place in China, where, owing to the influence of Confucianism, the whole population has gradually acquired the family institutions which were originally peculiar to the members of the feudal nobility.

insisted for the first time on the mutual and bilateral character of sexual obligations. The husband belonged to the wife as exclusively as the wife to the husband. This rendered marriage a more personal and individual relation than it had been under the patriarchal system. The family was no longer a subsidiary member of a larger unity—the kindred or "gens." It was an autonomous self-contained unit which owed nothing to any power outside itself.

It is precisely this character of exclusiveness and strict mutual obligation which is the chief ground of objection among the modern critics of Christian morality. But whatever may be thought of it, there can be no doubt that the resultant type of monogamous and indissoluble marriage has been the foundation of European society and has conditioned the whole development of our civilization. No doubt it involves a very severe effort of repression and discipline, but its upholders would maintain that it has rendered possible an achievement which could never have been equalled under the laxer conditions of polygamous or matrilinear societies. There is no historical justification of Bertrand Russell's belief that the Christian attitude to marriage has had a brutalizing effect on sexual relations and has degraded the position of woman below even the level of ancient civilization: on the contrary, women have always had a wider share in social life and a greater influence on civilization in Europe than was the case either in Hellenic or Oriental society. And this is in part due to those very ideals of asceticism and chastity which Bertrand Russell regards as the source of all our troubles. For in a Catholic civilization the patriarchal ideal is counterbalanced by the ideal of virginity. The family for all its importance does not control the whole existence of its members. The spiritual side of life belongs to a spiritual society in which all authority is reserved to a celibate class. Thus in one of the most important aspects of life the sexual relation is transcended, and husband and wife stand on an equal footing. I believe that this is the chief reason why the feminine element has achieved fuller expression in Catholic culture and why, even at the present day, the feminine revolt against the restrictions of family life is so much less marked in Catholic society than elsewhere.

In Protestant Europe, on the other hand, the Reformation, by abandoning the ideal of virginity and by the destruction of monasticism and of the independent authority of the Church, accentuated the masculine element in the family. The Puritan spirit, nourished on the traditions of the Old Testament, created a new patriarchalism and made the family the religious as well as the social basis of society. Civilization lost its communal and public character and became private and domestic. And yet, by a curious freak of historical development, it was this Puritan and patriarchal society which gave birth to the new economic order which now threatens to destroy the family. Industrialism grew up, not in the continental centres of urban culture, but in the most remote districts of rural England, in the homes of Nonconformist weavers and ironworkers. The new industrial society was entirely destitute of the communal spirit and of the civic traditions which had marked the ancient and the mediaeval city. It existed simply for the production of wealth and left every other side of life to private initiative. Although the old rural culture, based on the household as an independent economic unit, was passing away for ever, the strict ethos of the Puritan family continued to rule men's lives.

This explains the anomalies of the Victorian period both in England and America. It was essentially an age of transition. Society had already entered on a phase of intense urban industrialism, while still remaining faithful to the patriarchal ideals of the old Puritan tradition. Both Puritan morality and industrial mass economy were excessive and one-sided developments, and when the two were brought together in one society they inevitably produced an impossible situation.

The problem that faces us today is, therefore, not so much the result of an intellectual revolt against the traditional Christian morality; it is due to the inherent contradictions of an abnormal state of culture. The natural tendency, which is even more clearly visible in America than in England, is for the Puritan tradition to be abandoned and for society to give itself up passively to the machinery of modern cosmopolitan life. But this is no solution. It leads merely to the breaking down of the old structure of society and the loss of the traditional moral standards without creating anything which can take their place. As in the decline of the ancient world, the family is steadily losing its form and its social significance, and the state absorbs more and more of the life of its members. The home is no longer a centre of social activity; it has become merely a sleeping place for a number of independent wage-earners. The functions which were formerly fulfilled by the head of the family are now being taken over by the state, which educates the children and takes the responsibility for their maintenance and health. Consequently, the father no longer holds a vital position in the family: as Mr. Bertrand Russell says, he is often a comparative stranger to his children, who know him only as "that man who comes for week-ends." Moreover, the reaction against the restrictions of family life which in the ancient world was confined to the males of the citizen class, is today common to every class and to both sexes. To the modern girl marriage and motherhood appear not as the conditions of a wider life, as they did to her grandmother, but as involving the sacrifice of her independence and the abandonment of her career.

The only remaining safeguards of family life in modern urban civilization are its social prestige and the sanctions of moral and religious tradition. Marriage is still the only form of sexual union which is openly tolerated by society, and the ordinary man and woman are usually ready to sacrifice their personal convenience rather than risk social ostracism. But if we accept the principles of the new morality, this last safeguard will be destroyed and the forces of dissolution will be allowed to operate unchecked. It is true that Mr. Russell, at least, is willing to leave us the institution of marriage, on condition that it is strictly de-moralized and no longer makes any demands on continence. But it is obvious that these conditions reduce marriage to a very subordinate position. It is no longer the exclusive or even the normal form of sexual relations: it is entirely limited to the rearing of children. For, as Mr. Russell is never tired of pointing out, the use of contraceptives has made sexual intercourse independent of parenthood, and the marriage of the future will be confined to those who seek parenthood for its own sake rather than as the natural fulfilment of sexual love. But under these circumstances who will trouble to marry? Marriage will lose all attractions for the young and the pleasure-loving and the poor and the ambitious. The energy of youth will be devoted to contraceptive love and only when men and women have become prosperous and middle-aged will they think seriously of settling down to rear a strictly limited family.

It is impossible to imagine a system more contrary to the first principles of social well-being. So far from helping modern society to surmount its present difficulties, it only precipitates the crisis. It must lead inevitably to a social decadence far more rapid and more universal than that which brought about the disintegration of ancient civilization. The advocates of birth-control can hardly fail to realize the consequences of a progressive decline of the population in a society in which it is already almost stationary, but for all that their propaganda is entirely directed towards a further diminution in the birth rate. Many of them, like Dr. Stopes, are no doubt so much concerned with the problem of individual happiness that they do not stop to consider how the race is to be carried on. Others, such as Mr. Russell, are obsessed by the idea that over population is the main cause of war and that a diminishing birth rate is the best guarantee of international peace. There is, however, nothing in history to justify this belief. The largest and most prolific populations, such as the Chinese and the Hindus, have always been singularly unaggressive. The most warlike peoples are usually those who are relatively backward in culture and few in numbers, like the Huns and the Mongols, or the English in the fifteenth century, the Swedes in the seventeenth century, and the Prussians in the eighteenth century. If, however, questions of population should give rise to war in the future, there can be no doubt that it is nations with wide possessions and a dwindling population who will be most likely to provoke an attack. But it is much more likely that the process will be a peaceful one. The peoples who allow the natural bases of society to be destroyed by the artificial conditions of the new urban civilization will gradually disappear and their place will be taken by those populations which live under simpler conditions and preserve the traditional forms of the family.

—1933.

5

Stages in Mankind's Religious Experience

EVEN the crudest and most primitive forms of religion possess an element of transcendence without which they would cease to be religion. For since religion is the bond between man and God, between human society and the spiritual world, it always has a twofold aspect. To the outsider, whether he be a traveller or a rational critic, primitive religions seem like a dead weight of social convention and superstition which prevents the society from advancing; to the primitive himself, however, it is the Way of the Gods, the traditional consecrated order which brings human life into communion with the higher powers; and we see from the history of more developed religions that the most simple and elementary religious practices are capable, not merely of becoming charged with religious emotion, but of becoming the vehicle of profound religious ideas, as for example the ritual of sacrifice in ancient India or the ceremonial ordering of the calendar in ancient China.

On the other hand, when we come to the higher religions where there is a conscious effort to assert the absolute transcendence of God and the spiritual order, we still do not find any complete divorce between religion and culture. Even Buddhism, which seems at first sight to turn its back on human life and condemn all the natural values on which human culture is built, nevertheless has as great an influence on culture and impresses its character on the social life of the Tibetans or the Singalese no less than a religion which adopts a frankly positive, or as we say "pagan," attitude towards nature and human life. Religions of this type do, however, bring out more clearly the element of tension and conflict in the relation between religion and culture, which it is easy to ignore in a primitive religion which seems completely fused and identified with the social pattern.

Thus there are two factors to be considered in relation to any religion. Just as it is possible to conceive of a religion which will satisfy man's religious needs without being applicable to the social situation of modern Europe—as, for example, in Buddhism—so we can construct, at least in theory, a religion which would be adapted to the social needs of modern civilization, but which would be incapable of satisfying the purely religious demands of the human spirit. Such a religion was constructed with admirable ingenuity and sociological knowledge by Comte in the nineteenth century, and it proved utterly lacking in religious vitality, and consequently also in human appeal. And a similar experiment which is being carried out with far less knowledge and greater passion by the modern Communists in Russia threatens to be even more sterile and inimical to man's spiritual personality.

It is useless to judge a religion from the point of view of the politician or the social reformer. We shall never create a living religion merely as a means to an end, a way out of our practical difficulties. For the religious view of life is the opposite to the utilitarian. It regards the world and human life *sub specie æternitatis*. It is only by accepting the religious point of view, by regarding religion as an end in itself and not as a means to something else, that we can discuss religious problems profitably. It may be said that this point of view belongs to the past, and that we cannot return to it. But neither can we escape from it. The past is simply the record of the experience of humanity, and if that experience testifies to the existence of a permanent human need, that need must manifest itself in the future no less than in the past.

What, then, is man's essential religious need, judging by the experience of the past? There is an extraordinary degree of unanimity in the response, although, of course, it is not complete. One answer is God, the supernatural, the transcendent; the other answer is deliverance, salvation, eternal life. And both these two elements are represented in some form or other in any given religion. The religion of ancient Israel, for example, may seem to concentrate entirely on the first of these two elements—the reality of God—and to have nothing to say about the immortality of the soul and the idea of eternal life. Yet the teachings of the prophets is essentially a doctrine of salvation—a social and earthly salvation, it is true, but nevertheless a salvation which is essentially religious and related to the eternal life of God. Again, Buddhism seems to have no room for God and to put the whole emphasis of its teaching on the second element—deliverance. Nevertheless, it is based, as much as any religion can be, on the idea of Transcendence. Indeed, it was an exaggerated sense of Transcendence that led to its negative attitude towards the ideas of God and the Soul. "We affirm something of God, in order not to affirm nothing," says the Catholic theologian. The Buddhist went a step further on the *via negativa* and preferred to say nothing.

Now, a concentration on these two specifically religious needs produces an attitude to life totally opposed to the practical utilitarian outlook of the ordinary man. The latter regards the world of man—the world of sensible experience and social activity—as the one reality, and is sceptical of anything that lies beyond, whether in the region of pure thought or of spiritual experience, not to speak of religious faith. The religious man, on the contrary, turns his scepticism against the world of man. He is conscious of the existence of another and greater world of spiritual reality in which we live and move and have our being, though it is hidden from us by the veil of sensible things. He may even think, like Newman, that the knowledge of the senses has a merely symbolic value; that "the whole series of impressions made on us by the senses may be but a Divine economy suited to our need, and the token of realities distinct from them, and such as might be revealed to us, nay, more perfectly, by other senses as different from our existing ones as they are from one another." [1]

The one ultimate reality is the Being of God, and the world

---

[1] *University Sermons*, p. 350. In this remarkable passage he develops a parallelism between the symbolic character of sensible knowledge and that of mathematical calculi and musical notation.

of man and nature itself are only real in so far as they have their ground and principle of being in the supreme reality. In the words of a French writer of the seventeenth century: "It is the presence of God that, without cessation, draws the creation from the abyss of its own nothingness above which His omnipotence holds it suspended, lest of its own weight it should fall back therein; and serves as the mortar and bond of connection which holds it together in order that all that it has of its Creator should not waste and flow away like water that is not kept in its channel."

Thus, although God is not myself, nor a part of my being, "yet the relation of dependence that my life, my powers, and my operations bear to His Presence is more absolute, more essential, and more intimate than any relation I can have to the natural principles without which I could not exist . . . I draw my life from His Living Life . . . ; I am, I understand, I will, I act, I imagine, I smell, I taste, I touch, I see, I walk, and I love in the Infinite Being of God, within the Divine Essence and substance. . . .

"God in the heavens is more my heaven than the heavens themselves; in the sun He is more my light than the sun; in the air He is more my air than the air that I breathe sensibly. . . . He works in me all that I am, all that I see, all that I do or can do, as most intimate, most present, and most immanent in me, as the super-essential Author and Principle of my works, without whom we should melt away and disappear from ourselves and from our own activities." [2]

Or again, to quote Cardinal Bona, God is "the Ocean of all essence and existence, the very Being itself which contains all being. From Him all things depend; they flow out from Him and flow back to Him and *are* in so far as they participate in His Being." [3]

Thus the whole universe is, as it were, the shadow of God, and has its being in the contemplation or reflection of the Being of God. The spiritual nature reflects the Divine consciously, while the animal nature is a passive and unconscious mirror. Nevertheless, even the life of the animal is a living manifestation of the Divine, and the flight of the hawk

[2] *Chardon, la Croix de Jesus,* pp. 422, 423, in Bremond, *Histoire littéraire du sentiment religieux en France,* viii, pp. 21–22.

[3] Bona, *Via Compendii ad Deum.*

or the power of the bull is an unconscious prayer. Man alone stands between these two kingdoms in the strange twilight world of rational consciousness. He possesses a kind of knowledge which transcends the sensible without reaching the intuition of the Divine.

It is only the mystic who can escape from this twilight world; who, in Sterry's words, can "descry a glorious eternity in a winged moment of Time—a bright Infinite in the narrow point of an object, who knows what Spirit means—that spire-top whither all things ascend harmoniously, where they meet and sit connected in an unfathomed Depth of Life." But the mystic is not the normal man; he is one who has transcended, at least momentarily, the natural limits of human knowledge. The ordinary man is by his nature immersed in the world of sense, and uses his reason in order to subjugate the material world to his own ends, to satisfy his appetites and to assert his will. He lives on the animal plane with a more than animal consciousness and purpose, and in so far, he is less religious than the animal. The life of pure spirit is religious, and the life of the animal is also religious, since it is wholly united with the life-force that is its highest capacity of being. Only man is capable of separating himself alike from God and from nature, of making himself his last end and living a purely self-regarding and irreligious existence.

And yet the man who deliberately regards self-assertion and sensual enjoyment as his sole ends, and finds complete satisfaction in them—the pure materialist—is not typical; he is almost as rare as the mystic. The normal man has an obscure sense of the existence of a spiritual reality and a consciousness of the evil and misery of an existence which is the slave of sensual impulse and self-interest and which must inevitably end in physical suffering and death. But how is he to escape from this wheel to which he is bound by the accumulated weight of his own acts and desires? How is he to bring his life into vital relation with that spiritual reality of which he is but dimly conscious and which transcends all the categories of his thought and the conditions of human experience? This is the fundamental religious problem which has perplexed and baffled the mind of man from the beginning and is, in a sense, inherent in his nature.

I have intentionally stated the problem in its fullest and most classical form, as it has been formulated by the great minds of our own civilization, since the highest expression of an idea is usually also the most explicit and the most intelligible. But, as the writers whom I have quoted would themselves maintain, there is nothing specifically Christian about it. It is common to Christianity and to Platonism, and to the religious traditions of the ancient East. It is the universal attitude of the *anima naturaliter Christiana*, of that nature which the mediaeval mystics term "noble," because it is incapable of resting satisfied with a finite or sensible good. It is "natural religion" not, indeed, after the manner of the religion of naturalism that we have already mentioned, but in the true sense of the word.

It is, of course, obvious that such conceptions of spiritual reality presuppose a high level of intellectual development and that we cannot expect to find them in a pre-philosophic stage of civilization. Nevertheless, however far back we go in history, and however primitive is the type of culture, we do find evidence for the existence of specifically religious needs and ideas of the supernatural which are the primitive prototypes or analogues of the conceptions which we have just described.

Primitive man believes no less firmly than the religious man of the higher civilizations in the existence of a spiritual world upon which the visible world and the life of man are dependent. Indeed, this spiritual world is often more intensely realized and more constantly present to his mind than is the case with civilized man. He has not attained to the conception of an autonomous natural order, and consequently supernatural forces are liable to interpose themselves at every moment of his existence. At first sight the natural and the supernatural, the material and the spiritual, seem inextricably confused. Nevertheless, even in primitive nature-worship, the object of religious emotion and worship is never the natural phenomenon as such, but always the supernatural power which is obscurely felt to be present in and working through the natural object.

The essential difference between the religion of the primitive and that of civilized man is that for the latter the spiritual world has become a cosmos, rendered intelligible by philosophy and ethical by the tradition of the world religions, whereas to the primitive it is a spiritual chaos in which good and evil, high and low, rational and irrational elements are confusedly mingled. Writers on primitive religion have continually gone astray through their attempts to reduce the spiritual world of the primitive to a single principle, to find a single cause from which the whole development may be explained and rendered intelligible. Thus Tylor finds the key in the belief in ghosts, Durkheim in the theory of an impersonal *mana* which is the exteriorization of the collective mind, and Frazer in the technique of magic. But in reality there is no single aspect of primitive religion that can be isolated and regarded as the origin of all the rest. The spiritual world of the primitive is far less unified than that of civilized man. High gods, nature spirits, the ghosts of the dead, malevolent demons, and impersonal supernatural forces and substances may all coexist in it without forming any kind of spiritual system or hierarchy. Every primitive culture will tend to lay the religious emphasis on some particular point. In Central Africa witchcraft and the cult of ghosts may overshadow everything else; among the hunters of North America the emphasis may be laid on the visionary experience of the individual, and the cult of animal guardians; and among the Hamitic peoples the sky-god takes the foremost place. But it is dangerous to conclude that the point on which attention is focussed is the whole field of consciousness. The high gods are often conceived as too far from man to pay much attention to his doings, and it is lesser powers—the spirits of the field and the forest, or the ghosts of the dead—who come into closest relation with human life, and whose malevolence is most to be feared.

Consequently primitive religion is apt to appear wholly utilitarian and concerned with purely material ends. But here also the confusion of primitive thought is apt to mislead us. The ethical aspect of religion is not consciously recognized and cultivated as it is by civilized man, but it is none the less present in an obscure way. Primitive religion is essentially an attempt to bring man's life into relation with, and under the sanctions of, that other world of mysterious and sacred powers, whose action is always conceived as the ultimate and fundamental law of life. Moreover, the sense of sin and of the need for purification or catharsis is very real to primitive man. No doubt sin appears to him as a kind of physical contagion that seems to us of little moral value. Nevertheless, as we can see from the history of Greek religion, the sense of ritual defilement and that of moral guilt are very closely linked with one another, and the idea of an essential connection between moral and physical evil—between sin and death, for example—is found in the higher religions no less than among the primitives. *Libera nos a malo* is a universal prayer which answers to one of the oldest needs of human nature.

But the existence of this specifically religious need in primitive man—in other words, the naturalness of the religious attitude—is widely denied at the present day. It is maintained that primitive man is a materialist and that the attempt to find in primitive religion an obscure sense of the reality of spirit, or, indeed, anything remotely analogous to the religious experience of civilized man, is sheer metaphysical theorizing. This criticism is partly due to a tendency to identify any recognition of the religious element in primitive thought and culture with the particular theories of religious origins which have been put forward by Tylor and Durkheim. In reality, however, the theories of the latter have much more in common with those of the modern writers whom I have mentioned than any of them have with the point of view of writers who recognize the objective and autonomous character of religion. All of them show that anti-metaphysical prejudice which has been so general during the last generation or two, and which rejects on *a priori* grounds any objective interpretation of religious experience. On the Continent there is already a reaction against the idea of a "science of religion" which, unlike the other sciences, destroys its own object and leaves us with a residuum of facts that belong to a totally different order. In fact, recent German writers such as Otto, Heiler, and Carl Beth tend rather to exaggerate the mystical and intuitive character of religious experience, whether in its primitive or advanced manifestations. But in this country the anti-metaphysical prejudice is still dominant. A theory is not regarded as "scientific" unless it explains religion in terms of something else—as an artificial construction from nonreligious elements.

Thus Professor Perry writes: "The idea of deity has grown up with civilization itself, and in its beginnings it was constructed out of the most homely materials." He holds that religion was derived not from primitive speculation or symbolism nor from spiritual experience, but from a practical observation of the phenomena of life. Its origins are to be found in the association of certain substances, such as red earth, shells, crystals, etc., with the ideas of life and fertility and their use as amulets or fetishes in order to prolong life or to increase the sexual powers. From these beginnings religion was developed as a purely empirical system of ensuring material prosperity by the archaic culture in Egypt and was thence gradually diffused throughout the world by Egyptian treasure-seekers and megalith-builders. The leaders of these expeditions became the first gods, while the Egyptian practices of mummification and tomb-building were the source of all those ideas concerning the nature of the soul and the existence of a spiritual world that are found among primitive peoples.

It is needless for us to discuss the archaeological aspects of this pan-Egyptian hypothesis of cultural origins. From our present point of view the main objection to the theory lies in the naive Euhemerism of its attitude to religion. For even if we grant that the whole development of higher civilization has proceeded from a single centre, that is a very different thing from admitting that a fundamental type of human experience could ever find its origin in a process of cultural diffusion. It is not as though Professor Perry maintained that primitive man lived a completely animal existence before the coming of the higher culture. On the contrary, the whole tendency of his thought has been to vindicate the essential *humanity* of the primitive. It is the claim of "the new anthropology" that it rehabilitates human nature itself and "disentangles the original nature of man from the systems, tradition, and machinery of civilization which have modified it." [4] If, then, primitive man is non-religious, the conclusion follows that human nature itself is non-religious, and religion, like war, is an artificial product of later development.

But this conclusion has been reached only by the forced construction that has been arbitrarily put upon the evidence. Because the primitive fetish has no more religious value for us than the mascot that we put on our motor-cars, we assume that it can have meant nothing more to primitive man. This, however, is to fall into the same error for which Mr. Massingham rightly condemns the older anthropology—the neglect of the factor of degeneration. Our mascot is a kind of fetish, but it is a degenerate fetish, and it is degenerate precisely because it has lost its religious meaning. The religious man no longer uses mascots, though if he is a Catholic he may use the image of a saint. To the primitive man his

[4] H. J. Massingham, *The Heritage of Man*, p. 142.

fetish is more than the one and less than the other. It has the sanctity of a relic and the irrationality of a mascot. Professor Lowie has described how an Indian offered to show him "the greatest thing in the world"; how he reverently uncovered one cloth wrapper after another; and how at length there lay exposed a simple bunch of feathers—a mere nothing to the alien onlooker, but to the owner a badge of his convenant with the supernatural world. "It is easy," he says, "to speak of the veneration extended to such badges . . . as fetishism, but that label with its popular meaning is monstrously inadequate to express the psychology of the situation. For to the Indian the material object is nothing apart from its sacred associations." [5]

So, too, when Mr. Massingham speaks of primitive religion as "a purely supernatural machinery, controlled by man, for insuring the material welfare of the community," he is right in his description of facts, but wrong in his appreciation of values. To us, agriculture is merely a depressed industry which provides the raw material of our dinners, and so we assume that a religion that is largely concerned with agriculture must have been a sordid materialistic business. But this is entirely to misconceive primitive man's attitude to nature. To him, agriculture was not a sordid occupation; it was one of the supreme mysteries of life, and he surrounded it with religious rites because he believed that the fertility of the soil and the mystery of generation could only be ensured through the co-operation of higher powers. Primitive agriculture was in fact a kind of liturgy.

For us nature has lost this religious atmosphere because the latter has been transferred elsewhere. Civilization did not create the religious attitude or the essential nature of the religious experience, but it gave them new modes of expression and a new intellectual interpretation. This was the achievement of the great religions or religious philosophies that arose in all the main centres of ancient civilization about the middle of the first millennium B.C.[6] They attained to the two fundamental concepts of metaphysical being and ethical order, which have been the foundation of religious thought and the framework of religious experience

[5] R. H. Lowie, *Primitive Religion*, p. 19.

[6] I have discussed this movement at greater length in *Progress and Religion*, ch. vi.

ever since. Some of these movements of thought, such as Brahmanism, Taoism, and the Eleatic philosophy, concentrated their attention on the idea of Being, while others, such as Buddhism, Confucianism, Zoroastrianism, and the philosophy of Heraclitus, emphasized the idea of moral order; but all of them agreed in identifying the cosmic principle, the power behind the world, with a spiritual principle, conceived either as the source of being or as the source of ethical order.[7] Primitive man had already found the Transcendent immanent in and working through nature as the supernatural. The new religions found it in thought as the supreme Reality and in ethics as the Eternal Law. And consequently, while the former still saw the spiritual world diffused and confused with the world of matter, the latter isolated it and set it over against the world of human experience, as Eternity against Time, as the Absolute against the Contingent, as Reality against Appearance, and as the Spiritual against the Sensible.

This was indeed the discovery of a new world for the religious consciousness. It was thereby liberated from the power of the nature daimons and the dark forces of magic and translated to a higher sphere—to the Brahma-world—"where there is not darkness, nor day nor night, nor being nor not-being, but the Eternal alone, the source of the ancient wisdom," to the Kingdom of Ahura and the Six Immortal Holy Ones, to the world of the Eternal Forms, the true home of the soul. And this involved a corresponding change in the religious attitude. The religious life was no longer bound up with irrational myths and non-moral tabus; it was a process of spiritual discipline directed towards the purification of the mind and the will—a conversion of the soul from the life of the senses to spiritual reality. The religious experience of primitive man had become obscured by magic and diabolism, and the visions and trances of the Shaman belong rather to the phenomena of Spiritualism than of mysticism. The new type of religious experience, on the other hand, had reached a higher plane. It consisted in an intuition that was essentially spiritual and found its highest realization in the vision of the mystic.

[7] This may not appear obvious in the case of Buddhism. It is, however, implicit in the doctrine of Karma as the ground of the world process.

Thus each of the new religio-philosophic traditions, Brahmanism, Buddhism, Taoism, and Platonism—ultimately transcends philosophy and culminates in mysticism. They are not satisfied with the demonstration of the Absolute; they demand the experience of the Absolute also, whether it be the vision of the Essential Good and the Essential Beauty, through which the soul is made deiform, or that intuition of the nothingness and illusion inherent in all contingent being which renders a man *jivana mukti*, "delivered alive." But how is such an experience conceivable? It seems to be a contradiction in terms—to know the Unknowable, to grasp the Incomprehensible, to receive the Infinite. Certainly it transcends the categories of human thought and the normal conditions of human experience. Yet it has remained for thousands of years as the goal—whether attainable or unattainable—of the religious life; and no religion which ignores this aspiration can prove permanently satisfying to man's spiritual needs. The whole religious experience of mankind —indeed, the very existence of religion itself—testifies, not only to a sense of the Transcendent, but to an appetite for the Transcendent that can only be satisfied by immediate contact—by a vision of the supreme Reality. It is the goal of the intellect as well as of the will, for, as a Belgian philosopher has said, "The human mind is a *faculty in quest of its intuition,* that is to say, of assimilation with Being," and it is "perpetually chased from the movable, manifold and deficient towards the Absolute, the One and the Infinite, that is, towards *Being pure and simple*." [8]

A religion that remains on the rational level and denies the possibility of any real relation with a higher order of spiritual reality, fails in its most essential function, and ultimately, like Deism, ceases to be a religion at all. It may perhaps be objected that this view involves the identification of religion with mysticism, and that it would place a philosophy of intuition like that of the Vedanta higher than a religion of faith and supernatural revelation, like Christianity. In reality, however, the Christian insistence on the necessity of faith and revelation implies an even higher conception of transcendence than that of the Oriental religions. Faith transcends the sphere of rational knowledge even more than metaphys-

[8] J. Maréchal, *Studies in the Psychology of the Mystics,* trans. Algar Thorold (Benziger, 1927), pp. 101, 133.

ical intuition, and brings the mind into close contact with super-intelligible reality. Yet faith also, at least when it is joined with spiritual intelligence, is itself a kind of obscure intuition—a foretaste of the unseen [9]—and it also has its culmination in the mystical experience by which these obscure spiritual realities are realized experimentally and intuitively.

Thus Christianity is in agreement with the great Oriental religions and with Platonism in its goal of spiritual intuition, though it places the full realization of the goal at a further and higher stage of spiritual development than the rest. For all of them religion is not an affair of the emotions, but of the intelligence. Religious knowledge is the highest kind of knowledge, the end and coronation of the whole process of man's intellectual development.

If we accept the necessity of an absolute and metaphysical foundation for religion and religious experience, we still have to face the other aspect of the problem—namely, how this spiritual experience is to be brought into living relation with human life and with the social order. The ecstasy of the solitary mind in the presence of absolute reality seems to offer no solution to the actual sufferings and perplexities of humanity. And yet the religious mind cannot dissociate itself from this need, for it can never rest with a purely individual and self-regarding ideal of deliverance. The more religious a man is, the more is he sensitive to the common need of humanity. All the founders of the world religions—even those, like Buddha, who were the most uncompromising in their religious absolutism—were concerned not merely with their private religious experience, but with the common need of humanity. They aspired to be the saviours and path-finders —ford-makers, as the Indians termed them—who should rescue their people from the darkness and suffering of human life.

Nowhere is this social preoccupation more insistent than in the religious tradition of the West, and it is to be found even in the most abstract and intellectualist type of religious thought. It is to be seen above all in Plato, the perfect example of the pure metaphysician, who, nevertheless, made his metaphysics the basis of a programme of political and social reform. Indeed, according to his own description in the

[9] Cf. Rousselot, *Les Yeux de la Foi*.

Seventh Epistle it was his political interests and his realization of the injustice and moral confusion of the existing state which were the starting point of his metaphysical quest. But though Plato realized as fully as any purely religious teacher the need for bringing social life into contact with spiritual reality and for relating man's rational activity to the higher intuitive knowledge, he failed to show how this could be accomplished by means of a purely intellectual discipline. He saw that it was necessary on the one hand to drag humanity out of the shadow world of appearances and false moral standards into the pure white light of spiritual reality, and, on the other hand, that the contemplative must be forced to leave his mountain of vision and "to descend again to these prisoners and to partake in their toils and honours." [10] But, as he says, the spiritual man is at a disadvantage in the world of politics and business. The eyes that have looked upon the sun can no longer distinguish the shadows of the cave. The man who cares only for eternal things, who seeks to fly hence and to become assimilated to God by holiness and justice and wisdom, is unable to strive for political power with the mean cunning of the ordinary "man of affairs." [11] In fact nothing could show the impossibility of curing the ills of humanity by pure intelligence more completely than Plato's own attempt to reform the state of Sicily by giving a young tyrant lessons in mathematics. The political problems of the Greek world were solved not by the philosopher-king, but by condottieri and Macedonian generals, and the gulf between the spiritual world and human life grew steadily wider until the coming of Christianity.

In the East, however, the religious conception of life was victorious and dominated the whole field of culture. In India, above all, the ideal of spiritual intuition was not confined to a few philosophers and mystics, but became the goal of the whole religious development. It was, as Professor de la Vallée Poussin has said, "the great discovery that has remained for at least twenty-five centuries the capital and most cherished truth of the Indian people." The man who cannot understand this cannot understand the religion of India or the civilization with which it is so intimately connected. It is, however, only too easy for the Western mind to miscon-

[10] *Republic*, 519.
[11] *Theætetus*, 176.

ceive the whole tendency of Indian thought. It is apt to interpret the teaching of the Upanishads on the lines of Western idealist philosophy, and to see in the Indian doctrine of contemplation a philosophic pantheism that is intellectualist rather than religious. In reality it is in Western mystics such as Eckart or Angelus Silesius rather than in philosophers such as Hegel or even Spinoza that the true parallel to the thought of the Vedanta is to be found. It leads not to pantheism in our sense of the word, but to an extreme theory of transcendence which may be termed super-theism. Western pantheism is a kind of spiritual democracy in which all things are equally God; but the "nondualism" of the Vedanta is a spiritual absolutism in which God is the only reality. At first sight there may seem to be little practical difference between the statement that everything that exists is divine and the statement that nothing but the divine exists. But from the religious point of view there is all the difference in the world. For "if this transitory world be the Real," says a mediaeval Vedantist, "then there is no liberation through the Atman, the holy scriptures are without authority and the Lord speaks untruth . . . The Lord who knows the reality of things has declared 'I am not contained in these things, nor do beings dwell in Me.' " [12]

God is the one Reality. Apart from Him, nothing exists. In comparison with Him, nothing is real. The universe only exists in so far as it is rooted and grounded in His Being. He is the Self of our selves and the Soul of our souls. So far the Vedanta does not differ essentially from the teaching of Christian theology. The one vital distinction consists in the fact that Indian religion ignores the idea of creation and that in consequence it is faced with the dilemma that either the whole universe is an illusion—Maya—a dream that vanishes when the soul awakens to the intuition of spiritual reality, or else that the world is the self-manifestation of the Divine Mind, a conditional embodiment of the absolute Being.

Hence there is no room for a real intervention of the spiritual principle in human life. The Indian ethic is, above all, an ethic of flight—of deliverance from conditional existence and from the chain of re-birth. Human life is an object of compassion to the wise man, but it is also an

[12] *Vivekachudamani* (attributed to Sankara), trans. C. Johnston, p. 41.

object of scorn. "As the hog to the trough, goes the fool to the womb," says the Buddhist verse; and the Hindu attitude, if less harsh, is not essentially different. "Men are held by the manifold snares of the desires in the world of sense, and they fall away without winning to their end like dykes of sand in water. Like sesame-grains for their oil, all things are ground out in the mill-wheel of creation by the oil-grinders, to wit, the taints arising from ignorance that fasten upon them. The husband gathers to himself evil works on account of his wife; but he alone is therefore afflicted with taints, which cling to man alike in the world beyond and in this. All men are attached to children, wives and kin; they sink down in the slimy sea of sorrows, like age-worn forest-elephants." [13]

It is true that orthodox Hinduism inculcates the fulfilment of social duties, and the need for outward activity, but this principle does not lead to the transformation of life by moral action, but simply to the fatalistic acceptance of the established order of things. This is the theme of the greatest work of Indian literature, the Bhagavad-Gita, and it involves a moral attitude diametrically opposed to that of the Western mind. When Arjuna shrinks from the evils of war and declares that he would rather die than shed the blood of his kinsfolk, the god does not commend him. He uses the doctrine of the transcendence and impassibility of true being to justify the ruthlessness of the warrior.

"Know that that which pervades this universe is imperishable; there is none can make to perish that changeless being.

". . . This Body's Tenant for all time may not be wounded, O Thou of Bharata's stock, in the bodies of any beings. Therefore thou dost not well to sorrow for any born beings. Looking likewise in thine own Law, thou shouldst not be dismayed; for to a knight there is no thing more blest than a lawful strife." [14]

The sacred order that is the basis of Indian culture is no true spiritualization of human life; it is merely the natural order seen through a veil of metaphysical idealism. It can incorporate the most barbaric and non-ethical elements equally with the most profound metaphysical truths; since in the

[13] *Mahabharata*, xii, ch. 174, trans. L. D. Barnett.
[14] *Bhagavad-Gita*, ii, pp. 17, 30–31, trans. L. D. Barnett.

presence of the absolute and the unconditioned all distinctions and degrees of value lose their validity.

The experience of India is sufficient to show that it is impossible to construct a dynamic religion on metaphysical principles alone, since pure intuition affords no real basis for social action. On the other hand, if we abandon the metaphysical element and content ourselves with purely ethical and social ideals, we are still further from a solution, since there is no longer any basis for a spiritual order. The unity of the inner world dissolves in subjectivism and scepticism, and society is threatened with anarchy and dissolution. And since social life is impossible without order, it is necessary to resort to some external principle of compulsion, whether political or economic. In the ancient world this principle was found in the military despotism of the Roman Empire, and in the modern world we have the even more complete and far-reaching organization of the economic machine. Here indeed we have an order, but it is an order that is far more inhuman and indifferent to moral values than the static theocratic order of the Oriental religion-cultures.

But is there no alternative between Occidentalism and Orientalism, between a spiritual order that takes no account of human needs and a material order that has no regard for spiritual values? There still remains the traditional religion of our own civilization: Christianity, a religion that is neither wholly metaphysical nor merely ethical, but one that brings the spiritual world into vital and fruitful communion with the life of man.

In the ancient world its faith in a holy society and in a historical process of redemption distinguished Christianity from all its religious rivals and gave it the militant and unyielding quality that enabled it to triumph in its struggle with secular civilization. But this is not sufficient to explain its religious appeal. In addition to the social and historical side of its teaching, Christianity also brought a new doctrine of God and a new relation of the human soul to Him. Judaism had been the least mystical and the least metaphysical of religions. It revealed God as the Creator, the Lawgiver and the Judge, and it was by obedience to His Law and by the ritual observances of sacrifice and ceremonial purity that man entered into relations with Him. But the transformation by Jesus of the national community into a new universal spiritual society brought with it a corresponding change in the doctrine of

God. God was no longer the national deity of the Jewish people, localized, so to speak, at Sinai and Jerusalem. He was the Father of the human race, the Universal Ground of existence "in Whom we live and move and are." And when St. Paul appealed to the testimony of the Stoic poet, he recognized that Christianity was prepared to accept the metaphysical inheritance of Hellenic thought as well as the historic revelation of Jewish prophecy.

This is shown still more clearly in St. John's identification of the Logos and the Messiah in the prologue to the Fourth Gospel. Jesus of Nazareth was not only the Christ, the Son of the Living God; He was also the Divine Intelligence, the Principle of the order and intelligibility of the created world. Thus the opposition between the Greek ideal of spiritual intuition and the Living God of Jewish revelation—an opposition that Philo had vainly attempted to surmount by an artificial philosophical synthesis—finally disappeared before the new revelation of the Incarnate Word. As St. Augustine has said, the Fourth Gospel is essentially the Gospel of contemplation, for while the first three evangelists are concerned with the external mission of Jesus as Messianic King and Saviour and teach the active virtues of Christian life, St. John is, above all, "the theologian" who declares the mysteries of the Divine Nature and teaches the way of contemplation.[15] Jesus is the bridge between Humanity and Divinity. In Him God is not only manifested to man, but vitally participated. He is the Divine Light, which illuminates men's minds, and the Divine Life, which transforms human nature and makes it the partaker of Its own supernatural activity.

Hence the insistence of the Fourth Gospel on the sacramental element in Christ's teaching,[16] since it is through the sacraments that the Incarnation of the Divine Word is no longer merely a historical fact, but is brought into vital and sensible contact with the life of the believer. So far from being an alien magical conception superimposed from without upon the religion of the Gospel, it forms the very heart of Christianity, since it is only through the sacramental principle that the Jewish ideal of an external ritual cult becomes transformed into a worship of spiritual communion. The modern idea that sacramentalism is inconsistent with the "spiritual"

[15] *De Consensu Evangelistarum* i, cap. 3–5.

[16] E.g. John iii, 5; vi, 32–58.

or mystical element in religion, is as lacking in foundation as the allied belief in an opposition between religion and theology. It is only when we reduce theology to religious rationalism and spiritual religion to a blend of ethics and emotion that there is no place left for sacramentalism; but under these conditions genuine mysticism and metaphysical truth equally disappear. Each of them forms an essential element in the historical development of Christianity. In the great age of creative theological thought, the development of dogma was organically linked with sacramentalism and mysticism. They were three aspects of a single reality—the great mystery of the restoration, illumination and deification of humanity by the Incarnation of the Divine Word. This is clearly recognized by Ritschl and his followers such as Harnack, although they involve mysticism, sacramentalism and scientific theology in a common condemnation.

Nevertheless, their criticism of the development of Greek Christianity is not entirely unjustified, for the historical and social elements, on which Ritschl laid so exclusive an emphasis, form an integral part of the Christian tradition, and apart from them the mystical or metaphysical side of religion becomes sterile or distorted. The tendency of the Byzantine mind to concentrate itself on this aspect of Christianity did actually lead to a decline in moral energy and in the spiritual freedom and initiative of the Church, and Eastern Christianity has tended to become an absolute static religion of the Oriental type.

It is true that this ideal, since it is a purely religious one, has much more in common with Catholic Christianity than have the secularized ideals of modern European culture. Catholicism and Orientalism stand together against the denial of metaphysical reality and of the primacy of the spiritual, which is the fundamental Western error. As Sir Charles Eliot has truly said, "The opposition is not so much between Indian thought and the New Testament. . . . the fundamental contrast is rather between both India and the New Testament, on the one hand, and, on the other, the rooted conviction of European races, however much orthodox Christianity may disguise their expression of it, that this world is all-important. The conviction finds expression not only in the avowed pursuit of pleasure and ambition, but in such sayings as that the best religion is the one that does most good, and in such ideals as self-realization or the full development of one's motive and powers. Though monasteries and monks still exist, the great majority of Europeans instinctively disbelieve in asceticism, the contemplative life and contempt of the world." [17]

And yet, for all this, there is no getting over the profound differences that separate Christianity from the purely metaphysical and intuitive type of religion.

Against the Oriental religions of pure spirit, which denied the value and even the reality of the material universe, the Church has undeviatingly maintained its faith in a historical revelation that involved the consecration not only of humanity but even of the body itself. This was the great stumbling-block to the Oriental mind, which readily accepted the idea of an Avatar or of the theophany of a divine Aeon, but could not face the consequences of the Catholic doctrine of the Two Natures and the full humanity of the Logos made flesh. This conception of the Incarnation as the bridge between God and Man, the marriage of Heaven and Earth, the channel through which the material world is spiritualized and brought back to unity, distinguishes Christianity from all the other Oriental religions, and involves a completely new attitude to life. Deliverance is to be obtained not by a sheer disregard of physical existence and a concentration of the higher intellect on the contemplation of pure Being, but by a creative activity that affects every part of the composite nature of man. And this activity is embodied in a definite society, which shares in the divine life of the Spirit, while at the same time it belongs to the visible order of social and historical reality.

Thus Catholic Christianity occupies an intermediate position between the two spiritual ideals and the two conceptions of reality which have divided the civilized world and the experience of humanity. To the West its ideals appear mystical and otherworldly, while in comparison with the Oriental religions it stands for historical reality and moral activity. It is a stranger in both camps and its home is everywhere and nowhere, like man himself, whose nature maintains a perilous balance between the worlds of spiritual and sensible reality, to neither of which it altogether belongs. Yet by reason of this ambiguous position the Catholic Church stands as the one mediator between East and West, between

[17] C. Eliot, *Hinduism and Buddhism*, Vol. I, p. ix.

the ideal of spiritual intuition and that of moral and social activity. She alone possesses a tradition that is capable of satisfying the whole of human nature and one that brings the transcendent reality of spiritual Being into relation with human experience and the realities of social life.

—1931.

SECTION III: URBANISM AND THE ORGANIC NATURE OF CULTURE

1

The Evolution of the Modern City

THE problem of the industrial city is so essentially a modern one that we are only just beginning to appreciate its full meaning. In all the centuries since first men began to build cities the world has seen nothing resembling the movement which, in a few generations, has covered whole regions of Europe and America with a black network of towns. At the beginning of the last century the cities of Germany, for example, had hardly changed since the end of the Middle Ages. They were still self-sufficing, separated each by its own customs barrier from the surrounding country; their craftsmen were still bound by the old guild regulations; their citizens were an hereditary caste sharply divided from the nobles on the one hand and the peasants on the other. Of all the 1,000 corporate towns of Prussia only seventeen numbered more than 10,000 inhabitants, while many of them were mere villages of a few hundred souls. By the end of the century the whole face of society was changed. Great industrial cities, numbering their inhabitants by the hundred thousand, were springing up in every part of Germany. The descendant of the eighteenth-century serf had become a socialist factory hand or a commercial traveller. Great trusts and cartels controlling vast resources had taken the place of the old guild-regulated handicrafts.

Thus the new industrial movement was nothing less than a transformation of civilization. The old city life of Europe, which had possessed an unbroken tradition from the age of the Carolingians down to the eighteenth century, had come to an end. The city that was destined to take its place was a new creation without a civic past or any organic connection with the old civic tradition of Europe.

This new type of city first arose in eighteenth-century England—that is to say, in the age and the country in which the old city life had become most decadent. In England and in the northwest of Europe generally the city had never become the normal type of social organization as in the Mediterranean lands. In the latter, civilization has always preserved the city character imprinted on it by the Graeco-Roman city-state. There, even now, the provincial capitals keep much of their vitality as regional centres, and a man's first patriotism still goes to his city. There, too, the educated and ruling classes are almost exclusively city dwelling—the noble no less than the true "bourgeois"—and even the landowner makes his home in his city "palace" rather than his country villa. But in Northern Europe this was never the case. There the normal social unit has been the village with its centre in the church and the manor house. In the Middle Ages the ruling classes lived isolated in their own fiefs, given up to hunting and war, and despising the inhabitants of the cities as an inferior caste of tradesmen and artisans. And whilst in France and the countries under French influence the Renaissance monarchy gradually changed all this, and converted the nobility into a new class of courtier-townsman, in England the Renaissance monarchy was defeated, and the landed aristocracy gained control of the whole political order. The country squires, the lineal descendants of the mediaeval landowners, still lived on their own estates, with a true feudal contempt of the city, and a more than mediaeval passion for the chase. As Justices of the Peace they were the true rulers of the country; and, as members of Parliament, they absorbed the power formerly possessed by the Court on the one hand, and the yeomanry and the corporate towns on the other. The whole evolution of English society from the seventeenth to the eighteenth century was the inverse of that of the continent: it moved from urban monarchy to rural aristocracy. And it was the England that followed these traditions and was governed by this class that was suddenly precipitated into the full current of the Industrial Revolution.

This alone is sufficient to explain the haphazard and inorganic development of the new towns. The living social organs were those of the national state, and were rural and aristocratic in character. The rulers of the country looked on the development of the new coal mines and factories in somewhat the same way as a Roman senator would have viewed the work of his slave gangs on his provincial estates —as something outside and below civic life. The mediaeval constitutions of the municipalities were no longer functioning. The craft regulations were mere antiquarian survivals. The body of Freemen had practically disappeared; the essential work of the Common Council was being taken over by the Borough Justices of the Peace, and by a number of anomalous bodies—Paving Commissioners, Police Commissioners and the like—created by special Acts of Parliament. Some of the greatest industrial towns were not even corporate cities. Manchester itself was governed by a manorial court—convoked and presided over by the steward of the Lord of the Manor—right down to 1846. At the beginning of the nineteenth century there were still no resident magistrates, and that great city was as dependent on the authority of the neighbouring county justices as any country village.

Moreover, as the ruling classes were not city-dwellers, there was no opportunity for contact and adjustment between the new raw industrial city and the contemporary standards of civilized living. Even the rich manufacturers themselves did not make a permanent home in the towns which produced their wealth. It was their ambition to climb out of their town into the society of the country, which preserved all its social prestige, even in districts where the material advance of the new towns was greatest. In mediaeval Florence the nobles came into the city, as it grew rich, but in nineteenth-century Leeds and Manchester the merchants and manufacturers went into the country. There was none of that civic patriotism which caused the mediaeval merchant to spend so large a proportion of his wealth in the service and adornment of the city. And, in the same way, the semi-servile class of wage-labourers, who formed the true population of the new towns, grew up without traditions or ideals, with no share in the national franchise or in the government of their city. Their standards of life were even lower, and their interests more limited, than those of the rural class from which they had sprung. No doubt the mediaeval artisan had no high standard of life, but at least he shared in the living organic life of his city; and the gulf between his existence and that of the collier or cotton spinner of the later eighteenth century is almost that which separates civilization from barbarism. The whole life of the mediaeval townsman, whether rich or poor, was in his city and he took part in the life of the outer world only as a member of the civic organism; on the other hand the rich townsman of the industrial age was primarily a citizen of the national state, while the wage-earner could hardly be reckoned as a citizen at all.

Thus it is useless to seek to understand the rise of the industrial city by looking for an internal process of development, such as we can find in the history of the Greek or the mediaeval city. The new towns were not self-conscious and self-determining societies; they were the organs of a nationalist-imperialist movement of economic expansion. And, as the great age of Roman imperial expansion brought with it the decay of the old municipal life and a terrible degradation of slave labour, so, too, the industrial movement in eighteenth-century England brought with it a similar deterioration, alike in the civic life of the town and in the status of the wage-labourer. The same spirit that manifested itself in the ruthless daring and harsh discipline of the eighteenth-century navy, caused the sacrifice of the amenities of life in the new cities to the national wealth. At the cost of two or three generations of pitiless toil on the part of the people, and of demoniac energy on the part of the organizers and employers, England established her position as the workshop of the world.

The true character of this movement has been obscured by the false diagnosis of the economists. For a century after Adam Smith, the preachers of Free Trade and *laissez faire* in industry gave a liberal and individualistic interpretation to a process which was essentially due to half a century of disciplined national effort. The economic freedom that English trade and industry had secured for themselves was not the abstract liberty of the eighteenth-century philosophers, it was the freedom of the young giant who strips himself of the armour of antiquated restrictions in order to wrestle more freely with his opponents. The real note of the period was not liberty, but economic conquest and exploitation. England possessed an almost complete monopoly in the new industrial methods and her naval and mercantile power enabled her to find an opening for the new products in all the markets of the world—even in those of India and West Africa—while her potential rivals were still hampered by the old economic restrictions or by the pre-occupation of war and revolution. The economists failed to see that this advantage was essentially temporary. They attributed it to necessary working out of economic laws; and, as they believed in the providentially established harmony between individual gain and national welfare, it was natural for them also to suppose that the British industrial monopoly was ideally adapted to the true needs of humanity in general.

Finally, towards the middle of the nineteenth century, the new system achieved its consummation by the revolution of the means of transport and communication and by the consequent realization in practice of the economists' ideal of the world market. This change, while bringing an enormous accession of force to the industrial movement generally, had a special importance in the development of the industrial city. All the ancient limitations in the size of a city were removed, and the last links that bound the industrial town to its rural environment were broken. The city now lived entirely for and by the world market. It drew its food from one continent, the raw materials for its industries from another, and exported the finished product, perhaps, to a third.

Thus it was no longer in any sense a part or servant of its own region, nor was it organized primarily as a place for its own citizens to live in. It was a cosmopolitan ergastulum for the production of wealth. The desire for gain, which was the creative force behind this new city-development, showed itself in every aspect of its life. Thus the interests alike of the producer and the consumer were subordinated to those of the middleman, the class of financiers, bankers, brokers and merchants, which represented the vital principle of this order in the same way that the knight and the ecclesiastic represented that of the mediaeval state. And the same spirit governed the actual construction of the industrial town: it was built neither for beauty nor for convenience, but for the immediate profit of the ground landlord and the speculative builder. The exploitation ethos, the spirit of Dickens' Gradgrind and Matthew Arnold's Mr. Bottles, was a very real force during the nineteenth century, and in its time it moulded civilization

In England no less effectually than did the militarist ethos in Prussia.

The typical cities of the industrial age—the Lancashire cotton town of a century ago, the Pittsburgh or Chicago of the last generation or the new Russian factory towns of 1914—were like the great mining camps which grew up on the Californian and Australian goldfields; not cities, but fortuitous collections of individuals drawn together to exploit the new source of wealth, and one another, and living in chaotic disorder and discomfort without any thought beyond the gain of the moment. And, as the mining camp gave place in time to a comparatively settled and orderly town, so we can see the industrial order gradually passing into something different.

During the second half of the nineteenth century new factors began to appear, which pointed towards the ending of the period of successful economic monopoly. Industrialism was no longer limited to those societies which had first understood how to apply it profitably; it spread over the world with amazing rapidity. The statesmen and economists of the continental countries realized that the doctrines of *laissez faire* and Free Trade only tended to accentuate the economic inferiority of the less developed countries, and they began to use all the resources of statecraft and science in order to organize and protect the industrial powers of their own nations. Thus there arose the new Germanic type of industrialism—so different in its ordered and bureaucratic co-ordination from the haphazard disorder of our own Industrial Revolution. Yet this advance was dearly purchased by the growing intensification of international competition and the desperate struggle for markets and colonies, which went hand in hand with the development of vast armaments and culminated in the general European War.

The development of rival industrialisms, like that of rival armaments, is a process which contains in itself the causes of its own destruction. It has become increasingly evident that it is possible for industrial production to expand out of all proportion to the growth of the world markets. The prosperity of industrial England of the Victorian age, with its cheap labour and high profits, rested, on the one hand, on the cheap produce of the newly opened farm lands of America and, on the other, on the control of the markets of India and the other lands that were not yet industrialized. The universalization of industrialism imperils both these factors.

No country is now either too old or too new to become an industrial power. The cities of the United States are already almost numerous enough to absorb the harvests of the Middle West; India aspires to industrial self-sufficiency and Japan to industrial imperialism. And this vast development of world industry and population makes correspondingly heavy demands on the natural resources of the world. A century ago it might well seem that British coal and American timber would last for ever; but the following generations spent the accumulated wealth of ages with such reckless haste that, by the beginning of the twentieth century, it became clear that the wasteful exploitation of coal and timber and the extensive cultivation of virgin prairie soils, would have to give place to a policy of conservation, to new methods of economy and to a more intensive agriculture.

Moreover, at the same time that the weaker countries were revolting against the economic exploitation of the great industrial powers, the weaker classes were asserting their right to an equal share in the control and profits of industry. If the wage-earner was never a contented partner in the industrial system, it is only recently that education and organization have given him the power to make his claims felt. The fluidity and docility of labour were essential factors in the old industrial system, and if labour were to achieve the position of an equal partner in industry it would inevitably give rise to a new system. Behind all the ephemeral phenomena of labour disputes and socialist propaganda there lies a really significant change in social mentality—the revolt of the popular mind against the exploitation ethos and the coming of a new humanist ethos which places vital and aesthetic considerations in front of mechanical and financial ones.

This change had also begun to show itself during the last quarter of the nineteenth century in a widespread movement towards better conditions of life in the industrial town. There was a renewal of the municipal spirit, and men once more began to think of the city as a place to live in and not merely as a place out of which to make money. This spirit showed itself in housing and sanitary reform, in the rise of municipal enterprises and institutions, and finally in the town planning movement. Nevertheless the social reformers, like their contemporaries, the Socialists, did not envisage the possibility of any great change in the industrial movement. They all took the giant city for granted, and thought only of how to make

it more habitable. Their attitude towards the rural environment of the city was suburban rather than regional—that is to
say they looked on it as so much empty space for town-
expansion, not as the social complement of the city with
which it stands in organic connection.

It is only during the last twenty years that it has become
possible to understand the meaning of the new economic and
social factors, and to discern the rise of a new type of industrialism, a "neo-technic order," which brings with it the prospect of a new industrial city. We are witnessing on the one
hand that universalization of industrialism that I have just
described and, on the other, an agrarian revival which has
restored the prosperity of the continental and Irish peasantry
and has given them economic strength to resist the exploitation of the middleman. The same process, in a somewhat
different form, is taking place in the United States and Can-
ada, where the farmers are organizing themselves both economically and politically. Everywhere the agricultural producer is gaining strength against the urban consumer. Already
in Central Europe we have seen the country beginning to
take its revenge by exploiting the towns; and the time is not
far distant when the giant city, which has no regular source
of food supply, but is dependent on the surplus of the world
markets, will find its position becoming increasingly difficult.

In the long run, the general levelling-out process that these
changes involve will favour a smaller type of industrial city
and one that is more in contact with its rural neighbourhood.
There is no longer sufficient justification for huddling all the
factories of a nation round the mouths of the coal pits. The
obvious advantage in saving coal freights is largely counterbalanced by the waste and disorder with which this system
has been accompanied; and there are great compensatory advantages, even of the economic order, in the opposite policy
of a decentralized industry. If industrialism ever attains stable
equilibrium it is probable that every town will possess factories but that the pure factory-town will become a thing of
the past. The future is not with the giant hive of cosmopolitan industry but rather with the medium-sized city of 50,000
to 100,000 inhabitants which possesses a high industrial development but which is also a true centre to the rural districts in which it is placed. For the more closely a town is
knit up with its agricultural environment, both socially and
economically, the stronger it will be and the richer will be the

resources on which it can draw. Hitherto this contact has been notably lacking. Both in Europe and America there is an extraordinary social and intellectual cleavage between the country and the town—even the small town, like Mr. Sinclair Lewis' "Main Street," which is parasitically dependent on the farmer. But it is hardly conceivable that this cleavage can long continue. In England we already see the effects of the new road transport in bringing the villager into close contact with his country town; and everywhere the worker on the land has so far acquired the tastes and mentality of the townsman that the old peasant life and character, which hardly changed from the fifteenth to the nineteenth century, is now completely vanishing. And this process of interpenetration need not stop with the mere urbanization of the rustic. As it progresses we may hope that the town will receive as well as give; that it will once more recover its contacts with the country around it and with the natural occupations of the countryside for lack of which the industrial town has suffered so grievously.

This brings us close to the ideal of the Garden City, but the Garden City movement, in its actual development, has tended towards the substitution of satellite towns for suburbs rather than towards the creation of regional city centres. It may indeed be questioned whether the latter is possible in so highly developed and thickly populated a country as England, and whether our true policy does not lie in the reformation and development of the existing country towns. Up to the present the problems of the market town have been almost completely neglected; but there is no doubt that a small part of the effort and expenditure that have been spent, both on the improvement of the giant industrial city and on the creation of the garden town, might produce remarkable results if it were applied to a market town like Evesham or to a county centre like Salisbury or York. In the case of most of these towns there are none of the heartbreaking masses of material difficulty which meet the town planner in the great industrial city. They are not an amorphous chaos like the latter. They have preserved their organic form, and there is usually sufficient space for secondary replanning and expansion. The obstacles to improvement are rather moral than material—the dead weight of traditional apathy and the absence of a corporate and civic spirit. And these are mainly due to the conditions of the industrial age which have sucked the vitality from the countryside and from the towns that served it. The passing of these conditions, and the rise of a different type of industrialism, would bring about an economic revival of the lesser towns and consequently a renewal of civic life.

It is true that this country has committed itself to the earlier type of industrialism in so wholesale a fashion that the possibilities of further development are not so great as they are either in the new lands across the seas or in the older countries that were left behind by the Industrial Revolution. Nevertheless agrarian England still exists, and our cities cannot long continue to ignore it. The progress of modern science and modern technique is not hostile, but favourable, to a closer contact between the city and its rural environment. There is every reason to believe that the city of the future, no less than those of Antiquity and of the Middle Ages, will be a regional city—the civic expression of the local society. For the greater is man's control and knowledge of nature the more will he be led to make a full utilization of all the potentialities, both for wealth and life, of the natural region with which his life is bound up.

—1923.

2

Catholicism and the Bourgeois Mind

THE question of the bourgeois involves a real issue which Christians cannot afford to shirk. For it is difficult to deny that there is a fundamental disharmony between bourgeois and Christain civilization and between the mind of the bourgeois and the mind of Christ.

But first let us admit that it is no use hunting for the bourgeois. For we are all more or less bourgeois and our civilization is bourgeois from top to bottom. Hence there can be no question of treating the bourgeois in the orthodox communist fashion as a gang of antisocial reptiles who can be exterminated summarily by the revolutionary proletariat; for in order to "liquidate" the bourgeoisie modern society would have to "liquidate" itself.

This is where Marx went wrong. His theory of increasing misery led him to suppose that the line of class division would become sharper and more strongly defined, until the rising tide of popular misery broke the dykes and swept away the closed world of privileged bourgeois society. Instead of this we have seen the bourgeois culture, the bourgeois mind, even the bourgeois standards of life advancing and expanding until they became diffused throughout the whole social organism and dominated the whole spirit of modern civilization.

And so in order to understand the essential character of

the bourgeois, it is necessary to disregard for the moment this universalized bourgeois culture which is part of the very air we breathe and turn back to the time when the bourgeois was still a distinct social type which could be isolated from the other elements in society and studied as an independent phenomenon.

Now the bourgeois was in origin the member of a small and highly specialized class which had grown up within the wall of the mediaeval city commune. Far from being the average European man, he was an exceptional type standing somewhat outside the regular hierarchy of the mediaeval state, which was primarily an agrarian society consisting of the nobility, the clergy, and the peasantry. His very existence was guaranteed by a charter of privileges which constituted the city-commune as a *régime d'exception*. Thus there was a sharp division of material interests and social culture between the bourgeois and the countryman, a division which was deepened in Eastern Europe, including Eastern Germany, by the fact that the towns were often islands of German speech and civilization amidst a population that was predominantly Slav. And so while the peasant laboured and the noble fought, the bourgeois was free to lead his own life, to mind his own business and to grow rich within the narrow limits of the mediaeval urban economy.

All this seems infinitely remote from the modern world. But we must remember that it was not so remote from the society to which the founders of modern socialism—Lassalle and Marx and Engels—belonged. The German bourgeoisie had only just emerged from a régime of corporate rights and privileges which bound the bourgeois to his corporation, the craftsman to his guild, the peasant to his land, and the Jew to his ghetto. The generation before that of Marx had seen this structure collapse like a house of cards, so that the world was suddenly thrown open to any man who possessed money and enterprise—that is to say to every good bourgeois.

Thus the process which had taken centuries to develop in Western Europe was completed in Central and Eastern Europe within a single lifetime. Whereas in England and the United States, the bourgeois spirit had already become a fluid element that interpenetrated the whole social organism; in Germany, or Austria, or Russia, it was still a new factor in social life and so it was easy for Marx to separate it from the rest of society and regard it as the distinctive mark of a definite limited class.

And this explains why class hatred comes more easily to the Eastern than to the Western European. Croce has an amusing story of how an Italian delegate to a German socialist congress was obliged to apologize for the lack of class hatred in the Italian socialist movement. "We do not hate," he admitted, "but we are quite willing to." And in English socialism even the will to hatred has been lacking in spite of the fact that the proletariat in England suffered far more than the proletariat in Germany from the coming of industrialism. For the leaders of English socialism have been idealists, whether bourgeois idealists like Robert Owen and William Morris or Christian socialists like Keir Hardie and George Lansbury.

But while we may well congratulate ourselves that English social life has not been poisoned by class hatred and class war, it does not follow that the complete penetration of English culture by bourgeois standards and ideals is a good or admirable thing. It is even possible that the victory of the bourgeois has meant the destruction of elements that are not merely valuable but essential to English life, since the English tradition is something much wider and deeper than the machine-made urban and suburban culture by which it has been temporarily submerged.

Actually we have only to open our eyes to see that this criticism is justified. The devastated areas of industrial England and the cancerous growth of the suburbs are not merely offensive to the aesthetic sense, they are symptoms of social disease and spiritual failure. The victory of bourgeois civilization has made England rich and powerful, but at the same time it has destroyed almost everything that made life worth living. It has undermined the natural foundations of our national life, so that the whole social structure is in danger of ruin.

Looked at from this point of view the distinctive feature of the bourgeois culture is its *urbanism*. It involves the divorce of man from nature and from the life of the earth. It turns the peasant into a minder of machines and the yeoman into a shopkeeper, until ultimately rural life becomes impossible and the very face of nature is changed by the destruction of the countryside and the pollution of the earth and the air and the waters.

This is characteristic of modern bourgeois civilization in general, but nowhere is it more striking than in England. And since English culture has been historically a peculiarly rural one, the victory of bourgeois civilization involves a more serious breach with the national tradition and a more vital revolution in ways of life and thought than in any other country of Western Europe.

But if the bourgeois is the enemy of the peasant, he is no less the enemy of the artist and the craftsman. As Sombart has shown in his elaborate study of the historic evolution of the bourgeois type, the craftsman like the artist has an organic relation to the object of his work. "They see in their work a part of themselves and identify themselves with it so that they would be happy if they could never be separated from it." For in the precapitalist order "the production of goods is the act of living men who, so to speak, incarnate themselves in their works: and so it follows the same laws that rule their physical life, in the same way as the growth of a tree or the act of reproduction of an animal, obeys in its direction and measure and end the internal necessities of the living organism." [1] The attitude of the bourgeois on the other hand is that of the merchant whose relation to his merchandise is external and impersonal. He sees in them only objects of exchange, the value of which is to be measured exclusively in terms of money. It makes no difference whether he is dealing in works of art or cheap ready-made suits: all that matters is the volume of the transactions and the amount of profit to be derived from them. In other words, his attitude is not qualitative, but quantitative.

It is easy enough to see why this should be. For the bourgeois was originally the middleman who stood between the producer and the consumer, as merchant or salesman or broker or banker. And thus there is not merely an analogy, but an organic connection between the role of the bourgeois in society and the economic function of money. One is the middleman and the other is the medium of exchange. The bourgeois lives for money, not merely as the peasant or the soldier or even the artist often does, but in a deeper sense, since money is to him what arms are to the soldier and land is to the peasant, the tools of his trade and the medium through which he expresses himself, so that he often takes

[1] Sombart, *Le Bourgeois* (French trans.), pp. 25–7.

an almost disinterested pleasure in his wealth because of the virtuosity he has displayed in his financial operations. In short the bourgeois is essentially a *money-maker*, at once its servant and its master, and the development of his social ascendancy shows the degree to which civilization and human life are dominated by the money power.

This is why St. Thomas and his masters, both Greeks and Christians, look with so little favour on the bourgeois. For they regarded money simply as an instrument, and therefore held that the man who lives for money perverts the true order of life.

"Business," says St. Thomas, "considered in itself, has a certain baseness (*turpitudo*) inasmuch as it does not of itself involve any honourable or necessary end."

We find this criticism repeated at the time of the Renaissance by humanists like Erasmus; indeed, it is the basis of that aristocratic prejudice against the bourgeois which has never entirely disappeared and which reappears in all sorts of forms from sheer idealism to pure snobbery in the most unlikely times and places.

Thus the classical Marxian opposition of bourgeois and proletarian is but one of a whole series of oppositions and class conflicts which the rise of the bourgeoisie has aroused. There is the aristocratic opposition of which I have just spoken. There is the opposition of the artist which did so much to bring the name of the "bourgeois" into disrepute in the nineteenth century. There is the opposition to the bourgeois in so far as he is the representation and incarnation of the money power—an opposition which has found a new expression in the Social Credit movement. And finally there is the opposition between bourgeois and peasant, which is more fundamental and deep-rooted than any of them.

But while all these oppositions are real and each implies a genuine criticism of bourgeois culture, none of them is absolute or exhaustive. There is a more essential opposition still, which has been pointed out by Sombart and which goes beyond economics and sociology to the bedrock of human nature. According to Sombart, the bourgeois type corresponds to certain definite psychological predispositions. In other words there is such a thing as a *bourgeois soul* and it is in this rather than in economic circumstance that the whole development of the bourgeois culture finds its ultimate root. In the same way the opposite pole to the bourgeois is not to be found in a particular economic function of interest, as for instance the proletarian or the peasant, but rather in the anti-bourgeois temperament, the type of character which naturally prefers to spend rather than to accumulate, to give rather than to gain. These two types correspond to Bergson's classi-fication of the "open" and "closed" temperaments and they represent the opposite poles of human character and human experience. They are in eternal opposition to one another and the whole character of a period or a civilization depends on which of the two predominates. Thus we are led back from the external and material class conflict of the Marxians to a conception not far removed from that of St. Augustine, "Two loves built two cities"; the essential question is not the ques-tion of economics, but the question of love. "Looking at the matter closely," writes Sombart, "we get the impression that the opposition between these two fundamental types rests in the final analysis on an opposition of erotic life, for it is clear that this dominates the whole of human conduct as a superior and invisible power. The bourgeois and the erotic tempera-ments constitute, so to speak, the two opposite poles of the world." Sombart's use of the word "erotic" is of course wider than the current English term. Unsatisfactory as the word "erotic" is, it is the best we have, for "charitable" is even more miserably inadequate. Our bourgeois culture has re-duced the heavenly flame of St. Paul's inspired speech to a dim bulb that is hardly strong enough to light a mothers' meeting. But Sombart expressly distinguishes it from sensu-ality, which may be found in either of the two types of temperament. Indeed, the erotic type par excellence in Som-bart's view is the religious mystic, the "man of desire," like St. Augustine or St. Francis.

Seen from this point of view, it is obvious that the Christian ethos is essentially antibourgeois, since it is an ethos of love. This is particularly obvious in the case of St. Francis and the mediaeval mystics, who appropriated to their use the phrase-ology of mediaeval erotic poetry and used the antibourgeois concepts of the chivalrous class-consciousness, such as *"adel,"* *"noble,"* and *"gentile"* in order to define the spiritual charac-ter of the true mystic.

But it is no less clear in the case of the Gospel itself. The spirit of the Gospel is eminently that of the "open" type which gives, asking nothing in return, and spends itself for others. It is essentially hostile to the spirit of calculation, the spirit of worldly prudence and above all to the spirit of religious self-seeking and self-satisfaction. For what is the Pharisee but a spiritual bourgeois, a typically "closed" nature, a man who applies the principle of calculation and gain not to economics but to religion itself, a hoarder of merits, who reckons his accounts with heaven as though God was his banker? It is against this "closed," self-sufficient moralist ethic that the fiercest denunciations of the Gospels are directed. Even the sinner who possesses a seed of generosity, a faculty of self-surrender, and an openness of spirit is nearer to the kingdom of heaven than the "righteous" Pharisee; for the soul that is closed to love is closed to grace.

In the same way the ethos of the Gospels is sharply opposed to the economic view of life and the economic virtues. It teaches men to live from day to day without taking thought for their material needs. "For a man's life does not consist in the abundance of things which he possesses." It even condemns the prudent forethought of the rich man who plans for the future: "Thou fool, this night do they require thy soul of thee, and whose shall those things be which thou hast provided?"

Thus so long as the Christian ideal was supreme, it was difficult for the bourgeois spirit to assert itself. It is true, as Sombart insists, that the bourgeois class and the bourgeois view of life had already made their appearance in mediaeval Europe, but powerful as they were, especially in the Italian cities, they always remained limited to a part of life and failed to dominate the whole society or inspire civilization with their spirit. It was not until the Reformation had destroyed the control of the Church over social life in Northern Europe that we find a genuine bourgeois culture emerging. And whatever we may think of Max Weber's thesis regarding the influence of the Reformation on the origins of capitalism, we cannot deny the fact that the bourgeois culture actually developed on Protestant soil, and especially in a Calvinist environment, while the Catholic environment seemed decidedly unfavourable to its evolution.

It is indeed impossible to find a more complete example in history of the opposition of Sombart's two types than in the contrast of the culture of the Counter Reformation lands with that of seventeenth-century Holland and eighteenth-century England and Scotland and North America. The Baroque culture of Spain and Italy and Austria is the complete social embodiment of Sombart's "erotic" type. It is not that it was a society of nobles and peasants and monks and clerics which centred in palaces and monasteries (or even palace-monasteries like the Escorial), and left a comparatively small place to the bourgeois and the merchant. It is not merely that it was an *uneconomic* culture which spent its capital lavishly, recklessly and splendidly whether to the glory of God or for the adornment of human life. It was rather that the whole spirit of the culture was passionate and ecstatic, and finds its supreme expressions in the art of music and in religious mysticism. We have only to compare Bernini with the brothers Adam or St. Teresa with Hannah More to feel the difference in the spirit and rhythm of the two cultures. The bourgeois culture has the mechanical rhythm of a clock, the Baroque the musical rhythm of a fugue or a sonata.

The ideal of the bourgeois culture is to maintain a respectable average standard. Its maxims are: "Honesty is the best policy," "Do as you would be done by," "The greatest happiness of the greatest number." But the Baroque spirit lives in and for the triumphant moment of creative ecstasy. It will have all or nothing. Its maxims are: "All for love and the world well lost," *"Nada, nada, nada,"* "What dost thou seek for, O my soul? All is thine, all is for thee, do not take less, nor rest with the crumbs that fall from the table of thy Father. Go forth, and exult in thy glory, hide thyself in it and rejoice, and thou shalt obtain all the desires of thy heart."

The conflict between these two ideals of life and forms of culture runs through the whole history of Europe from the Reformation to the Revolution and finds its political counterpart in the struggle between Spain and the Protestant Powers. It is hardly too much to say that if Philip II had been victorious over the Dutch and the English and the Huguenots, modern bourgeois civilization would never have developed and capitalism in so far as it existed would have acquired an entirely different complexion. The same spirit would have ruled at Amsterdam as at Antwerp, at Berlin as at Munich, in North America as in South, and thus the moment when Alexander Farnese turned back a dying man from his march on Paris may be regarded as one of the greatest turning points in world history. Even so it is quite conceivable that Europe might have fallen apart into two closed worlds, as alien and opposed to one another as Christendom and Islam, had it not been that neither culture was strong enough to assimilate France. For a time during the first half of the seventeenth century, the Counter Reformation and its culture carried everything before them, but the bourgeois spirit in France was already too strong to be eliminated and it allied itself with the monarchy and the Gallican church against ultramontane Catholicism and Baroque culture.

Although the classicist and Gallican culture of the age of Louis XIV was far from being genuinely bourgeois, it contained a considerable bourgeois element and owed a great deal to men of bourgeois class and bourgeois spirit, such as Boileau, Nicole and even perhaps Bossuet himself. The resultant change in the spirit of French religion and culture is to be seen in that "retreat of the mystics" of which Bremond speaks, and in the victory of a rather hard and brilliant Nationalism which prepared the way for the rationalism of the Enlightenment. Thus French eighteenth-century culture became an open door through which the bourgeois spirit penetrated the closed world of Baroque Catholicism, first as a leaven of criticism and new ideas, and finally as a destructive flood of revolutionary change which destroyed the moral and social foundations of the Baroque culture. The uneconomic character of that culture left it powerless to withstand the highly organized financial power of the new commercialist bourgeois society. It went in the same way that the Hellenistic world succumbed to the superior organization of Roman imperialism. Nevertheless it did not succumb without a struggle, for wherever the common people possessed the power of organization and the means of defence, and wherever the religious tradition of the Counter Reformation had struck deep roots in the soil, they fought with desperate resolution and heroism in defence of the old Catholic order,[2] as in La Vendée in 1793, in Tirol in 1809, and in the Basque provinces till late in the nineteenth century.

With the passing of the Baroque culture a vital element went out of Western civilization. Where its traditions survived into the nineteenth century, as in Austria and Spain and parts of Italy and South Germany, one still feels that life has a richer savour and a more vital rhythm than in the lands

---

[2] These popular risings may be compared with the peasant risings against the Reformation in sixteenth-century England. In each case it was the common people and not the privileged classes who were the mainstay of the resistance.

where the bourgeois spirit is triumphant. Unfortunately the breach with the past seems too great for Europe to recover this lost tradition even when the bourgeois civilization is decadent and exhausted. Men look for an alternative not to the humane culture of the immediate Catholic past but to the inhuman mass civilization of Russia or the barbaric traditions of German paganism, while in our own country we are abandoning the competitive selfishness of the older capitalism only to adopt a bourgeois version of socialism which is inspired by a humanitarian policy of social reform, derived from the liberal-democratic tradition. It aims not at the proletarian revolutionary ideal of the communists, but rather at the diffusion of bourgeois standards of life and culture among the whole population—the universalizing of the bourgeois *rentier* type.

Whatever may be the future of these movements there can be little doubt that they mark an important change in the history of the bourgeois civilization and that the age of the free and triumphant progress of Western capitalism is ended. Capitalism may well survive, but it will be a controlled and socialized capitalism which aims rather at maintaining the general standard of life than at the reckless multiplication of wealth by individuals. Yet the mere slowing down of the tempo of economic life, the transformation of capitalism from a dynamic to a static form will not in itself change the spirit of our civilization. Even if it involves the passing of the bourgeois type in its classical nineteenth-century form, it may only substitute a post-bourgeois type which is no less dominated by economic motives, though it is more mechanized and less dominated by the competitive spirit. It may even be, as so many Continental critics of English society suggest, the bourgeois capitalist order in a senile and decadent form. As we have already pointed out, the character of a culture is determined not so much by its form of economic organization as by the spirit which dominates it. Socialization and the demand for a common standard of economic welfare, however justified it may be, do not involve a vital change in the spirit of a culture. Even a proletarian culture of the communist type, in spite of its avowed hatred of the bourgeois and all his works, is post-bourgeois rather than anti-bourgeois. Its spiritual element is a negative one, the spirit of revolution, and when the work of destruction is accomplished, it will inevitably tend to fall back into the traditions of the bourgeois culture, as appears to be happening in Russia at present. Thus, while Western communism is still highly idealistic and represents a spiritual protest against the bourgeois spirit and a reaction against the victorious industrial capitalism of the immediate past, Russian communism is actually doing for Russia what the Industrial Revolution did for Western Europe, and is attempting to transform a peasant people into a modern urban industrial society.

No economic change will suffice to change the spirit of a culture. So long as the proletarian is governed by purely economic motives, he remains a bourgeois at heart. It is only in religion that we shall find a spiritual force that can accomplish a spiritual revolution. The true opposite to the bourgeois is not to be found in the communist, but in the religious man—the man of desire. The bourgeois must be replaced not so much by another class as by another type of humanity. It is true that the passing of the bourgeois does involve the coming of the worker, and there can be no question of a return to the old régime of privileged castes. Where Marx was wrong was not in his dialectic of social change, but in the narrow materialism of his interpretation which rules out the religious factor.

The fact is that Marx was himself a disgruntled bourgeois, and his doctrine of historic materialism is a hang-over from a debauch of bourgeois economics and bourgeois philosophy. He was no great lover, no "man of desire," but a man of narrow, jealous, unforgiving temperament, who hated and calumniated his own friends and allies. And consequently he sought the motive power for the transformation of society not in love but in hatred and failed to recognize that the social order cannot be renewed save by a new principle of spiritual order. In this respect Marxian socialism is infinitely inferior to the old Utopian socialism, for Saint-Simon [3] and his followers with all their extravagances had at least grasped this essential truth. They failed not because they were too religious but because they were not religious enough and mistook the shadows of idealism for the realities of genuine religion. Yet we must admit that the Church of their day with its reactionary Gallicanism and its official alliance with the secular power gave them some excuse for their end.

[3] Saint-Simon himself is an extreme example of Sombart's "erotic" type with all its faults and weaknesses.

Today Christians are faced with a no less heavy responsibility. There is always a temptation for religion to ally itself with the existing order, and if we today ally ourselves with the bourgeois because the enemies of the bourgeois are often also the enemies of the Church, we shall be repeating the mistake that the Gallican prelates made in the time of Louis XVIII. The Christian Church is the organ of the spirit, the predestined channel through which the salvific energy of divine love flows out and transforms humanity. But it depends on the Christians of a particular generation, both individually and corporately, whether this source of spiritual energy is brought into contact with the life of humanity and the needs of contemporary society. We can hoard our treasure, we can bury our talent in the ground like the man in the parable who thought that his master was an austere man and who feared to take risks. Or, on the other hand, we can choose the difficult and hazardous way of creative spiritual activity, which is the way of the saints. If the age of the martyrs has not yet come, the age of a limited, self-protective, bourgeois religion is over. For the kingdom of heaven suffers violence and the violent take it by force.

—1935.

3

The World Crisis and the English Tradition

THE crisis that has arisen in the modern world during the postwar period is not merely an economic one. It involves the future of Western culture as a whole, and, consequently, the fate of humanity. But it is not a simple or uniform phenomenon. It is not confined to any one state or any one continent. It is world-wide in its incidence and shows itself in a different form in every different society. The problem of Russia is essentially different from that of America, and that of Germany from that of England. And yet all are inextricably interwoven in an immense and complicated tangle which politicians and economists are vainly struggling to unravel.

Hence it is useless to hope to find the solution of the world crisis in some simple remedy that can be applied to every society indifferently. The problem is a real one, and it cannot be solved by the manipulation of credit and currency. It is a question of how to adjust the traditional forms of social and political order which are the result of a long and gradual process of historical evolution to the new economic forces that have transformed the world during the last century, and above all during the last forty years.

Thus each people has to find the individual solution that is in conformity with its own sociological and historical structure.

And nowhere is this more necessary than in England, for while the English situation is one of the key positions of the world crisis, it has no exact analogy with anything that exists in any other country. It shows a peculiarly abrupt contrast between a highly individual national culture and an exceptionally highly developed system of world trade and finance. Of all countries England is at once the most national and insular in its cultural tradition and the most cosmopolitan in its economic and imperial position. In this it resembles Rome, the peasant state that became the organizer of a world empire and the centre of a cosmopolitan civilization.

And as the development of Roman culture was late and backward in comparison with the Hellenic world, so was it with the English national culture as compared with that of continental Europe. The development of a native English culture was checked by the Norman Conquest, and during the best part of the Middle Ages England was under the dominion of an alien culture that had its roots across the channel. England first began to become herself in the fourteenth century, when the mediaeval unity was passing away, and it was only in the three centuries that followed the Renaissance and the Reformation that the English national culture acquired its characteristic form.

At that time civilization on the Continent was following in a remarkable way in the footsteps of the great Mediterranean civilization of the past. Renaissance Italy inherited the traditions of Hellenism, while Spain and Baroque Austria and the France of Louis XIV inherited the Roman Byzantine tradition of state absolutism and sacred monarchy. But in England there is no room for such comparisons. Partly, though not entirely, as a result of the Reformation, she remained apart from the main current of European life, following her own path and jealously guarding against any influence from outside somewhat after the fashion of Japan in the Far East during this very period. Her development was, in fact, the exact opposite to that of Germany during the seventeenth and eighteenth centuries, open as the latter was to all the cultural and political currents in Europe, receiving French influence from across the Rhine, Italian influence through Austria, and Swedish influence from the Baltic.

It was this accentuation of her island position which was

the essential condition of England's achievement. She was a little world, secure behind the guardian barrier of the narrow seas, the most peaceful land in Europe, almost the only spot in the world that was free from the constant menace of war and invasion. Hence there was a general relaxation of tension in the social organism. There was no need for the rigid centralization, the standing armies, the bureaucratic organization, which on the Continent were absolutely necessary for national survival. And so, while in other countries culture concentrated itself in cities and in the courts of kings, in England it spread itself abroad over the open country. A new type of civilization grew up that was not urban or courtly, but essentially rural and based upon the life of the family.

It was this characteristic that was the source of the exceptional stability and strength of the English social organism which so impressed Continental observers in the eighteenth and nineteenth centuries. On the Continent ever since the time of the Roman Empire every people and every state was divided within itself by a duality of culture. On the one hand there were the traditions of the court and the city which, finally, after the Renaissance, fused with one another; on the other the peasant tradition, which to a greater or less extent preserved an older and more primitive culture and possessed its own art, its own costume, its own social customs, almost its own laws. We have an extreme instance of this in Russia during the last two centuries, where the contrast of the French-speaking official or courtier of Petersburg, living by the culture of modern Europe, and the patriarchal peasant, living in a half-Slavonic, half-Byzantine, wholly mediaeval world, was so intense as to be unbearable, and ultimately caused the dissolution of Russian society. But in England, at least since the close of the Middle Ages, there has been no such contrast. Our society and culture have been single and homogeneous. We have not had a special peasant art and costume because our whole culture has been a rural culture. That characteristic figure, the eighteenth-century squire, was not the member of a noble class as was even the smallest German baron or French count, he was a glorified yeoman. No doubt he, too, was sometimes an oppressor, but he was never a stranger, and when he was most high-handed, as in the enclosure of the commons, he was fighting the last stage of the peasant's long battle for the Plough against the Waste.

Like Tennyson's Lincolnshire Farmer, he thought that a few moral deficiencies would be overlooked in the man who "stubbed Thurnaby Waste."

Thus the English culture and the social discipline that went with it were not a civilization imposed from above but grew up from below out of the very soil of England. When all the great states of the Continent were shaken by revolution and disorder, England alone stood firm and preserved an unbroken continuity with her past. Her constitution was not a paper document, based on the most admirable abstract principles and entirely altered every few years, it was herself; she could not throw it aside any more than a man can discard his own personality.

One of the most original Catholic sociologists of the nineteenth century, Frederic Le Play, devoted a work to the study of English society. He had been impressed when first he visited England in 1836 by the stability of the social organism and by the weakness of the forces of irreligion and disorder which were then in the ascendant throughout Western Europe; and he found the source of England's greatness in the characteristics that we have just described. It was not simply the strength of family life and the home, but the way in which a whole culture and social order had been built up on these foundations. Elsewhere in those households that he studied so devotedly in the six volumes of his *Ouvriers Européens*, he had seen family life that was as strong or stronger, from a moral and economic point of view, but nowhere else was it the centre of the national culture and polity to the same extent as it was in England.

This development had its roots far back in the Middle Ages. Long before the Reformation English society had begun to acquire its characteristic rural aspect. The English village, with its pacific manor-house and its richly adorned parish church, was already far different from those of the war-harried castle-studded countrysides of France and Germany. But it was only in the centuries which followed the Renaissance that this English society began to bear fruit in an equally distinctive style and culture. How incomparably English are the typical Tudor and Jacobean manor and farmhouse, and how rich is their social content. They make us understand how it was possible for England to produce men like Herrick and Herbert and Henry Vaughan, poets who lived out of the world, far from the possibilities of the city and its culture, but whose art had a purity and freshness as far from that of the poets of the same period in Italy and France as an English meadow from a Neapolitan street.

And with the following century the contrast between English and Continental culture becomes even stronger. It is true that the hard brilliance and rationalism of the French eighteenth century had its parallel here in Pope and Bolingbroke, and later in Chesterfield and Gibbon, but the victory was not with them. More and more their spirit was felt to be alien, their spiritual home was at Paris and Lausanne. The heart of England was with the solid traditionalism of Dr. Johnson or the intense pietism of Cowper and the Wesleys. Moreover, the coming of the house of Hanover, so far from introducing continental influences, served rather to weaken the prestige of the court and to make the country more obstinately English than ever. Neither our society nor our art served the court and the capital, both alike centred in the family, in the country houses or in the homes of the merchants. And this is true of both the chief manifestations of English art during this period, the great portrait painters and the late Georgian school of architecture and decoration, of which the typical representatives are the brothers Adam.

In the latter the English tradition has reached maturity. It is no longer purely rural, it has begun to impress its image on the town and on urban life. The ordinary London house of this type, with the reserved severity of its exterior and the intimate refinement and grace of the interior, is a true type of the society that produced it. A society whose civilization was essentially private, bound up with the family and the home, and which brings with it even into the city and its suburbs something of the quiet and retirement of the countryside. It is the complete antithesis of the Latin social ideal, which is communal and public, which finds its artistic expression in the Baroque town square, with its fountains and statuary and monumental façades, a fitting background to the open-air life of a many-coloured voluble crowd.

So if one compares the London of a hundred years ago, when this English culture was still practically intact, with the great cities of the Continent with their ancient tradition of a splendid civic life, the comparison is at first all in their favor. In England there was a rustic individualism and a boorishness which sink at times to downright callousness and brutality, as in the penal code and the treatment of the poor.

But as soon as we leave public life and look behind the severe and sometimes dingy façade, what treasures does the interior life of that late Georgian London reveal! The harvest of Renaissance Florence was greater, may be, but there the resources of a brilliant court called together the talent of all Italy. In London it was a spontaneous flowering from the poorest and most unpromising soil. Blake, Keats, Charles Lamb, Thomas Girtin, and the Varleys, Turner and Dickens, were all of them poor men, for the most part completely without any of the advantages of birth or education. Yet each of them is unique, each of them is a voice of England, and some of their work possesses the same unearthly beauty and spirituality which marked English poetry in the seventeenth century.

But with the close of the Georgian period a profound change begins to pass over English society. England ceases to be an agrarian state, and the new industry, which had been developing for more than half a century, becomes the dominant element in the life of the nation. The centre of gravity shifts from the village and the country house to the industrial town, the mine and the factory.

This change was not a gradual modification of the older non-industrial civilization, it was an independent growth. For the new industry developed in just those districts of England that were most backward and furthest removed from the centres of the old culture. Great masses of population began to settle on the wild moorlands of north-western England and in the valleys of the Welsh hills, and new cities grew up, like mushrooms, without plan and forethought, without corporate responsibility of civil tradition. Thus two Englands stood over against one another without social contact. As long as the Georgian era lasted the old England still ruled, and the new nation of industrial workers lived a disenfranchised existence as a mere wealth-producing caste. Then came the ferment of the years after the Napoleonic War, the rise of Liberalism and the passing of the Reform Bill. Finally, with the repeal of the Corn Laws, the old rural England passed into the background, and a new financial industrial state took its place.

Thus the nineteenth century and the Victorian age can be looked on from two points of view: as the last phase of the old rural domestic culture—the culmination of the English tradition; or as the revolt against it—the growth of a new urban-industrial civilization with its centre in the group-work of the mine and the factory, bringing with it the disintegration of the family into a number of independent wage earners and the degeneration of the home into a workers' dormitory.

Yet, in spite of all, the English were faithful to their old ideal. The clerk and the workman clung to their rural tradition of a separate home, and the English industrial town to this day stands apart from its fellows on the Continent as a separate type by reason of its square miles of little brick boxes—each the home of a single family—in which it houses its workers. But a tree cannot continue to bear fruit, even of this stunted and unbeautiful kind, when the roots are gone. With the twentieth century we see the coming of a new urban civilization, which has no contact with the English tradition. The old ideals have grown discredited, and the Englighman no longer disdains to dwell in flats. And with the flat comes a corresponding new anti-domestic ethos; divorce, birth control, the turning to outer society for all vital needs.

England, in fact, has been going through the same social crisis as ancient Rome experienced at the end of the Republic.

Rome, too, had been founded on the life of the family and the rural community, and the loss of the agrarian foundations of Roman society caused a profound revolution in Roman culture and in the Roman polity. The national Roman tradition was only saved by an immense effort for social regeneration which was indeed but partially successful. And the parallel is all the more instructive, because in both cases the essential problem was the same—namely, how to reconcile the national tradition of an agrarian state with the imperial responsibilities of a world empire.

For in modern England, no less than in ancient Rome, the disintegration of the agrarian foundations of the old national culture was accompanied by the formation of a great imperial state. As Rome unified the Mediterranean world by her work of military conquest and organization, so England by her maritime and commercial expansion became the great organizer of the new cosmopolitan economic unity. Everywhere in the nineteenth century the English financiers, engineers, colonists, explorers, seamen and administrators were breaking down the geographical, social and economic barriers that separated continents and civilizations, and were binding the world together by an intricate structure of world trade and world finance on the summit of which the new English industrial society was poised. We have a classical example of this in the Lancashire cotton industry, depending as it did on the three-fold relation of American raw material, English industry and Oriental markets, bound together by English shipping and financial organization, and secured by English sea power and imperial adminstration. Nevertheless, this new economic imperialism was not the result of the unaided enterprise of the new industrial society. Its foundations had already been laid in the eighteenth century by the old agrarian state. The British Empire owes its creation not to the England of the mill-owners, but to the England of the squires, the England of Walpole and the Pitts, which also produced the merchants and the seamen who created the East India Company and the mercantile marine. The spirit of the new society is to be seen in the cosmopolitan Free Trade ideals of the Manchester school, which disavowed the old mercantile imperialism, even though it actually owed to it the possibility of its own existence. And, consequently, these ideals never dominated English policy. The prosperity of nineteenth-century England was due to a working compromise between the two societies and the two traditions which is represented by the Free Trade imperialism of Palmerston and Disraeli, a compromise which was essentially unstable since it concealed latent contradictions.

Today these contradictions have worked themselves out, and the instability of the nineteenth-century compromise is patent to all. It is no longer possible to reconcile Free Trade and imperialism or to combine the old national agrarian tradition with that of a completely industrialized society. The English achievement is threatened both within and without: within, by the almost complete dissolution of the rural life from which our national culture derived its inner vitality; and without, by the crumbling of the whole edifice of world trade and world finance on which the economic prosperity of English industrialism was based. Consequently, we seem faced by a dilemma between two alternatives, each of which promises to be equally disastrous. Either we can attempt to restore the agrarian foundations of our culture by a return to agricultural self-sufficiency, in which case we destroy the economic foundation of the urban industrialism by which the vast majority of our population lives; or we can sacrifice everything to maintaining the cosmopolitan mechanism of world industry and trade, which would mean the final destruction not only of our agriculture, but of our national tradition and our social vitality.

While the spread of industrialism and its growing perfection of technique are steadily increasing the volume of actual and potential production, the world market is being increasingly restricted by economic nationalism and the political control of trade. England is faced with the prospect of being the workshop of a world that does not need her services. At the very moment when the existence of the world market is being threatened, our whole population is becoming dependent on the world market for its very existence. English agriculture is at its last gasp, and any serious effort to revive it would be opposed by the united forces of capital and labour as involving either a rise in the costs of labour or a decline in the standard of living.

But if we cannot afford the economic cost of preserving our agricultural population, can we afford the social cost of destroying it? It is impossible to decide the question by purely economic considerations. A landlord might find it more profitable to clear his estate of its farming population and to let it to a game syndicate, but that does not mean that it would be in the national interest for him to do so. And in the same way our present abundant supplies of cheap food may be bought too dear, if they involve the sacrifice of the agrarian foundation of our national culture. The land of England is not just a food factory that can be dismantled at will, it is a part of ourselves, and if it becomes derelict, our whole social life is maimed. The first consideration for a society is not to maintain the volume of its industrial production or even "the standard of life" in the current sense of the expression, but the quality of its population, and that cannot be secured by the mere expenditure of money on the so-called "social services," but only by the preservation of the natural foundations of society: the family and the land.

It is, of course, obvious that we cannot disregard economic factors, and that a society which cannot pay its way cannot exist. Nevertheless, the system that produces the largest profits is not necessarily the most efficient in the long run, even from the economic point of view. A purely urban industrialism is at its best a wasteful system, for it destroys the natural mechanism of social life, and is forced to construct at immense cost an artificial mechanism to take its place. For example, under the old order the land-owning class was also the ruling class, and provided the permanent "cadres" from which the administrators and the servants of the state were recruited. But in an industrial state the wealthy class is a plutocracy that possesses no definite social function, and a separate governing class of paid bureaucrats has to be created and trained at the expense of the state. And thus the plutocracy of the industrialist order actually costs the country more than did the old ruling class, while it is decidedly inferior to the latter, from the non-economic point of view, as an organ of national culture.

Such considerations as these, however, have no influence on modern politics, which invariably sacrifice sociology to economics, and which even in economics prefer immediate profit to ultimate advantage. Socialism alone possesses any kind of a sociology, and it derives considerable advantage from the fact. But it is a naive and rudimentary sociology which shuts its eyes to the existence of any but economic values, and seeks national salvation in the complete subordination of the social organism to the economic machine. In fact, socialism and industrial capitalism both share the same economic fallacy and the same urbanist and mechanical ideals: both alike lead to the disintegration of the social organism and to the destruction of its agrarian foundation.

If England is to be saved, it is necessary to abandon the economic fatalism that has dominated our thought for a hundred years and to base our national policy on sound sociological principles. We must recognize that our national culture is our greatest asset, and the true foundations of society are to be found neither in commerce nor in financial and industrial mechanism, but in nature.

Instead of exploiting nature for financial profit and forcing society into the strait waistcoat of a mechanical order, we must adapt our economic mechanism to the needs of the social organism and the safeguarding of its vital functions. Science and technology can be used in the service of rural life as well as of urban industry, and the recovery of some measure of equilibrium between the agrarian and the urban elements in our national life would strengthen the whole structure of the social organism. It is true that we cannot transform England into a self-sufficient peasant state, but it is possible to restore the life of the English countryside if we seriously wished to do so. The obstacles to recovery are not merely economic, they are also in an even greater degree political and social. If in the England of the eighteenth century the towns were governed in the interests of the country, today the county is governed in the interests of the towns, and rural society is forced to adapt itself to the educational and social legislation that is a product of the utterly different social environment of urban industrialism. And at the same time the rural society is being deprived of social leadership. The old land-owning class filled so large a place in rural society that its disappearance leaves an immense gap in the social and cultural life of the countryside, and nothing is being done to fill it, owing to the concentration of all the vital forces of the nation in the great cities. Here again there is a pressing need for the restoration of social equilibrium by a measure of cultural decentralization and by a more even distribution of the non-economic resources of the nation between city and countryside. And all these changes are not merely desirable: they are absolutely necessary if England is to survive.

No civilization hitherto has been able to resist the destructive effect of urban and bureaucratic centralization. It has been well said that the great city is the grave of a culture, and in the same way the substitution of a centralized bureaucratic control for the spontaneous activity of normal social life involves a process of ossification and the senile decay of the whole social organism.

The only question is whether the process has already gone too far to be checked in this country. There is no *a priori* reason why a society should not recover its health and social stablity by reversing the drift towards centralization and deliberately strengthening its foundations in the life of the family and the country. But such a movement of social regeneration requires a vigorous moral effort and a consciousness of our responsibility. We cannot do anything so long as we are hypnotized by economic fatalism and so long as we cannot free ourselves from the decaying remains of nineteenth-century philosophy. It is necessary for us to revise our whole scheme of social values and to educate the nation in the ideas that have some relation to the realities of the modern situation. The work of social restoration must be preceded and accompanied by the reconstitution of our intellectual and spiritual traditions.

—1933.

4

Bolshevism and the Bourgeoisie

WHILE Bolshevism is in the concrete a Russian phenomenon, its theoretic basis and its absolute claims have given it a much wider significance than any purely national revolution could have. It reflects in the distorted and exaggerated medium of Russian society a crisis that is common to the whole of the modern world. As primitive peoples succumb more easily than white men to the diseases of civilization, so the spiritual maladies of European civilization become more deadly in a simpler social environment. The influence of revolutionary ideas, the loss of spiritual order, the substitution of private interests for public authority and of individual opinions for social beliefs are factors common to the modern world, but the Western peoples have been in some degree immunized by two centuries of experience and they have hitherto been able to preserve their social stability in spite of the prevalence of subversive ideas. In Russia, however, this was not the case. The Russian bourgeoisie possessed in an exaggerated form all the weaknesses of their Western counterparts. They were a source of weakness rather than of strength to the social order, which they undermined spiritually at the same time that they exploited it economically. They showed a platonic sympathy for every kind of subversive ideal, and even the Bolsheviks themselves received financial support from prominent industrialists, such as Sava Morosov. Above all, it is in Russia that we can study in its purest form the phenomenon of an intelligentsia—that is to say, an educated class—that is entirely detached from social responsibilities and provides a seed bed for the propagation of revolutionary ideas. It was not from the peasants or the industrial proletariat, but from the ranks of the lesser nobility and the bourgeois intelligentsia that the leaders of the revolutionary and terrorist movement arose from the time of Herzen and Bakunin to that of Lenin himself.

Hence it is not surprising that the same society that has seen the most extreme development of the subversive elements in bourgeois culture should also produce the most extreme type of reaction against that culture. The disintegration of bourgeois society has worked itself out to its logical conclusion and has given place to a movement in the reverse direction. The futility and emptiness of Russian bourgeois existence as described, for instance, by Chekhov, or still earlier in Goncharov's *Oblomov*, is such that any régime which offers a positive and objective end of life becomes attractive. Man cannot live in a spiritual void; he needs some fixed social standards and some absolute intellectual principles. Bolshevism at least replaces the spiritual anarchy of bourgeois society by a rigid order and substitutes for the doubt and scepticism of an irresponsible intelligentsia the certitude of an absolute authority embodied in social institutions. It is true that the Bolshevik philosophy is a poor thing at best. It is philosophy reduced to its very lowest terms, a philosophy with a minimum of spiritual and intellectual content. It impoverishes life instead of enriching it, and confines the mind in a narrow and arid circle of ideas. Nevertheless, it is enough of a philosophy to provide society with a theoretical basis, and therein lies the secret of its strength. The lesson of Bolshevism is that any philosophy is better than no philosophy, and that a régime which possesses a principle of authority, however misconceived it may be, will be stronger than a system that rests on the shifting basis of private interests and private opinions.

And this is the reason why Bolshevism with all its crudity constitutes a real menace to Western society. For although our civilization is stronger and more coherent than that of pre-war Russia, it suffers from the same internal weakness. It needs some principle of social and economic order and yet it has lost all vital relation to the spiritual traditions on which the old order of European culture was based.

It may be plausibly argued that the faults of the bourgeois are no greater than those of the leading classes in other ages, while his virtues are all his own. But the fact remains that the typical leaders of bourgeois society do not arouse the same respect as that which is felt for the corresponding figures in the old régime. We instinctively feel that there is something honourable about a king, a noble, or a knight, which the banker, the stockbroker or the democratic politician does not possess. A king may be a bad king, but our very condemnation of him is a tribute to the prestige of his office. Nobody speaks of a "bad bourgeois"; the Socialist may indeed call him a "bloody bourgeois," but that is a set formula that has nothing to do with his personal vices or virtues.

This distrust of the bourgeois is no modern phenomenon. It has its roots in a much older tradition than that of Socialism. It is equally typical of the mediaeval noble and peasant, the romantic Bohemian and the modern proletarian. The fact is that the bourgeoisie has always stood somewhat apart from the main structure of European society, save in Italy and the Low Countries. While the temporal power was in the hands of the kings and the nobles and the spiritual power was in the hands of the Church, the bourgeoisie, the Third Estate, occupied a position of privileged inferiority which allowed them to amass wealth and to develop considerable intellectual culture and freedom of thought without acquiring direct responsibility or power.[1] Consequently, when the French Revolution and the fall of the old régime made the bourgeoisie the ruling class in the West, it retained its inherited characteristics, its attitude of hostile criticism towards the traditional order and its enlightened selfishness in the pursuit of its own interests. But although the bourgeois now possessed the substance of power, he never really accepted social responsibility as the old rulers had done. He remained a private individual —an *idiot* in the Greek sense—with a strong sense of social conventions and personal rights, but with little sense of social

[1] The same conditions obtained in a highly accentuated form in the case of the Jews, who are, so to speak, bourgeois *par excellence,* and this explains how it is that the East European Jew can adapt himself so much more rapidly and successfully than his Christian neighbour to modern bourgeois civilization.

solidarity and no recognition of his responsibility as the servant and representative of a super-personal order. In fact, he did not realize the necessity of such an order, since it had always been provided for him by others, and he had taken it for granted.

This, I think, is the fundamental reason for the unpopularity and lack of prestige of bourgeois civilization. It lacks the vital human relationship which the older order with all its faults never denied. To the bourgeois politician the electorate is an accidental collection of voters; to the bourgeois industrialist his employees are an accidental collection of wage earners. The king and the priest, on the other hand, were united to their people by a bond of organic solidarity. They were not individuals standing over against other individuals, but parts of a common social organism and representatives of a common spiritual order.

The bourgeoisie upset the throne and the altar, but they put in their place nothing but themselves. Hence their régime cannot appeal to any higher sanction than that of self-interest. It is continually in a state of disintegration and flux. It is not a permanent form of social organization, but a transitional phase between two orders.

This does not, of course, mean that Western society is inevitably doomed to go the way of Russia, or that it can find salvation in the Bolshevik ideal of class dictatorship and economic mass civilization. The Bolshevik philosophy is simply the *reductio ad absurdum* of the principles implicit in bourgeois culture and consequently it provides no real answer to the weaknesses and deficiencies of the latter. It takes the nadir of European spiritual development for the zenith of a new order.

The bourgeois culture, in spite of its temporary importance, is nothing but an episode in European history. This is why the current Socialist opposition of communist and bourgeois society is in reality a false dilemma. Western civilization is not merely the civilization of the bourgeois; it is the old civilization of Western Christendom that is undergoing a temporary phase of disorganization and change. It owes its strength not to its bourgeois politics and economics, but to the older and more permanent elements of its social and spiritual tradition. In no country, save perhaps in the United States, does the bourgeois culture exist in the pure state as a self-subsistent whole. England, above all, which seems at first sight to be the most thoroughly bourgeois society of all, has in reality never possessed a bourgeoisie in the true sense. Its ruling class down to modern times was agrarian in character and incorporated considerable elements of the older aristocratic tradition. Ever since Tudor times it was the aim of the successful merchant to "found a family" and leave the city for the country, and even the city man remained to a great extent a countryman at heart, as we see as late as the Victorian period in Surtees Jorrocks. The English Nonconformists did indeed possess a tradition of cultural separatism analogous to that of the Continental bourgeoisie; but even they were not pure bourgeois, since their basis of social unity was a religious and not an economic one.

In the same way the government in England has never been completely transformed by the bourgeois revolution, but still preserves the monarchical principle as the centre of national solidarity and order.

And the same state of things exists in varying degrees in every Western state. Even France, which politically is an almost pure type of bourgeois culture, is sociologically far from simple and owes its strength to the delicate equilibrium that it has established between two different social types— the peasant and the bourgeois—and two opposite spiritual traditions—that of the Catholic Church and that of the Liberal Enlightenment.

Consequently, it is impossible to solve the problem of Western society by disregarding the social and spiritual complexity of European civilization. Bourgeois civilization is not the only European tradition, and Rousseau and Marx are not the only European thinkers. The new order must be conceived not in terms of bourgeois exploiter and exploited proletarian, but as a unity that incorporates every element in European culture and that does justice to the spiritual and social as well as to the economic needs of human nature. In Russia such a solution was impossible owing to the profound gulf that divided the bourgeoisie and the intelligentsia with their imported Western culture from the governmental tradition of Byzantine autocracy and Orthodoxy and from the peasant culture of a semi-barbaric peasantry. But Western civilization is still fundamentally homogeneous. Our intelligentsia has not entirely lost its roots in a common spiritual order, and our bourgeoisie is not entirely divorced from social responsibility. It is still not too late to restore the integrity of European culture on the basis of a comprehensive and catholic order. We must go back to an older and more fundamental social tradition and to a wider and more perennial philosophy, which recognize the depth and complexity of human nature and the existence of a moral order that must govern political and economic relations no less than private behaviour. As Dr. Gurian has observed, Bolshevism itself is an unintentional and therefore most impressive witness to the existence of such an order, since its attempt to treat society as a closed and self-sufficient order has led not to Utopia but to tyranny. Man is first mutilated by being deprived of some of his most essential activities, and this maimed and crippled human nature is made the standard by which civilization and life itself are judged.[2]

—1932.

[2] Waldemar Gurian, *Bolshevism: Theory and Practice* (Sheed & Ward); cf. pp. 237–42.

PART II CONCEPTIONS OF WORLD HISTORY

SECTION I: CHRISTIANITY AND THE MEANING OF HISTORY

1

The Christian View of History

THE problem of the relations of Christianity to History has been very much complicated and, I think, obscured by the influence of nineteenth-century philosophy. Almost all the great idealist philosophers of that century, like Fichte and Schelling and Hegel, constructed elaborate philosophies of history which had a very considerable influence on the historians, expecially in Germany, and on the theologians also. All these systems were inspired or coloured by Christian ideas and they were consequently eagerly accepted by Christian theologians for apologetic purposes. And thus there arose an alliance between idealist philosophy and German theology which became characteristic of the Liberal Protestant movement and dominated religious thought both on the Continent and in this country during the later nineteenth century.

Today the situation is entirely changed. Both philosophic idealism and liberal Protestantism have been widely discredited and have been replaced by logical positivism and by the dialectic theology of the Barthians. The result is that the idea of a Christian philosophy of history has also suffered from the reaction against philosophic idealism. It is difficult to distinguish the authentic and original element in the Christian view of history from the philosophic accretions and interpretations of the last century and a half, so that you will find modern representatives of orthodox Christianity like Mr. C. S. Lewis questioning the possibility of a Christian interpretation of history, and declaring that the supposed connection between Christianity and Historicism is largely an illusion.[1]

If we approach the subject from a purely philosophical point of view there is a good deal to justify Mr. Lewis's scepticism. For the classical tradition of Christian philosophy as represented by Thomism has devoted comparatively little attention to the problem of history, while the philosophers who set the highest value on history and insist most strongly on the close relation between Christianity and history, such as Collingwood and Croce and Hegel, are not themselves Christian and may perhaps have tended to interpret Christianity in terms of their own philosophy.

Let us therefore postpone any philosophical discussion and consider the matter on the basis of the original theological data of historic Christianity without any attempt to justify or criticize them on philosophical grounds. There is no great difficulty in doing this, since the classical tradition of Christian philosophy as represented by Thomism has never devoted much attention to the problem of history. Its tradition has been Hellenic and Aristotelian, whereas the Christian interpretation of history is derived from a different source. It is Jewish rather than Greek, and finds its fullest expression in the primary documents of the Christian faith—the writings of the Hebrew prophets and in the New Testament itself.

Thus the Christian view of history is not a secondary element derived by philosophical reflection from the study of history. It lies at the very heart of Christianity and forms an integral part of the Christian faith. Hence there is no Christian "philosophy of history" in the strict sense of the word. There is, instead, a Christian history and a Christian theology of history, and it is not too much to say that without them there would be no such thing as Christianity. For Christianity, together with the religion of Israel out of which it was born, is an historical religion in a sense to which none of the other world religions can lay claim—not even Islam, though this comes nearest to it in this respect.

Hence it is very difficult, perhaps even impossible, to explain the Christian view of history to a non-Christian, since it is necessary to accept the Christian faith in order to under-

[1] In his article on "Historicism" in *The Month*, October, 1950.

stand the Christian view of history, and those who reject the idea of a divine revelation are necessarily obliged to reject the Christian view of history as well. And even those who are prepared to accept in theory the principle of divine revelation—of the manifestation of a religious truth which surpasses human reason—may still find it hard to face the enormous paradoxes of Christianity.

That God should have chosen an obscure Palestinian tribe—not a particularly civilized or attractive tribe either—to be the vehicle of his universal purpose for humanity, is difficult to believe. But that this purpose should have been finally realized in the person of a Galilean peasant executed under Tiberius, and that this event was the turning point in the life of mankind and the key to the meaning of history—all this is so hard for the human mind to accept that even the Jews themselves were scandalized, while to the Greek philosophers and the secular historians it seemed sheer folly.

Nevertheless, these are the foundations of the Christian view of history, and if we cannot accept them it is useless to elaborate idealistic theories and call them a Christian philosophy of history, as has often been done in the past.

For the Christian view of history is not merely a belief in the direction of history by divine providence, it is a belief in the intervention by God in the life of mankind by direct action at certain definite points in time and place. The doctrine of the Incarnation which is the central doctrine of the Christian faith is also the centre of history, and thus it is natural and appropriate that our traditional Christian history is framed in a chronological system which takes the year of the Incarnation as its point of reference and reckons its annals backwards and forwards from this fixed centre.

No doubt it may be said that the idea of divine incarnation is not peculiar to Christianity. But if we look at the typical examples of these non-Christian theories of divine incarnation, such as the orthodox Hindu expression of it in the Bhagavad-Gita, we shall see that it has no such significance for history as the Christian doctrine possesses. It is not only that the divine figure of Khrishna is mythical and unhistorical, it is that no divine incarnation is regarded as unique but as an example of a recurrent process which repeats itself again and again *ad infinitum* in the eternal recurrence of the cosmic cycle.

It was against such ideas as represented by the Gnostic

theosophy that St. Irenaeus asserted the uniqueness of the Christian revelation and the necessary relation between the divine unity and the unity of history—"that there is one Father the creator of Man and one Son who fulfils the Father's will and one human race in which the mysteries of God are worked out so that the creature conformed and incorporated with his son is brought to perfection."

For the Christian doctrine of the Incarnation is not simply a theophany—a revelation of God to Man; it is a new creation—the introduction of a new spiritual principle which gradually leavens and transforms human nature into something new. The history of the human race hinges on this unique divine event which gives spiritual unity to the whole historic process. First there is the history of the Old Dispensation which is the story of the providential preparation of mankind for the Incarnation when "the fulness of time," to use St. Paul's expression, had come. Secondly there is the New Dispensation which is the working out of the Incarnation in the life of the Christian Church. And finally there is the realization of the divine purpose in the future: in the final establishment of the Kingdom of God when the harvest of this world is reaped. Thus the Christian conception of history is essentially unitary. It has a beginning, a centre, and an end. This beginning, this centre, and this end transcend history; they are not historical events in the ordinary sense of the word, but acts of divine creation to which the whole process of history is subordinate. For the Christian view of history is a vision of history *sub specie æternitatis,* an interpretation of time in terms of eternity and of human events in the light of divine revelation. And thus Christian history is inevitably apocalyptic, and the apocalypse is the Christian substitute for the secular philosophies of history.

But this involves a revolutionary reversal and transposition of historical values and judgments. For the real meaning of history is not the apparent meaning that historians have studied and philosophers have attempted to explain. The world-transforming events which changed the whole course of human history have occurred as it were under the surface of history unnoticed by the historians and the philosophers. This is the great paradox of the gospel, as St. Paul asserts with such tremendous force. The great mystery of the divine purpose which has been hidden throughout the ages has now been manifested in the sight of heaven and earth by the apostolic ministry. Yet the world has not been able to accept it, because it has been announced by unknown insignificant men in a form which was inacceptable and incomprehensible to the higher culture of the age, alike Jewish and Hellenistic. The Greeks demand philosophical theories, the Jews demand historical proof. But the answer of Christianity is Christ crucified—*verbum crucis*—the story of the Cross: a scandal to the Jews and an absurdity to the Greeks. It is only when this tremendous paradox with its reversal of all hitherto accepted standards of judgment has been accepted that the meaning of human life and human history can be understood. For St. Paul does not of course mean to deny the value of understanding or to affirm that history is without a meaning. What he asserts is the mysterious and transcendent character of the true knowledge—"the hidden wisdom which God ordained before the world to our glory which none of the rulers of this world know." [2] And in the same way he fully accepted the Jewish doctrine of sacred history which would justify the ways of God to man. What he denied was an external justification by the manifest triumph of the Jewish national hope. The ways of God were deeper and more mysterious than that, so that the fulfilment of prophecy towards which the whole history of Israel had tended had been concealed from Israel by the scandal of the Cross. Nevertheless the Christian interpretation of history as we see it in the New Testament and the writings of the Fathers follows the pattern which had already been laid down in the Old Testament and in Jewish tradition.

There is, in the first place, a sacred history in the strict sense, that is to say, the story of God's dealings with his people and the fulfilment of his eternal purpose in and through them. And, in the second place, there is the interpretation of external history in the light of this central purpose. This took the form of a theory of successive world ages and successive world empires, each of which had a part to play in the divine drama. The theory of the world ages, which became incorporated in the Jewish apocalyptic tradition and was ultimately taken over by Christian apocalyptic, was not however Jewish in origin. It was widely diffused throughout the ancient world in Hellenistic times and probably goes back in origin to the tradition of Babylonian cosmology and astral theology. The

[2] Col. ii; cf. Eph. iii.

theory of the world empires, on the other hand, is distinctively Biblical in spirit and belongs to the central message of Hebrew prophecy. For the Divine Judgment which it was the mission of the prophets to declare was not confined to the chosen people. The rulers of the Gentiles were also the instruments of divine judgment, even though they did not understand the purposes that they served. Each of the world empires in turn had its divinely appointed task to perform, and when the task was finished their power came to an end and they gave place to their successors.

Thus the meaning of history was not to be found in the history of the world empires themselves. They were not ends but means, and the inner significance of history was to be found in the apparently insignificant development of the people of God. Now this prophetic view of history was taken over by the Christian Church and applied on a wider and universal scale. The divine event which had changed the course of history had also broken down the barrier between Jews and the Gentiles, and the two separated parts of humanity had been made one in Christ, the corner-stone of the new world edifice. The Christian attitude to secular history was indeed the same as that of the prophets; and the Roman Empire was regarded as the successor of the old world empires, like Babylon and Persia. But now it was seen that the Gentile world as well as the chosen people were being providentially guided towards a common spiritual end. And this end was no longer conceived as the restoration of Israel and the gathering of all the exiles from among the Gentiles. It was the gathering together of all the spiritually living elements throughout mankind into a new spiritual society. The Roman prophet Hermas in the second century describes the process in the vision of the white tower that was being built among the waters, by tens of thousands of men who were bringing stones dragged from the deep sea or collected from the twelve mountains which symbolize the different nations of the world. Some of these stones were rejected and some were chosen to be used for the building. And when he asks "concerning the times and whether the end is yet," he is answered: "Do you not see that the tower is still in process of building? When the building has been finished, the end comes."

This vision shows how Christianity transfers the meaning of history from the outer world of historic events to the inner world of spiritual change, and how the latter was conceived as the dynamic element in history and as a real world-transforming power. But it also shows how the primitive Christian sense of an imminent end led to a foreshortening of the time scale and distracted men's attention from the problem of the future destinies of human civilization. It was not until the time of the conversion of the Empire and the peace of the Church that Christians were able to make a distinction between the end of the age and the end of the world, and to envisage the prospect of a Christian age and civilization which was no millennial kingdom but a field of continual effort and conflict.

This view of history found its classical expression in St. Augustine's work on *The City of God* which interprets the course of universal history as an unceasing conflict between two dynamic principles embodied in two societies and social orders—the City of Man and the City of God, Babylon and Jerusalem, which run their course side by side, intermingling with one another and sharing the same temporal goods and the same temporal evils, but separated from one another by an infinite spiritual gulf. Thus St. Augustine sees history as the meeting point of time and eternity. History is a unity because the same divine power which shows itself in the order of nature from the stars down to the feathers of the bird and the leaves of the tree also governs the rise and fall of kingdoms and empires. But this divine order is continually being deflected by the downward gravitation of human nature to its own selfish ends—a force which attempts to build its own world in those political structures that are the organized expression of human ambition and lust for power. This does not, however, mean that St. Augustine identifies the state as such with the *civitas terrena* and condemns it as essentially evil. On the contrary, he shows that its true end—the maintaining of temporal peace—is a good which is in agreement with the higher good of the City of God, so that the state in its true nature is not so much the expression of self-will and the lust for power as a necessary barrier which defends human society from being destroyed by these forces of destruction. It is only when war and not peace is made the end of the state that it becomes identified with the *civitas terrena* in the bad sense of the word. But we see only too well that the predatory state that lives by war and conquest is an historical reality, and St. Augustine's judgment on secular history is a predominantly pessimistic one which sees the kingdoms of this world as founded in injustice and extending themselves by war and oppression. The ideal of temporal peace which is inherent in the idea of the state is never strong enough to overcome the dynamic force of human self-will, and therefore the whole course of history *apart from divine grace* is the record of successive attempts to build towers of Babel which are frustrated by the inherent selfishness and greed of human nature.

The exception, however, is all-important. For the blind forces of instinct and human passion are not the only powers that rule the world. God has not abandoned his creation. He communicates to man, by the grace of Christ and the action of the Spirit, the spiritual power of divine love which alone is capable of transforming human nature. As the natural force of self-love draws down the world to multiplicity and disorder and death, the supernatural power of the love of God draws it back to unity and order and life. And it is here that the true unity and significance of history is to be found. For love, in St. Augustine's theory, is the principle of society, and as the centrifugal and destructive power of self-love creates the divided society of the *civitas terrena,* so the unitive and creative power of divine love creates the City of God, the society that unites all men of good will in an eternal fellowship which is progressively realized in the course of the ages.

Thus St. Augustine, more perhaps than any other Christian thinker, emphasizes the social character of the Christian doctrine of salvation. For "whence," he writes, "should the City of God originally begin or progressively develop or ultimately attain its end unless the life of the saints were a social one?" [3] But at the same time he makes the individual soul and not the state or the civilization the real centre of the historic process. Wherever the power of divine love moves the human will there the City of God is being built. Even the Church which is the visible sacramental organ of the City of God is not identical with it, since, as he writes, in God's foreknowledge there are many who seem to be outside who are within and many who seem to be within who are outside.[4] So there are those outside the communion of the Church "whom the Father, who sees in secret, crowns in

[3] *De Civ. Dei,* xix, V.

[4] *De bapt.,* V, 38.

secret." [5] For the two Cities interpenetrate one another in such a way and to such a degree that "the earthly kingdom exacts service from the kingdom of heaven and the kingdom of heaven exacts service from the earthly city." [6]

It is impossible to exaggerate the influence of St. Augustine's thought on the development of the Christian view of history and on the whole tradition of Western historiography, which follows quite a different course from that of Eastern and Byzantine historiography. It is true that the modern reader who expects to find in St. Augustine a philosophy of history in the modern sense, and who naturally turns to the historical portions of his great work, expecially Books XV to XVIII, is apt to be grievously disappointed, like the late Professor Hearnshaw who wrote that the *De Civitate Dei* contains neither philosophy nor history but merely theology and fiction. But though St. Augustine was never a Christian historian such as Eusebius, his work had a far more revolutionary effect on Western thought. In the first place, he impressed upon Christian historians his conception of history as a dynamic process in which the divine purpose is realized. Secondly, he made men realize the way in which the individual personality is the source and centre of this dynamic process. And finally, he made the Western Church conscious of its historical mission and its social and political responsibilities so that it became during the following centuries the active principle of Western culture.

The results of St. Augustine's work find full expression three centuries later in the Anglo-Saxon Church. Unlike St. Augustine, St. Bede was a true historian, but his history is built on the foundations that St. Augustine had laid, and thus we get the first history of a Christian people in the full sense of the word—a history which is not primarily concerned with the rise and fall of kingdoms—though these are not omitted; but with the rise of Christ's kingdom in England, the *gesta Dei per Anglos*. Of course Bede's great work can hardly be regarded as typical of mediaevel historiography. It was an exceptional, almost a unique, achievement. But at any rate his historical approach is typical, and, together with his other chronological works, it provided the pattern which was followed by the later historians of the

[5] *De Vera Religione*, vi, II.

[6] *In Psalmos*, li, 4.

Christian Middle Ages. It consists in the first place of a world chronicle of the Eusebian type which provided the chronological background on which the historian worked. Secondly there were the histories of particular peoples and Churches of which St. Bede's *Ecclesiastical History* is the classical example, and which is represented in later times by works like Adam of Bremen's *History of the Church of Hamburg* or Ordericus Vitalis's *Ecclesiastical History*. And thirdly there are the biographies of saints and bishops and abbots, like Bede's life of St. Cuthbert and the lives of the abbots of Wearmouth.

In this way the recording of contemporary events in the typical mediaeval chronicle is linked up on the one hand with the tradition of world history and on the other with the lives of the great men who were the leaders and heroes of Christian society. But the saint is not merely an historical figure; he has become a citizen of the eternal city, a celestial patron and a protector of man's earthly life. So that in the lives of the saints we see history transcending itself and becoming part of the eternal world of faith.

Thus in mediaeval thought, time and eternity are far more closely bound up with one another than they were in classical antiquity or to the modern mind. The world of history was only a fraction of the real world and it was surrounded on every side by the eternal world like an island in the ocean. This mediaeval vision of a hierarchical universe in which the world of man occupies a small but central place finds classical expression in Dante's *Divina Commedia*. For this shows better than any purely historical or theological work how the world of history was conceived as passing into eternity and bearing eternal fruit.

And if on the one hand this seems to reduce the importance of history and of the present life, on the other hand it enhances their value by giving them an eternal significance. In fact there are few great poets who have been more concerned with history and even with politics than Dante was. What is happening in Florence and in Italy is a matter of profound concern, not only to the souls in Purgatory, but even to the damned in Hell and to the saints in Paradise, and the divine pageant in the Earthly Paradise which is the centre of the whole process is an apocalyptic vision of the judgment and the reformation of the Church and the Empire in the fourteenth century.

Dante's great poem seems to sum up the whole achievement of the Catholic Middle Ages and to represent a perfect literary counterpart to the philosophical synthesis of St. Thomas. But if we turn to his prose works—the *Convivio* and the *De Monarchia*—we see that his views on culture, and consequently on history, differ widely from those of St. Thomas and even more from those of St. Augustine. Here for the first time in Christian thought we find the earthly and temporal city regarded as an autonomous order with its own supreme end, which is not the service of the Church but the realization of all the natural potentialities of human culture. The goal of civilization—*finis universalis civitatis humani generis*—can only be reached by a universal society and this requires the political unification of humanity in a single world state. Now it is clear that Dante's ideal of the universal state is derived from the mediaeval conception of Christendom as a universal society and from the tradition of the Holy Roman Empire as formulated by Ghibelline lawyers and theorists. As Professor Gilson writes, "if the *genus humanum* of Dante is really the first known expression of the modern idea of Humanity, we may say that the conception of Humanity first presented itself to the European consciousness merely as a secularized imitation of the religious notion of a Church." [7]

But Dante's sources were not exclusively Christian. He was influenced most powerfully by the political and ethical ideals of Greek humanism, represented above all by Aristotle's *Ethics* and no less by the romantic idealization of the classical past and his devotion to ancient Rome. For Dante's view of the Empire is entirely opposed to that of St. Augustine. He regards it not as the work of human pride and ambition but as a holy city specially created and ordained by God as the instrument of his divine purpose for the human race. He even goes so far as to maintain in the *Convivio* that the citizens and statesmen of Rome were themselves holy, since they could not have achieved their purpose without a special infusion of divine grace.

In all this Dante looks forward to the Renaissance rather than back to the Middle Ages. But he carries with him so much of the Christian tradition that even his secularism and his humanism have a distinctively Christian character which make them utterly different from those of classical antiquity.

[7] E. Gilson, *Dante the Philosopher,* p. 179.

And this may also be said of most of the writers and thinkers of the following century, for, as Karl Burdach has shown with so much learning, the whole atmosphere of later mediaeval and early Renaissance culture was infused by a Christian idealism which had its roots in the thirteenth century and especially in the Franciscan movement. Thus the fourteenth century which saw the beginnings of the Italian Renaissance and the development of Western humanism was also the great century of Western mysticism; and this intensification of the interior life with its emphasis on spiritual experience was not altogether unrelated to the growing self-consciousness of Western culture which found expression in the humanist movement. Even in the fifteenth and sixteenth centuries the humanist culture was not entirely divorced from this mystical tradition; both elements co-exist in the philosophy of Nicholas of Cusa, in the culture of the Platonic Academy at Florence and in the art of Botticelli and finally in that of Michelangelo. But in his case we feel that this synthesis was only maintained by an heroic effort, and lesser men were forced to acquiesce in a division of life between two spiritual ideals that became increasingly divergent.

This idealization of classical antiquity which is already present in the thought of Dante developed still further with Petrarch and his contemporaries until it became the characteristic feature of Renaissance culture. It affected every aspect of Western thought, literary, scientific and philosophic. Above all, it changed the Western view of history and inaugurated a new type of historiography. The religious approach to history as the story of God's dealings with mankind and the fulfilment of the divine plan in the life of the Church was abandoned or left to the ecclesiastical historians, and there arose a new secular history modelled on Livy and Tacitus and a new type of historical biography influenced by Plutarch.

Thus the unity of the mediaeval conception of history was lost and in its place there gradually developed a new pattern of history which eventually took the form of a threefold division between the ancient, mediaeval and modern periods, a pattern which in spite of its arbitrary and unscientific character has dominated the teaching of history down to modern times and still affects our attitude to the past.

This new approach to history was one of the main factors in the secularization of European culture, since the idealization of the ancient state and especially of republican Rome influenced men's attitude to the contemporary state. The Italian city-state and the kingdoms of the West of Europe were no longer regarded as organic members of the Christian community, but as ends in themselves which acknowledged no higher sanction than the will to power. During the Middle Ages the state as an autonomous self-sufficient power structure did not exist—even its name was unknown. But from the fifteenth century onwards the history of Europe has been increasingly the history of the development of a limited number of sovereign states as independent power centres and of the ceaseless rivalry and conflict between them. The true nature of this development was disguised by the religious prestige which still surrounded the person of the ruler and which was actually increased during the age of the Reformation by the union of the Church with the state and its subordination to the royal supremacy.

Thus there is an inherent contradiction in the social development of modern culture. Inasmuch as the state was the creation and embodiment of the will to power, it was a Leviathan—a sub-moral monster which lived by the law of the jungle. But at the same time it was the bearer of the cultural values which had been created by the Christian past, so that to its subjects it still seemed a Christian state and the vice-gerent of God on earth.

And the same contradiction appears in the European view of history. The realists like Machiavelli and Hobbes attempted to interpret history in non-moral terms as a straightforward expression of the will to power which could be studied in a scientific (quasi-biological) spirit. But by so doing they emptied the historical process of the moral values that still retained their subjective validity so that they outraged both the conscience and the conventions of their contemporaries. The idealists, on the other hand, ignored or minimized the sub-moral character of the state and idealized it as the instrument of divine providence or of that impersonal force which was gradually leading mankind onwards towards perfection.

It is easy to see how this belief in progress found acceptance during the period of triumphant national and cultural expansion when Western Europe was acquiring a kind of world hegemony. But it is no less clear that it was not a purely rational construction, but that it was essentially nothing else but a secularized version of the traditional Christian view. It inherited from Christianity its belief in the unity of history and its faith in a spiritual or moral purpose which gives meaning to the whole historical process. At the same time its transposition of these conceptions to a purely rational and secular theory of culture involved their drastic simplification. To the Christian the meaning of history was a mystery which was only revealed in the light of faith. But the apostles of the religion of progress denied the need for divine revelation and believed that man had only to follow the light of reason to discover the meaning of history in the law of progress which governs the life of civilization. But it was difficult even in the eighteenth century to make this facile optimism square with the facts of history. It was necessary to explain that hitherto the light of reason had been concealed by the dark forces of superstition and ignorance as embodied in organized religion. But in that case the enlightenment was nothing less than a new revelation, and in order that it might triumph it was necessary that the new believers should organize themselves in a new church whether it called itself a school of philosophers or a secret society of *illuminati* or freemasons or a political party. This was, in fact, what actually happened, and the new rationalist churches have proved no less intolerant and dogmatic than the religious sects of the past. The revelation of Rousseau was followed by a series of successive revelations—idealist, positivist and socialistic, with their prophets and their churches. Of these today only the Marxist revelation survives, thanks mainly to the superior efficiency of its ecclesiastical organization and apostolate. None of these secular religions has been more insistent on its purely scientific and non-religious character than Marxism. Yet none of them owes more to the Messianic elements in the Christian and Jewish historical traditions. Its doctrine is in fact essentially apocalyptic—a denunciation of judgment against the existing social order and a message of salvation to the poor and the oppressed who will at last receive their reward after the social revolution in the classless society, which is the Marxist equivalent of the millennial kingdom of righteousness.

No doubt the Communist will regard this as a caricature of the Marxist theory, since the social revolution and the coming of the classless society is the result of an inevitable economic and sociological process and its goal is not a spiritual but a material one. Nevertheless the cruder forms of Jewish and Christian millenniarism were not without a materialistic element since they envisaged an earthly kingdom in which the saints would enjoy temporal prosperity, while it is impossible to ignore the existence of a strong apocalyptic and Utopian element in the Communist attitude towards the social revolution and the establishment of a perfect society which will abolish class conflict and social injustice.

There is in fact a dualism between the Marxist myth, which is ethical and apocalyptic, and the Marxist interpretation of history, which is materialist, determinist and ethically relativistic. But it is from the first of these two elements that Communism has derived and still derives its popular appeal and its quasi-religious character which render it such a serious rival to Christianity. Yet it is difficult to reconcile the absolutism of the Marxist myth with the relativism of the Marxist interpretation of history. The Marxist believer stakes everything on the immediate realization of the social revolution and the proximate advent of the classless society. But when these have been realized, the class war which is the dialectical principle of historical change will have been suppressed and history itself comes to an end. In the same way there will no longer be any room for the moral indignation and the revolutionary idealism which have inspired Communism with a kind of religious enthusiasm. Nothing is left but an absolute and abject attitude of social conformism when the revolutionary protest of the minority becomes transformed into the irresistible tyranny of mass opinion which will not tolerate the smallest deviation from ideological orthodoxy. By the dialectic of history the movement of social revolution passes over into its totalitarian opposite, and the law of negation finds its consummation.

Thus, in comparison with the Christian view of history, the Marxist view is essentially a short-term one, the significance of which is concentrated on the economic changes which are affecting modern Western society. This accounts for its immediate effectiveness in the field of political propaganda, but at the same time it detracts from its value on the philosophical level as a theory of universal history. The Marxist doctrine first appeared about a century ago, and could not have arisen at any earlier time. Its field of prediction is limited to the immediate future, for Marx himself seems to have expected the downfall of capitalism to take place in his own lifetime, and the leaders of the Russian revolution took a similar view. In any case the fulfilment of the whole Marxist programme is a matter of years, not of centuries, and Marxism seems to throw no light on the historical developments which will follow the establishment of the classless society.

The Christian view, on the other hand, is co-extensive with time. It covers the whole life of humanity on this planet and it ends only with the end of this world and of man's temporal existence. It is essentially a theory of the interpenetration of time and eternity: so that the essential meaning of history is to be found in the growth of the seed of eternity in the womb of time. For man is not merely a creature of the economic process—a producer and a consumer. He is an animal that is conscious of his mortality and consequently aware of eternity. In the same way the end of history is not the development of a new form of economic society, but is the creation of a new humanity, or rather a higher humanity, which goes as far beyond man as man himself goes beyond the animals. Now Christians not only believe in the existence of a divine plan in history, they believe in the existence of a human society which is in some measure aware of this plan and capable of co-operating with it. Thousands of years ago the Hebrew prophet warned his people not to learn the ways of the nations who were dismayed at the signs of the times. For the nations were the servants of their own creatures—the false gods who were the work of delusion and who must perish in the time of visitation. "But the portion of Jacob is not like these, for he that formed all things has made Israel to be the people of his inheritance." The same thing is true today of the political myths and ideologies which modern man creates in order to explain the signs of the time. These are our modern idols which are no less bloodthirsty than the gods of the heathen and which demand an even greater tribute of human sacrifice. But the Church remains the guardian of the secret of history and the organ of the work of human redemption which goes on ceaselessly through the rise and fall of kingdoms and the revolutions of social systems. It is true that the Church has no immediate solution to offer in competition with those of the secular ideologies. On the other hand, the Christian solution is the only one which gives full weight to the unknown and unpredictable element in history; whereas the secular ideologies which attempt to eliminate this element, and which almost invariably take an optimistic view of the immediate future are inevitably disconcerted and disillusioned by the emergence of this unknown factor at the point at which they thought that it had been finally banished.

—1951.

2

History and the Christian Revelation

THE Christian interpretation of history is inseparable from the Christian faith. It is not a philosophic theory which has been elaborated by the intellectual effort of Christian scholars. It is an integral part of the Christian revelation; indeed that revelation is essentially an historic one, so that the most metaphysical of its dogmas are based upon historic facts and form part of that great dispensation of grace in which the whole temporal process of the life of humanity finds its end and meaning. In this respect Catholicism and Communism agree, in spite of the absolute contradiction that characterizes their several interpretations of history. For Communism is also an historic faith and the materialist interpretation of history is no less fundamental to Communism than is the spiritual interpretation of history to Christianity. The economic doctrines of Marxism are based on history to an almost greater extent than the theological doctrines of Catholicism; and a Socialism which professes Communism and Materialism without the historic doctrine of Marx has no more right to be called Marxism than a religion which accepts the ethical and theological teachings of Christianity while rejecting the historic elements of the faith has the right to the name of Catholicism.

In spite of this parallelism, however, no real comparison is possible between a theory deliberately constructed by an individual thinker as part of his economic system and a doctrine which is older than history itself and which has developed organically with the greatest religious tradition of the world.

For if we wish to find the roots of the Catholic interpretation of history, we must go back behind the Fathers, behind the New Testament, behind even the Hebrew prophets to the very foundation of the religion of Israel. It has its root in the solemn *berith* or covenant by which at a particular point in time and space Israel became a *theophoric* nation, the People of Jahweh. To the rationalistic critic this strange ceremony which took place in the Arabian desert some 3,400 years ago cannot seem anything more than a somewhat abnormal instance of the primitive conception of the solidarity between the tribal god and his worshippers. To the Christian, however, it is nothing less than the first act in that marriage of God with humanity which was to be consummated in the Incarnation and to bear fruit in the creation of a new humanity. Even the critics, however, admit the unique character of the relations between Israel and its God. In the case of the other Semitic peoples this relation is a natural one and consists in the kinship of the people with its god. Only in the case of Israel is the relation an adoptive one that had its origin in a particular series of historical events.

And as the convenant of Jahweh had an historic origin, it also found an historic fulfilment. Only in so far as Israel fulfilled its theophoric mission could it enjoy its theophoric privileges. The misfortunes of Israel were the judgments of Jahweh and every historic crisis was a call for Israel to return to the laws of Jahweh and thus to renew the validity of the covenant. And in the writings of the prophets we see how the successive crises of Jewish history were the occasion of fresh revelations of the divine vocation of Israel and of the divine purpose in history. The vision of the prophets was no longer limited to the Kingdoms of Judah and Israel; it extended to the surrounding nations and the world empires that were eating them up. Even the kingdoms that were the enemies of the people of Jahweh were the instruments of Jahweh and had their part to play in working out his purpose. Assyria was the rod of his anger, which would be broken and cast aside when its work was done. And thus the judgment of Jahweh was no longer confined to the offences of Israel, it was a world judgment against the injustice but above all against the pride of man.

For the day of the Lord of Hosts shall be upon every one that is proud and lofty and upon every one that is lifted up and he shall be brought low: and upon all the cedars of Lebanon and upon all the oaks of Bashan; and upon all the great mountains and upon all the high hills, and upon every high tower and upon every fenced wall, and upon all the ships of Tarshish and upon all that is fair to behold. And the loftiness of man shall be brought down and the haughtiness of man shall be humbled: and the Lord alone shall be exalted in that day.[1]

But through this denunciation of divine wrath, there is an increasing revelation of the hope of Israel. The new Jerusalem will not be a kingdom like the kingdoms of the Gentiles, but an eternal and universal one, founded on a new spiritual covenant. Israel was destined to be a theophoric people in a fuller sense than when it received the law of Jahweh at Sinai. It was to be the vehicle of divine revelation to the world.

This Jewish interpretation of history finds its most systematic expression in the book of Daniel which formed a model for the later apocalyptic literature. It no longer takes the form of isolated prophecies and denunciations of particular judgments, but of a synthetic view of world history as seen in the series of world empires which occupy "the latter times." Each empire has its allotted time and when "the sentence of the watchers" has gone forth its kingdom is numbered and finished. And at the same time the transcendent character of the Messianic hope is brought out more clearly than before. The Kingdom of God does not belong to the series of the world empires, it is something that comes in from outside and replaces them. It is the stone cut out of the mountain without hands that crushes the fourfold image of world empire to powder and grows till it fills the whole world. It is the universal kingdom of the Son of Man which will destroy the Kingdoms of the four beasts and will endure for ever.

This is the tradition that was inherited by the Christian Church. Indeed it may be said that it was precisely this

[1] Isaiah ii, 12–17.

prophetic and apocalyptic element in Judaism to which Christianity appealed. To the modern Protestant the essence of the Gospel is to be found in its moral teaching: its doctrine of the brotherhood of man and the fatherhood of God. But to the primitive Christian it was in the literal sense the Good News of the Kingdom. It was the announcement of a cosmic revolution, the beginning of a new world order: the dispensation of the fullness of the times to re-establish all things in Christ.

In order to understand the resultant attitude to history we must study the Apocalypse, which is at once the culmination of the Jewish apocalyptic tradition and the first Christian interpretation of history. It is marked by an historical dualism of the most uncompromising kind, which even accentuates the contrast between the Kingdom of God and the kingdoms of men which we find already in the prophets and in the book of Daniel. The city of God is not built up on earth by the preaching of the Gospel and the labour of the saints: it descends from God out of heaven like a bride adorned for her husband. But before it comes the mystery of iniquity must fulfil itself on earth and the harvest of human power and pride must be reaped. This is the significance of the judgment of Babylon, which appears in the Apocalypse not as a conquering military power as in the earlier prophets, but as the embodiment of material civilization and luxury, the great harlot, whose charms bewitch all the nations of the earth; the world market whose trade enriches the merchants and the shipowners.

At first sight there may seem little in common between all this lurid apocalyptic imagery and the teaching of the Gospels. Nevertheless the same fundamental conceptions underlie both of them. The dualism of the Kingdom and the World in the Gospels and the Epistles is no less uncompromising than that of the two apocalyptic cities. This is especially so in the case of the fourth Gospel with its insistence on the enmity of the World as the necessary condition for the children of the Kingdom. "I pray not for the world, but for those that thou hast given me." And again —"The prince of this world cometh and in me he has not anything." [2]

So too the supernatural and catastrophic character of the

---

[2] John xvii, 9; xiv, 30.

coming of the Kingdom is insisted on in the Synoptic Gospels no less than in the Apocalypse. There also, in what may be called the apocalypse of Jesus, we find the same prophecies of coming woe and the same conception of a world crisis which is due to the ripening of the harvest of evil rather than the progress of the forces of good. "And as it was in the days of Noah, so it shall be also in the days of the Son of Man. They ate and drank, they married and gave in marriage until the day when Noah entered into the ark and the flood came and destroyed them all." [3]

It does not follow, however, that the faithful are powerless to affect the course of events. It is their resistance that breaks the power of the world. The prayers of the saints and the blood of the martyrs, so to speak, force the hand of God and hasten the coming of the Kingdom. If the unjust judge listens to the importunity of the widow, will not God much more avenge his elect who cry to him night and day?

These are the foundations of the Christian view of history as it has been incorporated in the Catholic tradition. It is true that it seems at first sight a doctrine of the end of history which leaves no room for future development. As Newman writes, history seemed to have changed its direction with the coming of Christ. It no longer runs straight forward, but is, as it were, continually verging on eternity. "The Jews had a grant of this world: they had entered the vineyard in the morning; they had time before them; they might reckon on the future. . . . But it is otherwise with us. Earth and sky are ever failing; Christ is ever coming; Christians are ever lifting up their heads and looking out, and therefore it is the evening." Nevertheless "the evening is long and the day was short." "This last age though ever-failing has lasted longer than the ages before it, and Christians have more time for a greater work than if they had been hired in the morning." [4]

This was the great problem before the ancient church, and on its solution the Catholic interpretation of history depends. The millenniarists solved it in one way by a literalist interpretation of the Apocalyptic traditions, the Gnostics and the Origenists solved it in another way by eliminating history

[3] Luke xvii, 7.

[4] Sermons on Subjects of the Day, 10.

altogether in the interests of metaphysics and subsituting theosophy for apocalyptic.

But the Catholic solution which found its classical expression in St. Augustine retained the Hebrew sense of the significance and uniqueness of history, while rejecting the literalism and materialism of the extreme millenniarists and adopting the spiritual interpretation of the Greek theologians. The conflict between the Church and the Roman Empire was not the last act in the world drama; it was but one chapter of a long history in which the opposition and tension between the two social principles represented by the Church and the World would repeat themselves successively in new forms.

History was no longer a mere unintelligible chaos of disconnected events. It had found in the Incarnation a centre which gave it significance and order. Viewed from this centre the history of humanity became an organic unity. Eternity had entered into time and henceforward the singular and the temporal had acquired an eternal significance. The closed circle of time had been broken and a ladder had been let down from heaven to earth by which mankind can escape from the "sorrowful wheel" which had cast its shadow over Greek and Indian thought, and go forward in newness of life to a new world.

Thus the Catholic interpretation of history differs from any other in its combination of universalism with a sense of the uniqueness and irreversibility of the historic process. Its rejection of millenniarism frees it from the short views and the narrow fanaticisms of the sectarian tradition, as well as from the provincialism and partiality of the national historian who is a part of the political unit of which he writes. But the Catholic historian is the heir of a universal tradition. As Orosius writes, "Everywhere is my country, everywhere my law and my religion. . . . The breadth of the east, the fullness of the north, the extent of the south and the islands of the west are the wide and secure home of my citizenship, for it is as a Roman and a Christian that I address Christians and Romans."

And on the other hand the Catholic interpretation of history no less avoids the false universalism of the rationalist historians who insist on the fundamental identity of human nature in all circumstances; and who believe, like Hume, that the object of history is "only to discover the constant and universal principles of human nature by showing men in all variety of circumstances and situations." "The same motives always produce the same actions; the same events always follow from the same causes." [5]

But the Catholic interpretation of history preserves the prophetic and apocalyptic sense of mystery and divine judgment. Behind the rational sequence of political and economic cause and effect, hidden spiritual forces are at work which confer on events a wholly new significance. The real meaning of history is something entirely different from that which the human actors in the historical drama themselves believe or intend. For example, to a contemporary "scientific" historian the rise of the world empires in the Near East from the 8th to the 6th centuries B.C. would have seemed the only historical reality. He could not have even imagined that 2,000 years later all this drama of world history would only be remembered in so far as it affected the spiritual fortunes of one of the smallest and least materially civilized of the subject peoples. And in the same way what contemporary observer could have imagined that the execution of an obscure Jewish religious leader in the first century of the Roman Empire would affect the lives and thoughts of millions who never heard the names of the great statesmen and generals of the age?

It is this mysterious and unpredictable aspect of history which is the great stumbling block to the rationalist. He is always looking for neat systems of laws and causal sequences from which history can be automatically deduced. But history is impatient of all such artificial constructions. It is at once aristocratic and revolutionary. It allows the whole world situation to be suddenly transformed by the action of a single individual like Mohammed or Alexander. No doubt the situation in each case was ripe for change, but it would not have changed in that particular way without the intervention of that particular individual. If Alexander had turned his eyes to the West instead of to Persia, the course of world history would have been altered. There would have been no Roman Empire and consequently either no Europe or else a different Europe and a different modern civilization.

Now the Catholic interpretation, on the other hand, finds no difficulty in accepting the arbitrary and unpredictable character of historical change, since it sees everywhere the

[5] *Enquiry*, pp. 84 *et seq.*

signs of a divine purpose and election. The will of God chooses a barbarous Semitic tribe and makes of it the vehicle of his purposes towards humanity. Nor is the divine choice determined by human merit or by the internal logic of events. "Many widows were in Israel in the days of Elias but unto none of them was Elias sent save unto Sarepta of Sidon to a woman that was a widow. And many lepers were in Israel in the time of Eliseus the prophet and none of them was cleansed saving Naaman the Syrian." The house of the world seems closed and guarded; its masters have no rivals left to fear. But suddenly the wind of the spirit blows and everything is changed. No age has ever been able to foresee the age to come. The Augustan age could not have foretold the triumph of Christianity, nor the Byzantine age the coming of Islam. Even in our own generation, the best political observer of twenty years ago never guessed the possibility of the destruction of Parliamentarism in Central Europe by the advent of Fascism. But while all this is a scandal and reproach to historical rationalism, it offers no difficulties to the Catholic who lives in the presence of mysteries and who knows that "the way of man is not in himself."

To the ordinary educated man looking out on the world in A.D. 33 the execution of Sejanus must have appeared much more important than the crucifixion of Jesus, and the attempts of the Government to solve the economic crisis by a policy of free credit to producers must have seemed far more promising than the doings of the obscure group of Jewish fanatics in an upper chamber at Jerusalem. Nevertheless there is no doubt today which was the most important and which availed most to alter the lot of humanity. All that Roman world with its power and wealth and culture and corruption sank into blood and ruin—the flood came and destroyed them all—but the other world, the world of apostles and martyrs, the inheritance of the poor, survived the downfall of ancient civilization and became the spiritual foundation of a new order.

Christianity literally called a new world into existence to redress the balance of the old. It did not attempt to reform the world, in the sense of the social idealist. It did not start an agitation for the abolition of slavery, or for peace with Parthia. It did not support the claims of the Jews to national self-determination, or the Stoic propaganda for an ideal world state. It left Caesar on his throne and Pilate and Gallio on their judgment seats and went its own way to the new world.

The Christian solution was a fundamentally different one from that of social idealism. And this was not simply due to the fact that the world of the first century A.D. was not yet ripe for idealism. On the contrary, it had to meet the rivalry of the social millenniarism of the Jews, which was more intense, because it was more genuinely religious than the social millenniarism of modern socialism; and on the other hand it had to meet the humanitarian idealism of Hellenism, which was even more rational and even more humane than any form of modern idealism. Christianity refused each of these alternatives, it offered men the answer of the Cross—to the Jews a scandal and to the Greeks foolishness, just as today it is a scandal to the secular reformer and foolishness to the rational idealist. In the life of Christ the power of the world —the "torrent of human custom"—at last met with another power which it could neither overcome nor circumvent,—the irresistible power met the immovable obstacle, and the result was the tragedy of the Cross, a tragedy which seemed at first sight to manifest the triumph of the forces of evil and the victory of the flesh over the spirit, but which was in reality the turning point in the history of humanity and the starting point of a new order.

Not that this new order was itself the new world to which Christianity had looked. Christendom is not Christianity. It is not the City of God and the Kingdom of Christ. Humanity remains much the same as it has always been. To quote Newman:

The state of great cities now is not so very different from what it was of old; at least not so different as to show that the main work of Christianity has lain with the face of society, or what is called the world. Again the highest class in the community and the lowest are not so different from what they would be respectively without the knowledge of the Gospel as to allow it to be said that Christianity has succeeded with the world as the world in its several ranks and classes.[6]

In reality no age has the right to call itself Christian in an absolute sense: all stand under the same condemnation. The

[6] *Parochial Sermons* (1st ed.), iv, pp. 175–76.

one merit of a relatively Christian age or culture—and it is no small one—is that it recognizes its spiritual indigence and stands open to God and the spiritual world; while the age or culture that is thoroughly non-Christian is closed to God and prides itself on its own progress to perfection. No doubt there is a real leaven of spiritual progress at work in mankind and the life of the world to come is already stirring in the womb of the present. But the progress of the new world is an invisible one and its results can only be fully seen at the end of time. Apparent success often means spiritual failure, and the way of failure and suffering is the royal road of Christian progress. Wherever the Church has seemed to dominate the world politically and achieves a victory within the secular sphere, she has had to pay for it in a double measure of temporal and spiritual misfortune. Thus the triumph of the Orthodox Church in the Byzantine Empire was followed first by the loss of the East to Islam and then by the schism with the West. The mediaeval attempt to create a Christian theocracy was followed by the Reformation and the destruction of the religious unity of Western Europe, while the attempt that was made both by the Puritans and by the monarchies of the Counter-Reformation to dragoon society into orthodoxy and piety was followed by the incredulity and anti-clericalism of the eighteenth century and the secularization of European culture.

It is necessary that Christians should remember that it is not the business of the Church to do the same thing as the State—to build a Kingdom like the other kingdoms of men, only better; nor to create a reign of earthly peace and justice. The Church exists to be the light of the world, and if it fulfills its function, the world is transformed in spite of all the obstacles that human powers place in the way. A secularist culture can only exist, so to speak, in the dark. It is a prison in which the human spirit confines itself when it is shut out of the wider world of reality. But as soon as the light comes, all the elaborate mechanism that has been constructed for living in the dark becomes useless. The recovery of spiritual vision gives man back his spiritual freedom. And hence the freedom of the Church is in the faith of the Church and the freedom of man is in the knowledge of God.

—1935.

3

Christianity and Contradiction in History

Is history a reasonable process or is it essentially incalculable and irrational? It seems to me that the Christian is bound to believe that there is a spiritual purpose in history—that it is subject to the designs of Providence and that somehow or other God's will is done. But that is a very different thing from saying that history is rational in the ordinary sense of the word. There are, as it were, two levels of rationality, and history belongs to neither of them. There is the sphere of completely rationalized human action—the kind of rationality that we get in a balance sheet or in the plans and specifications of an architect or an engineer. And there is the higher sphere of rationality to which the human mind attains, but which is not created by it—the high realities of philosophy and abstract truth.

But between these two realms there is a great intermediate region in which we live, the middle earth of life and history; and that world is submitted to forces which are both higher and lower than reason. There are forces of nature in the strict sense and there are higher forces of spiritual good and evil which we cannot measure. Human life is essentially a warfare against unknown powers—not merely against flesh and blood, which are themselves irrational enough, but against principalities and powers, against "the Cosmocrats of the Dark Aeon," to use St. Paul's strange and disturbing expression; powers which are more than rational and which make use of lower things, things below reason, in order to conquer and rule the world of man.

Of course if we were pure spirits, the whole process of history and human life might be intelligible and spiritually transparent. We should be like a man in calm weather on a clear tropical lagoon who can look down and see the lower forms of life in their infinite variety and the powers of evil like the sharks that move silently and powerfully through the clear water, and who can also look up and see the ordered march of the stars.

But this is not given to man. The actor in history is like the captain who sees nothing but clouds above and waves below, who is driven by the wind and the current. He must trust in his chart and his compass, and even these cannot deliver him from the blind violence of the elements. If he makes a mistake, or if the chart fails him, he dies in a blind flurry of dark water and with him the crew who have no responsibility except to obey orders and to trust their officers.

It is true that the theologian and the philosopher aspire to the spiritual state but they only attain to it partially and momentarily; for the rest of their lives, outside their science, they belong to the world of other men. But the politician and the man of action are like the sailor, and the State is like the ship which may be wrecked by an error of a single man; and it makes no difference if it is a democracy or a dictatorship, just as it makes no difference whether the ship is sailed by the owner or whether the captain is chosen by the officers and the officers by the crew.

It seems the very nature of history that individuals and apparently fortuitous events have an incalculable effect upon the fortunes of the whole society. As Burke wrote: "It is often impossible to find any proportion between the apparent force of any moral cause or any assigned, and their known operation. We are therefore obliged to deliver up their operation to mere chance, or more piously (perhaps more rationally) to the occasional interposition and the irresistible hand of the Great Disposer. The death of a man at a critical juncture, his disgust, his retreat, his disgrace, have brought innumerable calamities on a whole nation. A common soldier, a child, a girl at the door of an inn have changed the face of the future and almost of Nature." [1]

This has always been so, but it is seen in the most striking way when it comes to a question of moralizing politics or realizing social ideals in practice. It is here that we see most clearly and tragically the contradiction between human aims and historical results and the way in which fate seems to bring so much that is best in social endeavour to sterility or to disaster. Take two examples from the period of modern history connected with the French Revolution. First, frustration of social idealism. The great Revolution a hundred and fifty years ago was a deliberate attempt to moralize political relations and to create a new order based on moral principles which would vindicate the human rights of every individual whatever his economic or social position. Under the guidance of men who believed most wholeheartedly in these ideals, it led nevertheless to as complete a subversion and denial of those rights as it is possible to conceive. It led to the denial of freedom of conscience and freedom of opinion; it led to terrorism and wholesale judicial murder, until every man of principles, whatever his principles were, had been exterminated or outlawed, and society returned with gratitude and relief to the absolute dictatorship of an unscrupulous military despot. For Bonaparte appeared to his contemporaries as an angel of light in comparison with the idealists and social reformers who, instead of creating a Utopia, had made a hell on earth.

In the second place, to take an example from the opposite side, there is the case of the war in La Vendée which brings up both the question of the just war and that of the conscientious objector. The men of La Vendée had every justification for their resistance to the revolutionary government, since it had clearly violated the rights of freedom of opinion and religious liberty that were laid down in the constitution, and since the latter expressly admitted the right of the citizen to resist the government in such cases. The actual occasion of the rising was moreover the question of military service in defence of the revolution against which the men of La Vendée had a direct and simple conscientious objection. Hence the war in La Vendée was at once a just war if ever there was one and a case of spontaneous popular resistance

---

[1] *Letters on the Regicide Peace,* ed. E. J. Payne, p. 6.

to compulsory service in what they considered an unjust war.

Yet what was the result? Instead of sending 12,000 conscripts to the army, of whom a small proportion would have been killed or wounded, the whole population was involved in the most desperate struggle that any people ever experienced: a struggle which is said to have cost nearly a quarter of a million lives, which caused practically every town and village and farm to be destroyed, and which contributed largely, if indirectly, to the horrors of the Reign of Terror in the rest of France. And so their desire to keep out of a war they did not approve of caused another war of a far more atrocious kind, and their determination to vindicate their just rights led to every kind of injustice and cruelty.

These are extreme instances, but all through history we find plentiful evidence of the same non-moral and irrational tendency which causes idealists and humanitarians to despair. And at the present day humanitarianism and moral idealism have become so much a part of our tradition that Christians often unconsciously or even consciously accept the same point of view and are tempted to despair by the failure of Christian ideals to work out in practice.

Actually, however, Christianity has never accepted these postulates, and the Christian ought to be the last person in the world to lose hope in the presence of the failure of the right and the apparent triumph of evil. For all this forms part of the Christian view of life, and the Christian discipline is expressly designed to prepare us to face such a situation.

Christianity, to a far greater degree than any other religion, is a historical religion and it is knit up inseparably with the living process of history. Christianity teaches the existence of a divine progress in history which will be realized through the Church in the Kingdom of God. But at the same time it recognizes the essential duality of the historical process—the co-existence of two opposing principles, each of which works and finds concrete social expression in history. Thus we have no right to expect that Christian principles will work in practice in the simple way that a political system may work. The Christian order is a supernatural order. It has its own principles and its own laws which are not those of the visible world and which may often seem to contradict them. Its victories may be found in apparent defeat and its defeats in material success.

We see the whole thing manifested clearly and perfectly once and once only, i.e. in the life of Jesus, which is the pattern of the Christian life and the model of Christian action. The life of Jesus is profoundly historical; it is the culminating point of thousands of years of living historical tradition. It is the fulfilment of an historical purpose, towards which priests and prophets and even politicans had worked, and in which the hope of a nation and a race was embodied. Yet, from the worldly point of view, from the standpoint of a contemporary secular historian, it was not only unimportant, but actually invisible. Here was a Galilean peasant who for thirty years lived a life so obscure as to be unknown even to the disciples who accepted his mission. Then there followed a brief period of public action, which did not lead to any kind of historical achievement but moved swiftly and irresistibly towards its catastrophic end, an end that was foreseen and deliberately accepted.

And out of the heart of this catastrophe there arose something completely new, which even in its success was a deception to the very people and the very race that had staked their hopes on it. For after Pentecost—after the outpouring of the Spirit and the birth of the infant Church—there was an event as unforeseen and inexplicable as the Incarnation itself, the conversion of a Cilician Jew, who turned away from his traditions and from his own people so that he seemed a traitor to his race and his religion. So that ultimately the fulfilment of the hope of Israel meant the rejection of Israel and the creation of a new community which was eventually to become the State religion of the Roman Empire which had been the enemy of Jew and Christian alike.

If you look on all this without faith, from the rationalist point of view, it becomes no easier to understand. On the contrary it becomes even more inexplicable; *credo quia incredibile*.

Now the life of Christ is the life of the Christian and the life of the Church. It is absurd for a Christian who is a weak human vehicle of this world-changing force to expect a quiet life. A Christian is like a red rag to a bull—to the force of evil that seeks to be master of the world and which, in a limited sense, but in a very real sense, is, as St. John says, the Lord of this world. And not only the individual but the Church as an historic community follows the same pattern and finds its success and failure not where the politician finds them, but where Christ found them.

The Church lives again the life of Christ. It has its period of obscurity and growth and its period of manifestation, and this is followed by the catastrophe of the Cross and the new birth that springs from failure. And what is most remarkable is that the enemies of the Church—the movements that rend and crucify her—are in a sense her own offspring and derive their dynamic force from her. Islam, the Protestant Reformation, the Liberal Revolution, none of them would have existed apart from Christianity—they are abortive or partial manifestations of the spiritual power which Christianity has brought into history. "I have come to cast fire on the earth and what will I, but that it be kindled."

It is easy to give way to the dominant tendency to surrender to the spirit of the age and the spirit of the world by shutting our eyes to the errors of public opinion and the evils and injustice of popular action; it is the same temptation which in the past made religious men flatter the pride of the great and overlook the injustice of the powerful. But it is also easy, and it is a more insidious temptation, to adopt an attitude of negative hostility to the spirit of the age and to take refuge in a narrow and exclusive fanaticism which is essentially the attitude of the heretic and the sectarian and which does more to discredit Christianity and render it ineffective than even worldliness and time-serving. For the latter are, so to speak, external to the Church's life, whereas the former poisons the sources of its spiritual action and causes it to appear hateful in the eyes of men of good will.

It is the nature of heresy to sacrifice Catholic truth and Christian unity by concentrating its attention on the immediate solution of some pressing contemporary problem of Christian thought or action. The heretic goes astray by attempting to take a short cut, owing to a natural human impatience at the apparent slowness and difficulty of the way of pure faith.

But the Church also has to take the difficult way of the Cross to incur the penalties and humiliations of earthly failure without any compensating hope of temporal success. She is not an alternative and a rival to the State, and her teaching does not take the place of political needs and ideologies; yet she cannot disinterest herself in the corporate life of the community and confine her attentions to the individual soul. The Church is no human society, but she is the channel by which divine life flows into human society and her essential task is the sanctification of humanity as a whole in its corporate as well as in its individual activities.

Human society today is in a state of rapid change. The life is going out of the old political and juridical forms and a new community is being created whose appearance marks a new epoch in history. It is not the Church's business to stop this great social change, and she could not if she would, but neither can she abdicate her essential mission, which remains the same in the new circumstances as of old. The new social forms offer new opportunities—new openings for the action of grace.

We are perhaps too much inclined to look to authority to lay down beforehand a programme of action when the initiative must come in the first place from the spontaneous personal reaction of individuals to the circumstances of the moment. Even in the natural sphere the statesmen and organizers of this world do not know what is going to happen from one day to another.

But whereas this obscurity and incalculability is inevitably a source of discouragement to the statesman, whose whole business is to achieve temporal success, it should be of no great importance to the Christian who sees the end of history as dawn and not as night.

When Our Lord spoke of the future He gave His disciples no optimistic hopes, no visions of social progress; He described all the things that we are afraid of today and more—wars, persecutions, disasters and the distress of nations. But strange to say He used this forecast of calamity as a motive for hope. "When you see these things," He said, "look up and lift up your heads for your redemption is at hand."

That may seem a strange philosophy of history, but it is the authentic philosophy of Christ, and if the prospect of these things causes us to hang down our heads instead of lifting them up, it shows that there is something wrong with our point of view. I know we are apt to feel this does not apply to us—that it merely refers to the end of the world. But to the Christian the world is always ending, and every historical crisis is, as it were, a rehearsal for the real thing.

—1939.

4

The Kingdom of God and History

The development of an historical sense—a distinct consciousness of the essential characteristics of different ages and civilizations—is a relatively recent achievement; in fact it hardly existed before the nineteenth century. It is above all the product of the Romantic movement which first taught men to respect the diversity of human life, and to regard culture not as an abstract ideal but as the vital product of an organic social tradition. No doubt, as Nietzsche pointed out, the acquisition of this sixth sense is not all pure gain, since it involves the loss of that noble self-sufficiency and maturity in which the great ages of civilization culminate—"the moment of smooth sea and halcyon self-sufficiency, the goldenness and coldness which all things show that have perfected themselves." It was rendered possible only by the "democratic mingling of classes and races" which is characteristic of modern European civilization. "Owing to this mingling the past of every form and mode of life and of cultures which were formerly juxtaposed with or superimposed on one another flow forth into us," so that "we have secret access above all to the labyrinth of imperfect civilizations and to every form of semi-barbarity that has at any time existed on earth."[1]

[1] F. Nietzsche, *Beyond Good and Evil*, 224.

Yet it is impossible to believe that the vast widening of the range and scope of consciousness that the historical sense has brought to the human race is an ignoble thing, as Nietzsche would have us believe. It is as though man had at last climbed from the desert and the forest and the fertile plain onto the bare mountain slopes whence he can look back and see the course of his journey and the whole extent of his kingdom. And to the Christian, at least, this widening vision and these far horizons should bring not doubt and disillusionment, but a firmer faith in the divine power that has guided him and a stronger desire for the divine kingdom which is the journey's end.

It is in fact through Christianity above all that man first acquired that sense of a unity and a purpose in history without which the spectacle of the unending change becomes meaningless and oppressive.

"The rational soul," writes Marcus Aurelius, "traverses the whole universe and the surrounding void, and surveys its form, and it extends itself with the infinity of time and embraces and comprehends the periodical revolutions of all things, and it comprehends that those who come after us will see nothing new, nor have those before us seen anything more, but in a manner he who is forty years old, if he has any understanding at all, has seen by virtue of the uniformity that prevails all things that have been or that will be." [2]

This denial of the significance of history is the rule rather than the exception among philosophers and religious teachers throughout the ages from India to Greece and from China to Northern Europe. Even Nietzsche, who grew up in the tradition of the modern historical movement and himself possessed so delicate and profound an historical sense, could not escape the terrifying vision of The Return of All Things, even though it seemed to nullify his own evolutionary gospel of the superman. "Behold," he wrote, "this moment. Two roads meet here and none has ever reached their end. . . ." "From this gateway a long eternal road runs back: behind us lies an eternity. Must not all things that can run have run this road? Must not all that can happen have already happened, have already been done and passed through? And if all has already been, what . . . of this moment? Must not this gateway also have been before? And are not all things

---

[2] *Marcus Aurelius*, xi, i, trans. G. Long.

knotted together in such a way that this moment draws after it all that is to come, and therefore also itself? For all that can run—even in this long road behind, must run it yet again.

"And this slow spider that crawls in the moonlight and this moonlight itself, and you and I whispering together in the gateway, must we not all have been before?

"And must we not come again and run that other long road before us—that long shadowy road—must we not return eternally?" [3]

As St. Augustine said,[4] it is only by Christ the Straight Way that we are delivered from the nightmare of these eternal cycles which seem to exercise a strange fascination over the human mind in any age and clime.

Nevertheless, Christianity does not itself create the historical sense. It only supplies the metaphysical and theological setting for history and an attempt to create a theory of history from the data of revealed truth alone will give us not a history but a theodicy like St. Augustine's *City of God* or the *Praeparatio Evangelica* of Eusebius. The modern historical consciousness is the fruit of Christian tradition and Christian culture but not of these alone. It also owes much to humanism, which taught the European mind to study the achievements of ancient civilization and to value human nature for its own sake. And it was the contact and conflict of these two traditions and ideals—Christianity and humanism —classical and mediaeval culture—that found expression in the Romantic movement in which the modern historical sense first attained full consciousness. For it was only then and thus that the human mind realized that a culture forms an organic unity, with its own social traditions and its own spiritual ideals, and that consequently we cannot understand the past by applying the standards and values of our own age and civilization to it, but only by relating historical facts to the social tradition to which they belong and by using the spiritual beliefs and the moral and intellectual values of that tradition as the key to their interpretation.

Hence the essence of history is not to be found in facts but in traditions. The pure fact is not as such historical. It only becomes historical when it can be brought into relation

---

[3] *Also Sprach Zarathustra*, 30:2, 2.
[4] *De Civitate Dei*, XII, xx.

with a social tradition so that it is seen as part of an organic whole. A visitor from another planet who witnessed the Battle of Hastings would possess far greater knowledge of the facts than any modern historian, yet this knowledge would not be historical for lack of any tradition to which it could be related; whereas the child who says "William the Conqueror 1066" has already made his atom of knowledge an historical fact by relating it to a national tradition and placing it in the time-series of Christian culture.

Wherever a social tradition exists, however small and unimportant may be the society which is its vehicle, the possibility of history exists. It is true that many societies fail to realize this possibility, or realize it only in an unscientific or legendary form, but on the other hand this legendary element is never entirely absent from social tradition, and even the most civilized society has its national legend or myth, of which the scientific historian is often an unconscious apologist. No doubt it is the ideal of the modern historian to transcend the tradition of his own society and to see history as one and universal, but in fact such a universal history does not exist. There is as yet no history of humanity, since humanity is not an organized society with a common tradition or a common social consciousness. All the attempts that have hitherto been made to write a world history have been in fact attempts to interpret one tradition in terms of another, attempts to extend the intellectual hegemony of a dominant culture by subordinating to it all the events of other cultures that come within the observer's range of vision. The more learned and conscientious a historian is, the more conscious he is of the relativity of his own knowledge, and the more ready he is to treat the culture that he is studying as an end in itself, an autonomous world which follows its own laws and owes no allegiance to the standards and ideals of another civilization. For history deals with civilizations and cultures rather than civilization, with the development of particular societies and not with the progress of humanity.

Consequently if we rely on history alone we can never hope to transcend the sphere of relativity; it is only in religion and metaphysics that we can find truths that claim absolute and eternal validity. But as we have said, non-Christian and pre-Christian philosophy tend to solve the problem of history by a radical denial of its significance.

The world of true Being which is man's spiritual home

is the world that knows no change. The world of time and change is the material world from which man must escape if he would be saved. For all the works of men and the rise and fall of kingdoms are but the fruits of ignorance and lust—*mala vitae cupido*—and even the masters of the world must recognize in the end the vanity of their labours like the great Shogun Hideyoshi who wrote on his death-bed:

> Alas, as the grass I fade
> As the dew I vanish
> Even Osaka Castle
> Is a dream within a dream.

Yet even the religion that denies the significance of history is itself a part of history and it can only survive in so far as it embodies itself in a social tradition and thus "makes history." The spiritual experience from which a religion receives its initial impetus—like the contemplation of Buddha under the Bo tree or Mohammed's vision in the cavern on Mt. Hira—may seem as completely divested of historical and social reference as any human experience can be. Yet as soon as the teacher comes down among men and his followers begin to put his teachings into practice a tradition is formed which comes into contact with other social traditions and embraces them or is absorbed by them, until its very nature seems to be changed by this chemistry of history. Thus we see Buddhism passing from India to Central Asia and China, and from China to Korea and Japan and again to Ceylon and Burma and Siam. We see it taking different forms in different cultures and at the same time changing the cultures themselves, while all the while the religion itself ignores historical change and remains with its gaze averted from life, absorbed in the contemplation of Nirvana.

Now at first sight it may seem that this is true of Christianity; that it also has been absorbed against its will in the stream while its attention has been concentrated on eternal truths and its hopes fixed on eternal life. It is easy to find examples in Christianity of world flight and world denial no less extreme than that of the Indian *sannyasi*: the fathers of the desert, St. Simeon on his pillar, Thomas à Kempis in his cell and the countless pious Christians of every age and country who have regarded this life as an exile in the vale of tears and have oriented their whole existence towards death and immortality. In fact the current criticism of Christianity is based on this conception and the communist sneer about "pie in the sky when you die" is merely a crude and malicious statement of what has always been an essential element of the Christian faith and one which is nowhere more prominent than in the gospel itself.

Nevertheless this is only one side of the Christian view of life, for Christianity has always possessed an organic relation to history which distinguishes it from the great Oriental religions and philosophies. Christianity can never ignore history because the Christian revelation is essentially historical and the truths of faith are inseparably connected with historical events. The Sacred Scriptures of our religion are not made up of expositions of metaphysical doctrines like the Vedanta, they form a sacred history, the record of God's dealings with the human race from the creation of man to the creation of the Church. And the whole of this history finds its centre in the life of an historic personality who is not merely a moral teacher or even an inspired hierophant of divine truth, but God made man, the Saviour and restorer of the human race, from whom and in whom humanity acquires a new life and a new principle of unity.

Thus the Christian faith leaves no room for the relativism of a merely historical philosophy. For here at one moment of time and space there occurs an event of absolute value and incomparable significance for all times and all peoples. Amid the diversity and discontinuity of human civilizations and traditions there appears One who is one and the same for all men and for all ages: in whom all the races and traditions of man find their common centre.

Yet on the other hand the Incarnation does not involve any denial of the significance of history such as we find in the Gnostic and Manichaean heresies. It is itself in a sense the fruit of history, since it is the culminating point of one tradition, and the starting point of another. The appeal to tradition is one of the most characteristic features of the gospel. The New Testament opens with "the book of the generation of Jesus Christ the son of David, the son of Abraham," and the first preaching of the apostles starts with an appeal to a tradition that goes back to Ur of the Chaldeans and the earliest origins of the Hebrew people.

Thus, the Christian Church possessed its own history, which was a continuation of the history of the chosen people, and this history had its own autonomous development which was independent of the currents of secular history. We have the age of the apostles and the age of the martyrs and the age of the fathers, each of them built on the same foundations and each contributing its part to the building up of the City of God.

The chief problem, therefore, which we have to study is that of the relations between this sacred tradition and the other countless traditions that make up human history. For Christianity, no less than the other world religions, has entered the stream of historical change and has passed from one race to another, from civilization to barbarism and from barbarism to civilization. Men of different periods with different historical backgrounds and different national or racial traditions all belong to the all-embracing tradition of the Christian Church. We have Hellenistic Christians and Byzantine Christians, Romans and Syrians, Mediaeval Christians and Renaissance Christians, seventeenth-century Spaniards and nineteenth-century Englishmen. Are these differences of culture and race accidental and ephemeral—details that have no relevance to the Christian view of life and the Christian interpretation of History? Or are they also of spiritual significance as elements in the divine plan and forms through which the providential purpose of God in history is manifested?

Now from the early Christian point of view, at least, it would seem that the whole significance of history was entirely comprised in that sacred tradition of which we have spoken. The key to history—the mystery of the ages—was to be found in the tradition of the chosen people and the sacred community, and outside that tradition among the Gentiles and the kingdoms of men there is a realm of endless strife and confusion, a succession of empires founded by war and violence and ending in blood and ruin. The Kingdom of God is not the work of man and does not emerge by a natural law of progress from the course of human history. It makes a violent inruption into history and confounds the work of man, like the stone hewn from the mountain without human agency which crushes the image of the four world empires into dust.

One of the most striking features of the Christian tradition is, in fact, its historical dualism: in the Old Testament the opposition between the chosen people and the Gentiles; in the New, the opposition between the church and the world—in the Augustinian theodicy, the two cities, Jerusalem and Babylon—the community of charity and the community of self-will. Yet this dualism is never an absolute one. Even the Old Testament, in spite of its insistence on the unique privilege of Israel as the exclusive bearer of the divine promise, also recognizes the hand of God in the history of the Gentiles. Even the powers that seem most hostile to the people of God are the instrument by which God works out his purpose. This is shown most remarkably in the Isaianic prophecy with regard to Cyrus, for here a Gentile ruler is addressed by the messianic title as chosen and anointed by God to do his will and to deliver his people. No doubt here and elsewhere the divine action in history always has a direct reference to the fortunes of the people of God. But the converse is also true, for God's dealings with his people are of profound significance for the future of the Gentiles. In the end the Holy City will be the resort of all peoples; the Gentiles will bring their riches into it, and from it there will go forth the law of justice and grace to all the nations of the earth.

And in the New Testament there is a still further recognition of a limited but intrinsic value in the social order and social traditions that lie outside the dispensation of grace. Even the pagan state is God's servant in so far as it is the guardian of order and the administrator of justice. And in the higher sphere of grace, the passing of the old racial restrictions and the opening of the Kingdom to all nations involved at least in principle the consecration of every nation and of every social tradition in so far as they were not corrupted by sin. And so we have the reception into the church of Greek philosophy and scholarship, and of Roman law and leadership, until the whole civilized world found itself Christian. The vital thing was not the conversion of the Empire and the union of church and state, but the gradual penetration of culture by the Christian tradition, until that tradition embraced the whole of the life of Western man in all its historic diversity and left no human activity and no social tradition unconsecrated.

With this coming in of the nations and the establishment of the Kingdom of Christ among the Gentiles the Christian interpretation of prophecy seemed to have been fulfilled. From the time of St. Augustine Christian millenniarism was generally abandoned and the Messianic kingdom was identified with the triumph of the church—*"ecclesia et nunc est regnum Christi regnumque coelorum."* It seemed to the men of that age witnessing the fall of the Empire and the ruin of civilization that nothing remained to be accomplished except the last things. Consequently the Christian interpretation of history became mainly retrospective, and the present and the future of man's attention were concentrated not on history but on the end of history which seemed close at hand.

But with the passing of ages and the birth of new nations and new forms of culture, new problems presented themselves to the Christian conscience. The Augustinian theology with its intense realization of the inherited burden of evil which weighs down the human race and its conception of divine grace as a supernatural power which renews human nature and changes the course of history, continued to inspire the mediaeval outlook, and the mediaeval interpretation of history is still based on the Augustinian conception of the two cities. But whereas St. Augustine presents this opposition primarily as a conflict between the Christian Church and the heathen world, the Middle Ages saw it above all as a struggle between the forces of good and evil within Christian society. The reform of the church, the restoration of moral order, and the establishment of social justice—these were the vital problems that occupied the mind of mediaeval Christendom from the tenth century onwards; and the whole movement of reform from the time of St. Odo of Cluny to that of St. Bernard and Otto of Freising was consciously based on an interpretation of history which applied the Augustinian concept of the two cities to the contemporary crisis between church and state or rather between the religious and secular forces that were at war within the Christian community. This neo-Augustinian view of history finds its most direct expression in the writings of Odo of Cluny in the tenth century, Bonizo of Sutri in the eleventh and Otto of Freising in the twelfth, but it also inspired some of the ablest partisans of the Empire such as the author of the treatise *De Unitate Ecclesiae conservanda.* For the mediaeval empire and indeed the mediaeval kingship were not regarded by their supporters as secular institutions in our sense of the word. They were the leaders of the Christian people and the defenders of the Christian faith, and it was to them rather than to the papacy and the priesthood that the government of Christendom as an historical "temporal" order had been committed by God.

This tradition of Christian imperialism was not destroyed by the victory of the papacy over the Empire. In fact it found its most remarkable expression in the fourteenth century in Dante's theory of the providential mission of the Roman Empire as the society through which the human race would realize its potential unity and attain universal peace, and of the particular vocation of the Messianic prince, the mystical *Dux* who would be the saviour of Italy and the reformer of the Church. Here for the first time we have a Christian interpretation of history which looks beyond the sacred Judaeo-Christian tradition and admits the independent value and significance of the secular tradition of culture. There are in fact two independent but parallel dispensations—the dispensation of grace, which is represented by the Church, and the natural dispensation by which humanity attains its rational end by the agency of the Roman people, which was ordained by nature and elected by God for universal empire.

Thus while on the one hand Dante's interpretation of history looks back to the mediaeval tradition of the Holy Roman Empire and the Augustinian ideal of the City of God, on the other hand it looks forward to the humanism of the Renaissance and the modern liberal ideal of universal peace as well as the modern nationalist ideal of the historical mission of a particular people and state. And this idea of a predestined correspondence between the secular tradition of human civilization embodied in the Roman Empire and the religious tradition of supernatural truth embodied in the Catholic Church finds its philosophical basis in the Thomist doctrine of the concordance of nature and grace. If it had been adopted by Thomism as the basis of the interpretation of history, it might well have developed with the growth of historical knowledge into a really catholic philosophy of history in which the different national traditions were shown, on the analogy of that of Rome, as contributing each according to its own mission and its natural aptitudes towards the building up of a Christian civilization. Actually, however, Dante's attachment to the dying cause of Ghibelline imperialism prevented his philosophy from exercising any wide influence on Catholic thought. It remained an impressive but eccentric witness to the universalism of mediaeval thought and the lost spiritual unity of mediaeval culture.

For the close of the Middle Ages was marked by the great religious revolution which destroyed the unity of Western Christendom and divided the peoples of Europe by the strife of sects and the conflict of opposing religious traditions. There was no longer one common Catholic faith and consequently there was no longer a common sacred tradition or a common interpretation of history. It is true that the Reformers inherited far more from the Middle Ages than they themselves realized, and this was particularly the case with regard to the interpretation of history. Their conception of history, no less than that of the Middle Ages, is based on the Bible and St. Augustine, and the Augustinian scheme of world history, based on the opposition and conflict of the two cities, had as great an influence on Luther and Calvin and the seventeenth-century Puritan divines as it had on the Catholic reformers five centuries earlier.

Nevertheless the Catholic interpretation of history is organically related to the Catholic conception of the nature and office of the church, and in so far as Protestantism formed a new conception of the church, it ultimately involved a new interpretation of history. Thus already, long before the emergence of the new schools of Biblical criticism and ecclesiastical history that have so profoundly affected the modern Protestant attitude to the Catholic tradition, a divergence between the Catholic and Protestant interpretations of history is plainly visible.

At first sight the difference between sixteenth-century Catholicism and Protestantism is the difference between the traditional and the revolutionary conceptions of Christianity and of the church. To the Catholic the church was the Kingdom of God on earth—*in via*—the supernatural society through which and in which alone humanity could realize its true end. It was a visible society with its own law and constitution which possessed divine and indefectible authority. It remained through the ages one and the same, like a city set on a hill, plain for all men to see, handing on from generation to generation the same deposit of faith and the same mandate of authority which it had received from its divine Founder and which it would retain whole and intact until the end of time.

The Reformers, on the other hand, while maintaining a

similar conception of the church as the community through which God's purpose towards the human race is realized, refused to identify this divine society with the actual visible hierarchical church, as known to history. Against the Catholic view of the church as the visible City of God, they set the apocalyptic vision of an apostate church, a harlot drunk with the blood of the saints, sitting on the seven hills and intoxicating the nations with her splendour and her evil enchantments. The true church was not this second Babylon, but the society of the elect, the hidden saints who followed the teaching of the Bible rather than of the hierarchy and who were to be found among the so-called heretics—Hussites, Wycliffites, Waldensians and the rest, rather than among the servants of the official institutional church.

The result of this revolutionary attitude to the historic church was a revolutionary, catastrophic, apocalyptic and discontinuous view of history. As Calvin writes, the history of the church is a series of resurrections. Again and again the church becomes corrupt, the Word is no longer preached, life seems extinct, until God once more sends forth prophets and teachers to bear witness to the truth and to reveal the evangelical doctrine in its pristine purity. Thus the Reformation may be compared to the Renaissance since it was an attempt to go back behind the Middle Ages, to wipe out a thousand years of historical development and to restore the Christian religion to its primitive "classical" form. Yet on the other hand this return to the past brought the Protestant mind into fresh contact with the Jewish and apocalyptic sources of the Christian view of history, so that the Reformation led to an increased emphasis on the Hebraic prophetic and apocalyptic elements in the Christian tradition as against the Hellenic, patristic and metaphysical elements that were so strongly represented alike in patristic orthodoxy and in mediaeval Catholicism.

Hence we find two tendencies in Protestant thought which find their extreme expression respectively in Socinianism and millenniarism. One represents the attempt to strip off all accretions, to separate religion from history and to recover the pure timeless essence of Christianity. The other represents a crude and vehement reassertion of the historical time-element in Christianity and an attempt to strip it of all its non-Jewish, mystical, philosophical and theological elements. The resultant type of religion was marked by some of the worst excesses of fanaticism and irrationality, yet on the other hand it was intensely social in spirit, as we see, for example, in the case of the Anabaptists, and it made an earnest, if one-sided and over-simplified, effort to provide a Christian interpretation of history.

But though these two tendencies seem hostile to one another, they were not in fact mutually exclusive. For example, John Milton could be at the same time a millenniarist and a Socinian, and eighteenth-century Unitarians, such as Priestley, who seem to represent the Socinian type of Protestantism in an almost pure state, acquired from the opposite tradition a kind of secularized millenniarism which found expression in the doctrine of progress. The development of this rationalized theology and of this secularized millenniarism, whether in its revolutionary-socialistic or revolutionary-liberal forms (but especially the latter), is of central importance for the understanding of modern culture. It was in fact a new reformation, which attempted to rationalize and spiritualize religion in an even more complete and drastic way than the first Reformation had done, but which ended in emptying Christianity of all supernatural elements and interpreting history as the progressive development of an immanent principle.

Thus it is not only the materialistic interpretation of history but the idealistic interpretation as well which is irreconcilable with the traditional Christian view, since it eliminates that sense of divine otherness and transcendence, that sense of divine judgment and divine grace which are the very essence of the Christian attitude to history. This holds true of Protestantism as well as of Catholicism. Nevertheless it must be admitted that the clash is much sharper and more painful in the case of the latter. Partly, no doubt, because the great idealist thinkers, such as Kant, were themselves men of Protestant origin who had preserved a strong Protestant ethos, it has been possible for Protestants to accept the idealist interpretation of history without any serious conflict, and in the same way it was on Protestant rather than on Catholic foundations that the new liberal theology of immanence developed itself.

Catholicism, on the other hand, showed little sympathy to the idealist movement which it tended to regard as an external and non-religious force. Its attitude to history was at once more traditionalist and more realist than that of Protestantism and it did not readily accept the idea of an inevitable law of progress which was accepted by both liberal and Protestant idealists as the background of their thought and the basic principle of their interpretation of history. Consequently there is a sharp contrast between the Catholic and the liberal-idealist philosophies such as hardly exists in the Protestant world. As Croce brings out so clearly in his *History of Europe in the Nineteenth Century,* it is not a conflict between religion and science or religion and philosophy, but between two rival creeds, based on an irreconcilable opposition of principles and resulting in a completely different view of the world. For, as Croce again points out, the idealist conceptions of monism, immanence and self-determination are the negation of the principles of divine transcendence, divine revelation, and divine authority on which the Catholic view of God and man, of creation and history and the end of history is based.

Hence the opposition between liberalism and Catholicism is not due, as the vulgar simplification would have it, to the "reactionary" tendencies of the latter but to the necessity of safeguarding the absolute Christian values, both in the theological and the historical spheres. For if Christianity is the religion of the Incarnation, and if the Christian interpretation of history depends on the continuation and extension of the Incarnation in the life of the church, Catholicism differs from other forms of Christianity in representing this incarnational principle in a fuller, more concrete, and more organic sense. As the Christian faith in Christ is faith in a real historical person, not an abstract ideal, so the Catholic faith in the church is faith in a real historical society, not an invisible communion of saints or a spiritual union of Christians who are divided into a number of religious groups and sects. And this historic society is not merely the custodian of the sacred Scriptures and a teacher of Christian morality. It is the bearer of a living tradition which unites the present and the past, the living and the dead, in one great spiritual community which transcends all the limited communities of race and nation and state. Hence, it is not enough for the Catholic to believe in the Word as contained in the sacred Scriptures, it is not even enough to accept the historic faith as embodied in the creeds and interpreted by Catholic theology, it is necessary for him to be incorporated as a cell in the living organism of the divine society and to enter into communion with the historic reality of the sacred tradition. Thus to the student who considers Catholicism as an intellectual system embodied in theological treatises, Catholicism may seem far more legalist and intellectualist than Protestantism, which emphasizes so strongly the personal and moral-emotional sides of religion, but the sociologist who studies it in its historical and social reality will soon understand the incomparable importance for Catholicism of tradition, which makes the individual a member of a historic society and a spiritual civilization and which influences his life and thought consciously and unconsciously in a thousand different ways.

Now the recognition of this tradition as the organ of the Spirit of God in the world and the living witness to the supernatural action of God on humanity is central to the Catholic understanding and interpretation of history. But so tremendous a claim involves a challenge to the whole secular view of history which is tending to become the faith of the modern world. In spite of the differences and contradictions between the progressive idealism of liberalism and the catastrophic materialism of communism all of them agree in their insistence on the immanence and autonomy of human civilization and on the secular community as the ultimate social reality. Alike to the liberal and to the communist the Catholic tradition stands condemned as "reactionary" not merely for the accidental reason that it has been associated with the political and social order of the past, but because it sets the divine values of divine faith and charity and eternal life above the human values—political liberty, social order, economic prosperity, scientific truth— and orientates human life and history towards a supernatural and super-historical end. And since the modern society is everywhere tending towards ideological uniformity which will leave no room for the private worlds of the old bourgeois culture, the contradiction between secularism and Catholicism is likely to express itself in open conflict and persecution.

No doubt the prospect of such a conflict is highly distasteful to the modern bourgeois mind, even when it is Christian. The liberal optimism which has been so characteristic of Anglo-Saxon religious thought during the last half century led men to believe that the days of persecution were over and that all men of good will would agree to set aside their differences of opinion and unite to combat the evils that were universally condemned—vice and squalor and ignorance. But from the standpoint of the Christian interpretation of history there is no ground for such hopes. Christ came not to bring peace but a sword, and the Kingdom of God comes not by the elimination of conflict but through an increasing opposition and tension between the church and the world. The conflict between the two cities is as old as humanity and must endure to the end of time. And though the church may meet with ages of prosperity, and her enemies may fail and the powers of the world may submit to her sway, these things are no criterion of success. She wins not by majorities but by martyrs and the cross is her victory.

Thus in comparison with the optimism of liberalism the Christian view of life and the Christian interpretation of history are profoundly tragic. The true progress of history is a mystery which is fulfilled in failure and suffering and which will only be revealed at the end of time. The victory that overcomes the world is not success but faith and it is only the eye of faith that understands the true value of history.

Viewing history from this standpoint the Christian will not be confident in success or despondent in failure. "For when you shall hear of wars and rumors of wars be not afraid, for the end is not yet." None knows where Europe is going and there is no law of history by which we can predict the future. Nor is the future in our own hands, for the world is ruled by powers that it does not know, and the men who appear to be the makers of history are in reality its creatures. But the portion of the Church is not like these. She has been the guest and the exile, the mistress and the martyr, of nations and civilizations and has survived them all. And in every age and among every people it is her mission to carry on the work of divine restoration and regeneration, which is the true end of history.

—1938.

SECTION II: THE VISION OF THE HISTORIAN

1

The Problem of Metahistory

METAHISTORY is a new word and one which is as yet unfamiliar to the ordinary reader, so that it is perhaps necessary to define what we mean by it before any discussion of its function and value. I take it that the term was coined on the analogy of Metaphysics which is itself by no means an easy word to define. When Aristotle had written his books on Physics, he proceeded to discuss the ultimate concepts that underlie his physical theories: the nature of matter, the nature of being and the cause of motion and change. In the same way Metahistory is concerned with the nature of history, the meaning of history and the cause and significance of historical change. The historian himself is primarily engaged in the study of the past. He does not ask himself why the past is different from the present or what is the meaning of history as a whole. What he wants to know is what actually happened at a particular time and place and what effect it had on the immediate future. The facts may be of little importance, but if they are true facts, they are important to him if he is a true historian. The historian studies the past for its own sake with a disinterested passion that is its own reward.

But if this is so, what difference is there between history and antiquarianism? I think the difference is less than is generally supposed. For it was the great antiquaries of the seventeenth century—Ducange and Mabillon and the Maurists —who were the real founders of modern historical scholarship, and if we wish to find a typical example of the pure historian uncontaminated by any extraneous metahistorical or sociological elements, it is to these men that we should look. Nevertheless, one must admit that if history had been left to these pure historians, it would never have attained the position that it holds in the modern world. It was only when history entered into relations with philosophy and produced the new types of philosophic historians, like Montesquieu and Voltaire, Hume, Robertson and Gibbon, that it became one of the great formative elements in modern thought. This alliance endured throughout the nineteenth century. It was strongest in Germany where it assumed a new form under the influence of German philosophic idealism but it was also dominant elsewhere—in Russia and in Italy above all. In France it was sociology rather than metaphysics that had the greatest influence on the historians from Alexis de Tocqueville and Fustel de Coulanges to Elie Halévy in our own days, while in this country and in the United States the older eighteenth-century tradition of philosophic liberalism persisted throughout the nineteenth century and is not altogether extinct even today.

When modern historians like Mr. Alan Bullock pass a sweeping condemnation on metahistory (*History Today,* February 1951) and demand that it should be banished from the field of historical study, I do not think that they do justice to the part that metahistory has played in the modern historical development or fully realize how pervasive and how inevitable is its influence. For if an age has strong philosophic interests, it is surely inevitable that its philosophy will affect its study of history and that it will not only influence its attitude to history but will determine the choice of the subjects of historical study. If you believe in the theory of progress, for instance, you will see history as the story of progress and you will tend to study that aspect of progress which seems to you the most important, as Lord Acton studied the history of the idea of freedom. And if you are a good historian, as Acton was, your preconceived metahistorical idea will not destroy the value of the historical research which has been motivated by it.

But the influence of metahistory is not confined to periods

of philosophic activity. There is also a theological metahistory which plays a similar role in societies and periods dominated by religious faith. Even the great antiquary historians of whom I have spoken professed a theological metahistory of this kind, though it was so much taken for granted that it does not obtrude upon our attention. Nevertheless, a great historical scholar like Tillemont undoubtedly shared the same metahistorical preconceptions as Bossuet, and all his ponderous tomes were to him nothing more than a series of laborious footnotes inscribed at the foot of a page of divine revelation.

But if all historiography is so pervaded by metahistorical influences, what is the reason for the strong reaction against metahistory which is now so common among English academic historians and which was so well expressed in Mr. Alan Bullock's article? I think this is part of a wider change affecting every side of modern thought and which is philosophical rather than historical in origin. The great movement of philosophic idealism that dominated the nineteenth century has come to an end and consequently the idealist interpretations of history have become discredited. Historians today are in revolt against the metahistory of Hegel and Croce and Collingwood, not because it is metahistorical, but because they feel it to be the expression of a philosophical attitude that is no longer valid; just as the liberal historians of the eighteenth century revolted against the theological metahistory of the previous period. The effect of this great change on historical thought has been very fully discussed by Professor Renier in his remarkable book on *History: Its Purpose and Method,* published in 1950. But Professor Renier does not condemn metahistory as such. On the contrary, he argues that every historian has his philosophy of history, whether he recognizes it or not. Consequently his revolt against the idealist philosophies of history does not lead him to assert the independence of history against philosophy but rather to establish a new relation between history and the current nonidealist forms of philosophy as represented by the pragmatism of Professor Dewey and the logical positivism of Professor Ayer.

Mr. Alan Bullock, on the other hand, did not merely condemn the metahistory of the idealist, he wished to outlaw metahistory altogether. Above all his criticism was directed against all who attempt to find some kind of pattern in history, whether they are sociologists or students of comparative culture like Spengler and Toynbee. These last two writers are often regarded as the typical modern representatives of metahistory. They are the bugbears of the academic historian and it is against them rather than against Collingwood and Croce that the main attack of the critics of metahistory has been directed. Nevertheless, the reasons for this hostility are not so simple as they seem at first sight. Certainly both Spengler and Toynbee are metahistorians and both of them have been deeply influenced by the tradition of philosophic idealism which is today under a cloud. But they are also historians of culture who have ventured beyond the study of a single culture and have embarked on the difficult task of the comparative study of cultures. Now it may be argued that this task exceeds the powers of the historian and that we do not yet possess adequate knowledge to make it possible. But if it is possible, and insofar as it is possible, it belongs to the domain of history rather than of metahistory. The "pure" historian maintains that it is not his business to form general propositions about civilizations as such, but only to trace the rise and fall of such civilizations as the Hellenic and Chinese. But how is he to do this, until he has discovered what a civilization is? And how can he discover this unless he has made some comparative study of other civilizations? It seems to me that Toynbee's initial discussion of the field of historical study and his definition of a civilization as an independent entity that constitutes an intelligible field of historical study are genuinely historical conceptions providing a valuable and necessary criterion for modern historical study. If the academic historians are to criticize his system, it should not be on account of its metahistorical character, but because he has attempted too much with insufficient material; because he has not been content to lay the foundations of a comparative study of culture, but has tried to construct a complete all-embracing system of world history at a single stroke. If this is a mistake, it is one which has been made often enough by historians in the past. Universal history is not metahistory; although it is hardly less unpopular with modern academic historians.

There remains, however, a further possible objection to Toynbee's method. Even if we accept the comparative study of cultures as a legitimate form of knowledge, we may still say that this is not history but sociology; and in Mr. Bullock's view there is an essential difference between the function of the sociologist who is seeking for general laws governing human development and that of the historian who simply "wants to know what has happened." Though this distinction seems a reasonable one, it is one that is extremely difficult to maintain in practice. Mr. Bullock's definition of history, for example, is far too narrow to satisfy the historians themselves. As I have pointed out, French historiography has always had a strong sociological interest, and the best French historians are usually the most sociological. Mr. Bullock himself mentions Elie Halévy and Marc Bloch as representative historians, and I do not think there is anyone who would question this. Yet what is the first volume of Halévy's great *History of the English People* but a sociological study of English culture at the beginning of the nineteenth century? And the same is true of Marc Bloch's two volumes on *Feudal Society*.

Moreover, at the present time the rigid separation of sociology and history is being criticized from the side of the anthropologists. Dr. Evans-Pritchard, the Professor of Social Anthropology at Oxford and the President of The Royal Anthropological Institute, has recently made a masterly survey of the whole problem in the Marett Lecture for 1950; he arrives at the conclusion that sociology is a kind of historiography, and though it is a special kind of historiography it differs from that of the historian in technique and emphasis and perspective but not in method or aim. "When a social anthropologist writes about a society developing in time, he writes a history book, different it is true, from the ordinary narrative and political history, but in all essentials the same as social history." He believes that the present tendency of anthropological studies is in the direction of history and that in the future it will tend to approximate to culture history rather than to model itself on the natural sciences as in the past. Thus Dr. Evans-Pritchard is far from regarding sociology as a kind of metahistory. Indeed, there is a striking resemblance between the attitude of the academic historians to the idealistic metahistory of the nineteenth-century philosophers and that of Professor Evans-Pritchard towards the positivist "meta-sociology" of the nineteenth-century anthropologists, which he condemns in just the same way as Mr. Bullock, when the latter criticizes the attempt "to annex history to a metaphysical system, or to turn it into a science on that out-of-date nineteenth-century model on which the original expectation of the social sciences was founded."

Thus the problem of the relations between history and social anthropology is essentially different from that of their relations to metahistory, which is common to them both. The case of Toynbee is a difficult one because he is at the same time an historian, a sociologist of comparative culture and a metahistorian; his critics often go wrong by confusing his sociology of culture with his philosophy of history and treating both of them as equally metahistorical.

But Toynbee does not stand alone in this respect. Even more complex and more remarkable is the case of Tocqueville who is generally admitted by the academic historians to be one of the great historians of the nineteenth century. Yet Tocqueville is not only an historian and a sociologist: he is also a metahistorian, and his metahistory is religious as well as philosophical. He opens his greatest work by a bold profession of faith in the religious meaning of history and the religious vocation of the historian. "The whole book," he writes, "which is here offered to the public has been written under the impression of a kind of religious dread produced in the author's mind by the contemplation of the irresistible revolution that has advanced for centuries in spite of such amazing obstacles, and which is still proceeding in the midst of the ruins it has made. It is not necessary that God Himself should speak in order to disclose to us the unquestionable signs of His will; we can discern them in the habitual course of nature and in the invariable tendency of events." The modern reader may dismiss such utterances as mere conventional rhetoric. But if he does so he will be profoundly mistaken, for Tocqueville was expressing his deepest convictions. As he wrote to a friend, he regarded his work as "a holy task and one in which one must spare neither one's money nor one's time, nor one's life."

If the metahistorical approach is inconsistent with historical subjectivity, if, as Mr. Bullock writes, history will not "bear the weight of the systems of moral absolutism after which so many people hanker," then Tocqueville's preface to *Democracy in America* is enough to condemn his book from the start as morally pretentious and historically worthless. Yet, somehow he gets away with it, and his two great works still stand today as classical examples of the art of the historian. And he succeeds not in spite of his principles but because of them. If we compare his work with that of his contemporaries who wrote good, straight narrative history like Mignet or Thiers, one must admit that Tocqueville is incomparably the greater historian; he is greater because he is more profound and his profundity is due to the breadth of his spiritual vision and to the strength of his religious faith.

The only conclusion that I can draw from this is that metahistory is not the enemy of true history but its guide and its friend, provided always that it is good metahistory. There were other historians of Tocqueville's generation who also conceived their task in metahistorical terms—for example, Michelet and Carlyle, but the metahistory of the one consists of superficial generalizations and that of the other is a bombastic and interminable sermonizing. Better an antiquary or an annalist than a minor historian who writes like a minor prophet. The academic historian is perfectly right in insisting on the importance of the techniques of historical criticism and research. But the mastery of these techniques will not produce great history, any more than a mastery of metrical technique will produce great poetry. For this something more is necessary—intuitive understanding, creative imagination, and finally a universal vision transcending the relative limitations of the particular field of historical study. The experience of the great historians such as Tocqueville and Ranke leads me to believe that a universal metahistorical vision of this kind, partaking more of the nature of religious contemplation than of scientific generalization, lies very close to the sources of their creative power.

—1951.

2

St. Augustine and the City of God

St. Augustine's work of *The City of God* was, like all his books, a *livre de circonstance,* written with a definitely controversial aim in response to a particular need. But during the fourteen years—from 412 to 426—during which he was engaged upon it, the work developed from a controversial pamphlet into a vast synthesis which embraces the history of the whole human race and its destinies in time and eternity. It is the one great work of Christian antiquity which professedly deals with the relation of the state and of human society in general to Christian principles; and consequently it has had an incalculable influence on the development of European thought. Alike to Orosius and to Charlemagne, to Gregory I and Gregory VII, to St. Thomas and Bossuet, it remained the classical expression of Christian political thought and of the Christian attitude to history. And in modern times it has not lost its importance. It is the only one among the writings of the Fathers which the secular historian never altogether neglects, and throughout the nineteenth century it was generally regarded as justifying the right of St. Augustine to be treated as the founder of the philosophy of history.

Of late years, however, there had been a tendency, especially in Germany, to challenge this claim and to criticize St. Augustine's method as fundamentally anti-historical, since it interprets history according to a rigid theological scheme and regards the whole process of human development as predetermined by timeless and changeless transcendental principles.[1] Certainly *The City of God* is not a philosophical theory of history in the sense of rational induction from historical facts. He does not discover anything from history, but merely sees in history the working out of universal principles. But we may well question whether Hegel or any of the nineteenth-century philosophers of history did otherwise. They did not derive their theories from history, but read their philosophy into history.

What St. Augustine does give us is a synthesis of universal history in the light of Christian principles. His theory of history is strictly deduced from his theory of human nature, which, in turn, follows necessarily from his theology of creation and grace. It is not a rational theory in so far as it begins and ends in revealed dogma; but it is rational in the strict logic of its procedure and it involves a definitely rational and philosophic theory of the nature of society and law and of the relation of social life to ethics.

Herein consists its originality, since it unites in a coherent system two distinct intellectual traditions which had hitherto proved irreconcilable. The Hellenic world possessed a theory of society and a political philosophy, but it had never arrived at a philosophy of history. The Greek mind tended towards cosmological rather than historical speculation. In the Greek view of things, Time had little significance or value. It was the bare "number of movement," an unintelligible element which intruded itself into reality in consequence of the impermanence and instability of sensible things. Consequently it could possess no ultimate or spiritual meaning. It is intelligible only in so far as it is regular—that is to say, tending to a recurrent identity. And this element of recurrence is due to the influence of the heavenly bodies, those eternal and divine existences whose movement imparts to this lower world all that it has of order and intelligibility.

Consequently, in so far as human history consists of unique and individual events it is unworthy of science and philosophy. Its value is to be found only in that aspect of

[1] E.g. H. Grundmann, *Studien über Joachim von Floris* (1927), pp. 74–5; cf. also H. Scholz, *Glaube und Unglaube in der Weltgeschichte* (1911).

it which is independent of time—in the ideal character of the hero, the ideal wisdom of the sage, and the ideal order of the good commonwealth. The only spiritual meaning that history possesses is to be found in the examples that it gives of moral virtue or political wisdom or their opposites. Like Greek art, Greek history created a series of classical types which were transmitted as a permanent possession to later antiquity. Certainly Greece had its philosophical historians, such as Thucydides and, above all, Polybius, but to them also the power which governs history is an external necessity —Nemesis or Tyche—which lessens rather than increases the intrinsic importance of human affairs.

The Christian, on the other hand, possessed no philosophy of society or politics, but he had a theory of history. The time element, in his view of the world, was all-important. The idea, so shocking to the Hellenic mind or to that of the modern rationalist, that God intervenes in history and that a small and uncultured Semitic people had been made the vehicle of an absolute divine purpose, was to him the very centre and basis of his faith. Instead of the theogonies and mythologies which were the characteristic forms of expression in Greek and Oriental religion, Christianity from the first based its teaching on a *sacred history*.[2]

Moreover, this history was not merely a record of past events; it was conceived as the revelation of a divine plan which embraced all ages and peoples. As the Hebrew prophets had already taught that the changes of secular history, the rise and fall of kingdoms and nations, were designed to serve God's ultimate purpose in the salvation of Israel and the establishment of His Kingdom, so the New Testament teaches that the whole Jewish dispensation was itself a stage in the divine plan, and that the barrier between Jew and Gentile was now to be removed so that humanity might be united in an organic spiritual unity.[3] The coming of Christ is the turning-point of history. It marks "the fullness of times," [4] the coming of age of humanity and the fulfilment

[2] Cf. for example, the speech of Stephen in Acts vii.

[3] Eph. ii.

[4] St. Paul uses two expressions (Gal. iv, 4 and Eph. i, 10): $\pi\lambda\acute{\eta}\rho\omega\mu\alpha$ $\tau o\hat{\upsilon}$ $\chi\rho\acute{o}\nu o\upsilon$—the fullness of time in respect to man's age, and $\pi\lambda\acute{\eta}\rho\omega\mu\alpha$ $\tau\hat{\omega}\nu$ $\kappa\alpha\iota\rho\hat{\omega}\nu$—the completion of the cycle of seasons. Cf. Prat, *Théologie de S. Paul* (second edition), II, 151.

of the cosmic purpose. Henceforward mankind had entered on a new phase. The old things had passed away and all things were become new.

Consequently the existing order of things had no finality for the Christian. The kingdoms of the world were judged and their ultimate doom was sealed. The building had been condemned and the mine which was to destroy it was laid, though the exact moment of the explosion was uncertain. The Christian had to keep his eyes fixed on the future like a servant who waits for the return of his master. He had to detach himself from the present order and prepare himself for the coming of the Kingdom.

Now from the modern point of view this may seem to destroy the meaning of history no less effectively than the Hellenic view of the insignificance of time. As Newman writes, "When once the Christ had come . . . nothing remained but to gather in His Saints. No higher Priest could come, no truer doctrine. The Light and Life of men had appeared and had suffered and had risen again; and nothing more was left to do. Earth had had its most solemn event, and seen its most august sight; and therefore it was the last time. And hence, though time intervene between Christ's first and second coming, it is not *recognized* (as I may say) in the Gospel Scheme, but is, as it were, an accident. . . . When He says that He will come soon, 'soon' is not a word of time but of natural order. This present state of things, 'the present distress,' as St. Paul calls it, is ever *close upon* the next world and resolves itself into it." [5]

But on the other hand, although the kingdom for which the Christian hoped was a spiritual and eternal one, it was not a kind of abstract Nirvana, it was a real kingdom which was to be the crown and culmination of history and the realization of the destiny of the human race. Indeed, it was often conceived in a temporal and earthly form; for the majority of the early Fathers interpreted the Apocalypse in a literal sense and believed that Christ would reign with His saints on earth for a thousand years before the final judgment. [6] So vivid and intense was this expectation that the

[5] *Parochial Sermons*, VI, xvii.

[6] Tixeront: *Histoire des Dogmes* I, 217 ff. On millenniarism at Rome in the third century cf. d'Alès, *La Théologie de S. Hippolyte*, v.

new Jerusalem seemed already hovering over the earth in readiness for its descent, and Tertullian records how the soldiers of Severus' army had seen its walls on the horizon, shining in the light of dawn, for forty days, as they marched through Palestine. Such a state of mind might easily lead, as it did in the case of Tertullian, to the visionary fanaticism of Montanism. But even in its excesses it was less dangerous to orthodoxy than the spiritualistic theosophy of the Gnostics, which dissolved the whole historical basis of Christianity, and consequently it was defended by apologists, such as Justin Martyr and Irenaeus, as a bulwark of the concrete reality of the Christian hope.

Moreover, all Christians, whether they were millenniarists or not, believed that they already possessed a pledge and foretaste of the future kingdom in the Church. They were not, like the other religious bodies of the time, a group of individuals united by common beliefs and a common worship, they were a true people. All the wealth of historical associations and social emotion which were contained in the Old Testament had been separated from its national and racial limitations and transferred to the new international spiritual community. Thereby the Church acquired many of the characteristics of a political society; that is to say, Christians possessed a real social tradition of their own and a kind of patriotism which was distinct from that of the secular state in which they lived.

This social dualism is one of the most striking characteristics of early Christianity. Indeed, it is characteristic of Christianity in general; for the idea of the two societies and the twofold citizenship is found nowhere else in the same form. It entered deeply into St. Augustine's thought and supplied the fundamental theme of *The City of God*. In fact, St. Augustine's idea of the two cities is no new discovery but a direct inheritance from tradition. In its early Christian form, however, this dualism was much simpler and more concrete than it afterwards became. The mediaeval problem of the coexistence of the two societies and the two authorities within the unity of the Christian people was yet to arise. Instead there was the abrupt contrast of two opposing orders—the Kingdom of God and the kingdom of this world—the present age and the age to come. The Empire was the society of the past, and the Church was the society of the future, and, though they met and mingled physically, there was no spiritual contact between them. It is true, as we have seen, that the Christian recognized the powers of this world as ordained by God and observed a strict but passive obedience to the Empire. But this loyalty to the state was purely external. It simply meant, as St. Augustine says, that the Church during her commixture with Babylon must recognize the external order of the earthly state which was to the advantage of both—*utamur et nos sua pace*.[7]

Hence there could be no bond of spiritual fellowship or common citizenship between the members of the two societies. In his relations with the state and secular society the Christian felt himself to be an alien—*peregrinus;* his true citizenship was in the Kingdom of Heaven. Tertullian writes, "Your citizenship, your magistracies and the very name of your *curia* is the Church of Christ. . . . We are called away even from dwelling in this Babylon of the Apocalypse, how much more from sharing in its pomps? . . . For you are an alien in this world, and a citizen of the city of Jerusalem that is above." [8]

It is true that Tertullian was a rigorist, but in this respect, at any rate, his attitude does not differ essentially from that of St. Cyprian or of the earlier tradition in general. There was, however, a growing tendency in the third century for Christians to enter into closer relations with the outer world and to assimilate Greek thought and culture. This culminated in Origen's synthesis of Christianity and Hellenism, which had a profound influence, not only on theology, but also on the social and political attitude of Christians. Porphyry remarks that "though Origen was a Christian in his manner of life, he was a Hellene in his religious thought and surreptitiously introduced Greek ideas into alien myths."

This is, of course, the exaggeration of a hostile critic; nevertheless it is impossible to deny that Origen is completely Greek in his attitude to history and cosmology. He broke entirely, not only with the millenniarist tradition, but also with the concrete realism of Christian eschatology, and substituted in its place the cosmological speculations of later Greek philosophy. The Kingdom of God was conceived by him in a metaphysical sense as the realm of spiritual reality

---

[7] *De Civitate Dei*, XIX, xxvi. "That the peace of God's enemies is useful to the piety of His friends as long as their earthly pilgrimage lasts." Cf. also *ibid.*, xvii.

[8] *De Corona*, xiii.

—the supersensuous and intelligible world. The historical facts of Christian revelation consequently tended to lose their unique value and became the symbols of higher immaterial realities—a kind of Christian *Mythos*. In place of the *sacred history* of humanity from the Fall to the Redemption we have a vast cosmic drama like that of the Gnostic systems, in which the heavenly spirits fall from their immaterial bliss into the bondage of matter, or into the form of demons. Salvation consists not in the redemption of the body, but in the liberation of the soul from the bondage of matter and its gradual return through the seven planetary heavens to its original home. Consequently there is no longer any real unity in the human race, since it consists of a number of individual spirits which have become men, so to speak, accidentally, in consequence of their own faults in a previous state of existence.

No doubt these ideas are not the centre of Origen's faith. They are counterbalanced by his orthodoxy of intention and his desire to adhere to Catholic tradition. Nevertheless, they inevitably produced a new attitude to the Church and a new view of its relation to humanity. The traditional conception of the Church as an objective society, the new Israel, and the forerunner of the Kingdom of God fell into the background as compared with a more intellectualist view of the Church as the teacher of an esoteric doctrine or *gnosis* which leads the human soul from time to eternity. Here again Origen is the representative of the Graeco-Oriental ideals which found their full expression in the mystery religions.

The result of this change of emphasis was to reduce the opposition which had previously existed between the Church and secular society. Unlike the earlier Fathers, Origen was quite prepared to admit the possibility of a general conversion of the Empire, and in his work against Celsus he paints a glowing picture of the advantages that the Empire would enjoy if it was united in one great "City of God" under the Christian faith. But Origen's City of God, unlike Augustine's, has perhaps more affinity with the world state of the Stoics than with the divine Kingdom of Jewish and Christian prophecy. It found its fulfilment in the Christian Empire of Constantine and his successors, as we can see from the writings of Eusebius of Cæsarea, the greatest representative of the tradition of Origen in the following age.

Eusebius goes further than any of the other Fathers in his rejection of millenniarism and of the old realistic eschatology. For him prophecy finds an adequate fulfilment in the historical circumstances of his own age. The Messianic Kingdom of Isaiah is the Christian Empire, and Constantine himself is the new David, while the new Jerusalem which St. John saw descending from heaven like a bride adorned for her husband means to Eusebius nothing more than the building of the Church of the Holy Sepulchre at Constantine's orders.[9]

Such a standpoint leaves no room for the old Christian and Jewish social dualism. The emperor is not only the leader of the Christian people, his monarchy is the earthly counterpart and reflection of the rule of the Divine Word. As the Word reigns in heaven, so Constantine reigns on earth, purging it from idolatry and error and preparing men's minds to receive the truth. The kingdoms of this world have become the Kingdom of God and of His Christ, and nothing more remains to do this side of eternity.[10]

It is not enough to dismiss all this as mere flattery on the part of a courtier prelate. The Eusebian ideal of monarchy has a great philosophical and historical tradition behind it. It goes back, on the one hand, to the Hellenistic theory of kingship, as represented by Dio Chrysostom, and, on the other, to the Oriental tradition of sacred monarchy which is as old as civilization itself. It is true that it is not specifically Christian and it is entirely irreconcilable with the strictly religious attitude of men like Athanasius, who were prepared to sacrifice the unity of the Empire to a theological principle. Nevertheless, it was ultimately destined to triumph, at least in the East, for it finds its fulfilment in the Byzantine Church-State indissolubly united under the rule of an Orthodox emperor.

In the West, however, Christian thought followed an entirely different course of development. At the time when

[9] *Life of Constantine*, III, xxxiii. So too he applies the passage in Dan. vii, 17. ("And the saints of the Most High shall receive the Kingdom") to Dalmatius and Hannibalianus, who were made Cæsars by Constantine (*Oration on the Tricennalia of Constantine*, iii.).

[10] Eusebius develops the parallel at great length in his *Oration on the Tricennalia of Constantine*, ii—x.

Origen was creating a speculative theology and a philosophy of religion, the attention of the Western Church was concentrated on the concrete problems of its corporate life. From an intellectual point of view the controversies on discipline and Church order which occupied the Western mind seem barren and uninteresting in comparison with the great doctrinal issues which were being debated in the East. But historically they are the proof of a strong social tradition and of an autonomous and vigorous corporate life.

Nowhere was this tradition so strong as in Africa; indeed, so far as its literary and intellectual expression is concerned, Africa was actually the creator of the Western tradition. By far the larger part of Latin Christian literature is African in origin, and the rest of the Latin West produced no writers, save Ambrose and Jerome, who are worthy to be compared with the great African doctors. This, no doubt, was largely due to the fact that Africa possessed a more strongly marked national character than any other Western province. The old Libyo-Phoenicean population had been submerged by the tide of Roman culture, but it still subsisted, and during the later Empire it began to reassert its national individuality in the same way as did the subject nationalities of the Eastern provinces. And, as in Syria and Egypt, this revival of national feeling found an outlet through religious channels. It did not go so far as to create a new vernacular Christian literature, as was the case in Syria, for the old Punic tongue survived mainly among the peasants and the uneducated classes,[11] but though it expressed itself in a Latin medium, its content was far more original and characteristic than that of the Syriac or Coptic literatures.

This is already apparent in the work of Tertullian, perhaps the most original genius whom the Church of Africa ever produced. After the smooth commonplaces of Fronto or the florid preciosity of Apuleius the rhetoric of Tertullian is at once exhilarating and terrific.[12] It is as though one were to go out of a literary *salon* into a thunderstorm. His work is marked by a spirit of fierce and indomitable hostility to

---

[11] Although the emperor Severus, according to his biographer, found it easier to express himself in Punic than in Latin.

[12] It is true that Tertullian's style is no less artificial than that of Apuleius, by whom he was perhaps influenced, but the general effect that it produces is utterly different.

the whole tradition of pagan civilization, both social and intellectual. He has no desire to minimize the opposition between the Church and the Empire, for all his hopes are fixed on the passing of the present order and the coming of the Kingdom of the Saints. Similarly he has no sympathy with the conciliatory attitude of the Alexandrian School towards Greek philosophy. "What has Athens to do with Jerusalem?" he writes. "What concord is there between the Academy and the Church?" . . . "Our instruction comes from the Porch of Solomon who taught that the Lord should be sought in simplicity of heart. Away with all attempts to produce a mottled Christianity of Stoic, Platonic and dialectic composition. We want no curious disputation after possessing Christ Jesus. . . ." [13]

This uncompromising spirit remained characteristic of the African Church, so that Carthage became the antithesis of Alexandria in the development of Christian thought. It remained a stronghold of the old realistic eschatology and of millenniarist ideas, which were held not only by Tertullian, but by Arnobius and Lactantius and Commodian. The work of the latter, especially, shows how the apocalyptic ideas of the Christians might become charged with a feeling of hostility to the injustice of the social order and to the Roman Empire itself. In his strangely barbaric verses, which, nevertheless, sometimes possess a certain rugged grandeur, Commodian inveighs against the luxury and oppression of the rich and exults over the approaching doom of the heathen world-power.

> *"Tollatur imperium, quod fuit inique repletum,*
> *Quod per tributa mala diu macerabat omnes*
>
> .   .   .   .
>
> *Haec quidem gaudebat, sed tota terra gemebat;*
> *Vix tamen advenit illi retributio digna,*
> *Luget in æternum quæ se jactabat æterna."* [14]

And the same intransigent spirit shows itself in the cult of martyrdom, which attained an extraordinarily high devel-

[13] *De Praescriptione*, vii (Homes's trans.).

[14] *Carmen apologeticum*, 889–90 and 921–3. "May the Empire be destroyed which was filled with injustice and which long afflicted the world with heavy taxes. . . . Rome rejoiced while the whole earth groaned. Yet at last due retribution falls upon her. She who boasted herself eternal shall mourn eternally."

opment in Africa, especially among the lower classes. Cultivated pagans saw in the martyrs the rivals and substitutes of the old gods and regarded their cult as typical of the barbarous anti-Roman or anti-Hellenic spirit of the new religion. Maximus, the old pagan scholar of Madaura, protested to St. Augustine that he could not bear to see Romans leaving their ancestral temples to worship at the tombs of lowborn criminals with vile Punic names, such as Mygdo and Lucitas and Namphanio "and others in an endless list with names abhorred both by gods and men." And he concludes: "It almost seems to me at this time as if a second battle of Actium had begun in which Egyptian monsters, doomed soon to perish, dare to raise their weapons against the gods of the Romans." [15]

In fact the conversion of the Empire had not altered the fierce and uncompromising spirit of African Christianity. On the contrary, the peace of the Church was in Africa merely the occasion of fresh wars. The Donatist movement had its origin, like so many other schisms, in a local dispute on the question of the position of those who had lapsed or compromised their loyalty under the stress of persecution. But the intervention of the Roman state changed what might have been an unimportant local schism into a movement of almost national importance, and roused the native fanaticism of the African spirit. To the Donatists the Catholic Church was "the Church of the traitors," [16] which had sold its birthright and leagued itself "with the princes of this world for the slaughter of the saints." They themselves claimed to be the true representatives of the glorious tradition of the old African Church, for they also were persecuted by the world, they also were a martyr Church, the faithful remnant of the saints.

The African Church had been called by Christ to share in His passion, and the persecution of the Donatists was the first act of the final struggle of the forces of evil against the Kingdom of God. *"Sicut enim in Africa factum est,"* writes Tyconius, *"ita fieri oportet in toto mundo, revelari Anti-*

---

[15] *Ep.* xvi.

[16] *Traditores*—primarily those who had delivered (*tradere*) the sacred books to the authorities during the persecution of Diocletian, but the word also has the evil association of our "traitor."

*christum sicut et nobis ex parte revelatum est." "Ex Africa
manifestabitur omnis ecclesia."* [17]

But the Donatist movement was not only a spiritual protest against any compromise with the world; it also roused
all the forces of social discontent and national fanaticism.
The wild peasant bands of the Circumcellions, who roamed
the country, with their war-cry of *"Deo laudes,"* were primarily religious fanatics who sought an opportunity of martyrdom. But they were also champions of the poor and the
oppressed, who forced the landlords to enfranchise their
slaves and free their debtors, and who, when they met a rich
man driving in his chariot, would make him yield his place
to his footman, as a literal fulfillment of the words of the
Magnificat, *deposuit potentes de sede et exaltavit humiles.*
In fact, we have in Donatism a typical example of the results
of an exclusive insistence on the apocalyptic and antisecular
aspects of Christianity, a tendency which was destined to
reappear at a later period in the excesses of the Taborites, the
Anabaptists and some of the Puritan sects.

The existence of this movement, so powerful, so self-confident, and so uncompromising, had a profound effect on
Augustine's life and thought. The situation of the Church in
Africa was essentially different from anything which existed
elsewhere. The Catholics were not, as in many of the Eastern
provinces, the dominant element in society, nor were they,
as in other parts of the West, the acknowledged representatives of the new faith against paganism. In numbers they
were probably equal to the Donatists, but intellectually they
were the weaker party, since with the exception of Optatus
of Milevis the whole literary tradition of African Christianity
had been in the hands of the Donatists; indeed, from the
schism to the time of Optatus, a space of more than fifty
years, not a single literary representative of the Catholic
cause had appeared.

Hence during the thirty years of his ecclesiastical life St.
Augustine had to fight a continuous battle, not only against

---

[17] From the *Commentary on the Apocalypse* of Beatus in
Monceaux. *Hist. Litt. de l'Afrique Chrétienne,* V, p. 288,
notes 2 and 3: "For as it has been done in Africa, so it must
be done in the whole world and Antichrist must be revealed, as
has been revealed to us in part." "Out of Africa all the Church
shall be revealed."

the paganism and unbelief of the open enemies of Christianity, but also against the fanaticism and sectarianism of his fellow-Christians. The extinction of the Donatist schism was the work to which before all others his later life was dedicated, and it inevitably affected his views of the nature of the Church and its relation to the secular power. The Catholics had been in alliance with the state since the time of Constantine, and relied upon the help of the secular arm both for their own protection and for the suppression of the schismatics. Consequently, Augustine could no longer maintain the attitude of hostile independence towards the state which marked the African spirit, and which the Donatists still preserved. Nevertheless, he was himself a true African. Indeed, we may say that he was an African first and a Roman afterwards, since, in spite of his genuine loyalty towards the Empire, he shows none of the specifically Roman patriotism which marks Ambrose or Prudentius. Rome is to him always "the second Babylon," [18] the supreme example of human pride and ambition, and he seems to take a bitter pleasure in recounting the crimes and misfortunes of her history.[19] On the other hand, he often shows his African patriotism, notably in his reply to the letter of Maximus of Madaura to which I have already referred, where he defends the Punic language from the charge of barbarism.[20]

It is true that there is nothing provincial about Augustine's mind, for he had assimilated classical culture and especially Greek thought to a greater extent than any other Western Father. But for all that he remained an African, the last and greatest representative of the tradition of Tertullian and Cyp-

[18] *De Civitate Dei,* XVIII, ii, xxii.

[19] E.g. the passage on Rome after Cannae in *De Civitate Dei,* III, xix.

[20] "Surely, considering that you are an African and that we are both settled in Africa, you could not have so forgotten yourself when writing to Africans as to think that Punic names were a fit theme for censure. . . . And if the Punic language is rejected by you, you virtually deny what has been admitted by most learned men, that many things have been wisely preserved from oblivion in books written in the Punic tongue. Nay, you ought even to be ashamed of having been born in the country in which the cradle of this language is still warm." *Ep.* xvii. (trans. J. G. Cunningham). Julian of Eclanum often sneers at St. Augustine as "a Punic Aristotle" and "*philosophaster Paenorum.*"

rian, and when he took up the task of defending Christianity against the attacks of the pagans, he was carrying on not only their work, but also their spirit and their thought. If we compare *The City of God* with the works of the great Greek apologists, the *Contra Celsum* of Origen, the *Contra Gentes* of Athanasius and the *Praeparatio Evangelica* of Eusebius, we are at once struck by the contrast of his method. He does not base his treatment of the subject on philosophic and metaphysical arguments, as the Greek Fathers had done, but on the eschatological and social dualism, which, as we have seen, was characteristic of the earliest Christian teaching and to which the African tradition, as a whole, had proved so faithful.

Moreover, the particular form in which Augustine expresses this dualism, and which supplies the central unifying idea of the whole work, was itself derived from an African source, namely from Tyconius, the most original Donatist writer of the fourth century.[21] Tyconius represents the African tradition in its purest and most uncontaminated form. He owes nothing to classical culture or to philosophic ideas; his inspiration is entirely Biblical and Hebraic. Indeed, his interpretation of the Bible resembles that of the Jewish Midrash far more than the ordinary type of patristic exegesis. It is a proof of the two-sidedness of Augustine's genius that he could appreciate the obscure and tortuous originality of Tyconius as well as the limpid classicism of Cicero. He was deeply influenced by Tyconius, not only in his interpretation of scripture,[22] but also in his theology and in his attitude to history; above all, in his central doctrine of the Two Cities. In his commentary on the Apocalypse, Tyconius had written, "Behold two cities, the City of God and the City of the Devil. . . . Of them, one desires to serve the world, and the other to serve Christ; one seeks to reign in this world, the other to fly from this world. One is afflicted, and the other rejoices; one smites, and the other is smitten; one slays, and the other is slain; the one in order to be

[21] Strictly speaking, Tyconius was not a Donatist, but an "Afro-Catholic," since he believed not that the Donatists were the only true Church but that they formed part of the Catholic Church, although they were not in communion with it.

[22] Cf. especially Augustine's incorporation of the "Rules" of Tyconius in his *De Doctrina Christiana*.

the more justified thereby, the other to fill up the measure of its iniquities. And they both strive together, the one that it may receive damnation, the other that it may acquire salvation." [23]

This idea had entered deeply into Augustine's thought from the first. He was already meditating on it at Tagaste in 390; in 400 he makes use of it in his treatise *On Catechizing the Unlearned,* and finally, in *The City of God,* he makes it the subject of his greatest work. In his mind, however, the idea had acquired a more profound significance than that which Tyconius had given it. To the latter, the Two Cities were apocalyptic symbols derived from the imagery of the Bible and bound up with his realistic eschatological ideas. To Augustine, on the other hand, they had acquired a philosophic meaning and had been related to a rational theory of sociology. He taught that every human society finds its constituent principle in a common will—a will to life, a will to enjoyment, above all, a will to peace. He defines a people as a "multitude of rational creatures associated in a common agreement as to the things which it loves." [24] Hence, in order to see what a people is like we must consider the objects of its love. If the society is associated in a love of that which is good, it will be a good society; if the objects of its love are evil, it will be bad. And thus the moral law of individual and social life are the same, since both to the city and to the individual we can apply the same principle—*non faciunt bonos vel malos mores nisi boni vel mali amores.*

And thus the sociology of St. Augustine is based on the same psychological principle which pervades his whole thought—the principle of the all-importance of the will and the sovereignty of love. The power of love has the same importance in the spiritual world as the force of gravity possesses in the physical world.[25] As a man's love moves him, so must he go, and so must he become; *pondus meum amor meus, eo feror quocumque feror.*

And though the desires of men appear to be infinite they

[23] Beatus, *Comm. in Apocalypsin,* ed. Florez, pp. 506–7.

[24] *De Civitate Dei,* XIX, xxiv.

[25] Following the Aristotelian theory according to which every substance naturally tends to its "proper place"—τόπος οἰκεῖος, cf. Augustine, *Confessions,* XIII, i, x; *De Civitate Dei,* XI, xxviii.

are in reality reducible to one. All men desire happiness, all seek after peace; and all their lusts and hates and hopes and fears are directed to that final end. The only essential difference consists in the nature of the peace and happiness that are desired, for, by the very fact of his spiritual autonomy, man has the power to choose his own good; either to find his peace in subordinating his will to the divine order, or to refer all things to the satisfaction of his own desires and to make himself the centre of his universe—"a darkened image of the divine Omnipotence." It is here and here only that the root of dualism is to be found: in the opposition between the "natural man" who lives for himself and desires only a material felicity and a temporal peace, and the spiritual man who lives for God and seeks a spiritual beatitude and a peace which is eternal. The two tendencies of will produce two kinds of men and two types of society, and so we finally come to the great generalization on which St. Augustine's work is founded. "Two lives built two Cities—the earthly, which is built up by the love of self to the contempt of God, and the heavenly, which is built up by the love of God to the contempt of self." [26]

From this generalization springs the whole Augustinian theory of history, since the two cities "have been running their course mingling one with the other through all the changes of times from the beginning of the human race, and shall so move on together until the end of the world, when they are destined to be separated at the last judgment." [27]

In the latter part of *The City of God* (Books xv to xviii) St. Augustine gives a brief synopsis of world history from this point of view. On the one hand he follows the course of the earthly city—the mystical Babylon—through the ages, and finds its completest manifestation in the two world empires of Assyria and Rome "to which all the other Kingdoms are but appendices." On the other hand, he traces the development of the heavenly City: from its beginnings with the patriarchs, through the history of Israel and the holy city of the first Jerusalem down to its final earthly manifestation in the Catholic Church.

[26] *De Civitate Dei*, XIV, xxviii.

[27] *De Catechizandis Rudibus*, XXI, xxxvii; cf. *ibid.*, XIX, xxxi and *De Civitate Dei*, XIV, i, xxviii, XV, i, ii.

The rigid simplification of history which such a sketch demands necessarily emphasizes the uncompromising severity of St. Augustine's thought. At first sight he seems, no less than Tertullian or Commodian, to condemn the state and all secular civilization as founded on human pride and selfishness, and to find the only good society in the Church and the Kingdom of the Saints. And in a sense this conclusion does follow from the Augustinian doctrine of man. The human race has been vitiated at its source. It has become a waste product—a *massa damnata*. The process of redemption consists in grating a new humanity on to the old stock, and in building a new world out of the *débris* of the old. Consequently, in the social life of unregenerate humanity St. Augustine sees a flood of infectious and hereditary evil against which the unassisted power of the individual will struggles in vain. "Woe to thee," he cries, "thou river of human custom! Who shall stop thy course? How long will it be before thou art dried up? How long wilt thou roll the sons of Eve into that great and fearful ocean which even they who have ascended the wood (of the Cross) can scarcely cross?" [28]

This view of human nature and of the social burden of evil finds still further confirmation in the spectacle of universal history. St. Augustine, no less than St. Cyprian,[29] sees the kingdoms of the world founded in injustice and prospering by bloodshed and oppression. He did not share the patriotic optimism of writers like Eusebius and Prudentius, for he realized, more keenly perhaps than any other ancient writer, at what a cost of human suffering the benefits of the imperial unity had been purchased. "The imperial city," he writes, "endeavours to communicate her language to all the lands she has subdued to procure a fuller society and a greater abundance of interpreters on both sides. It is true, but how many lives has this cost! and suppose that done, the worst is not past, for . . . the wider extension of her empire produced still greater wars. . . . Wherefore he that does but consider with compassion all these extremes of sorrow and bloodshed must needs say that this is a mystery. But he that endures them without a sorrowful emotion or thought thereof, is

[28] *Confessions*, I, xxv.
[29] Cf. especially St. Cyprian's *Epistle to Donatus*.

far more wretched to imagine he has the bliss of a god when he has lost the natural feelings of a man." [30]

In the same way the vaunted blessings of Roman law are only secured by an infinity of acts of injustice to individuals, by the torture of innocent witnesses and the condemnation of the guiltless. The magistrate would think it wrong not to discharge the duties of his office, "but he never holds it a sin to torture innocent witnesses, and when he has made them their own accusers, to put them to death as guilty." [31] Consequently the consideration of history leads Augustine to reject the political idealism of the philosophers and to dispute Cicero's thesis that the state rests essentially on justice. If this were the case, he argues, Rome itself would be no state; in fact, since true justice is not to be found in any earthly kingdom, the only true state will be the City of God. [32] Accordingly, in order to avoid this extreme conclusion he eliminates all moral elements from his definition of the state, and describes it, in the passage to which I have already referred, as based on a common will, whether the object of that will be good or bad. [33]

The drastic realism of this definition has proved shocking to several modern writers on Augustine. Indeed, so distinguished a student of political thought as Dr. A. J. Carlyle is unwilling to admit that St. Augustine really meant what he said, [34] and he cites the famous passage in Book iv, chapter 4, "Set justice aside and what are kingdoms but great robberies," [35] to show that the quality of justice is essential to any real state. The actual tendency of the passage, however, appears to be quite the contrary. St. Augustine is arguing that there is no difference between the conqueror and the robber except the scale of their operations, for, he continues, "What is banditry but a little kingdom?" and he approves the reply

[30] *De Civitate Dei,* XIX, vii (trans. J. Healey).

[31] *De Civitate Dei,* XIX, vi.

[32] *De Civitate Dei,* II, xxi.

[33] Cf. note 24 above.

[34] "If he did," he writes, "I cannot but feel that it was a deplorable error for a great Christian teacher." *Social and Political Ideas of Some Great Mediæval Thinkers,* ed. F. J. C. Hearnshaw, p. 51.

[35] *Remota justitia quid regna nisi magna latrocinia?*

of the pirate to Alexander the Great, "Because I do it, with a little ship, I am called a robber, and you, because you do it with a great fleet, are called an emperor."

In reality there is nothing inconsistent or morally discreditable about St. Augustine's views. They follow necessarily from his doctrine of original sin; indeed, they are implicit in the whole Christian social tradition and they frequently find expression in later Christian literature. The famous passage in the letter of Pope Gregory VII to Hermann of Metz, which has been regarded by many modern writers as showing his belief in the diabolic origin of the state, is simply an assertion of the same point of view; while Newman, who in this, as in so many other respects, is a faithful follower of the patristic tradition, affirms the same principle in the most uncompromising terms. "Earthly kingdoms," he says, "are founded, not in justice, but in injustice. They are created by the sword, by robbery, cruelty, perjury, craft and fraud. There never was a kingdom, except Christ's, which was not conceived and born, nurtured and educated, in sin. There never was a state, but was committed to acts and maxims which is its crime to maintain and its ruin to abandon. What monarchy is there but began in invasion or usurpation? What revolution has been effected without self-will, violence or hypocrisy? What popular government but is blown about by every wind, as if it had no conscience and no responsibilities? What dominion of the few but is selfish and unscrupulous? Where is military strength without the passion for war? Where is trade without the love of filthy lucre, which is the root of all evil?" [36]

But from this condemnation of the actual reign of injustice in human society it does not follow that either Newman or Augustine intended to suggest that the state belonged to a non-moral sphere and that men in their social relations might follow a different law to that which governed their moral life as individuals. On the contrary, St. Augustine frequently insists that it is Christianity which makes good citizens, and that the one remedy for the ills of society is to be found in the same power which heals the moral weakness of the individual soul. "Here also is security for the welfare and renown of a commonwealth; for no state is perfectly estab-

[36] From "Sanctity the Token of the Christian Empire" in *Sermons on Subjects of the Day* (1st ed.), p. 273.

lished and preserved otherwise than on the foundations and by the bond of faith and of firm concord, when the highest and truest good, namely God, is loved by all, and men love each other in Him without dissimulation because they love one another for His sake." [37]

Moreover, though St. Augustine emphasizes so strongly the moral dualism which is inherent in the Christian theory of life, he differs from the earlier representatives of the African school in his intense realization of a universal reasonable order which binds all nature together and which governs alike the stars in their courses and the rise and fall of kingdoms. This belief is one of the fundamental elements in Augustine's thought. It dominated his mind in the first days of his conversion, when he composed the treatise *De Ordine,* and it was preserved unimpaired to the last. It finds typical expression in the following passage in *The City of God:* "The true God from Whom is all being, beauty, form and number, weight and measure; He from Whom all nature, mean and excellent, all seeds of forms, all forms of seeds, all motions both of forms and seeds, derive and have being; . . . He (I say) having left neither heaven nor earth, nor angel nor man, no, nor the most base and contemptible creature, neither the bird's feather, nor the herb's flower, nor the tree's leaf, without the true harmony of their parts, and peaceful concord of composition; it is in no way credible that He would leave the kingdoms of men and their bondage and freedoms loose and uncomprised in the laws of His eternal providence." [38]

Here Augustine is nearer to Origen than Tertullian; in fact this fundamental concept of the Universal Law—*lex æterna*—is derived from purely Hellenic sources. It is the characteristically Greek idea of cosmic order which pervades the whole Hellenic tradition from Heraclitus and Pythagoras to the later Stoics and neo-Platonists, and which had reached Augustine by way of Cicero and Plotinus.[39] This Hellenic influence is to be seen above all in Augustine's profound sense of the æsthetic beauty of order and in his

[37] *Ep.* cxxxvii, 5, 18 (trans. Cunningham); cf. *Ep.* cxxxviii, 15 and 17.

[38] *De Civitate Dei,* V, xi (trans. J. Healey).

[39] Cf. P. A. Schubert, *Augustins Lex Æterna Lehre nach Inhalt und Quellen* (1924).

doctrine that even the evil and suffering of the world find their aesthetic justification in the universal harmony of creation, an idea which had already found classic expression in the great lines of Cleanthes' Hymn to Zeus:

"Thou knowest how to make even that which is uneven and to order what is disordered, and unlovely things are lovely to Thee. For so Thou bringest together all things in one, the good with the bad, that there results from all one reasonable order abiding for ever."

Thus St. Augustine was able to view history from a much wider standpoint than that of Tertullian or the Donatists. He can admit that the Earthly City also has its place in the universal order, and that the social virtues of the worldly, which from a religious point of view are often nothing but "splendid vices," yet possess a real value in their own order, and bear their appropriate fruits in social life. And in the same way he believes that the disorder and confusion of history are only apparent, and that God orders all events in His Providence in a universal harmony which the created mind cannot grasp.

This philosophic universalism is not confined to Augustine's conception of the order of nature; it also affects his eschatology and his doctrine of the Church. Above all, it determined his treatment of the central theme of his great work—*The City of God*—and entirely alienated him from the realistic literalism of the old apocalyptic tradition. To Augustine, the City of God is not the concrete millennial kingdom of the older apologists, nor is it the visible hierarchical Church. It is a transcendent and timeless reality, a society of which "the King is Truth, the law is Love and the duration is Eternity." [40] It is older than the world, since its first and truest citizens are the angels. It is as wide as humanity, since "in all successive ages Christ is the same Son of God, co-eternal with the Father, and the unchangeable Wisdom by Whom every rational soul is made blessed." Consequently, "from the beginning of the human race whosoever believed in Him and in any way knew Him, and lived in a pious and just manner according to His precepts, was undoubtedly saved by Him in whatsoever time and place he may have lived." [41]

---

[40] *Ep.* cxxxviii, 3, 17.
[41] *Ep.* cii, 2, 11 and 12.

Thus the City of God is co-extensive with the spiritual creation in so far as it has not been vitiated by sin. It is, in fact, nothing less than the spiritual unity of the whole universe, as planned by the Divine Providence, and the ultimate goal of creation.

These conceptions are quite irreconcilable with the old millenniarist belief which was still so strong in the West, and which Augustine himself had formerly accepted. They led him to adopt Tyconius's interpretation of the crucial passage in the Apocalypse, according to which the earthly reign of Christ is nothing else but the life of the Church militant: an explanation which henceforth gained general acceptance in the West. Moreover, he went further than Tyconius himself and the great majority of earlier writers by abandoning all attempts to give the data of prophecy an exact chronological interpretation with regard to the future, and by discouraging the prevalent assumption of the imminence of the end of the world.[42]

Thus St. Augustine influenced Christian eschatology in the West no less decisively than Origen had done in the East almost two centuries earlier, and to some extent their influences tended in the same direction. To Augustine, as to Origen, the ideal of the kingdom of God acquired a metaphysical form, and became identified with the ultimate timeless reality of spiritual being. The Augustinian City of God bears a certain resemblance to the neo-Platonic concept of the Intelligible World—κόσμος νοητὸς: indeed, the Christian Platonists of later times, who were equally devoted to Augustine and Plotinus, deliberately make a conflation of the two ideas. Thus John Norris of Bemerton writes of his "Ideal World": "Thou art that Glorious Jerusalem, whose foundations are upon the Holy Hills, the everlasting Mountains, even the Eternal Essences and Immutable Ideas of Things. . . . Here are τὰ ὄντα—the Things that are and that truly and chiefly are *quae vere summeque sunt*, as St. Austin speaks and that because they necessarily and immutably are, and cannot either not be or be otherwise. Here live, flourish

---

[42] *Ep.* cxcix. In another passage he even goes so far as to entertain the hypothesis of the world being still in existence 500,000 years hence (*De Civitate Dei*, XII, xii); elsewhere, however, he speaks of the world having reached old age (e.g. *Sermo* xxxi. 8; *Ep.* cxxxvii, 16).

and shine those bright and unperishing Realities whereof the Things of this World are but the Image, the Reflection, the Shadow, the Echo." [43]

This Platonic idealism did indeed leave a deep imprint on St. Augustine's thought. Nevertheless, he never went so far in this direction as Origen had done, for his Platonism did not destroy his sense of the reality and importance of the historical process. To Origen, on the contrary, the temporal process had no finality. There was an infinite succession of worlds through which the immortal soul pursued its endless course. Since "the soul is immortal and eternal, it is possible that, in the many and endless periods of duration in the immeasurable and different worlds, it may descend from the highest good to the lowest evil, or be restored from the lowest evil to the highest good." [44] This is not precisely the classical Hellenic doctrine, since, as I have pointed out elsewhere,[45] Origen expressly rejects the theory of the Return of All Things as irreconcilable with a belief in free will. It has a much closer resemblance to the Hindu doctrine of *samsara* —the endless chain of existences, which are the fruit of the soul's own acts. But although this theory allows for the freedom of the will, it is destructive of the organic unity of humanity and of the significance of its social destinies to an even greater extent than the purely Hellenic doctrine. Consequently, St. Augustine rejected it no less firmly than the theory of cyclic recurrence. He admits that the idea of a perpetual return is a natural consequence of the belief in the eternity of the world, but if we once accept the doctrine of Creation, as Origen himself did, there is no further need for the theory of "the circumrotation of souls," or for the belief that nothing new or final can take place in time. Humanity has had an absolute beginning and travels to an absolute goal. There can be no return. That which is begun in time is consummated in eternity.[46] Hence time is not a perpetually revolving image of eternity; it is an irreversible process moving in a definite direction.

[43] J. Norris, *An Essay Towards the Theory of the Ideal or Intelligible World*, I, 430–6 (1701).

[44] Origen: *De Principiis*, III, i, 21 (trans. I. Crombie).

[45] *Progress and Religion* (London, 1929), p. 156.

[46] *De Civitate Dei*, XII, xi–xx, XXI, xvii.

This recognition of the uniqueness and irreversibility of the temporal process—this "explosion of the perpetual cycles" —is one of the most remarkable achievements of St. Augustine's thought. It is true that the change of attitude was implicit in Christianity itself, since the whole Christian revelation rests on temporal events which nevertheless possess an absolute significance and an eternal value. As St. Augustine says, Christ is the straight way by which the mind escapes from the circular maze of pagan thought.[47] But although this change had been realized by faith and religious experience, it still awaited philosophic analysis and definition. This it received from St. Augustine, who was not only founder of the Christian philosophy of history, but was actually the first man in the world to discover the meaning of time.

His subtle and profound mind found a peculiar attraction in the contemplation of the mystery of time which is so essentially bound up with the mystery of created being.[48] He was intensely sensitive to the pathos of mutability—*omnis quippe iste ordo pulcherrima rerum valde bonarum modis suis peractis transiturus est; et mane quippe in eis factum est et vespera* [49] but he felt that the very possibility of this act of contemplation showed that the mind in some sense transcended the process which it contemplated. Consequently he could not rest satisfied with the naïve objectivism of Greek science which identified time with the movement of the heavenly bodies.[50] If the movement of bodies is the only measure of time, how can we speak of past and future? A movement which has passed has ceased to exist, and a movement which is to come has not begun to exist. There remains only the present of the passing moment, a moving point in nothingness. Therefore, he concludes, the measure of time is not to be found in things, but in the soul—time is spiritual extension—*distentio animæ*.

Thus the past is the soul's remembrance, the future is its

[47] "*Viam rectam sequentes, quae nobis est Cristus, eo duce et salvatore a vano et inepto impiorum circumitu iter fidei mentemque avertamus.*" *De Civitate Dei,* XII, xx.

[48] Cf. *De Civitate Dei,* XII, xv, xi, vi.

[49] *Confessions,* XIII, xxxv. "For all this most fair order of things truly good will pass away when its measures are accomplished, and they have their morning and their evening."

[50] *Confessions,* XI, xxiii.

expectation, and the present is its attention. The future, which does not exist, cannot be long; what we mean by a long future is a long expectation of the future, and a long past means a long memory of the past. "It is, then, in thee, my soul, that I measure time. . . . The impression which things make upon thee as they pass and which remains when they have passed away is what I measure. I measure this which is present, and not the things which have passed away that it might be. Therefore this is time (*tempora*) or else I must say that I do not measure time at all." [51]

Finally, he compares the time-process with the recitation of a poem which a man knows by heart. Before it is begun the recitation exists only in anticipation; when it is finished it is all in the memory; but while it is in progress, it exists, like time, in three dimensions—"the life of this my action is extended into the memory, on account of what I have said, and into expectation, on account of what I am about to say; yet my attention remains present and it is through this that what was future is transposed and becomes past." And what is true of the poem holds good equally of each line and syllable of it, and of the wider action of which it forms part, and also of the life of man which is composed of a series of such actions, and of the whole world of man which is the sum of individual lives.[52]

Now this new theory of time which St. Augustine originated also renders possible a new conception of history. If man is not the slave and creature of time, but its master and creator, then history also becomes a creative process. It does not repeat itself meaninglessly; it grows into organic unity with the growth of human experience. The past does not die; it becomes incorporated in humanity. And hence progress is possible, since the life of society and of humanity itself possesses continuity and the capacity for spiritual growth no less than the life of the individual.

How far St. Augustine realized all this may indeed be questioned. Many modern writers do, in fact, deny that he conceived of the possibility of progress or that he had any real historical sense. They argue, as I said before, that *The City of God* conceives humanity as divided between two

[51] *Ibid.*, XI, xxvii.
[52] *Confessions*, XI, xxviii.

static eternal orders whose eternal lot is predestined from the beginning. But this criticism is, I think, due to a misconception of the Augustinian attitude to history. It is true that Augustine did not consider the problem of secular progress, but then secular history, in Augustine's view, was essentially unprogressive. It was the spectacle of humanity perpetually engaged in chasing its own tail. The true history of the human race is to be found in the process of enlightenment and salvation by which human nature is liberated and restored to spiritual freedom. Nor did Augustine view this process in an abstract and unhistorical way. For he constantly insists on the organic unity of the history of humanity, which passes through a regular succession of ages, like the life of an individual man; [53] and he shows how "the epochs of the world are linked together in a wonderful way" by the gradual development of the divine plan.[54] For God, who is "the unchangeable Governor as He is the unchangeable Creator of mutable things, orders all events in His providence until the beauty of the completed course of time, of which the component parts are the dispensations adapted to each successive age, shall be finished, like the grand melody of some ineffably wise master of song." [55]

It is true, as we have already seen, that in *The City of God* St. Augustine always emphasizes the eternal and transcendent character of the Heavenly City in contrast to the mutability and evil of earthly life. It is impossible to identify the City of God with the Church as some writers have done, since in the Heavenly City there is no room for evil or imperfection, no admixture of sinners with the saints. But, on the other hand, it is an even more serious error to separate the two concepts completely and to conclude that St. Augustine assigned no absolute and transcendent value to the hierarchical Church. Certainly the Church is not the eternal City of God, but it is its organ and representative in the world. It is the point at which the transcendent spiritual order inserts itself into the sensible world, the one bridge by which the creature can pass from Time to Eternity. St. Augustine's point of view is, in fact, precisely the same as that

---

[53] E.g. *De Vera Religione*, XXVII, 1.

[54] *Ep.* cxxxvii, 15.

[55] *Ep.* cxxxviii, 5 (trans. Cunningham).

which Newman so often expresses, though their terminology is somewhat different. Like Augustine, Newman emphasizes the spiritual and eternal character of the City of God and regards the visible Church as its earthly manifestation. "The unseen world through God's secret power and mercy encroaches upon this; and the Church that is seen is just that portion of it by which it encroaches, it is like the islands in the sea, which are in truth but the tops of the everlasting hills, high and vast and deeply rooted, which a deluge covers." [56]

And neither in the case of St. Augustine nor in that of Newman does this emphasizing of the transcendence and spirituality of the City of God lead to any depreciation of the hierarchical Church. The latter describes the Christian Church as an Imperial power—"not a mere creed or philosophy but a *counter kingdom.*" "It occupied ground; it claimed to rule over those whom hitherto this world's governments ruled over without rival; and it is only in proportion as things that are brought into this kingdom and made subservient to it; it is only as kings and princes, nobles and rulers, men of business and men of letters, the craftsman and the trader and the labourer humble themselves to Christ's Church and (in the language of the prophet Isaiah) 'bow down to her with their faces toward the earth and lick up the dust of her feet,' that the world becomes living and spiritual, and a fit object of love and a resting-place for Christians." [57]

The late Dr. Figgis, in his admirable lectures: *The Political Aspects of St. Augustine's "City of God,"* has referred to this sermon of Newman as showing how far later Western tradition carried "the political way of thinking about the Church, which had been inaugurated by St. Augustine." But here again Newman's teaching really represents, not the views of his own time nor even those of the Middle Ages, but a deliberate revival of the patristic Augustinian doctrines. We have seen how primitive Christianity, and the early Western tradition in particular, showed an intense social realism in their eschatology and in their conception of the Church and the Kingdom of God. St. Augustine definitely abandoned

[56] "The Communion of Saints" in *Parochial Sermons* (1st ed.), IV, p. 201.

[57] *Sermons on Subjects of the Day* (1st ed.), pp. 257 and 120.

the millenniarist tradition and adopted a thoroughly spiritual eschatology. But he preserved the traditional social realism in his attitude to the Church: indeed, he reinforced it by his identification of the Church with the millennial kingdom of the Apocalypse. *Ecclesia et nunc est regnum Christi regnumque cælorum.*[58] Consequently it is in the Church that the prophecies of the kingdom find their fulfilment, and even those which seem to refer to the last Judgment may really be applied to "that advent of the Saviour by which He is coming through all the present time in His Church, that is to say in His members, gradually and little by little, for it is all His Body." [59]

"O beata ecclesia," he writes, *"quodam tempore audisti, quodam tempore vidisti. . . . Omnia enim quæ modo complentur antea prophetata sunt. Erige oculos ergo, et diffunde per mundum: vide jam hereditatem usque ad terminos orbis terræ. Vide jam impleri quod dictum est: Adorabunt eum omnes reges terræ, omnes gentes servient illi."* [60]

The grain of mustard-seed has grown until it is greater than all the herbs, and the great ones of this world have taken refuge under its branches. The yoke of Christ is on the neck of kings, and we have seen the head of the greatest empire that the world has known laying aside his crown and kneeling before the tomb of the Fisherman.[61]

Hence Augustine bases his claim to make use of the secular power against the Donatists, not on the right of the state to intervene in religious matters, but on the right of the Church to make use of the powers of this world which God has subdued to Christ according to His prophecy: "All

[58] *De Civitate Dei*, XX, x.

[59] *De Civitate Dei*, XX, v.

[60] *Enarrationes in Psalmos*, LXVII, vii. "O blessed Church, once thou hast heard, now thou hast seen. For what the Church has heard in promises, she now sees manifested. For all things that were formerly prophesied, are now fulfilled. Lift up thine eyes and look abroad over the world. Behold now thine inheritance even to the ends of the earth. See now fulfilled what was spoken: 'All the kings of the earth shall worship Him, all nations shall do Him service.'"

[61] *Sermo* xliv, 2; *Ep.* ccxxxii, 3. We may observe that the same facts on which Eusebius rests his glorification of the Emperor are used by Augustine to exalt the Church.

the kings of the earth shall adore Him and all nations shall serve Him"—"*et ideo hac Ecclesiæ potestate utimur, quam ei Dominus et promisit et dedit.*" [62]

To some—notably to Reuter and Harnack—this exaltation of the visible Church has seemed fundamentally inconsistent with the Augustinian doctrine of grace. It is indeed difficult to understand Augustine's theology if we approach it from the standpoint of the principles of the Reformation. But if we ignore modern developments, and study Augustine's doctrine of grace and the Church from a purely Augustinian standpoint, its unity and consistency are manifest.

St. Augustine never separates the moral from the social life. The dynamic force of both the individual and the society is found in the will, and the object of their will determines the moral character of their life. And as the corruption of the will by original sin in Adam becomes a social evil by an hereditary transmission through the flesh which unites fallen humanity in the common slavery of concupiscence, so too the restoration of the will by grace in Christ is a social good which is transmitted sacramentally by the action of the Spirit and unites regenerate humanity in a free spiritual society under the law of charity. The grace of Christ is only found in "the society of Christ." "Whence," says he, "should the City of God originally begin or progressively develop or ultimately attain its end, unless the life of the saints was a social one?" [63] Thus the Church is actually the new humanity in process of formation, and its earthly history is that of the building of the City of God which has its completion in eternity, "*Adhuc ædificatur templum Dei.*" [64] "*Vos tanquam lapides vivi coædificamini in templum Dei.*" [65] Hence, in spite of all the imperfections of the earthly Church, it is nevertheless the most perfect society that this world can know. Indeed, it is the only true society, because it is the only society which has its source in a spiritual will. The kingdoms of the earth seek after the goods of the earth; the

[62] *Ep.* cv, 5, 6; cf. *Ep.* xxxv, 3. "And, therefore, we are making use of this power which the Lord both promised and gave to the Church."

[63] *De Civitate Dei*, XIX, v.

[64] *Sermo* clxiii, 3.

[65] *Ibid.*, clvi, 12, 13.

Church, and the Church alone, seeks spiritual goods and a peace which is eternal.

Such a doctrine may seem to leave little room for the claims of the state. In fact, it is difficult to deny that the state does occupy a very subordinate position in St. Augustine's view. At its worst it is a hostile power, the incarnation of injustice and self-will. At its best, it is a perfectly legitimate and necessary society, but one which is limited to temporary and partial ends, and it is bound to subordinate itself to the greater and more universal spiritual society in which even its own members find their real citizenship. In fact, the state bears much the same relation to the Church that a Friendly Society or a guild bears to the state: it fulfils a useful function and has a right to the loyalty of its members, but it can never claim to be the equal of the larger society or to act as a substitute for it.

It is on the ground of these conceptions that St. Augustine has so often been regarded as the originator of the mediaeval theocratic ideal, and even (by Reuter) as "the founder of Roman Catholicism." [66] And indeed it is to him more than any other individual that we owe the characteristically Western ideal of the Church as a dynamic social power in contrast to the static and metaphysical conceptions which dominated Byzantine Christianity. But it does not necessarily follow that the influence of St. Augustine tended to weaken the moral authority of the state or to deprive ordinary social life of spiritual significance. If we consider the matter, not from the narrow standpoint of the juristic relations of Church and state, but as St. Augustine himself did, from the point of view of the relative importance of the spiritual and material element in life, we shall see that his doctrine really made for moral freedom and responsibility. Under the Roman Empire, as in the sacred monarchies of the Oriental type, the state is exalted as a superhuman power against which the individual personality had no rights and the individual will had no power. In the East, even Christianity proved powerless to change this tradition, and alike in the Byzantine Empire and in Russia the Church consecrated anew the old Oriental ideal of an omnipotent sacred state

[66] Cf. C. H. Turner in the *Cambridge Mediaeval History*, I, 173: "St. Augustine's theory of the *Civitas Dei* was, in germ, that of the mediaeval papacy, without the name of Rome."

and a passive people. In the West, however, St. Augustine broke decisively with this tradition by depriving the state of its aura of divinity and seeking the principle of social order in the human will. In this way the Augustinian theory, for all its otherworldliness, first made possible the ideal of a social order resting upon the free personality and a common effort towards moral ends. And thus the Western ideals of freedom and progress and social justice owe more than we realize to the profound thought of the great African who was himself indifferent to secular progress and to the transitory fortunes of the earthly state, "for he looked for a city that has foundations whose builder and maker is God."

—1930.

3

Edward Gibbon and the Fall of Rome

I

THE eighteenth century is not usually regarded as an historically minded age. Indeed there is an anti-historical quality in the mind of the eighteenth century which is not to be found in either of the centuries that preceded and followed it. It possessed neither the antiquarian and traditionalist spirit of the seventeenth century nor the romantic spirit which inspired the historical achievement of the nineteenth century. The leaders of eighteenth-century thought often show a positive contempt and hatred for the past. Or else they write as though they had transcended the limitations of time by an effort of pure reason so that they could look down on history from the summit of their philosophy with an Olympian detachment and calm.

Nevertheless the eighteenth century was in its own way profoundly interested in history. There has never been an age when history was more fashionable or when the man of letters was more often an historian. Practically all the leading thinkers and writers of the age devoted themselves to the theory and practice of the art of history from Montesquieu and Voltaire to Mably and Raynal and from Bolingbroke and Hume to Goldsmith and Adam Ferguson.

This literary tendency in eighteenth-century historiography was not without its advantages. It brought history out of the study and the cell into the world—at least into the rather limited world of polite society. The new historians of the school of Voltaire were not content to dig for facts among dusty archives. They aspired to trace the history of the human spirit and the development of human civilization. They were the first to conceive the ideal of a history that was not a mere chronicle of events, but which should embrace every aspect of social life and which would deal with the intellectual as well as the political achievements of society: in short, the ideal of culture history. On the other hand the gain in breadth of treatment was compensated by a loss of depth. The literary historian was more anxious to be considered a man of taste and wit than a man of learning. Too often he wrote history as we write historical biography today, and though he made ample use of the works of his great predecessors of the school of Tillemont and Mabillon he referred to their laborious scholarship with a shade of contempt. Voltaire's most ambitious historical essay—the *Essai sur les Mœurs*—was written for the entertainment of a lady who professed her distaste for history,[1] and he was not afraid to profess his contempt for historical details, which he even refers to on one occasion as "the vermin that destroy books." [2]

II

To this tendency there is, however, one great exception. Edward Gibbon is the classical representative of eighteenth-century historiography, yet he was no less great as a man of learning than as a man of letters. He shared the presuppositions of Hume and Voltaire: he also aspired to write history as a philosopher and a man of taste; but whereas with Voltaire or Montesquieu philosophy often overpowers history and learning is sacrificed to literature, Gibbon achieves a complete fusion between history and literature and the mastery of his style only reflects a no less perfect mastery over his material. To the other philosophic historians, with the exception of Robertson, the writing of history was a parergon and often only the amusement of their leisure

[1] *Essai sur les Mœurs*, ch. 1.
[2] Letter to the Abbé Dubos.

hours, to Gibbon it was his life's work. In this at least he resembles the historians of an earlier time, such as Tillemont and Mabillon rather than Hume and Voltaire. Yet at the same time, no man could belong more utterly to his own age. He is the perfect representative of the eighteenth-century spirit in all its strength and weakness: its self-confidence and self-satisfaction, its classicism and formalism, its mature and cosmopolitan civilization. Indeed he is in a sense more eighteenth century than his age, for his classicism and rationalism are still undisturbed by the revolutionary spirit of romanticism that was invading and conquering European society. He belongs to the immediate past, to the age of Bolingbroke and Montesquieu, rather than to the world of Rousseau and Burke and Cowper and Herder and Möser, who were actually his contemporaries. Both by temperament and education Gibbon was out of touch with English national culture. His mind was more French than English, and as much European as French. He is perhaps the greatest representative of that international or rather cosmopolitan culture which had grown up under the shadow of the *Grand Siècle*. For the breakdown of the political supremacy of France in the last years of Louis XIV had in no way affected its cultural hegemony, which had steadily increased throughout the first two-thirds of the eighteenth century. Indeed the chief agents of the latter were the enemies of the former. They were exiles and rebels like Bayle and Leclerc and Voltaire himself.

Now Gibbon had come under the influence of this culture during his most impressionable years and he fully realized how much he owed to the "fortunate banishment" which resulted from his early conversion to Catholicism.

If my childish revolt against the religion of my country [he writes] had not stripped me in time of my academic gown, the five important years so liberally improved in the studies and conversation of Lausanne would have been steeped in port and prejudice among the monks of Oxford. Had not the fatigue of idleness compelled me to read, the path of learning would not have been enlightened by a ray of philosophic freedom. I should have grown to manhood, ignorant of the life and language of Europe, and my knowledge of the world would have been confined to an English cloister.

But my religious error fixed me at Lausanne, in a state of banishment and disgrace. The rigid course of discipline and abstinence to which I was condemned invigorated the constitution of my mind and body; poverty and pride estranged me from my fellow countrymen.[3]

At Lausanne Gibbon soon ceased to be a Catholic, but at the same time, as he confesses, he "ceased to be an Englishman," his "opinions, thoughts and sentiments were cast in a foreign mould," so that he became the most cosmopolitan and un-English of all the great English writers.

This emancipation from national culture and traditional religion was Gibbon's true conversion and determined all his subsequent development. His adhesion to Catholicism was but the first step in his journey from the Oxford of the Wartons to the Lausanne of Voltaire.

French Switzerland at the period of Gibbon's residence was becoming the centre of the European Enlightenment. At the very moment when Gibbon was making up his mind to return to Protestantism, an even more famous convert, Jean Jacques Rousseau, was taking the same step at Geneva, and a few months later Voltaire arrived as a voluntary exile to establish his permanent headquarters by the Lake of Geneva.[4] Nevertheless, though Gibbon came into contact with Voltaire himself during his first sojourn at Lausanne and subsequently became acquainted with practically all the leaders of French thought, he never entered into contemporary French society and French thought so completely as did Hume. He belonged to an older tradition. He was not the disciple of Voltaire and the Encyclopaedists but of their forerunners, the Protestant exiles Bayle and Leclerc. The former always shocked him by their contempt for erudition and their preference for philosophic generalizations instead of historical facts. In his journals he contrasts the "taste for true learning which prevailed in the seventeenth century with the present taste uniting much indifference about theology with superficiality of learning and boldness in phi-

---

[3] *Autobiography*, p. 81.

[4] Rousseau made his abjuration at Geneva in July 1754 and Gibbon at Lausanne on December 25 of the same year. Voltaire settled at Prangins near Nyon in December 1754 and bought a house close to Lausanne.

losophy." Yet on the other hand he had no less distaste for the strict orthodoxy and the reverence for tradition that characterized the great Gallican scholars. For while he criticized the superficiality and partisanship of the French philosophers, he shared their fundamental ideals and prejudices, and it is impossible to find any European writer, not even Voltaire himself, whose work reflects more perfectly the spirit of what is called "The Enlightenment" in all its strength and all its limitations.

In Bayle and Leclerc, however, he found the happy mean between seventeenth-century traditionalism and eighteenth-century rationalism, and he owed more to them than perhaps to any other teachers. Bayle's Dictionary and the *Bibliothèques* of Leclerc provided Gibbon with light reading during his years of service with the Hampshire militia and stimulated his encyclopaedic tastes and his omnivorous appetite for books.

III

During the fifteen years between his return to England in 1758 and the commencement of his History in 1773 Gibbon continued to pursue his intellectual vocation in the unfavourable circumstances of his life as a country gentleman and an officer in the militia. Nothing indeed is more impressive than the contrast between his easygoing adaptability to an uncongenial environment and the indomitable persistence with which he continued to pursue his distant goal. In this respect, at least, his life and method of work were totally unlike those of the French philosophers, as Byron points out so well in his famous parallel between Voltaire and Gibbon,

> The other deep and slow, exhausting thought
> And hiving wisdom with each passing year
> In meditation dwelt, with learning wrought
> And shaped his weapon with an edge severe
> Sapping a solemn creed with solemn sneer; . . .

After his father's death, Gibbon came to London in 1772 and began to take an active part in public life, entering Parliament in 1774 and obtaining office in Lord North's government in 1779. It was during these active years that he wrote and published the first three volumes of the *Decline and Fall*. Finally in 1784 after the fall of Lord North's government, he decided to carry out his long meditated plan of retiring to his beloved Lausanne. There in ideal surroundings he completed the History and prepared to enjoy that "autumnal felicity" in which "our passions are supposed to be calmed, our duties fulfilled, our ambitions satisfied, our fame and fortune established on a solid basis." But the sands were running out. The History was hardly completed before the world of the Enlightenment collapsed in the storm and ruin of the Revolution, and Gibbon himself died at the age of fifty-six during his last visit to England on the 16th of January, 1794.

He was perhaps fortunate in the moment of his death. His age was finished and his work was done, and nothing he might have added to it could have added to his fame. From the moment that the first volume of his History was published in 1776, it had been accepted as a classic, and thenceforward for a century and more his work has continued to be published and sold and read in spite of all the changes of literary taste and the progress of historical knowledge.

What is the explanation of this extraordinary success? Above all, no doubt, it is due to his extraordinary literary gift, which surpasses that of every other English historian with the exception of Macaulay. It was the classical age of the literary historian, and Gibbon was the greatest and most learned of them all. But this is not the only explanation. In addition to his literary gift, he had found a theme which was precisely adapted to that gift and to the spirit of the age. The field of classical antiquity had been cultivated until the soil had become exhausted, and the later eighteenth century was awakening to the existence of the new world of mediaeval culture which had still to be explored. It was Gibbon's achievement to provide the link between these two worlds. As Carlyle wrote in one of his happiest moments, "Gibbon is a kind of bridge that connects the ancient with the modern ages. And how gorgeously does it swing across the gloomy and tumultuous chasm of these barbarous centuries." To a generation that had been reared on Livy and Tacitus and which was anxious to explore the world of Froissart and Villehardouin, Gibbon provided the necessary introduction and his work was read as eagerly as the latest novel. To the present generation his style is too ornate, his pace too slow and his philosophy too antiquated to make an immediate appeal. But his own contemporaries and the two generations that followed were enchanted by the music of his style and enthralled by the imaginative power with which he marshalled the pageantry of thirteen centuries of history.

Where Gibbon stands without a peer, alike among the literary historians of the eighteenth century and the scientific historians of later times, is in the supreme architectonic power with which he disposes of his vast material and creates out of the shapeless mass an ordered and intelligible whole.

It is true that he does not follow a uniform scheme of treatment and the two main parts of his work differ in plan as well as in scale, as he explains in the important introduction to the second part. The first four volumes contain a consecutive history of the Empire from the Antonines to Heraclius—a period of some five centuries. But in the last two volumes he abandons this method and deals with the last eight hundred years from Mohammed to the fall of Constantinople in a series of brilliant but discontinuous surveys. This method put Gibbon's remarkable powers of synthesis to a very severe test. Nevertheless with the exception of the two chapters which form the introduction to the second part, Gibbon is justified in his claim that "the seeming neglect of chronological order is surely compensated by the superior merits of interest and perspicuity," produced by "the method of grouping my picture by nations."

The real fault of these later volumes lies not in their discontinuity, but in his complete lack of sympathy with his main subject—the Byzantine Empire itself. No modern historian can agree with Gibbon's supercilious dismissal of Byzantine history. The fact is that Gibbon's clarity of vision and unity of design have been achieved at the cost of the depth of his understanding and the width of his sympathies. His thought had been so moulded by the culture of the Enlightenment that he could recognize no other values. Everything that was of value in the world came from antiquity or from the modern classical culture that was rooted in antiquity. The world between was a world of darkness and disorder, of superstition and barbarism. Hence he could not see the Byzantine world as a new form of culture with its own specific character and achievements and values. It was to him merely the ghost of a vanished majesty—a spectre reigning over a world of shadows.

This failure of understanding is even more disastrous when he has to deal with the problem of the rise of Christianity. For Christianity was essentially something new—the spiritual source of new life which came into a declining civilization "like the dayspring from on high: to give life to those who live in darkness in the shadow of death and to guide our feet into the way of peace."

All this was invisible and unintelligible to Gibbon. He had no understanding of specifically religious values. They were for him an unknown dimension. That is his real difficulty in dealing with Christianity: not the scientific incredibility of miracles, or the metaphysical absurdity of dogmas, but the fundamental concepts of religious faith and divine revelation—in short the idea of what Christianity was about.

Consequently Gibbon's famous chapters on the Rise of Christianity (chapters xv and xvi) entirely fail to touch the root of the matter. Assuming that Christianity in the religious sense of the word does not exist, the historian still has to account for the vast development of creeds and sects and ecclesiastical establishments which play such a large part in Byzantine and mediaeval history. This Gibbon proceeds to do by describing the five secondary causes which favoured the spread of the new religion. But, as Leslie Stephen, who was himself no believer, points out, these secondary causes are much more satisfactory to one who accepts the reality of the Christian revelation than to the religious sceptic. For Gibbon's causes, on his own showing, are essentially secondary, and "the true causes of the greatest of all spiritual movements lay in a region altogether inscrutable by his methods of enquiry." "Gibbon, indeed, is as incapable of understanding the spiritual significance of the phenomenon as of assigning a cause for it." [5]

It has often been said that Gibbon's attitude to Christianity is marked by a note of personal animosity, and the cause of this has sometimes been sought in the circumstances of his early conversion to Catholicism and his later reaction against it. But it seems to me that the real explanation is to be found in the intellectual discomfort caused by the

[5] Leslie Stephen, *History of English Thought in the 18th Century* (3d ed.), Vol. I, p. 449.

constant intervention in his history of a factor which he had eliminated from his philosophy and which is essentially inexplicable. And since Christianity has no place in his philosophy, he is compelled to reduce its place in history by treating it with irony and seeking to discredit it with sneers and innuendoes. The most notorious example of this method is to be seen in his treatment of the martyrs and the great persecutions, but it runs through the whole work and reaches its climax in his chapter on mediaeval heresy and the Reformation in the last volume, where he contrives to inflict the maximum of damage on both parties, concluding with a surprisingly bitter attack on the Unitarians, such as Dr. Priestley, "men who preserve the name without the substance of religion, who indulge the license without the temper of philosophy." [6]

This complete lack of sympathy and understanding for the religious forces which have exerted such an immense influence on Western culture is Gibbon's great defect as an historian: and it is a very serious one, since it invalidates his judgment on the very issues which are most vital to his subject. His most learned modern editor, the late J. B. Bury, cannot be suspected of any partiality in this matter, but on the two chief issues his judgment agrees with that of Gibbon's Christian critics. On the theological issue he writes, "Neither the historian nor the man of letters will any longer subscribe, without a thousand reserves, to the theological chapters of the Decline and Fall, and no discreet enquirer would go there for his ecclesiastical history." [7] And on the historical issue he says: "Gibbon's account of the internal history of the Empire after Heraclius is not only superficial; it gives an entirely false impression of the facts." "The designation of the later Empire as a 'uniform tale of weakness and misery' is one of the most untrue, and most effective, judgments ever uttered by a thoughtful historian." [8]

---

[6] Vol. V (Everyman's ed.), pp. 501–505. Here Gibbon even goes so far as to suggest that Priestley's opinions were so subversive as to require the attention of the government, a deplorable lapse from his own standards of toleration and enlightenment.

[7] *The Decline and Fall of the Roman Empire*, ed. by J. B. Bury (4th ed.), Vol. I, xxxix.

[8] *Ibid.*, Vol. I, lii–liii.

If this is true, how can Gibbon retain his position as the classical historian of the Decline of the Roman Empire? It is not simply due to his superb literary gifts, nor yet to his remarkably high standard of historical accuracy which distinguishes him from other literary historians. I believe the reason is that he has identified himself with his subject, as no other historian has done. A contemporary critic said of him that he came at last to believe he was the Roman Empire, and though this was said in jest by an unfriendly critic, it contains a real element of truth. For this somewhat absurd little man, "Monsieur Pomme de Terre," with his pug face and his pot belly, was possessed and obsessed by the majestic spirit of Rome. His conversion to the Church may have been transitory and superficial, but his conversion to the City and the Empire was profound and governed his whole life and work. He felt as a Roman; he thought as a Roman, he wrote as a Roman. Even when he is most representative of the spirit of his own age, as in the famous pages which conclude the first part of the History where he makes his profession of faith in the permanence and progress of European civilization, he sees that civilization as a kind of revived and extended *pax Romana:* "one great republic whose various inhabitants have attained almost the same level of politeness and cultivation."

Anyone who lives in his subject, as Gibbon has done, is bound to be a partisan, and Gibbon was a partisan of Rome, of antiquity and of the classical tradition. No doubt this makes him unjust to Christianity, the Catholic Church and the Byzantine Empire, for all of them were guilty in his eyes of *lèse majesté* against the indivisible authority of Rome and Reason and Civilization. Nevertheless the cause with which he identified himself was neither trifling nor imaginary. It represents a permanent element in history, though it is not the whole of history. If Gibbon was a bad Christian, he was a good European, and we may apply to him the great verse of the Christian poet concerning his hero, the Emperor Julian:

Perfidus ille Deo quamvis non perfidus Urbi.
(He was faithless to God, but he was not faithless to Rome.)

IV

It is not easy for us to realize the strength of this classical tradition in the eighteenth century. For three hundred years men had lived a double life. The classical world was the standard of their thought and conduct. In a sense, it was more real to them than their own world, for they had been taught to know the history of Rome better than that of England or modern Europe; to judge their literature by the standard of Quintilian, and to model their thought on Cicero and Seneca. Ancient history was history in the absolute sense, and the ages that followed were a shadowy and unreal world which could only be rationalized by being related in some way to the classical past.

Consequently when Gibbon conceived the plan of the great work to the fulfilment of which his whole life was dedicated, he was the heir and perhaps the last true representative of a great European tradition. Although he owed so much to the thought and culture of the Enlightenment, his History stands apart from the typical products of the eighteenth-century philosophic movement. He was not the disciple of Voltaire, he was the last of the Humanists.

This is to be seen above all in the very subject and form of his work. The same theme which Gibbon had chosen had inspired some of the earliest efforts of Renaissance historiography. The first literary histories of mediaeval Europe were the work of humanists who wished to throw a bridge over the formless chaos of the Dark Ages. They were essentially histories of the Decline and Fall of the Roman Empire. The earliest of these and the one which corresponds most closely in subject with Gibbon's work is the Decades of Favio Biondo, *Historiarum ab inclinatione Romanorum imperii decades,* which was written about the middle of the fifteenth century. Still more important are the two works of Sigonius, the last of the great Italian humanists of the Cinquecento, the *History of the Western Empire from Diocletian to the Death of Justinian* and the *History of Italy from 565 to 1286,* a work which could still be regarded as an authority on its subject when Gibbon wrote.[9]

Thus Gibbon found his theme already set by the Renais-

---

[9] We may also mention the *Storia d'Europa* of Giambullari (1495–1555), which only deals with the ninth and tenth centuries, but which is notable as the first venacular work on general history, as well as the first history dealing with Europe as a whole.

sance. Like the humanists, he saw mediaeval Europe only in the light of Rome's decline. Like them, he is sensitive to the pathos of the contrast between the greatness of Rome and the Gothic barbarism into which the later empire descended. Even the moment of imaginative vision when he conceived the idea of his work as he sat musing amid the ruins of the Capitol while the barefooted friars were singing Vespers in the temple of Jupiter, was the same vision which Poggio had experienced on the same spot three centuries before.[10]

But if Gibbon is the disciple of the humanists, he far surpassed their achievement. Even on their own ground, as a humanist and a rhetorician, he was their master. The Renaissance scholars might imitate the external forms of Ciceronian diction, but Gibbon's style, stately and ornate as a Roman triumph, possesses the authentic and living spirit of classical rhetoric. And this superiority is to be seen not only in his mastery of style but in his mastery of his subject. The humanists held only one end of the chain in their hands and consequently their history tends to dwindle away into a formless annalistic compilation. Gibbon, however, had seen the wheel of civilization come full circle again. Although in his essay on literature he sides with the ancients against the moderns, he had assimilated the essential principle of the modern development. He was conscious of the European achievement and he felt himself to be a member of a society that was not inferior in culture and politeness to that of classical Rome. He stood on the summit of the Renaissance achievement and looked back over the waste of history to ancient Rome, as from one mountain top to another.

V

But if Gibbon surpassed his masters, it was not simply because he united the humanist tradition with the philosophic culture of the eighteenth century. He was also indebted to another tradition, and though he was spiritually hostile to it, he made full use of its resources. The central tradition of European historiography is that of the Catholic Church. It is here and not in humanism that we find the true highway

[10] Poggio's *de Varietate Fortunae*. Cf. Gibbon, *Decline and Fall*, ch. lxxi.

that leads from the ancient to the modern world. By this road we can travel without a break from Eusebius and Jerome and Augustine to Bede and Marianus Scotus and Otto of Freising, and the patristic culture which supplies the key to the mind of the later Empire also forms the intellectual background of the monastic annalists and historians of the Middle Ages.

Nor was this tradition permanently interrupted by the coming of humanism. The classical renaissance was followed by a renaissance of ecclesiastical culture which found its chief expression in a new flowering of historical studies. The exigencies of theological controversy forced the ecclesiastical historians to be more careful than were the humanists to refer to their authorities and to quote original documents; and consequently the historiography of the Counter-Reformation, as represented by Baronius and the first Bollandists, in spite of its complete lack of literary form, marks an epoch in historical studies.

But it was in the French historians of the seventeenth century that the ecclesiastical tradition reached its highest point of development. For sheer learning and devotion to research no historians of any epoch can be compared to Tillemont and Mabillon and Ducange, by the side of whom the historians of the Enlightenment seem journalists and amateurs. And they are but the leaders of an army of scholars —Sirmond and Labbe, Petavius and Thomassin, d'Achery and Baluze—whose folios were the inexhaustible mine from which the writers of the following century drew their material. Not that this tradition was exhausted in the eighteenth century, for it was carried on to Gibbon's own time by monastic scholars like Montfaucon and Dom Bouquet and Dom Rivet, while in Italy Muratori was hardly inferior to the greatest names of the seventeenth century.

It is impossible to exaggerate Gibbon's debt to this tradition, and almost every page of his work bears traces of it. Gibbon was the most conscientious of historians; his critics never caught him out in a single false reference or second-hand quotation. But though he went direct to his sources, he was not an historian who worked from documents or one who could dispense with secondary authorities. He followed the steps of the older historians, and he went to the sources rather in order to verify their references and to correct their judgments than to build up anew from the foundations. That is why Gibbon is at his best when he has a sure guide to follow, and why, when he is left to his own resources, as in later Byzantine history or in the history of the later crusades, his touch becomes less sure and his mastery of his material less complete.

Fortunately in the earlier part of his work Gibbon possessed the best of guides in Tillemont, who led him over the rocky paths of later Roman history, to use Gibbon's own metaphor, with the sure-footed sagacity of an Alpine mule. There is something very incongruous in the collaboration of two such opposite types, each of them the perfect representative of his own tradition: the eighteenth-century man of the world whose sensitive vanity could not bear the shadow of an unfavourable criticism, and the solitary of Port Royal who wrote history as a means of sanctification and whose scrupulous self-repression forbade him to read the first review of his own work. Tillemont deliberately confined himself to preparing the materials for a history that he would never write. He did not possess "that fire of genius and that noble ardour of piety which are necessary to write of such great matters in a manner proportionate to the dignity and holiness of God Himself in the greatest of all His works." [11] "It was enough for him to offer to God the little that he had received" and to prepare the way for the historian of the future by his humble and laborious researches into matters of historic fact, which, as he remarks in a perfectly ingenuous way,[12] are often beneath the notice of men of genius. Tillemont carried out the task he had set himself in a thoroughly conscientious and adequate manner, but by the irony of fate the historian who entered into the fruit of his labours was not an orthodox genius like Bossuet but the "infidel" Gibbon who despised all that Tillemont revered and who used the material which Tillemont had so laboriously collected in order to explain away Christianity and to rationalize the history of the Church.

VI

Gibbon's famous chapters on the causes of the success of Christianity are perhaps the most triumphant example

[11] Lenain de Tillemont, *Mémoires pour servir à l'histoire ecclésiastique*, t. i, p. viii.

[12] Id., *Histoire des Empereurs*, t. i, pp. iv–v.

of his powers of historic exposition. With masterly ease he swept away the assumptions on which Tillemont's conception of history was based. What had seemed to the latter the most convincing and palpable proof of the supernatural origins of Christianity, the victory of divine weakness over human strength and the insertion of eternity in the world of time, dwindled away under Gibbon's cool survey into a very human development determined by the circumstances of the age and the perennial influences of religious credulity and enthusiasm. And yet the apparent completeness of Gibbon's success points to the fundamental weakness of his treatment. His essentially negative explanation of Christianity leaves the post-classical world devoid of form and meaning. He is forced to write his history in terms of the past, and the more complete is the victory of the new forces, the more lacking in content does his history become and the central theme of his work is the shadow of a great name. Consequently, if we wish to understand the spirit of the Christian Empire, it is to Tillemont rather than to Gibbon that we should go. Tillemont has not a spark of Gibbon's literary genius. He is dry and laborious and narrow-minded, bound by all the prejudices of the most rigid orthodoxy. But he has a profound veneration for the past and his only ambition is to be the faithful interpreter of its spirit. Even his prejudices are the prejudices of the age of which he writes and of themselves do something to re-create the mental atmosphere of a vanished civilization. And so one feels that he succeeds in the essential task of history—in the understanding of the past, while Gibbon only succeeds in explaining it away. To Gibbon the story of the Christian Empire and the civilization to which it gave birth is nothing but the history of an illusion. The world had conceived emptiness and brought forth wind. There was nothing left to write about but the battles of kites and crows and the aimless procession of phantom emperors. There remained only the shadow of the great name of Rome, like the shadow of a great rock in an empty land.

The result of this conception of history is to be seen at its worst in Gibbon's treatment of the Byzantine Empire. If only Gibbon could have perceived the true significance of the Byzantine development, his later volumes would have found the centre of unity which they actually lack. But all that he could perceive was "a tedious and uniform tale of weakness and misery." "The subjects of the Byzantine empire, who assume and dishonour the names both of Greeks and Romans, present a dead uniformity of abject vices which are neither softened by the weakness of humanity nor animated by the vigour of memorable crimes." [13] Consequently he treats Byzantine history merely as a frame for the series of brilliant but discontinuous historical surveys which fills his last three volumes. The history of the Byzantine Empire from the seventh to the twelfth centuries is contained in a single chapter which is little more than a catalogue of rulers. In the following chapter he returns to the eighth century to relate the rise of the Western empire and takes a rapid glance at its subsequent fortunes down to the fourteenth century. Next he turns back to the seventh century and to the East to describe the rise of Islam and gives two more chapters to the history of its expansion and the decline of the Khalifate of Bagdad. This is followed by four chapters dealing respectively with the state of the Byzantine Empire in the tenth century, the Paulician heresy, the Bulgarians and the other Northern enemies of the empire, the Saracens and Normans in Sicily and the history of the Seljuk Turks. This brings us to the Crusades, and from this point we have once more a continuous narrative that carries us down to the final conquest of Constantinople by the Turks. But this is not the conclusion of his work, for Gibbon returns once more to the city from which he had set out and the last three chapters of the *Decline and Fall of the Roman Empire* are devoted to the changing fortunes of mediaeval Rome.

Only the majestic order of Gibbon's style and his infallible sense of literary unity could overcome the difficulties of such a method, and it is possible to sympathize with Horace Walpole when he complains that he was "a little confounded by his leaping backwards and forwards and could not recollect all those fainéant Emperors of Constantinople who come again and again like the same ships in a moving picture." [14]

But even so severe a critic as Walpole admitted that "the sixth volume made ample amends. Mahomet and the Popes

[13] Gibbon, *Decline and Fall,* ch. xlviii.
[14] Letter to the Countess of Ossory, 10 February, 1789.

were gentlemen and good company," [15] and Gibbon's excursions into Oriental history are marred by none of the coldness and lack of imagination that characterize his treatment of ecclesiastical and Byzantine subjects.

VII

At first sight it may seem surprising that a humanist and a rationalist like Gibbon should have delighted in the exotic colours of Oriental history and should have written with sympathy and appreciation of a religion that was even fiercer and more uncompromising than the most militant form of traditional Christianity. But the eighteenth-century deist could appreciate the apparent simplicity of Moslem theology and the indulgence that it showed to what he terms "the most amiable weaknesses of human nature," while Gibbon's vestigial Protestantism approved the Puritanism of the soldiers of Islam in comparison with the iconolatry and asceticism of Byzantine Christendom. "More pure than the system of Zoroaster, more liberal than the law of Moses, the religion of Mahomet might seem less inconsistent with reason than the creed of mystery and superstition which in the seventh century disgraced the simplicity of the Gospel." [16]

Most of all, however, it was the exotic romance of Oriental history which appealed to Gibbon's imagination. Here at least we can trace the influence of an incipient romanticism in Gibbon's taste and style. In the Arabic and Persian historians, though he knew them only through the stiff Latin translations of Reiske and Gagnier, or the second-hand anecdotes of d'Herbelot and Ockley and Petit de la Croix, he felt the same sense of liberation and new experience which his contemporaries found in Macpherson's *Ossian*. If only Gibbon could have realized the exotic and Oriental elements in Byzantine culture, if he could have studied it as a strange phenomenon

---

[15] It is interesting to note that Walpole's further criticisms are based on diametrically opposite grounds to those of Gibbon's modern critics. While we deplore his lack of understanding of Byzantine history, Walpole complains that he spends his talents on the dreary wastes of Constantinopolitan history, and where we feel his lack of interest in religion Walpole wishes "that he had never heard of Monophysites or Nestorians or any such fools."

[16] *Decline and Fall*, ch. li.

comparable to Sassanian Persia rather than to ancient Rome, he would have been more sympathetic in his treatment and more just in his verdict. Unfortunately he was unable to escape from his theological and humanist prejudices. He judged Byzantine religion by the standards of eighteenth-century deism, and Byzantine culture by the standards of Renaissance classicism. The later empire was simply the degraded successor of classical Greece and Rome. It was like a slum tenement that had grown up in the ruins of a deserted palace. It was nothing in itself: all its significance came from the broken shell in which it was housed.

Gibbon's treatment of the Christian West falls half-way between the contemptuous indifference of his attitude to Byzantium and the imaginative sympathy that he shows for Oriental history. His historic sense was strong enough to cause him to realize the civilizing influence of Christianity on the barbarians and his devastating characterization of monasticism is followed by a not wholly inadequate appreciation of the part that the Church played in the making of Europe. He shows how the ecclesiastical use of Latin involved the preservation of the elements of classical culture so that "the flame of science was secretly kept alive to enlighten and warm the mature age of the Western world," how the authority of religion "preserved in the downfall of the empire a permanent respect for the name and institutions of Rome," and how religious intercourse and "the growing authority of the Popes cemented the union of the Christian republic; and gradually produced the similar manners and common jurisprudence, which have distinguished from the rest of mankind the independent and even hostile nations of modern Europe." [17]

Nevertheless Gibbon's religious prejudices rendered it impossible for him to understand the positive achievements of mediaeval religion and culture. His summary of the intellectual development of the greatest of mediaeval centuries is inadequate, even when judged by eighteenth-century standards.

The numerous vermin of mendicant friars [he writes], Franciscans, Dominicans, Augustins, Carmelites, who

[17] *Op. cit.*, chs. xxxvii, ii, "The Conversion of the Barbarians."

swarmed in this century with habits and institutions variously ridiculous, disgraced religion, learning and common sense. They seized on scholastic philosophy as a science peculiarly suited to their minds; and excepting only Friar Bacon, they preferred words to things. The subtle, the profound, the irrefragable, the angelic and the seraphic Doctors acquired those pompous titles by filling ponderous volumes with a small number of technical terms and a much smaller number of ideas. Universities arose in every part of Europe and thousands of students employed their lives upon these grave follies. The love songs of the Troubadores and Provençal bards were follies of a more pleasing nature, which amused the leisure of the greatest princes, polished the southern provinces of France and gave birth to the Italian poetry.[18]

This, however, is an extract from the *Outline of the History of the World* which Lord Sheffield printed among Gibbon's posthumous papers. Fortunately in his great work he passes lightly over the history of the mediaeval Church and concentrates his attention on those scenes of mediaeval history which he could best appreciate, the romantic story of the Crusades, Petrarch and Rienzo, and the dawn of the Renaissance.

VIII

This principle of selection which determines the character of Gibbon's later volumes is responsible alike for their literary unity and their historical discontinuity. It is to be justified by the fact that Gibbon did not conceive history according to the new liberal formula of an uninterrupted progress towards perfection, which inspired such works as Condorcet's *Esquisse d'un tableau historique des progrès de l'esprit humain*. It is true that Gibbon was not unaffected by the current ideas of human progress. Indeed they find matchless expression in the magnificent passage which closes his considerations on the Fall of the Roman Empire in the West and forms the conclusion of the first half of his great work.

The splendid days of Augustus and Trajan were eclipsed by a cloud of ignorance; and the barbarians subverted the

[18] *Miscellaneous Works* (1st ed.), ii, 422.

laws and palaces of Rome. But the scythe, the invention or emblem of Saturn, still continued annually to mow the harvest of Italy; and the human feasts of the Laestrygons have never been renewed on the coast of Campania.

Since the first discoveries of the arts, war, commerce, and religious zeal have diffused among the savages of the Old and New World these inestimable gifts; they have been successively propagated; they can never be lost. We may therefore acquiesce in the pleasing conclusion, that every age of the world has increased and still increases, the real wealth, the happiness, the knowledge and perhaps the virtue, of the human race.

Here speaks Gibbon the philosopher, but Gibbon the historian and humanist was inspired by a different and older conception of history. He believed like Voltaire that the human race had experienced a few moments of rare felicity, relatively equal to one another but separated by gulfs of barbarism and ignorance. In Voltaire's words, "Every age has produced heroes and politicians, every people has experienced revolutions, all history is almost equal for those who only wish to store their memories with facts. But whoever thinks, or (what is more rare) whoever possesses taste, only counts four centuries in the history of the world." [19] These four centuries are the classical age of Greece, the Augustan age of Rome, the age of the Renaissance in Italy, and the age of Louis XIV.

It was not, however, from Voltaire that Gibbon derived this aristocratic and discontinuous view of history, but from the historians of the Renaissance. The misfortunes of sixteenth-century Italy and the study of Tacitus and Thucydides led them to interpret history in a tragic or pessimistic spirit. Not the Christian Providence but the Hellenistic Τύχη— Fortune—was the deity that ruled the course of history. Every man and every state have their hour, and though genius and virtue could realize the possibilities of that happy moment, they could not preserve it or make the wheel of fortune to stand still.

This idea was developed by the publicists of the later Renaissance and the revolutions of states became one of the

[19] Voltaire, *Siècle de Louis XIV* (Introduction).

most popular themes of post-Renaissance historiography.[20] From Italy it passed to France in the later part of the seventeenth century. It was popularized by Vertot and Père J. d'Orleans and continued to flourish throughout the eighteenth century. Thus we have Père d'Orleans' *Revolutions of England* in 1689, Vertot's *Revolutions of Sweden* in 1695 and *of the Roman Republic* in 1719. In 1749 Levesque de Burigny published his *Revolutions of the Empire of Constantinople* and in the following year there appeared the first volume of Marigny's *Revolutions of the Empire of the Arabs*. Finally in 1769–70 there is Denina's *Revolutions of Italy*, and in 1783 Pilati de Tassulo produced his *History of the Revolutions in Government, Law, and the Human Mind from the Conversion of Constantine to the Fall of the Western Empire*, a theme very similar to that of Gibbon's own work.

IX

Consequently, when Gibbon set himself to write the history of "the memorable series of revolutions which in the course of about thirteen centuries gradually undermined, and at length destroyed the solid fabric of Roman greatness," [21] he was following an ancient and well-established tradition. Moreover, it was a tradition that was better suited to his purpose than the more ambitious programme of the historians of human progress. His purpose was to trace the declining curve of the cycle of ancient civilization. His history was not one of progress but of Decline and Fall. Consequently its theme was more in harmony with the tragic fatalism of the Renaissance historians than with the optimistic presuppositions of the theory of progress. It finds its ideal in the past and looks back to the golden age of the Antonines rather than forward to the glories of modern civilization.

In this respect Gibbon was no doubt somewhat out of touch with the dominant intellectual movement of his own age. To the men of the French Revolution he must have seemed a reactionary, and a representative of the discredited

[20] E.g. Gualdo Priorato's *Historia delle rivoluzioni di Francia* (1655), or Sammarco, *Delle mutazioni de' regni* (1628).
[21] *Decline and Fall* (Preface).

culture of the old régime. From the historical point of view, however, Gibbon was not the loser by this conservatism. History deals with particular cultures rather than with world civilization, with the life of peoples rather than with the progress of humanity. The historian of human progress is always tempted to falsify history by forcing its diversity into a unitary scheme of development and ordering it in an ascending series of moral and cultural values. George III was undoubtedly a more humane ruler than Jinghis Khan, but there is no ladder of progress that leads from one to the other. They stand on different ladders because they belong to different cultures, that is to say to different sociological time series. Thus the discontinuous conception of history is nearer to our own than is the unitary ideal of the liberal philosophy of history. We desire to appreciate every culture for its own sake and we do not attempt to judge the civilization of Yucatan by the standards of modern England.

Consequently if we criticize Gibbon it is not because he failed to bring out the progressive movement of civilizations from ancient Rome to modern Europe. Modern European civilization may be a better thing than that of the age of the Antonines, but it is essentially different, and Gibbon is perfectly justified in concentrating his attention on the declining curve of the one cycle rather than on the ascending curve of the other. Where Gibbon fails is in his inability to recognize the existence of the independent cycle of Byzantine civilization whose curves intersect both that of the fall of Rome and that of the rise of Europe. For although Gibbon did not try to force the facts of history into a unitary scheme of development he was still far too unitary in his conception of culture. He could appreciate Roman civilization because his own culture was thoroughly saturated with the Latin tradition. But that tradition was the only tradition and nothing outside it deserved the name of civilization. This cultural absolutism imparts a classical symmetry to Gibbon's treatment of history, but it is also responsible for a certain superficiality. It prevents him from understanding the profound cultural changes which are so intimately connected with the fall of the Empire. It has often been remarked that Gibbon's analysis of the causes of the Decline and Fall of Rome is lacking not only in profundity but in clarity. When he comes to the very heart of his subject, his mastery seems to fail him and he contents himself with a few general and rather fragmentary observations. In one chapter he lays emphasis on the decay of the military virtues during a long peace, in another on the oppression and heavy taxation of the government, while there is a veiled suggestion running through the whole work that the influence of Christianity did more than either the attacks of the barbarians or the weakness of the government to sap the vitality and lower the culture of the Roman Empire. But when we come to the pages entitled "General Considerations on the Fall of the Roman Empire in the West," we find that all these particular causes take a secondary place and that the fall of Rome is regarded as the result of an inevitable process of social dissolution.

The rise of a city that swelled into an empire may deserve as a singular prodigy the reflection of a philosophic mind. But the decline of Rome was the natural and inevitable effect of immoderate greatness. Prosperity ripened the principle of decay; the causes of destruction multiplied with the extent of conquest; and as soon as time or accident had removed the artificial supports, the stupendous fabric yielded to the pressure of its own weight. The story of its ruin is simple and obvious; and instead of inquiring why the Roman Empire was destroyed we should rather be surprised that it had subsisted so long.

X

This explanation differs little, if at all, from the historic fatalism of the classical and humanist tradition which Gibbon had expressly disavowed on a previous page. All earthly things are subject to mutability. Growth and decay, life and death, are the law of states as well as of individuals. As Voltaire puts it in his criticism of Montesquieu's *Considérations sur les causes de la grandeur des Romains et de leur décadence,* "Cet empire est tombé parce qu'il existait. Il faut bien que tout tombe." [22]

It is true that this conception only needs to be interpreted in a vitalistic sense in order to become an organic theory of social development. And though such theories are often re-

[22] *Dictionnaire philosophique,* s.v. *Gouvernement.*

garded as characteristically modern, they were by no means unknown in Gibbon's day. Already, a century before he wrote, Ducange had prefaced his great glossary of mediaeval Latin by a dissertation on the nature of language in which he argues that language is not a static thing but a living organism which goes through phases of adolescence, maturity, and senility.[23] And in Gibbon's own generation, the Italian Jesuit Bettinelli not only compares the task of the historian to that of the naturalist who traces the germination of the plant and the development of animal organisms, but applies his theory to history in what is perhaps the first satisfactory study of mediaeval culture.[24]

Gibbon himself, however, was too much under the influence of the static rationalist idealism of the Enlightenment to make use of these organic conceptions. Like Hume, he believed that human nature is always the same and that all historical events can be explained by a certain number of constant psychological motives which were the same among the Greeks and Romans as they are today. Consequently he saw the greatness and the decline of Rome as the result of the virtues and vices (and primarily the military virtues and vices) of the Romans, not as the growth and decay of a social organism.

XI

In reality, the Roman empire fell not by war or political incapacity but because of a process of sociological decay which destroyed the foundations of its strength. It was due to the victory of the Oriental theocratic monarchy over the Mediterranean city-state, and to the decline of the urban citizen class under the pressure of bureaucratic collectivism. The Roman Empire had never possessed a really homogeneous culture like that, for example, of China. It was an artificial union of alien social organisms which had been brought together by an amazing effort of military and administrative organization. In the East Rome inherited the debris of the

---

[23] Preface, *De causis corruptae latinitatis.*

[24] S. Bettinelli, *Storia del Risorgimento d'Italia dopo il Mille* (1773).

Oriental and Hellenistic monarchies, while in the West she conquered and assimilated the tribal society of the European barbarians. It is true that there was a real community of culture between the Latin cities of the West and the Hellenistic cities of the East. But it was a superficial cosmopolitan civilization which was limited to a privileged class, a society of consumers based on slave labour and the exploitation of subject classes and peoples. As soon as this privileged class was ruined by the economic crises of the third century and the loss of its political privileges, the underlying diversity between the barbarians of the East and the barbarians of the West emerged as strong as ever.

And this is the reason why the Empire survived in the East and not in the West. For the East was the home of the theocratic monarchy and when Constantine reorganized the Empire as a sacred monarchy united with a world religion and based on the twofold hierarchy of clergy and officials, it was a return to the underlying social tradition of the ancient East. In the West, however, this tradition was absent; the Western provincials had more community of social tradition with the warrior peoples of the North than with the theocracy of the East. The sacred monarchy of the Christian empire was an exotic growth which could only maintain itself at Ravenna, which was a window open to the Byzantine world, and the leadership of Western society fell into the hands of the barbarian warrior chieftains. Only the Church survived, because it was not bound up with the civic institutions of the Roman-Hellenistic urban culture. It could adapt itself alike to the theocratic imperialism of the East and to the barbaric monarchies of the West. It created new organs of culture to take the place of those of the city and it struck its roots far deeper into the soil of Europe than the urban civilization of the Empire had done, except in the Mediterreanean world.

All this complex process of sociological change was hidden from the eyes of Gibbon by the limitations of his historical vision. The constitutional changes of the third century which were the inevitable result of the social and economic crisis through which the Empire had passed, were regarded by him merely as the work of the pride and policy of "that artful prince" Diocletian. He does not seem to realize either the part played by municipal self-government in the early history of the Empire or the importance of the ruin of the citizen class and the transformation of the municipal constitution in its decline, though the Theodosian code supplied ample material for such a study. Moreover, his mind was so completely dominated by the humanist ideal that he was unable to understand either the Oriental tradition of the Sacred Monarchy to which the latter empire returned or the spirit of the new world religion which inspired both the Byzantine civilization and the nascent culture of Western Christendom. His gaze was concentrated on one side of the process—the passing of the classical culture—and he was oblivious of the new world that was coming into existence.

XII

Consequently we no longer read Gibbon in order to understand the causes that led to the decline and fall of the Roman Empire, nor yet to understand the nature of the new order that took its place. Nevertheless we do read him for his own sake and his work will remain a classic when the books of the scholars who corrected his mistakes and transcended his limitations are neglected and forgotten except by specialists. For we read history not only for the light that it throws on the past but also for the light that it throws on the world of the writer. We cannot fully understand an age unless we understand how that age regarded the past, for every age makes its own past, and this re-creation of the past is one of the elements that go to the making of the future. Few historians have possessed in so high a degree as Gibbon the power of transforming the chaos of the past into an intelligible order. No doubt it was an artificial order which contains only a part of the full content of the historic past. It is as it were a translation of the past into the language of eighteenth-century culture. But that culture was itself the product of the tradition that inspired his work—the tradition of the classical world transmitted through mediaeval Christendom and reinforced by the Humanism of the Italian Renaissance and the classicism of the seventeenth and eighteenth centuries; and consequently Gibbon's treatment still had a vital relation to its subject. If modern history with its romanticism and its relativity has immeasurably increased our understanding of the past, it has also lost something. It no longer shares that sense of living membership in a great tradition and a classical order which Gibbon with all his limitations of spiritual vision and historical imagination still possessed.

—1934; 1953.

Karl Marx and the Dialectic
of History

THERE is a natural affinity and concordance between the spirit of Catholicism and the spirit of history, and it is no accident that the modern historical tradition should have been born and nourished in the Catholic Church. The founders of modern historical scholarship were not the brilliant literary historians of the Renaissance but priests or monks like Tillemont and Muratori and Mabillon whose historical work is inspired by the same conscientious and disinterested piety as their religion.

The new rationalist and liberal school of history arising in the eighteenth century owed an immense and unacknowledged debt to this tradition. It is not merely that Gibbon is a pupil of Tillemont and that Voltaire wrote his essay on universal history as a continuation of Bossuet's *Discourse on Universal History*. The influence goes far deeper than this. It shows itself in the new doctrines of social progress and the education of humanity which are nothing but a secularization of the Catholic interpretation of history and a transposition of its essential motives to a new setting. "What," writes Croce—himself the last of the Liberal philosophers of history —"are our histories of culture, of civilization, of progress, of humanity, of truth, save the form of ecclesiastical history in harmony with our times—that is to say, of the triumph and propagation of the faith, of the strife against the powers of darkness, of the successive treatments of the new evangel made afresh with each succeeding epoch?" [1]

In fact, the Liberal interpretation of history has taken over from the Catholic tradition not only its universalism, its sense of a spiritual purpose which runs through the whole life of humanity, but also its dualism. The Liberal interpretation of history is also dominated by the image of the two cities. But it is now the Church which is the embodiment of those "reactionary forces" which are the Liberal equivalent of the powers of darkness, while the children of this world have become the children of light.

This transposition was not, however, altogether a new thing. It has behind it a somewhat similar emotional attitude to that which had already appeared in the Protestant tradition. It is true that that tradition was not remarkable for its historic achievements. It produced no historians worthy of being compared to the great scholars of the Counter-Reformation and the age of Louis XIV. But it was responsible for one innovation in the Christian interpretation of history which had momentous results. This was its identification of Papal Rome with the Babylon of the Apocalypse, which became practically an article of faith—and a very central one—in all the Reformed Churches. It is difficult for us today to realize the existence of this belief which dominated Protestant Europe for three hundred years and which still remains as a subconscious undercurrent in Protestant thought. But it is easy to see that it entirely altered the nature of the Christian dualism by transforming it from an opposition between the Church and the World to a conflict between two forms of Christianity. And when this step had once been taken, when the institutional Church for a thousand years had been relegated to the dominion of Antichrist and the Albigensians and Waldenses had been identified with the persecuted saints of Scripture, it was easy enough for the Enlightenment to take one step further by sending the Protestant Churches to join the Church of Rome outside the pale and by canonizing the apostles of free thought as the saints of rationalism.

This procedure was at least more logical than the Protes-

[1] B. Croce, *Theory and History of Historiography*, trans. D. Ainslie, p. 207.

tant synthesis of apocalypticism and private judgment. But it still retained a large residuum of mysticism which was incongruous with the dominant rationalist element in the liberal tradition. The religion of progress demands a basis in theology, even if it be only the etiolated natural theology of the Deist or the Freemason. This is why the compound has never been altogether a stable one. First one element in the synthesis attains predominance, and we have the idealist philosophy of history which in the hands of Schelling and Krause tends to become a genuinely religious mysticism; then the rationalist basis re-emerges and we have a reaction against idealism and an attempt to combine the doctrine of progress with a thoroughgoing materialism. But even in this materialistic form, the apocalyptic and millennial element in the theory is still clearly evident: indeed it is often at its strongest when the materialist basis is most pronounced.

The classical example of this is Marxian socialism and the materialistic interpretation of history which is its fundamental doctrine. There is no doubt about the pedigree of this doctrine. It is the child of the Revolutionary tradition on the one hand and on the other of German idealism, which in turn was the offspring of an illicit connection between the philosophy of the Enlightenment and the religion of Protestant Pietism.[2] Thus it goes back on both sides to a Catholic ancestry, since the philosophy of the Enlightenment derives its historic universalism from the Catholic tradition, while the tradition of Pietism goes back through the spiritual Reformers and the spiritual Franciscans to the ground stock of Christian millenniarism and apocalyptic. Moreover the other parent of Marxism, the Revolutionary tradition, has obvious links with the more sectarian and anti-Catholic forms of the same apocalyptic tradition. All these various elements are represented in the Marxian philosophy, and the real force that combines them is not so much the internal logic of his thought as the prophetic fervour and the burning conviction that inspired his message. For Karl Marx was of the seed of the prophets, in spite of his contempt for anything that savoured of mysticism or religious idealism. He was one of those exiles of Israel like Spinoza, whose isolation from the religious community of their fathers only serves to intensify their proud consciousness of a prophetic mission.

[2] Cf. J. Nadler, *Die Berliner Romantik*.

Thus the apocalyptic tradition which in its secularized form tended to degenerate into a vague idealism recovered its power and concrete reality by this renewed contact with the Jewish mind. The Messianic hope, the belief in the coming destruction of the Gentile power and the deliverance of Israel, were to the Jew not mere echoes of Biblical tradition; they were burnt into the very fibre of his being by centuries of thwarted social impulse in the squalid ghettos of Germany and Poland. And in the same way the social dualism between the elect and the reprobate, between the people of God and the Gentile world power, was a fact of bitter personal experience of which even the most insensitive was made conscious in the hundred petty annoyances of ghetto life.

Now the Revolution and the coming of liberalism had put an end to this state of things. The Jews had come out of the ghetto into the world and had received rights of citizenship in the new bourgeois civilization. It was at this point in Jewish history that Karl Marx makes his appearance. He had lost his membership of the Jewish community, for he was the son of a Christian convert, but he could not deny his Jewish heredity and his Jewish spirit and become the obedient servant of the Gentile civilization as his father had done. His whole soul revolted against the standards and ideals of the petty bourgeois society in which he had been brought up: yet he had tasted the forbidden fruit of the new knowledge and he could not go back to the Talmud any more than he could return to the ghetto. The only way of escape that remained open to him was by the revolutionary tradition, which was then at the height of its prestige and popularity. In this he found satisfaction at once for his conscious hostility to bourgeois civilization and for the deeper revolt of his repressed religious instincts.

The three fundamental elements in the Jewish historical attitude—the opposition between the chosen people and the Gentile world, the inexorable divine judgment on the latter and the restoration of the former in the Messianic kingdom—all found their corresponding principles in the revolutionary faith of Karl Marx. Thus the bourgeois took the place of the Gentiles and the economic poor—the proletariat—took the place of the spiritual poor of the Old Testament.

In the same way the approaching cataclysm of social revolution which was brought about not by human power and will, but by the immanent dialectic of history, corresponds to the Day of Jahweh and the judgment of the Gentiles; while the Messianic Kingdom finds an obvious parallel in the dictatorship of the proletariat which will reign till it has put down all rule and authority and power and in the end will deliver up its kingdom to the classless and stateless society of the future which will be all in all.

This social apocalyptic is one part, and I believe by far the most important part, of Marx's thought; the other part consists of the historical and philosophic theories which are its rational justification and which, whether they are in fact primary or secondary in the total system, must be judged on their own merits.

Now the Marxian interpretation of history is the most thoroughgoing system of historic materialism that has ever been invented. This is what Marx claimed for it, and in spite of the objections of the neo-Marxians, I believe that his claim was justified.

When Marx began to write, the metaphysical idealism of the great Romantic age had already gone out of fashion and science and positivism were becoming the order of the day. It was the age not only of Comte and Feuerbach but of thoroughgoing materialists like Büchner and Moleschott. Nevertheless it was also a great age of ethical and social idealism. Men might deny their God and scoff at all religious beliefs; they might even treat the idealist metaphysic as nothing else but sophisticated theology. But for all that, they still believed in the supremacy of spiritual values, and the power of moral ideals. Feuerbach, who had a decisive influence on the development of Marx's thought, was typical in this respect. He believed in the omnipotence of feeling and the illimitableness of the human heart and taught that even when faith in Christ has disappeared Christ's true essence remains in existence wherever love reigns. All this was highly antipathetic to Marx. And his hostility was not merely due to the natural contempt of a hard mind for soft ones, but to the knowledge that all this talk about moral ideals, this sloppy enthusiasm for a reign of universal love, was interfering with the coming of a real revolution which required hatred rather than love and hard knocks rather than lofty sentiments. Consequently Marx's objection to the materialists of his time is somewhat different from that of many of his followers today. The latter criticize the old materialism as too mechanical in its conceptions, and in a sense as too materialistic. Marx, on the other hand, criticized them on account of their residual idealism, i.e. because they were not materialistic enough. It was no use disproving the metaphysical truth of Christianity if you still remained in bondage to its moral ideals.

The chief failure of all materialism hitherto [he writes] including the materialism of Feuerbach, is that it conceives Reality or the sensible things only in the form of object or theory, but not as sensible human activity or Praxis, not as subject. Hence the active side develops in an abstract way in the opposition of Materialism to Idealism, which naturally knows no real sensible activity as such. Feuerbach wants sensible objects really different from objects of thought: but he does not conceive human action itself as material activity. Consequently in his *Essence of Christianity* he regards only the theoretic relation as the truly human one, while action or Praxis is conceived and remains fixed only in its dirty Jewish form. Hence he does not realize the meaning of revolutionary or practical-critical activity.[3]

For Marx there was no such thing as an essence of Christianity which could survive its outward forms, indeed strictly speaking there was no such thing as Christianity at all. All such phenomena were only the ideological reflections of actual social relations, and they could no more survive the passing of their sociological basis than a shadow on the hill can remain after the cloud passes by. In the same way there is no such thing as human nature in itself or spiritual consciousness, there is only the sum of economic relations which are the basis not only of social activity but of social being and social consciousness. "This sum of forces of production, capital resources and material circumstances which each individual and each generation finds already in existence as something given, is the real ground of that which appears to the philosophers as 'substance' and Being of Man, and which they have apotheosized and striven about, a real foundation which is not in the least weakened in its influence and effects on the development of men, because

[3] *Note on Feuerbach, Die Deutsche Ideologie,* p. 533, Sect. I, Vol. V of the Collected Edition of Marx and Engels, Berlin, 1932.

these philosophers set us instead self-consciousness or the One." [4]

Thus there is nothing absolute or transcendent in human life and thought and religion—everything is the product of history and all history is the history of the economic process. Moreover the economic process itself is not a stationary one. It consists in a series of revolutionary cycles, which bring with them corresponding changes in social and political institutions and in ideas. The great illusion of Liberalism, as seen in the bourgeois political economy, is that it is possible to base economic life on eternal and necessary laws and thus to transcend the category of history.

As Marx writes in his *Poverty of Philosophy*, "The economists regard bourgeois institutions as natural and based on eternal laws, and feudal institutions as artificial. Thus there has been history, but there is no longer any." Against this static conception Marx sets up his revolutionary theory of social dialectic, in which the element of conflict and social antagonism forms the very essence of the social process. "Feudal institutions," he writes, "have a good as well as a bad side. But it is the bad side that produces the movement of history by constituting the struggle." If it were possible to have eliminated the bad elements—serfdom, privilege, violence—and kept the good—patriarchalism, chivalry, guild organization—what would have been the result? "All the elements that constituted the struggle would have been annihilated and the development of the bourgeoisie would have been stifled in the germ. They would have set themselves the absurd task of *eliminating history*." [5] "Thus in order to judge fairly of feudal production, it is necessary to consider it as a system of production based on antagonism. It is necessary to show how wealth was produced within this antagonism, how the productive forces were developed at the same time as the antagonism of the classes, how one of the classes, the bad side, the inconvenience of society continued always to grow until the material conditions necessary for its emancipation arrived at maturity." [6]

Here we see the Marxian interpretation of history in its

[4] *Op. cit.*, p. 28.

[5] Marx, *The Poverty of Philosophy*, trans. Quelch (Chicago, 1910), p. 132.

[6] *Ibid.*, p. 133.

strongest and most incisive form. It recalls, as Marx himself was the first to emphasize, the Darwinian theory of evolution by struggle and the survival of the fittest. "From the war of nature, from famine and death, the most exalted object that we are capable of conceiving, namely the production of the higher animals, directly results."

But unfortunately this strong and logical theory is never carried out with full consistency. When we come to the next cycle, to that of the proletarian revolution, Marx's historical sense deserts him and he does exactly what he blames the liberals for doing—he eliminates history. The dictatorship of the proletariat, or rather the withering away of the state that follows it, is literally the end of history. The class conflict ceases, social antagonism disappears and with it the dynamic element in history goes too. There is no longer any force of change remaining, and the social dialectic has worked itself out to its final conclusion.

How are we to explain this apparent inconsistency? Clearly it is due to the victory of the Marxian apocalyptic over the Marxian philosophy. It is the essence of apocalyptic to look to the end of history and it can never be content with an endless movement of cyclical change. And the apocalyptic hope meant more to Marx than all his rational theories. That was the absolute of his thought, and the end of his action.

If he had followed out his theory dispassionately to its natural end, it is clear that he would have arrived at quite a different conclusion. The supreme significance of history would not have been found in any class, but in the class conflict itself. No class could be the bearer of absolute values, for apart from the fact that such values do not exist in Marx's philosophy, the intrusion of absolute values would have been fatal to the principle of progress. As Marx shows in the passage I have just quoted, the "bad" element in society is just as necessary to life as the good. And consequently it is not bad in any absolute sense, it is merely the negative pole in the historic process. Marx himself fully admitted this complete moral relativity in theory. He condemned the absolute ethical categories of the idealist as capitalistic fetishism. In this respect Bukharin is a good Marxian when he writes:

Ethics will ultimately in the case of the proletariat be

transformed into simple and easily understood rules of conduct, such as are required for communism, and thus it will really cease to be ethics at all. For the essence of ethics is the fact that it involves norms enveloped in a fetishistic raiment. Fetishism is the essence of ethics: when fetishism disappears, ethics also will disappear. For example, no one would think of designating the constitution of a consumer's store, or a party as "ethical" or moral, for anyone can see the human significance of these things.[7]

But if this is so, it is clear that every class and every economic order has its own morality and that the essential principle of morality is not to be found in any of these group or class ethics but rather in the conformity of the individual to the spirit of his own class and order. There is no such thing as a good *man*, there is only a good bourgeois or a good proletarian. And one is as good as the other, since each is a necessary factor in social progress. Thus too there is no absolute justice, since class interest is the ultimate criterion, and consequently it is no less just that the employer should exploit the worker in a capitalist society, than that the proletariat should liquidate the bourgeois in a communist state. Hence it would seem that the only real immorality is to betray the interests of one's own class, and that a man like Karl Marx himself, or F. Engels, who serves the interests of another class even if it be the class of the future, is no social hero, but an apostate and a traitor. He has become a bad bourgeois but he can never become a good proletarian unless he is economically and sociologically absorbed into the proletariat.

Now it is quite possible to imagine a moral and political system founded on this relativism and historical materialism, but it would be something entirely different from any existing form of socialism. It would entirely abjure the demon of the absolute and would take refuge in a philosophic detachment. It would recognize that conflict is the law of life and that men cannot do other than follow the dictates of class interest. It would recognize that revolution was not, as the liberals believed, the vindication of absolute rights and the liberation of humanity from the bondage of superstition and injustice but a part of the necessary cycle

[7] N. Bukharin, *Historical Materialism* (Eng. trans.), p. 239.

of change which governs the life of society, the destruction of the old order giving birth to a new one which will in turn pass away when its time is ripe. And this recognition of the naturalness and inevitability of social conflict and change would, in proportion as it was recognized, tend to purge the struggle of its bitterness. Men would recognize that their opponents were not inhuman monsters who were deliberately opposing the victory of truth, but that they were men like themselves, bound by circumstances to act as they did, and the more worthy of respect because they were loyal to their class and their order. And the philosopher himself would cease to share the naive passions of the mob and would turn like Heraclitus to the contemplation of the unseen harmony which runs through the apparent strife and confusion of life, since the harmonious structure of the world depends on its opposite tension, like that of the bow and the lyre, and if we could remove strife from the world, we should bring it to an end, since "strife is justice" and "war is the father and king of Gods and Men."

This is no unworthy conclusion, but it is not the conclusion which Marx himself drew from his doctrine, or any of his followers with the exception of Georges Sorel. As soon as Marx turns to action all his philosophy goes by the board and he adopts the naive absolutism of the fanatic. The exploitation of the proletariat arouses a genuinely moral indignation: he regards it not as a necessary phase in economic evolution, but as a sin that cries to heaven for vengeance. The cause of the proletariat is the cause of social justice in the most absolute sense. It is a cause for which the Communist is ready to suffer and die and to cause the suffering and death of others. All this is the fruit not of his philosophy or of his materialism but of the underlying religious impulse which finds expression in the revolutionary apocalyptic. It is a spiritual passion which has lost its theological object and has attempted to find independent justification in a purely rational theory. And the intrusion of this spiritual force falsifies Marx's whole theory by imparting to it an absolutism that is foreign to its real nature. Thus his historical relativism becomes contaminated by an apocalyptic determinism—a doctrine of the End of History—and his ethical relativism passes away before a Puritanical rigorism of a strictly dualist type. And this is why Marxism is characterized by a certain inhumanity which does not belong either to the religious apocalyptic tradition or to rationalism but which arises from the union of intense apocalyptic convictions with a materialist philosophy.

Now the Christian philosophy of history resembles that of Marxism in so far as it also has a revolutionary view of the historical process and an apocalyptic conception of the End of History. Like Marxism it rejects the static idealism of the Liberal tradition and the naive optimism of the humanitarian ethic. But on the other hand, while the historical dialectic of Marxism is essentially materialistic, that of Christianity is essentially spiritual, a dialogue between God and man, and the end of history is not found in history itself, but arises from the raising of history to a supertemporal plane.

Moreover, since the Christian dualism is a spiritual one, it does not find its solution in the class conflict or in any of the temporal conflicts of history, but in the mystery of the Cross which reverses the material values of history and gives a new meaning to victory and defeat. The true makers of history are not to be found on the surface of events among the successful politicians or the successful revolutionaries: these are the servants of events. Their masters are the spiritual men whom the world knows not, the unregarded agents of the creative action of the Spirit. The supreme instance of this—the key to the Christian understanding of history— is to be found in the Incarnation—the presence of the maker of the world in the world unknown to the world. And though this divine intervention in the course of history seems at first sight to empty secular history of all ultimate significance, in reality it gives history for the first time an absolute spiritual value. The Incarnation is itself in a sense the divine fruit of history—of the fullness of time—and it finds its extension and completion in the historic life of the Church.

For the redemption of humanity is not, as Protestantism tended to maintain, an isolated act which stands outside history and which involves on the part of humanity only the bare act of justifying faith. It is a vital process of regeneration which manifests itself in the corporate reality of a divine society. And the formation of this divine society—the creation of a new humanity—gives the historic process that absolute value and that transcendent end which Marxism vainly seeks in a social millenniarism which has no real relation to the materialistic theory on which it professes to base itself.

Thus there is no reconciliation possible between Marxian materialism, even in its most idealized form, and the Christian faith in God, the creator of heaven and earth, the Maker and Redeemer of man, the Lord and Giver of Life. Where that faith is absent, as it is so widely in the modern world, man is divorced from reality, he is living in the dark and all his intellectual and political systems become distorted and unreal. This is the case with Communism which, more than any other system in history, has attempted to build its new world in the dark. And consequently I believe that the ultimate verdict on Communism will be that the house it is building for the new humanity is not a palace but a prison, since it has no windows. For what man still needs and in his heart desires is the coming of "a dayspring from on high to give light to them that sit in darkness and the shadow of death, to guide our feet into the way of peace."

—1935.

5

H. G. Wells and the Outline of History

WELLS'S *Outline of History* was one of the outstanding successes of the years that followed the first World War. Its success even astonished its author, though few writers have possessed more abounding confidence in their universal powers. It was conceived at the same time as the League of Nations, when Wells's own mind was preoccupied with schemes for world organization and when he was exasperated by the failure of the specialists to grasp the total issues on which the life of humanity depended. Thus it was a kind of enormous pamphlet—"a sort of general report and handbook"—which was intended to give the common man a plain account of the whole human drama in which he was inextricably involved. "Multitudes of people," Wells wrote, "all the intelligent people of the world, indeed, were seeking more or less consciously to 'get the hang' of world affairs as a whole." They "tried to recall the narrow history teaching of their brief school days and found an uninspiring and partially forgotten list of national kings or presidents. They tried to read about these matters and found an endless wilderness of books." [1] And so Wells felt himself inspired to bring food to the hungry

---

[1] *The Outline of History*, rev. ed. by R. Postgate (New York, Garden City, 1949; London, Cassell, 1951), p. 2.

multitude in the wilderness. And he was right. He knew what they wanted and they accepted what he gave them, and the *Outline of History* sold by the million.

Wells accepted this amazing success with an un-Wellsian modesty. He admitted that he was no historian and that it was work for an historian rather than a novelist. "But there did not seem to be any historian available, who was sufficiently superficial, shall we say—sufficiently wide and sufficiently shallow to cover the vast range of the project." [2]

In face of all this, what is the historian to say? He cannot deny that the task, as Wells saw it, was a vital one. He cannot but admit that no historian was prepared to face the task, and that if it was to be performed by a non-historian no one could have done it better than Wells. For Wells was the last of the encyclopaedists—a belated child of the Enlightenment who still preserved its faith in progress and humanity and science with all its optimism and naïveté, even in the hostile climate of post-war Europe. Although he did not possess the intensive literary culture of Voltaire and his contemporaries, he had a similar universality of aim and he had the same gifts of intellectual synthesis and scientific popularization. Indeed, there was not one of the Encyclopaedists who achieved such an encyclopaedic feat as Wells performed in his trilogy *The Outline of History* (1920), *The Science of Life* (1931) and *The Wealth, Work and Happiness of Mankind* (1932).

No doubt it will be said that the feat was an impossible one and that what could be done in the eighteenth century is no longer possible in the twentieth. Certainly it will be generally agreed that if Wells survives it will be due to his early novels and not to his encyclopaedias and his essays in world reformation. But though he would have admitted this himself, he was a man who believed, like Tolstoi and Ruskin, that his mission as a teacher was more important than his work of artistic creation. For Wells was a frustrated evangelist who was always on the verge of producing an apocalypse or founding a new religion, but who was held back at the last moment by some obstacle which he never clearly understood.

The result was that for the last thirty years of his life, Wells's immense talents, which barely fell short of genius,

[2] *Ibid.*, p. 4.

were dissipated in this strange medley of encyclopaedias and novels with a purpose, of plans for world reformation and "open conspiracies" and cosmological speculations. *The Outline of History* is a characteristic product of their period, and it is also one of the most successful, because the labour of mastering so vast a body of material imposed on his mind that element of discipline which he was usually unwilling to accept. It was successful because it was an honest attempt to perform a necessary task, and because in this field at least he was willing to admit his limitations and to take the advice of men who knew more than himself. At the same time it shows the typical defects of Wells' mind, his Philistinism, his intolerance, the superficiality of his judgment, and the serious gaps in his knowledge and his intellectual sympathies. Moreover, his inevitable dependence on second-hand or third-hand sources is apt to interpose an artificial barrier between the author and his subject, so that there are times when Wells the prophet and Wells the artist are replaced by Wells the compiler.

Nevertheless, Wells had a real gift of historical vision and a power of synthesis that many eminent historians have lacked. This was due above all to his religious faith, to his conviction that history was not a record of dead events, but a creative process out of which a new world and a new humanity must ultimately emerge. Thus faith made him feel that there is nothing in the history of the past which is not relevant to the present and the future, so that he read and wrote history in order to discover the dynamic factors which had made and were transforming the world of man.

It is his attempt to trace these factors through the course of history that gives his work its unity and its originality. In the first place, he sees the social evolution of mankind since prehistoric times following two different lines of development which are continually conflicting with one another and thereby producing new social forms. On the one hand, there is the tradition of the ancient settled civilizations which were essentially *communities of obedience*, based on the labour of the peasant and united by the authority of the gods embodied in the person of the king and the institutions of the temple priesthood. On the other hand, there are the nomad pastoral societies which are essentially *communities of will*, based on the courage and energy of the individual warrior and united by the bond of loyalty to the chief who is chosen to lead his people in war and to judge them in peace.

The wealth and obedience of the settled civilizations inevitably invite the predatory attacks of the nomads. But, as soon as they are successful, they are incorporated by the settled civilization as a ruling aristocracy, the war leader becomes a king by divine right, and the community of will is absorbed in the community of obedience. According to Wells, these conflicting forces have continued to dominate the history of mankind. "Civilization, even in its most servile forms, has always offered much that is enormously attractive, convenient and congenial to mankind; but something restless and untamed in our race has striven to convert civilization from its original reliance on unparticipating obedience into a community of participating wills. And to this lurking nomadism in our blood, and particularly in the blood of monarchs and aristocracies which have no doubt contributed in a large proportion to the begetting of later generations, we must ascribe also that incessant urgency towards a wider range that forces every state to extend its boundaries if it can, and to spread its interests to the ends of the earth. The power of nomadic restlessness, that tends to bring all the earth under one rule, seems to be identical with the spirit that makes most of us chafe under direction and restraint and seek to participate in every government we tolerate." [3]

Now in Wells' view the modern state represents an attempt to combine these two apparently contradictory traditions—of society as a community of obedience and society as a community of will—in a new type of community which would be both civilized and free. The primitive precursor of this new form of life first emerges into history with the Roman republic, but it was not until 2,000 years later with the American and the French Revolutions that man first created a political order which consciously asserted the need for an association of the free will of the individual with the common purposes of civilization. And even then the fusion was still incomplete and was disguised in mythical formulae, like the Social Contract and the dogma that all men are by nature free and equal.

[3] *Ibid.*, pp. 737–738.

What is really needed in Wells' view is the conversion of the community of faith and obedience into a community of knowledge and will, a change which is more religious than political and which involves an intensive process of moral education. Hence the importance which he attributes to the role of the world religions. Rome could not succeed in the creation of a world republic, because Rome had no real religion. The historical importance of Christianity, and also of Islam, lies in the fact that for the first time in human experience they gave a common moral education to an unprecedented multitude of human beings and gave them a common idea of human purpose and destiny. In spite of Wells' notorious hostility to Catholicism, he pays a remarkable tribute to the idea of Christendom as the world-city of God, and especially to the Papacy, as the first clearly conscious attempt to provide a spiritual government for mankind—"a government ruling men through the educated coordination of their minds in a common conception of human history and human destiny." [4]

Wells fully accepted the validity of this ideal, although he rejected the specifically Christian form under which it first appeared. He believed that it would only be realized on the basis of the new scientific knowledge of nature and man and the new techniques of education and information which were developed in the eighteenth and nineteenth centuries. Even so, the modern scientific revolution still lacks its organ of world government and the moral power to unite mankind in a common purpose, and therefore its true goal is still unattained. Wells sees the last two centuries as a desperate race between the progress of world education and the danger of world catastrophe. From the days when he began to write his scientific thrillers, like the *War of the Worlds* and the *War in the Air*, Wells had always been acutely aware of this possibility of catastrophe—of the destruction of civilization by science; and it is still present in the concluding pages of the *Outline* in which he makes his final profession of faith in the gospel of progress. "Against the unifying effort of Christendom and against the unifying element of the mechanical revolution, catastrophe won. We cannot tell yet how much of the winnings of catastrophe

[4] *Ibid.,* p. 739.

still remain to be gathered in, what vast harvests of wasted lives still await the reaper." [5]

Thus the Wellsian view of history is neither as superficial nor as one-sided as many of his critics suppose. But it does suffer from a certain sectarian narrowness and intolerance of judgment which makes his detailed treatment of historical movements lag far behind the broad sweep of his historical vision. He is so conscious of the possibilities of human achievement, and so outraged by the continual failure of mankind to realize its opportunities, that he has no patience with man's actual historical achievements and scolds the makers of history as though they were a set of lazy and mischievous school boys. This is especially noticeable in the case of those movements which are most vital to his own interpretation of history and which one might have expected to evoke his sympathy, such as the Roman attempt to create a world state. He has a good word to say for the Huns, and he is warmly appreciative of the Mongols. But when he comes to the Romans, there is not a good word to be said for them. It is not merely that they were cruel, vulgar and avaricious. They did not even understand their own stupid business of war and empire. "It is absurd to write of its statecraft; it had none." "It was a colossally ignorant and unimaginative empire. It foresaw nothing. It had no strategic foresight, because it was blankly ignorant of geography and ethnology. It knew nothing of the conditions of Russia, Central Asia and the East," and by its destruction of Asia Minor and Babylonia (*sic.*) it destroyed the necessary basis for the eastern extension of culture. In the West, "it made no effort to Romanize Germany" and produced "no really intelligent account of Picts and Scots." It showed "an astonishing incapacity for novelty in methods of transport," and even proved inefficient as a military organization. Two hundred years after Caesar's time, "the Romans were still marching about, the same drilled and clanking cohorts they had always been, easily ridden round and shot to pieces." [6]

Nor is Wells much more sympathetic to the achievements of the modern European state and to the world expansion of Western civilization. It is true that this is of central importance for his general theory, since he regards the rise

[5] *Ibid.*, p. 1198.

[6] *Ibid.*, pp. 499–500.

of the modern state as marking a new epoch in human development and compares its relation to the great Oriental empires to the supersession of the tremendous fauna of the Mesozoic Age by the evolution of new and higher forms of life. But as soon as he begins to describe the process in detail, his moral and humanitarian feelings are too strong for his biological theories, and he denounces the whole process of Western expansion from his standpoint as a liberal idealist.

This inconsistency is natural enough. What is difficult to understand is his failure to do justice to the history of modern science which one would have expected to form the climax of the whole work. In this respect *The Wealth, Work and Happiness of Mankind* is decidedly superior to *The Outline of History*, but in both of them his attention is almost exclusively devoted to the technical and mechanical achievements of modern civilization and there is no adequate account of the movement of scientific thought that preceded those achievements and made them possible. In *The Outline of History* Darwin is almost the only man of science after Newton who receives serious attention. The great achievements of European science in the eighteenth and late seventeenth centuries are ignored. There is no mention of Huyghens and Pascal and Leibniz, of Euler and the Bernouillis, of Lagrange and Laplace and Lavoisier. Nor does the nineteenth century fare much better, for there is no mention of Dalton or Gauss or Clerk Maxwell and only a passing reference to Faraday and Mendel.

This cannot altogether be explained by lack of space. If there is room for James Branch Cabell and Sir James Barrie there is surely room for James Clerk Maxwell or even Lord Rutherford. The history of the intellectual revolution which has transformed man's whole conception of the nature of the world and has launched mankind on a new and perilous journey into the unknown was a subject which had always stirred Wells' imagination, and no man seemed better fitted to view it as a whole and to describe its progress in simple language to a popular audience. The *Outline of History* gave him a magnificent opportunity. Everything in his reading of history prepared the way for this, and as we read the book it seems to be moving steadily towards it as the climax of the whole work. But when the moment comes, he lets it slip through his fingers and disappear behind the complications of international politics and the causes and events of the first World War. No one believed more strongly than Wells that it is the thinkers who are the real makers of history, and that "compared to them the foreign ministers and statesmen and politicians are no more than a number of troublesome and occasionally incendiary schoolboys." But he fails to do justice to this idea in his treatment of recent history, and as his work draws to its close, his attention becomes increasingly absorbed in the mistakes of the politicians and the misdeeds of the warmongers, while science and the movement of thought fade into the background. In the final chapters it is Wells the journalist, not Wells the prophet nor Wells the sociologist, who has the last word.

—1951.

6

Oswald Spengler and the Life of Civilizations

IT is now about a dozen years since Professor Flinders Petrie in his little book on "Revolutions of Civilization" restated the theory of a cyclic movement in history, governing the rise and fall of cultures, a hypothesis which has attracted so many thinkers in the past—notably Vico and Campanella. Yet more recently this theory has become the centre of general interest and discussion on the Continent thanks to Herr Spengler's striking application of it to the present state of Europe in his now famous book *The Decline of the West*.

Herr Spengler's aim has been to create, not a philosophy of history in the old sense of the term, but a new, historical, kind of philosophy. It is by his intense feeling for the world as a living process, that the modern Western European differs most profoundly from the men of other ages and cultures. World history means infinitely more to him than it meant to the thinkers of ancient Greece or of India. To the latter at any rate, Time and consequently History, were without value or ultimate significance, to the modern European they are the very foundation of his conception of reality. Yet this sense of history has not found adequate expression in our philosophical systems. The metaphysicians of modern Europe, like their predecessors in classical antiquity, have viewed the world as a system, a great closed order resting on the principle of Causality, not a living organism. They have looked at the universe with the eyes of the physicist rather than with the eyes of the biologist, and have systematized it as the production of dead law instead of as the creation of living spirit. Nor have the historians themselves done better. They concentrate their attention on facts and events, they accumulate masses of detail without giving any heed to the informing Spirit which alone gives significance to the material circumstance. They view History "as a tape worm which tirelessly puts forth fresh 'Epochs,' instead of as a life-series of highly developed organisms."

In Herr Spengler's view World History is nothing less than a "Second Cosmos," with a different content and a different law of movement to that of the first Cosmos, Nature, which has hitherto absorbed the attention of the philosopher. It has its own internal law—*Schicksal* or Destiny, as distinguished from the law of Causality, which rules the world of Nature. That is to say, historical time is not mere numerical succession, it is the registration of a life process like the years of a man's life. Until the unities that lie behind the time-cycles of history have been grasped, it is useless to try and explain historical change by secondary causes. But if it is possible to attain an internal knowledge of history, if we grasp intuitively the principle that gives unity to an age or to a culture, then history will take an organic form, and we shall be able to see in all historic phenomena the expression of a moulding force behind the play of circumstances.

This unifying principle Herr Spengler finds in the spirit of the great world-cultures. He claims that each culture has an individual style or personality, which can be seized intuitively by whoever possesses a feeling for history, just as the individual genius of a great musician or artist can be recognized by the born critic in all his works. This individual style is not confined to the art or the social forms of a culture, as some have thought; it extends to philosophic thought, to science and to mathematics. Each culture has its distinctive *number,* so that there is a deep inner bond between the geometry of Euclid and the Greek tragedy, between algebra and arabesque, between the differential calculus and contrapuntal music. This principle of the organic interconnection of all the expressions of a particular culture is carried by Herr Spengler to paradoxical lengths. He maintains that there is an "intimate dependence of the most modern physical and chemical theories on the mythological conceptions of our Germanic forefathers": that Perspective in Painting, Printing, Credit, Long-Range Artillery and Contrapuntal Music, are all of them expressions of one psychic principle, while the city-state, the nude statue, Euclid and the Greek coin are alike expressions of another.[1] There is, in fact, no human activity which is not the vehicle of the cultural soul; the most abstract scientific thought and the most absolute ethical systems are partial manifestations of a process which is bound up with a particular people and a geographical region, and have no validity outside the domain of their own culture.

This leads to the most fundamental philosophic relativism. "There are no eternal truths. Each philosophy is an expression of its own age, and only of its own age, and there are no two ages which possess the same philosophical intentions."[2] The vital question for a philosopher is whether he embodies the Zeitgeist, "whether it is the soul of the age itself which speaks by his works and intuitions." Hitherto the philosophers have had no inkling of this truth. They have exalted the standards of conduct and the laws of thought of the modern Western European into absolute laws for humanity, they have not realized the possibility of a different soul and a different truth to their own. The historians have shared their error. The civilization that they saw around them was "Civilization," the movement that brought it to maturity was "Progress." They did not dream that European civilization was a limited episode like the civilizations of China and Yucatan.

The time has come, Herr Spengler says, to make a revolution comparable to the abandonment of the geocentric astronomy, to introduce a new "Copernican" philosophy of history, which will study each culture by the laws of its development, which will not subordinate the past to the present, or interpret the souls of other cultures by the standards that are peculiar to our own. The task of the true historian then must be to write the biographies of the great cultures

[1] *Der Untergang des Abendlandes* (2 vols., 1920–1922), Vol. I, p. 66.

[2] *Op. cit.*, I, p. 58.

as self-contained wholes, which follow a similar course of growth and decay, but are as unrelated to one another as different planetary systems. These great cultures are eight in number, Egypt, Babylonia, India, China, the Maya culture of Central America, the culture of classical antiquity, the Arabian culture and the culture of Western Europe. There are in addition a few cultures which have failed to attain full development, such as those of the Hittites, the Persians and the Quichua.

The dawn of a new culture is seen in the rise of a new mythology, which finds expression in the heroic saga and epic. Herr Spengler instances the Vedic mythology for India, the Olympian mythology and the Homeric poems for Antiquity, primitive Christianity and the Gospels for the "Arabian" culture, and "Germanic Catholicism" and the Nibelungenlied for Western Europe. In the next stage—"summer"—the culture attains to full self-consciousness. This is the time of the rise of the characteristic philosophies, and the building up of a new fundamental criterion by which to fathom the essence of a culture. Pythagoras and Descartes, Parmenides and Galileo are the representatives of this phase.

"Autumn" is marked by a loosening of social cohesion, by the growth of rationalism and individualism. At the same time the creative power of a culture finds its final expression in the great conclusive philosophical systems, and in the work of the great mathematicians. It is the period of Plato and Aristotle, of Goethe and Kant, but also of the Sophists and the Encyclopaedists.

In "Winter" the inner development of a culture is complete. After the triumph of the irreligious and materialistic *Weltanschauung,* "Culture" passes away into "Civilization," which is its inorganic, fossilized counterpart, and which finds its spiritual expression in a cosmopolitan and ethical propaganda, such as Buddhism, Stoicism and nineteenth-century Socialism. A similar course of development is traced in art, in economics and in political organization, and at the root of the whole process lies the Life of a People in its intimate connection with a definite geographical region, so that the passing of a culture is at the same time the passing of a people from the land that has fed and nursed it, into the melting pot of cosmopolitanism, the birth of a new population of *déracinés.*

Every historic culture must pass through this life-process,

just as every human being must pass through the same life-cycle from birth to death. And consequently each phase in the life of a particular culture finds its analogy in every other culture. Each event or personality possesses not only a local and temporary importance, it has also a symbolic meaning, as temporary representative of a universal type. There is not merely a superficial historical parallel, there is an organic identity between the place of Napoleon in our culture and that of Alexander in antiquity, between the Sophists and the Encyclopaedists, between the Ramessides and the Antonines. This principle is of the greatest importance for Herr Spengler's theory. By its use he claims that it will be possible not only to reconstruct vanished civilizations, as the palaeontologist reconstructs some prehistoric creature from a single bone, but even to establish a law for the "Predetermination of History," so that when once the underlying idea of a culture has been grasped, it will be possible to foretell the whole course of its growth and the actual dates of its principal phases.

Herr Spengler's aim throughout his work is in fact a practical one. He wishes to plot out the descending curve of Western Civilization, to make the present generation conscious of the crisis through which it is passing and of the true task that lies before it.

Der Untergang des Abendlandes is nothing else but the final passing of the Western Culture and the coming of "Civilization." Consequently the "architectonic" possibilities of the Western soul have been realized, and there remains only the practical task of conservation. The age has no more a need of artists and philosophers and poets, it calls for men of "Roman hardness," engineers, financiers, and organizers, of the type of Cecil Rhodes.

It is Herr Spengler's desire that the men of the new generation should turn to *"der Teknik statt der Lyrik, der Marine statt der Malerei, der Politik statt der Erkentnisskritik."* [3] The governing movement of the new age is to be Socialism, not the Socialism of the idealist or the revolutionary, but a practical, organizing, imperialist Socialism which stands as far from the latter, as did the world-city of the Roman

---

[3] *Op. cit.,* I, p. 57: "The technical instead of the lyrical; shipping instead of painting; politics instead of epistemology."

lawyer and government from the world-city of the Stoic theorists.

Here then is the final task of the German people. As the second century before Christ saw Rome step into the place of the Hellenistic monarchies, so Prussia takes over the direction of the world from France and England.[4] The hour of Cannae is past, the coming age will be the age of Caesar. And in the East there is a redness in the sky—the first sign of the dawn of the new Russian culture of the future.

To the English mind, ever suspicious of the theorists, and perhaps of the historical theorist more than others, Herr Spengler's views may seem so fantastic as to be hardly worth consideration. But this is largely due to a difference of outlook. Even in this cosmopolitan age the different European peoples have each preserved their own separate views of the past, and the man who has been brought up on the tradition of Macaulay and Freeman and Grote and Stubbs will never understand his contemporary who lives under the tradition of Treitschke and Mommsen. This opposition is sometimes softened by the existence of a liberal current of opinion in Germany which has been affected by the thought of the Western peoples, but Herr Spengler is a pure Central European, who views the whole history of Europe from the longitude of Munich and Berlin. The Baroque monarchies, which to the ordinary Englishman are a byway of history, are to him the characteristic expression of Western culture at the moment when it had achieved its final form, while parliamentarism and democracy, which to us are central, are to him the phenomena of decline. This difference of outlook makes his book all the more interesting for a foreigner, but it has the disadvantage of distracting the reader's attention from Herr Spengler's essential thesis to those details of his historical interpretation which arouse instinctive prejudice. If we disregard these accidental peculiarities, we shall see that *The Decline of the West* is only an extreme statement of the new relativist attitude to history which has become almost universal. During the last ten or twenty years there has been a general reaction against the old absolutist view of civilization and against that unquestioning faith in the transcendent value of our own Western culture which marked

[4] Herr Spengler's book was of course published during the course of the war (1917).

the nineteenth century. There are civilizations, but no *Civilization;* and the standards and achievements of each culture are valid only within the limits of that culture; they possess no absolute significance.

It is obvious that this philosophy of history can find no room for the conception of Progress. There is certainly a process of evolution, but it is a blind movement, which has no ethical meaning, such as was essential to the old idea of Progress. For Herr Spengler each culture is a fixed organism, which ends in itself, and it is no more possible to believe that the Hellenic culture and that of modern Europe are successive steps on the part of the Progress of Humanity than it would be to suppose that the pug and the Pomeranian are necessary stages in the upward progress of Doghood to perfection.

Hence the development of culture is not merely non-ethical; it is irrational. History is essentially unintelligible: for the law of Destiny, not that of Causality, is the law of life. The makers of history, the men and peoples of Destiny, are unconscious and instinctive in their creative activity, while the thinkers—philosophers and men of science—are sterile systematizers, "bloodless" men who have lost touch with the vital forces of their culture. Consequently, Spengler is continually depreciating Reason and scientific analysis, in comparison with instinctive feeling or "the physiognomic tact" which is the only means of approach to the positive aspect of reality which he so characteristically terms "the totemistic side of life." For him the roots of historical change —that is to say, of historical reality—lie not in the Reason but in "the blood."

If this is true, it is clear that culture is exclusively the result of racial growth, and owes nothing to Reason or to any tradition which transcends the limits of a single people's experience. For each culture is a world to itself, hermetically sealed against every influence from without, and impenetrable to the eyes of the rest of the world. And Herr Spengler fails to explain how he or anyone else can grasp the life process of a different organism from that of which he forms part, even by the exercise of "physiognomic tact." But this idea is irreconcilable with the whole course of human history, which is nothing but a vast system of intercultural relations.

I write, however, from the standpoint of one who is a firm

believer in the organic life of civilization and the existence of a cyclic movement in history which determines the main phases of the life of the peoples. The time is surely ripe for the abandonment of what Herr Spengler calls the Ptolemaic view of history, and for the beginnings of a scientific morphology of culture. But the new science is in its infancy, and it is a bold step to attempt at this early stage a detailed predetermination of history, such as we find in *Der Untergang des Abendlandes*. Such a scheme can only be carried through by a drastic selection of facts, and indeed Herr Spengler has not avoided the pitfall of oversimplification which has proved the ruin of so many earlier philosophies of history.

Thus while fully admitting that the principle of "the life of peoples" is at the root of the cyclic movement in history, one hesitates to confine all cultural achievement to the eight or twelve culture-peoples, each of which is responsible for a complete and independent civilization. There is little room in Herr Spengler's scheme for cultural interaction and admixture, still less for the co-operation of several peoples in one civilization.

Thus in the culture of the Ancient World everything must be explained as the life work of two culture peoples, the Greeks and the Romans. The last vital act of this culture was the building of the Roman Empire—a vast work of material organization. After that, there is nothing but petrifaction and death. How then are we to explain the cultural phenomena of the Imperial epoch—the rise of Christianity, the philosophy of Plotinus, the mathematics of Diophantus and the renewal of architecture and art? Herr Spengler answers that all this is the work of a new people, it belongs to the first stages of the Arab culture-cycle, which develops itself under the crust of the dying classical civilization.

The heroic mythus, which marks the dawn of the consciousness of this new people, is embodied in the Gospels and in primitive Christianity, as that of the Greeks was expressed in the Homeric poems and in the Olympian mythology. The Pantheon at Rome is the *Urmoschee*—the starting point of Arab architecture, and with Diophantus we first come into contact with a new mathematic as foreign from the Hellenic geometry, as is the "Magic" arabesque spirit of that culture from the "Olympian," statuesque spirit of Hellenism.

Is Herr Spengler justified in thus calling up a new racial culture like a *deus ex machina* to cut the knots of his historical problem? Certainly the new elements in later Hellenistic civilization may be explained as due to Oriental influences, but these influences come not from the budding energies of a new people, but from older peoples whose cultural development was even older than that of the Hellenes. The "heroic" phase of Arab culture is to be found in the stories of Antara the son of Sheddad, Hatim et-T'ai, Chanfara and the other open-handed bloodthirsty heroes of Arab legend—in the wars that sprang from the rivalry of the horse Dahis and the mare Ghabra, all of which is far more comparable to the spirit of the Homeric poems than the Sermon on the Mount. The Gospels and Primitive Christianity belong rather to the last stage of the Judaeo-Aramean culture—a culture which had expressed its "heroic" phase a thousand years earlier in the sagas of Samson, of Deborah, of Gideon and the like. All this results from Herr Spengler's over-simplification, which only allows him to take account of a single people in dealing with a particular civilization. In reality it is impossible to simplify to this degree any civilization except the most primitive ones. So long as a people exists it possesses a cultural tradition, and however depressed and passive this may seem in relation to the creative culture of the dominant people in a world civilization, it is nevertheless capable of far-reaching influences and reactions. Professor Flinders Petrie in his well-known study on the Revolutions of Civilization brings evidence to prove that a single people—such as the Egyptian—passes through successive culture-cycles; and though it is probable that without external influence or the infusion of fresh blood such cycles would tend to become stereotyped repetitions of the culture that has been previously worked out (as is perhaps the case in modern China), yet if once these stereotyped cultures were brought into contact with a new civilization, they would possess great potentialities for cultural influence.

Even in external things, we see how the life of a people can be transformed by some invention or art of life that has been borrowed from without, as in the case of the introduction of the horse among the American Indians by the Spaniards.

Far more important, however, is the spread of new forms of thought. It is true that a philosopher like Aristotle, or a religious leader like Mohammed, is the offspring of a particular culture, and could not have appeared in any other land, or at any other period but his own. Nevertheless, the influence of such men far transcends cultural and racial boundaries. It is true that by becoming a Moslem the Negro or the Turk undergoes a cultural transformation; a new cultural type arises which is neither that of Moslem Arabia nor that of the native pagan people. But the fact that such a process can occur at all is fatal to the Spenglerian theory of absolutely isolated and unrelated culture cycles. It readmits the principle of causality and the opportunity for rational analysis which Spengler professes to banish for ever. And even if he denies that such an admixture is a true culture, and relegates the peoples in question to his category of *Fellachenvolker*— "Fellahin peoples"—can he exclude the factor of alien intellectual influences from the very parent culture itself?

Thus, for example, in dealing with Islam we must not only take account of the culture of the Arabs of Arabia, who created the original Islamic State. There is also the Byzantine-Syro-Egyptian culture of the Levant, an old mature civilization which influenced Islam from the cradle; there is the Sassanian-Persian culture which had a vital influence on Islam even before the days of the Abbasids; there is the culture of Khorasan and Trans-Oxiana, mainly Persian, but possibly containing a Bactrian Greek element, and certainly affected by Indian Buddhist influence; finally there are the non-cultured peoples—the Turks, who were for centuries in contact with Persian and Chinese civilization, the Berbers, who had previously been under the influence of the Roman-Hellenistic culture, and last of all the Negroes. All these cultures and peoples brought their contributions to the civilization of mediaeval Islam, so that under the surface uniformity of Arabic language and religion and institutions, an extraordinary process of fermentation and change was taking place.

Again take the apparently much simpler case of our Western European culture. Here we have several peoples, composed of different racial elements, all co-operating in the development of a common culture heritage. The life-cycles of these peoples do not necessarily synchronize, nor do they all come under the influence of the common culture-heritage in the same measure. Italy was in the direct line of the Graeco-Roman tradition which only lightly affected the civilization of the Baltic lands. Yet Herr Spengler takes the view that the whole of our civilization is essentially the work of one people—the Germans. Consequently he begins its life-cycle, not with the Barbarian Invasions, as the parallel of the ancient world would suggest, but in the centuries which produced the Crusades, the Nibelungenlied and Wolfram von Eschenbach's Parsifal. This initial error falsifies his whole series of analogies between the ancient and modern cultures. He compares the Athenian democracy to the Bourbons instead of to Renaissance Italy, the age of Alexander to that of Napoleon instead of to the first European expansion in the sixteenth century, and the present age to that of the early Punic wars instead of to the Imperial epoch. Hence the depressing character of his forecast, since he would have us spend the next two centuries in that work of material organization which has actually occupied us for the last two hundred years.

In reality, since our civilization is the work of several peoples it embraces several parallel life-cycles. The most representative of these is no doubt that of the French, which stands mid-way between the early ripening of the Italians and the late maturity of the Germans. Indeed in many respects France has a similar importance for our culture to that which Hellas possessed for the culture of antiquity. Nevertheless this is but an average standard, and it can only be applied with exactitude to the French portion of the Western European culture-area.

Moreover it is clear that in order to explain the life-cycle of civilizations it is not sufficient to possess a formula for the life-cycle of individual peoples, we must also understand the laws of cultural interaction and the causes of the rise and fall of the great cultural syncretisms, which seem to overshadow the destinies of individual peoples. Considered from this point of view the last stage of a culture, the phase to which Herr Spengler confines the name of "Civilization," acquires peculiar importance. It is not merely a negative period of petrifaction and death, as he describes it; it is the time when civilization is most open to external influence. The true significance of the Roman Hellenistic period, for example, is not decay but syncretism. Two different streams of culture, which we describe loosely as "Oriental" and "Western," as "Asiatic" and "European" flowed for several centuries in the same bed, mingling with one another to such a degree that they seemed to form a new civilization. And this intermingling of culture was not merely of importance for the past as the conclusion of the old world, it had a decisive influence on the future. The passing of ancient civilization and the coming of a new age is marked, it is true, by these two streams once more separating and flowing out again to East and West as the new Daughter Cultures of Islam and Western Europe, though the central river bed is still occupied for a time by the dwindling stream of the Byzantine civilization. Nevertheless the two streams continued to bear witness to their common origin. The West was moulded by a religion of the Levant, the East carried on for centuries the tradition of Hellenic philosophy and science. Aristotle and Galen travelled to India with the Moslems, to Scotland and Scandinavia with the Christians. Roman law lived on alike with the mediaeval canonists and the Ulema of Islam. But because Islam inherited so largely from the Hellenistic-Oriental culture of Roman times Herr Spengler is not justified in giving an Arabic origin to the latter; the Arabs entered into the cultural inheritance in the East, just as the Germanic peoples did in the West, as heirs not as originators. And as East and West, each in its own measure, have received the inheritance of Hellenic culture, so too is it with the tradition of Israel. Without that tradition neither Christendom nor Islam is conceivable; each claims it as its peculiar birth-right. It is interwoven with the very texture of the Koran; it lives on in modern Europe; indeed it was nowhere stronger than it has been in the new countries—in Calvinist Scotland, in Lutheran Scandinavia; in Puritan New England. And it was in the same age of syncretism, the mature period of the Hellenistic-Oriental culture, that the Jewish tradition acquired these new contacts and opportunities for expression. Since then the different culture streams have been flowing away from one another, but they still bear the indelible character set upon them by that decisive period of intercourse and fusion.

All this network of cultural influences is viewed by Herr Spengler as essentially external, unreal, and non-vital. The Christianity of the Middle Ages and that of the Patristic period—"Faustian and Magian Christianity," to use his own expression—are for him two different religions, which possess a common terminology and common usages, but are nevertheless each the original expression of an individual soul. And this is the *reductio ad absurdum* of his whole theory, for it involves the conclusion that the culture of the West would have followed an identical course except for empty forms and names, if it had never become Christian, and had never received the inheritance of the Hellenic and Roman culture-traditions. The relativist philosophy of history ends by denying the very existence of relations, and dissolves the unity of history into an unintelligible plurality of isolated and sterile culture-processes.

Nevertheless the rejection of Herr Spengler's theory does not justify a denial of the objective reality of cultural unity. Philosophic critics of *The Decline of the West*, such as Mr. R. G. Collingwood,[5] tend to regard history as perpetual becoming, a single universal process of world development. Thus Mr. Collingwood maintains that the conception of a culture is purely subjective, and owes its existence to the observing mind. "The cycle is the historian's field of vision at the moment." "We fabricate periods of history by fastening upon some, to us, particularly luminous point and trying to study it as it actually came into being. We find our mind caught, as it were, by some striking phenomenon—Greek life in the fifth century or the like; and this becomes the nucleus of a group of historical inquiries asking how it arose and how it passed away; what turned into it and what it turned into."

In so far as a culture exists, it rests on the existence of some dominant idea; and since every idea involves its opposite, one culture necessarily passes into another by the natural evolution of thought. In other words two successive cultures are not independent organisms, they are merely the embodiment of a pair of complementary propositions in the process of Neo-Hegelian dialectic.

This idealistic conception of history is even less satisfactory than Spengler's anti-intellectualist relativism. Like the latter, it makes a complete divorce between History and Science and leaves no room for the contributions of the biologist and the anthropologist. For while Spengler regards a culture as an unconscious physical life-process which can only be grasped by a kind of instinctive sense, Mr. Collingwood eliminates the physical and material aspects altogether, and treats cultural development as a purely spiritual movement of ideas.

In reality a culture is neither a purely physical process nor

5 In *Antiquity*, I, 3, September 1927.

an ideal construction. It is a living whole from its roots in the soil and in the simple instinctive life of the shepherd, the fisherman and the husbandman, up to its flowering in the highest achievements of the artist and the philosopher; just as the individual combines in the substantial unity of his personality the animal life of nutrition and reproduction with the higher activities of reason and intellect. It is impossible to disregard the importance of a material and non-rational element in history. Every culture rests on a foundation of geographical environment and racial inheritance, which conditions its highest activities. The change of culture is not simply a change of thought, it is above all a change of life. The fall of the Hellenic culture was not due to the passing of the Hellenic idea, it was not, as Mr. Collingwood says, "a process that led to the Magian idea by its inner logic"; on the contrary, the Hellenic idea never died, it is eternal and imperishable, and the decline of the culture was due to a progress of social degeneration—the passing of the Greek people from the land that had fed and nursed it into the melting-pot of urban cosmopolitanism. It is even possible for one culture to kill another, as we see in the case of the destruction of the Peruvian civilization by the Spaniards, and in the countless instances in which primitive cultures have withered away on contact with modern European civilization. Nor is it only the lower cultures that are destroyed in this way. There are also instances of highly developed urban civilizations falling a victim to barbarian invaders, as when the flourishing culture of the Danube provinces was wiped out in the fifth century A.D., or when the cities of Eastern Iran were destroyed by the Mongols. The idealist attempt to see in history only the "glory of the Idea mirroring itself in the History of the World," [6] fares no better than the optimism of Dr. Panglos, and calls forth in the manner of Hegelian dialectic that opposite and complementary view of Candide, which looks on history as an irrational welter of cruelty and destruction in which brute force and blind chance are the only rulers.

Nevertheless though culture is essentially conditioned by material factors, these are not all. A culture receives its form from a rational or spiritual element which transcends

[6] Hegel, *Philosophy of History*, trans. J. Sibree (London, 1857) p. 477.

the limits of racial and geographical conditions. Religion and science do not die with the culture of which they formed part. They are handed on from people to people, and assist as a creative force in the formation of new cultural organisms.

There are, in fact, two movements in history, one of which is due, as Herr Spengler shows, to the life-process of an individual people in contact with a definite geographical environment, while the other is common to a number of different peoples, and results from political, intellectual and religious synthesis and interaction. Only by taking account of both these movements is it possible to understand the general movement of history and explain that real element of integration and progress, which causes different civilizations to be, not closed worlds without meaning for one another, but progressive stages in the life of humanity.

—1922; 1929.

7

Arnold Toynbee and the Study of History

Now that Dr. Toynbee's *Study of History* has been completed by the publication of the last four volumes (making ten in all), it is possible for us to take a comprehensive view of the whole work to form some opinion on its significance and value. But this is not an easy task. One cannot lightly pass judgment on a work of 6,000 pages which has been written with so much erudition and conviction. Nor can one get much help from the judgment of others working in the same field, for they hardly exist, at least in England.

What strikes one at first sight is the fact that the work on the one hand has been a great popular success, especially in the United States, and that, on the other, it has been judged unsympathetically, and often harshly, by the professional historians, especially in Great Britain. This is perhaps not surprising since, hitherto, civilizations have not been regarded as proper subjects for historical study. History has concerned itself with nations and empires, with states and institutions; while the study of civilization has been left to philosophers and sociologists.

This system answered well enough in the past, when the historians were concerned almost entirely with the States of the European world which all shared the same tradition of civilization, and when the study of the Oriental world was treated as a part of colonial history. But today this is no longer possible. Modern history has to take account of the conflicts and contacts between civilizations, as much as, or even more than, of those between the European nations. The ordinary man of today wants to know something about these great world societies which have now become the protagonists in the historical drama and the ordinary history book does very little to help him. That is the obvious justification of Dr. Toynbee's study and one of the main reasons for its wide popularity. For whether we agree or disagree with his conclusions we must, I think, admit that the study of history ought to include the study of civilizations, and that a history which confines itself to the study of States and peoples of Western Europe and America is both partial and incomplete.

If Dr. Toynbee had undertaken a compartive study of the existing civilizations of the East and the West and their antecedents, he would have been performing a very valuable service. Actually, however, he has done much more than this. He has attempted a study of all the civilizations that ever existed, in order to discover the laws that determine their rise and fall, and the prospects of civilization in the future. Now this is just what Oswald Spengler attempted to do more than thirty years ago and, in spite of the pronounced difference between the temperament and philosophy of the two writers, Toynbee's theory, in its original form, bears considerable resemblances to Spengler's morphology of culture. Both writers agree in their denial of the unity of civilization, and both regard civilizations as autonomous entities which are sharply distinguished from one another and from the world of primitive societies out of which they presumably arose. But while Tonybee regards his twenty-one civilizations as units of the same species which are philosophically equivalent and contemporaneous, he does not go so far as Spengler, who treats his cultures as organisms in the full biological sense, so that "the history of a culture is the exact counterpart of the history of an individual human being or of an animal or of a tree or of a flower."

One cannot but be impressed by the unflinching logic with which Spengler worked out his theory or by the verve and style with which he expounded it. Yet the whole brilliant construction is vitiated by an obvious fallacy. If cultures are completely self-contained microcosms, each with its own art and religion and philosophy and science which are unique and incommunicable, how can the historian ever get outside his own culture and see the whole process from the outside? Thus Spengler's philosophy of history is self-refuting. He shows how the individual can never, under any circumstances, transcend the limits of the culture to which he belongs and at the same time he breaks his own law by a titanic attempt to look at all the cultures of the world from outside and to discover the universal law which governs their rise and fall and the whole evolution of their life-cycles.

Toynbee recognized the absurdity of this philosophical *tour de force*; and though he does the same thing in a different way, he never attempts to deny the existence of elements that are common to all the civilizations, or the fact that science and ethics transcend the limitations of the individual civilization. But in that case it is difficult to see how the twenty-one civilizations can be regarded as in any sense equivalent, since it is obvious that they do not all stand on the same level with regard to their scientific achievement or their ethical development. Granted that every civilization is an intelligible field of study which deserves to be studied for its own sake as a whole and not merely on account of the contributions it may have made to some other civilization, this does not make all civilizations philosophically equivalent, any more than the fact that we study States as autonomous political entities need imply that they are all equal to one another in political value and social development.

Thus in reading Dr. Toynbee's early volumes, I was always perplexed by the difficulty of reconciling the moral absolutism of his judgments with the cultural relativism of his theory. But this difficulty, at least, has now been solved by the publication of his four concluding volumes. For in the first of these new volumes, in the parts which are devoted to the subject of Universal States and Universal Churches, he introduces the new principle which marks a fundamental modification of his earlier views and involves the transformation of his *Study of History* from a relativist phenomenology of equivalent cultures, after the fashion of Spengler, into a unitary philosophy of history comparable to that of the idealist philosophers of the nineteenth century.

This change, which was already foreshadowed in the fifth volume, marks the abandonment of his original theory of the philosophical equivalence of the civilizations and the introduction of a qualitative principle embodied in the Higher Religions which are regarded as representative of a higher species of society, and which stand in the same relation to the civilizations as the latter to the primitive societies. Thus Toynbee's theory of history ceases to be cyclical, like Spengler's, and becomes a progressive series of four world stages ascending from primitive societies, through the primary and secondary civilizations to the higher religions in which history finds its ultimate goal. In his own words the study of history reaches "a point at which the civilizations in their turn, like the parochial states of the Modern Western World at the outset of our investigation, have ceased to constitute intelligible fields of study for us and have forfeited their historical significance except in so far as they minister to the progress of Religion". (v. VII, p. 449).

This is a revolutionary change, and to appreciate its full significance we must study the more elaborate table of civilizations and religions arrayed in serial order in Table 7 to Volume VII which shows the way in which Dr. Toynbee's new theory transforms his original scheme of twenty-one independent equivalent culture cycles. It is arranged in six stages:

1. The Primitive Societies which are legion.
2. The Primary Civilizations which are now seven instead of five owing to the addition of the newly discovered archaic civilizations of the Indus Valley and Northern China.
3. The eight Secondary Civilizations, which are derived from the primary ones through their dominant minorities or through the external proletariats; these are the Hellenic, the Syriac, the Hittite, the Babylonic, the Indic, and the Sinic (or classical Chinese) in the Old World, and the Yucatic and Mexic in the New.
4. The Higher Religions which are apparently twelve in number, ranging from Christianity and Islam to the worship of Isis and Osiris.
5. The eight Tertiary Civilizations of which our own is one, and which also include two other Christian civilizations, Russian and Eastern Orthodox, two Muslim ones—Iranic and Arabic, two in the Far East, and India.
6. Finally there are the Secondary Higher Religions which developed out of the Tertiary Civilizations and include about a dozen later Oriental religious movements, like Sikhism, the Brahmo Samaj, Bahaiism and so forth.

This elaborate classification of civilizations and religions is extremely complex and it requires considerable study before we can understand it in detail. But this at least is clear, it means that the cyclical movements by which the civilizations rise and fall are not the whole of history. They are subordinated to a higher principle of spiritual universality represented by the world religions. Thus history becomes once more progressive and purposive—a process of spiritual evolution such as Hegel and the other nineteenth-century idealist philosophers of history had conceived.

Now this view is much nearer to the ordinary man's idea of history than the Spenglerian relativist theory. For though we may have abandoned the thoroughgoing optimism of the nineteenth-century doctrine of progress, we still find it hard to abandon a belief in the unity of history and in the existence of some common standard by which the achievements and failures of the different civilizations can be judged. And the same, I think, is true of the historians, for though they have lost Lord Acton's sublime vision of a universal history, which is something different from the combined history of all countries and which enlightens the mind and illuminates the soul, they nevertheless still believe in the unity of history and are almost unanimous in their rejection of a thoroughgoing historical relativism in the style of Herr Spengler.

Nevertheless I do not think that either the man in the street or the professional historian is likely to accept Dr. Toynbee's philosophy of history in its final form. It is too abstruse and learned for the former and too speculative and ideological for the latter. Few historians will be prepared to accept the system of classification by which he arrives at his total of twenty-one civilizations. It seems arbitrary to create three distinct civilizations out of the three or four successive phases of Chinese culture, and the same may be said of his three Christian civilizations—the Western, the Eastern Orthodox, and the Russian Orthodox. If all these are to be classified as distinct civilizations, why should the civilization of Korea be identified with that of Japan, or the very distinctive culture of Tibet or of Burma and Siam be denied any separate place in the list? One would have imagined that Russia was closer to Europe, and Muslim Persia to Muslim Syria, than Tibet or Burma were to India.

Most of all, however, the historian is likely to object to Dr. Toynbee's view of the supersession of the Tertiary Civilizations by the Higher Religions. According to this theory civilization has fulfilled its purpose during its secondary phase by the production of the Higher Religions. By doing so civilization, he says, had exhausted its mandate and had been replaced by a new and higher form of society—the Universal Churches. Thus the Tertiary Civilizations have no historical function: they are superfluous repetitions of an earlier historical phase and have no intrinsic value for the historian. As he explains (in Volume VII, p. 448) the historical process consists of four phases and four phases only—(1) Primitive Societies, (2) Primary Civilizations, (3) Secondary Civilizations, and (4) Higher Religions.

Now I cannot imagine any view more likely to arouse the antagonism of the average historian. For these Tertiary Civilizations are the main fields of historic research in its modern scientific form. If, as Toynbee says, these Tertiary Civilizations are "now right out of the picture" (v. VII, p. 449), for the purposes of his study, that is enough to condemn his theory of history in the eyes of the historians.

It is certainly difficult to believe that these recent and contemporary civilizations are more devoid of historical significance than the Hittite civilization or the civilization of Yucatan. Nor is Dr. Toynbee altogether consistent in this respect, since it is to these Tertiary Civilizations—especially to the two Islamic cultures and the three Christian ones—that a very large part of his study of history is devoted; and though much of what he says of modern Western civilization is negative and critical, it is not altogether so. There is still enough left on the credit side to justify a claim to historical significance.

Certainly I would agree with Dr. Toynbee against perhaps the majority of modern historians in his central theme that civilization exists to serve religion and not religion to serve civilization. But this does not mean that civilization must wither away and be replaced by a church, in the same way as the State withers away and is replaced by the classless society in the Marxian theory of history. So long as human life exists on earth, there must be civilizations and cultures, and the fact that a civilization accepts the truth of a world religion does not necessarily transform it into a church.

Nor can the Higher Religions disinterest themselves in the fate of civilization, for if a religion is a reality it must inevitably seek to transform the civilization with which it is in contact according to its ethical values and its spiritual ends. I think Dr. Toynbee's objection to such civilizations is that they are obstacles to world unity, but this is really a criticism of the Higher Religions rather than of the civilizations that they may inspire. In his view Christianity and Islam fail by their exclusiveness, and the true pathway to spiritual unity is that of Mahayana Buddhism, which accepts the multiplicity and equality of the different roads that lead to spiritual reality. Thus his original principle of the philosophic equivalence of the Civilizations is replaced by the principle of the theological equivalence of the Higher Religions.

Moreover I do not think that Dr. Toynbee's reduction of history to theology (to borrow an expression from Roger Bacon) will meet with any more favour from the theologians and the students of comparative religion, than it has done from the historians. In fact the criticisms of the theologians will follow somewhat similar lines to those of the historians. As the latter find it difficult to accept his list of civilizations, so the former will boggle at his lists of the primary and secondary religions. In the first place it is difficult to see why he limits his category of Living Religions to four only: Christianity, Islam, Hinduism, and Mahayana Buddhism. There are few students of religion who would deny the right of Judaism to be reckoned as a living religion. And in the case of Buddhism, it seems arbitrary to exclude that form of Buddhism which is still the dominant religion of Ceylon and Burma and Siam and Cambodia and which actually seems far more living at the present day than the Mahayana form of the religion, which is now almost moribund in China and Korea and survives only in Japan and Tibet and Nepal.

Dr. Toynbee explains his choice on the ground that this earlier Buddhism is not a living religion but only the fossil survivor of the Indic civilization, and in the same way he regards Judaism as a fossil of the Syriac civilization. But whatever sociological truth there may be in this view, it does not provide adequate basis for a religious judgment. If the Torah or the Noble Eight-Fold Path are spiritual ways still trodden in faith and devotion by living men, then these are still living religions, however ancient they are and however many traces they bear of extinct civilizations.

And if it seems unjustifiable to reduce religion to these four examples the theologian is likely to be even more critical of Dr. Toynbee's attempt to reduce these four to one by a process of psychological interpretation and theological syncretism. It is easy to understand that Dr. Toynbee's abandonment of the relativist principle of the philosophical equivalence of civilizations should make him look to the higher religions in order to find a principle which will unify his study. For as he writes, "The history of Religion appears to be unitary and progressive by contrast with the multiplicity and repetitiveness of the histories of civilizations" (v. VII, pp. 425–6). But when he goes beyond this and seeks to prove the substantial identity of all the existing forms of higher religion, he is oversimplifying the picture and is giving way to the temptation to force the evidence in order to make it fit in with his theories.

For if there were difficulties in his original thesis of the philosophical equivalence of civilizations, the objections to the theological equivalence of the higher religions are even more serious. In the study of civilizations, the historian is dealing with a field which is subject to temporal and spatial limitations and can be judged by historical criteria. But when it comes to the world religions, he is in a world which, of its nature, transcends the sphere of history and is not amenable to empirical study. These religions must be studied theologically, if at all, and when we survey the world religions from the theological point of view, we see that they are neither identical nor convergent, but represent at least two alternative and contradictory solutions to the religious problem.

On the one hand the religions of the Far East—Hinduism and Mahayana Buddhism—adapt themselves well enough to Dr. Toynbee's ideal of religious syncretism, but they do so by denying the significance of history and creating a dream world of cosmological and mythological fantasy in which aeons and universes succeed one another in dazzling confusion and where the unity of God and the historical personality of Buddha are lost in a cloud of mythological figures: Buddhas and Bodhisattvas, gods and saktis, demigods and spirits. On the other hand the three higher religions of the West—Judaism, Christianity, and Mohammedanism—have followed quite a different path. Their very existence is bound up with the historic reality of their founders, and with the establishment of a unique relation between the one God and His people.

Thus any syncretism between religions of these two different types would inevitably mean the abdication of the monotheistic religions and their absorption by the pantheistic or polytheistic ones. Such a process is not inconceivable, but we have no historical reason to suppose that it is possible and no theological reason for supposing it to be desirable or right. Hitherto the main trend of history has been in the opposite direction, and the exclusive monotheistic religions have been steadily extending their sphere of influence at the expense of their more accommodating rivals. It is true that Toynbee's Secondary Higher Religions are mostly of the syncretist type, but, with the exception of Sikhism, they have failed to establish themselves, and the success of Sikhism was military and political rather than purely religious.

Hence it seems that the principle of the theological equivalence of the higher religions finds no more justification in the study of history than the philosophical equivalence of civilizations has done. With regard to the latter, Dr. Toynbee has now come to accept the qualitative differentiation of cultures according to their degree of subordination to higher spiritual ends and in spite of his scepticism regarding the spiritual *raison d'être* of Western civilization, he admits the startling fact that this is now the only extant representative of the species which is not in process of disintegration. Though it is by no means certain that our civilization possesses either the strength or the wisdom to create a peaceful world order, it is difficult to see how its work can ever be altogether undone, except by the destruction of civilization itself.

Now as Western civilization has been the effective agent of world unity on the material, technological, and economic planes, so Christianity has worked for nearly 2,000 years towards the spiritual unification of humanity in the Kingdom of God. If Christianity fails, we have no reason to suppose that it will be replaced by an Oriental syncretism like Mahayana Buddhism or by a Christian Gnosticism. Its only effective rival is a secular counter-religion like Communism, which would mean the destruction of all the higher religions.

It is true that the political awakening of Asia and the resurgence of Oriental nationalism has been accompanied by an understandable reaction against Western missionary activities, but this is not due to any considerable revival of the higher religions of the Far East, least of all Mahayana

Buddhism. It is a political phenomenon which is inseparable from the reaction against Western imperialism and colonialism. On the level of the higher culture, the advance of Western ideas has been far more rapid during the last twenty or thirty years than at any time in the past. And while this does not mean any extension of the Western religions, it does involve the progressive decline of the ancient religious cultures of the East, as Mr. Nirad Chaudhuri has pointed out so strikingly in his book *The Autobiography of an Unknown Indian* (1951), which every historian who is interested in these questions will find invaluable.

Perhaps I have said too much on this question. But apart from its intrinsic interest and importance, it represents the climax of Dr. Toynbee's work, the whole of which must now be read in the light of its conclusion. But, personally, I cannot help feeling that this conclusion is premature. Dr. Toynbee has been guided in his immense task by two parallel motives; first by the Hellenic philosophic quest for a *theoria* —a synoptic vision of the whole course of human civilization, and secondly by the Hebraic prophetic mission to justify the ways of God to man and to find a religious solution to the riddle of history and the problems of modern civilization. Both these motives are so deeply rooted in the tradition of Western civilization that we can none of us ignore their force. But there is always a danger that the philosopher will be tempted to simplify the irrational multiplicity and idiosyncrasy of the world of history and that the prophet will attempt to anticipate the mystery of divine judgment, like the friends of Job—that symbol of humanity agonizing in the toils of history.

Practically every philosophy of history that has ever been elaborated errs in one or other of these ways, and frequently in both of them. The fact is that a comparative study of civilizations has only recently become possible, and even today, in spite of the progressive extension of our field of vision by archaeology and prehistory and Oriental studies, our knowledge is still fragmentary, uneven, and partial. This is no reason for discouragement. During the very years when Dr. Toynbee has been writing the present volumes, a whole series of discoveries has thrown new light on the most important of all historical problems, the origins of higher civilization in the Near East, the beginnings of agriculture and the domestication of animals and the rise of the village community and finally of the city. But until these discoveries have been completed and co-ordinated, it is impossible for us to write with assurance about the genesis of civilization and of the features which first differentiated civilization from primitive society.

And it is here precisely that the theorists of civilization are most unsatisfactory. Since their attention is concentrated on the higher civilizations in their highest manifestations, they tend to ignore or undervalue everything that lies outside or below or before them, so that they exaggerate the gulf that divides civilization from primitive culture. Thus Spengler writes: "A civilization is born at the moment when, out of the psychic conditions of a perpetually raw Humanity, a mighty soul awakes and extricates itself: a form out of the formless, a bounded transitory existence out of the boundless and the persistent." [1] In the same way Dr. Toynbee tends to make an absolute distinction between civilization and primitive societies—the former, in his original view, being all equivalent; and primitive societies, being also equivalent, and spread out indeterminately over the hundreds of thousands of years during which the human race has existed. They are even anterior to humanity, since, according to Dr. Toynbee, "the existence of primitive society is a condition which the evolution of Man out of Sub-Man presupposes" (v. I, p. 173; cf. v. VII, p. 420–1 and note).

But this seems a sheer misuse of terms. Certainly the societies of the ape-man must have been primitive, as primitive as can be. But they are not societies in the same sense as the human societies of the prehistoric world or of the non-civilized world today. All these belong to the same world of history as the higher civilizations. They possess language and culture and religion and art. And they differ from one another as much as or more than they differ from the civilizations. There is no excuse for lumping them all together at the bottom of the scale and grouping the civilizations all together at the top. They do not form a sort of amorphous mass of raw humanity such as Spengler imagines. The higher forms of neolithic culture, for example, stood midway between the culture of the hunters and the food-gatherers and that of the early civilizations, and the lowest form of primi-

[1] O. Spengler, *Der Untergang des Abendlandes* (Munich, 1923), Vol. 1, p. 153.

tive culture that we know at first hand, such as that of the Australians or that of the Bushmen, is infinitely removed from the highest forms of sub-human society.

Thus when we come to the study of the civilizations we cannot afford to disregard the existence of the neighbouring and related peoples of lower culture. We are likely to learn more about the nature of Mexican culture by a comparison with the Pueblo culture of the South Western United States, than by a comparison with another "secondary" civilization of the Old World, like that of the Hittites or the Greeks. By relegating these neighbouring cultures to the status of "external proletariats," Toynbee deprives them of much of their real significance and devalues their contribution to culture.

The fact is that a civilization of any but the most simple and archaic kind is a far more complex phenomenon than the philosophers of history have realized. No doubt it is always based on a particular original process of cultural creativity which is the work of a particular people. But at the same time it always tends to become a super-culture—an extended area of social communication which dominates and absorbs other less advanced or less powerful cultures and unites them in an "oecumene," an international and intercultural society; and it is this extension of the area of communication that is the essential characteristic of civilization as distinguished from lower forms of culture.

The higher civilizations usually represent a fusion of at least two independent traditions of culture, and while one of these is dominant and possibly more advanced, it is not enough to dismiss the sub-culture as an internal proletariat, as Dr. Toynbee does, since the word "proletariat" denotes a class within a society and not a culture or sub-culture within a civilization. Hence I do not believe it is possible to study the high civilizations satisfactorily until we have succeeded in analyzing their different cultural components. In other words, the essential basis of the study of history must be, not just a comparative study of the higher civilizations, but a study of their constituent cultures, and here we must follow, not the grand synoptic method of the philosophers of history, but the more laborious and meticulous scientific technique of the social anthropologists. It may be objected that this is not possible unless we possess authentic first-hand investigations similar to those of the modern ethnologist. But the prehistorian has adopted the anthropological method, not unfruitfully, in his study of the cultures of the remote past, and the same thing can be done by the historian, who possesses far richer sources of information.

Contemporary anthropologists, like Professor Evans-Pritchard, have accepted the principle of the essentially historical character of social anthropology, and in the same way it seems reasonable that the historians should begin to pay more attention to the methods and contribution of social anthropology. Now in his recent volumes Dr. Toynbee does expressly recognize the essential relation between the two disciplines and goes out of his way to reject many of the distinctions commonly made between civilizations and primitive societies (v. ix, pp. 188–9 and note).

But this only makes his neglect of the lower types of culture more incomprehensible. The only criteria of differentiation that he admits are quantitative ones—the civilizations are much fewer and larger than the primitive cultures, so that "the two species stand to one another like elephants and rabbits" (v. i, p. 148). But after all it is not just size and scarcity that distinguishes the elephant from the rabbit, and if elephants were simply gigantic rabbits, there would be no excuse for creating a new science of super-rabbits as distinct from the ordinary article. Moreover even this quantitative difference becomes less marked if, as I have suggested, a civilization is a community or concatenation of cultures. We know in the case of our own Western civilization how large a degree of cultural individuality and multiformity can coexist within a single civilization, so that we can talk of French and German cultures as distinct entities without denying their participation in a common civilization. In studying the civilizations of the past we are apt to neglect these internal differences, because we are viewing them through a telescope and not through a microscope. My fundamental criticism of Toynbee's great work is that it is too telescopic and that a true science of human cultures must be based on a more microscopic technique of anthropological and historical research.

Nevertheless, a telescopic survey of the whole field of study also has its value, especially when it is carried out by a scholar of immense learning and universal cultural interests like Dr. Toynbee. And I do not think that any historian or social anthropologist can read his work without gaining new insights into the nature of the problem of the relations between civilizations.

—1955.

8

Europe in Eclipse

EVER since the end of the first World War there has been a
growing demand for a universal history. The old national
histories no longer sufficed for an age which had seen historic empires falling like rotten trees and new states and
nationalities springing up like mushrooms. At the same time
it is doubtful whether it is yet possible to write a world history in the full sense of the word. There are still too many
tracts that are almost unexplored, and still more which have
only been explored in a partial and one-sided manner. Above
all, there exists no educated public which can compare the
histories of different civilizations and judge between them.
Oriental history is still the preserve of the comparatively
small number of specialists who are masters of the Oriental
languages, and there is little common ground between them.

Under the circumstances the history of a single civilization seems the most that we can hope to achieve. It is here
that European culture seems to offer the best starting point
for an approach to world history, for its transforming influence on the other world cultures has been far greater than
that of any of the Oriental civilizations. This is partly because
its geographic features have made Europe peculiarly open to
cultural contact, although one cannot ignore the dynamic
character which the European peoples themselves have mani-

fested. Nevertheless, it is possible to regard "Europe" from many points of view, and amongst these the geographical point of view is by no means the most important. Considered from the point of view of cultural inheritance, Europe is only a link between the ancient East, which was the source of higher civilization, and the new world of transoceanic cosmopolitan culture. Even if we exclude both the whole vast field of prehistoric antiquity and the cosmopolitan culture of the present century, we shall still find that what we are dealing with is not one civilization but three. First there is the culture of the Mediterranean *orbis terrarum* which was created by the Greeks and organized and extended to the West by the Romans; secondly there is the culture of mediaeval Christendom, and thirdly the culture of the European society of nations, as it existed from the fifteenth to the nineteenth centuries.

It is only this third culture which is European in the full sense of the word. In spite of the Greek origin of the word, and its occasional use in the Middle Ages, "Europe" is a peculiarly modern concept, which was introduced by the scholars of the Renaissance to distinguish the new *orbis terrarum* from the old. The cradle-lands of Hellenic culture were lost, but they dreamed of the re-flowering of the same classical tradition, first in Italy and then in the lands beyond the Alps. Thus for them "Europe" was not a continent but the comparatively small society of peoples who shared the same ideals of literary culture and civilized behaviour. And so "Europe" and "civilization" became interchangeable terms. The Turks were "barbarous," but so were the Muscovites. Sir Thomas More and Cardinal Pole were humane and civilized persons, but so was Bessarion, the Asiatic Greek.

This ideological conception of "Europe" has endured almost to our own times, so that as the area of communication grew the idea of Europe extended with it. But now the modern world is passing through a period of acute cultural crisis which affects every continent and race and people, and which is especially serious for those peoples who have inherited the tradition of Western culture. During the last centuries the expansion of the European peoples by conquest and colonization, by trade and industry, by science and technology, has unified the world as never before and laid the foundation for a world civilization. But at the moment when this process was approaching its climax, the political and economic power of Europe was shattered by forty years of world war and revolution. Today Europe has lost her political hegemony and the Great Powers of the nineteenth century have either ceased to exist or have become dwarfed and overshadowed by the rise of the new world powers which control whole continents and number their population by hundreds of millions.

Moreover, this end of the European age of history is not simply due to the decline in the political and economic power of the European peoples; it is also the result of a loss of faith in the uniqueness of European culture and of the claim of the Oriental and non-European peoples to an equality of cultural status. This is a revolutionary change, for hitherto, right down to our own times, the identification of European culture with Civilization in the absolute sense of the word has been accepted almost without question, not only by the man in the street but by the scholar and the man of science. Today all this is changed. Not only is Europe reduced to insignificance by the giant powers to which she has given birth, but it is difficult to find any people, however weak and backward, who will admit her claim to cultural superiority. Even peoples who emerged only yesterday from the darkness of African barbarism now regard themselves as culturally equal or superior to the old Western lords of the earth.

Nevertheless this new order of cultural equality is itself a European creation and part of the inheritance of Europe. The wave of defeatism which is affecting Western Europe and the aggressive nationalism of the non-European peoples are secondary phenomena in comparison with the vast changes which are transforming the life of humanity. But these changes are the work of Western man through the science and technology and the institutions and ideas that he has created or invented. Whether this is good or bad is another question. We still do not know whether this will be the foundation of a new world order or whether Western man, like Frankenstein, has created a monster that will destroy him.

To the Christian the answer must depend mainly on spiritual factors—above all on whether the new civilization is open or closed to the influence of Christianity. For Christianity has been the centre of the whole European culture-complex round which the other elements revolve, and so long as this centre remains, the continuity of culture and the preservation of its spiritual inheritance is secure. But at the present time the prospects of such a development are unfavourable. The great age of Western expansion has also been the age of the secularization of Western culture. What has expanded has been:—first, Western political and economic power; secondly, Western technology and science; and thirdly, Western political institutions and social ideals. Christianity has also expanded, but in a far lesser degree.

During the nineteenth century, Liberalism, the creed of progress and enlightenment, of liberty and humanity, was the effective religion of Western culture, and it succeeded in winning converts all over the world—in India and the Near East, in Japan and China. But now that Liberalism is in eclipse and no longer possesses the power to unite the world, the cosmopolitan culture of the modern world is like a body without a soul, and the void is being filled by new totalitarian ideologies like Communism, which threaten to divide the world rather than to unite it.

Thus at the present time it seems unlikely that Europe will succeed in handing on its cultural tradition to the new peoples in the way that ancient Rome handed on its tradition to the mediaeval world. Nevertheless it must be remembered that the prospects were no better in the third century A.D. A Roman of that age, witnessing the failure of the Empire to withstand the barbarian invasions in the West and the growing power of the Persian monarchy in the East, would never have imagined that Rome would become the centre of a new spiritual empire in the West or that the new Rome on the Bosphorus, which did not yet exist, was destined to maintain the tradition of the Empire and of Greek Christian culture for more than a millennium.

The fact is that the fate of civilization is not determined solely, or even predominantly, by political and economic causes. The age of the decline of the Roman Empire was also an age of spiritual rebirth, which prepared the way, not only for the coming of mediaeval Christendom, but also for the civilizations of Byzantium and Islam. It proved to be the great water-shed that divided the streams of Western and Eastern culture and determined the channels in which they were to flow for a thousand years.

Now our own age is also an age of transition, in which the frontiers between East and West are changing and a new world is painfully emerging from the ruins of the old. What is most important, however, is not the change in the balance of power and international relations, but the deeper changes that take place below the surface of political events and of which we may be almost unconscious. For the spiritual forces on which the vitality of a civilization depends often manifest themselves in unlooked-for ways which escape the attention of publicists and historians. In order to discover them it is necessary to look at our civilization as a whole, in the past as well as the present, and to see what have been the formative elements in the Western culture-process and how far they are still living today.

Now the civilization of the West is the embodiment of a twofold tradition. On the one hand it inherits the traditions of the classical culture of Rome and the Hellenistic world, and on the other it is the heir of Christendom and of a religious tradition which reaches back behind the classical world to the ancient East. From the one side, Europe has inherited the tradition of Greek philosophy and science and Roman law and literature; from the other, Europe has received its moral values and its spiritual ideals: its conception of God and Man, of divine providence and human responsibility. Both these elements coexist, whether in tension or balance, with one another at every stage of the development of Western culture. There are periods when one element seems to prevail over the other and almost excludes it, as the Christian tradition dominates the early Middle Ages, and the classical tradition dominates the age of the Renaissance. To borrow an expression from biology, there are dominant and recessive elements in every culture; and an element which is recessive during a whole age of civilization may later reemerge to dominate the civilization of the future. But the second recessive element is always present and contributes something essential to the achievement of the dominant partner, as the work of St. Thomas would have been impossible without the Hellenic contributions of Aristotle, and as the Renaissance drama in England and Spain is no less indebted to the Christian past than to the classical tradition.

But it may be objected that this is no longer the case when we come to the modern age; that the achievements of modern Western civilization in science and technology and in political and social reform represent a revolutionary change in human history which owes nothing to the past. It is certainly true that the secular ideology, which has done so much to form public opinion in the West during the last two centuries, inculcated this view and minimized or condemned the traditional elements in Western culture. Nevertheless this attitude was a partisan one, determined by the temporary needs of the parties and classes that were in conflict with the *ancien régime*. From the strictly historical angle there can be no doubt that the more recent developments of Western culture are deeply rooted in the European past.

Even the Liberal movement, with its humanitarian idealism and its belief in the law of nature and the rights of man, owes its origin to an irregular union between the humanist tradition and a religious ideal that was inspired by Christian moral values, though not by Christian faith. As I have shown in my book *Progress and Religion,* the whole development of liberalism and humanitarianism, which has been of such immense importance in the history of the modern world, derived its spiritual impetus from the Christian tradition that it attempted to replace, and when that tradition disappears this spiritual impetus is lost, and liberalism in its turn is replaced by the crudity and amoral ideology of the totalitarian state.

In the same way the modern scientific movement was a product of Western humanist culture and even today it still preserves the traces of its origin. No doubt modern technology can be detached from humanist culture and used in a purely instrumental way to serve the interests of any power that wishes to employ it for any purpose. Consequently it can be used for the destruction no less than for the service of man, as we see in the case of the development of atomic energy to create weapons of mass destruction. But this is not true of science as a whole, and there are many scientists who are fully conscious of the tragic contradiction between the humanist ideals that have been the inspiration of Western science and the inhuman consequences of the perversion of scientific technology when it is used simply as an instrument of power.

Moreover this is only one aspect of modern science. The same spirit which inspired the scientific conquest of nature by man, and led to the material unification of the world, has also led to a new understanding of human nature itself and to the discovery and investigation of the world of human culture.

One of the most fruitful results of this investigation of culture by Western science lies in the new knowledge it has afforded of the ancient civilizations of the Orient. Most histories of Western civilization do not give enough attention to this extra-European aspect of the European inheritance. If we compare our own culture with that of the Roman-Hellenistic world in its later stages, we see that what is most significant is not what happens in Europe itself but the changes that take place in the outer zone of Western expansion. For the later stages of Europe's cultural penetration of Asia constitute a process of no less importance than that of the Hellenistic penetration of the ancient East. But in most accounts of modern European history little or nothing is said of this process—as seen in the great expansion of the Christian missions in the East, or in the achievement of the great European archaeologists, philologists and Orientalists who have revealed and interpreted the Oriental literatures and cultures. Yet this great work, which was initiated in the sixteenth century when Matteo Ricci first brought Western science to China and revealed Chinese culture to Europe, is surely no less remarkable than that of the conquerors and the politicians. Not only did it immeasurably widen the frontiers of Western civilization and lay the foundations of a new understanding between East and West, it also gave the non-European peoples a new understanding of their own past. Without it, the East would be unconscious of the greatness of its own heritage, and the memory of the earliest Asiatic civilizations would still be buried in the dust.

This is an enduring inheritance for the whole world, East and West, which will outlast political ideologies and economic empires. At the present time it is the fashion to view the relations of East and West in terms of colonial exploitation or of nationalist reaction, and if this were all, the European inheritance could be written off like the oil concessions and capital investments which are being expropriated. But the cultural inheritance of Europe is not confined to Europe, any more than the inheritance of the classical world was confined to the Mediterranean. Even though the political hegemony of Europe has passed away, America and Asia still inherit the tradition of European culture, just as Western Europe and the Middle East still inherited the traditions of Roman and Hellenistic culture after the Empire had fallen. The permanent inheritance of Europe, like that of Hellenism, is a spiritual and intellectual one. It has changed the world because it has changed men's minds. Loss of power does not mean loss of knowledge, and even though Europe ceases to be a centre of world power, the spiritual and intellectual forces that had their origin in Europe will continue to influence the world, whether the new masters of the world acknowledge their debts or not. The influence of Hellenism did not end with the Roman conquest of Greece, nor yet with the fall of Rome or with the fall of the Byzantine Empire; and so it must be with the inheritance of Europe.

The creative development of this inheritance depends on the vitality of the spiritual forces which inspired the achievements of European culture—the religious tradition of Christianity and the intellectual tradition of Humanism; and these are still alive today. They live inside and outside Europe; on the one hand, in the Catholic Church, and on the other, in the Western tradition of science and scholarship and literature. And it is to these two powers that we must look for the creation of a new world civilization, which will unite the nations and the continents in an all-embracing spiritual community.

—1954.

CONTINUITY AND DEVELOPMENT IN CHRISTOPHER DAWSON'S THOUGHT

A Note by John J. Mulloy

IN considering the development of Christopher Dawson's thought over the span of thirty-five years which this volume encompasses, one is impressed by the remarkable continuity in fundamental conceptions with which he has approached the study of culture and world history.

A significant example of this continuity is afforded by his conception of the nature of a civilization, as this is applied in criticism of Spengler in 1922 and of Toynbee in 1955. In both writers Dawson finds an oversimplification of the concept and a failure to appreciate the contributions which a civilization receives from the peoples of lower culture who are its neighbors or who may have been incorporated by it.

First in 1922, speaking of the difficulties in which Spengler's theory of history results:

There is little room in Herr Spengler's scheme for cultural interaction and admixture, still less for the co-operation of several peoples in one civilization. . . .

. . . All this results from Herr Spengler's over-simplification, which only allows him to take account of a single people in dealing with a particular civilization. In reality it is impossible to simplify to this degree any civilization except the most primitive ones. So long as a people exists it possesses a cultural tradition, and however depressed and passive this may seem in relation to the creative culture of the dominant people in a world civilization, it is nevertheless capable of far-reaching influences and reactions.[1]

Thirty-three years later it is the same idea of the complexity of elements in a civilization which forms the basis for Dawson's criticism of Dr. Toynbee's view of history. And because of this complexity, the philosophers of history require the help of sociology and anthropology if they are to reach valid conclusions as to the nature and the historical development of the higher cultures.

The fact is that a civilization of any but the most simple and archaic kind is a far more complex phenomenon than the philosophers of history have realized. No doubt it is always based on a particular original process of cultural creativity which is the work of a particular people. But at the same time it always tends to become a super-culture—and extended area of social communication which dominates and absorbs other less advanced or less powerful cultures and unites them in an "oecumene," an international and intercultural society; and it is this extension of the area of communication that is the essential characteristic of civilization as distinguished from lower forms of culture.

The higher civilizations usually represent a fusion of at least two independent traditions of culture, and while one of these is dominant and possibly more advanced, it is not enough to dismiss the sub-culture as an internal proletariat, as Dr. Toynbee does, since the word "proletariat" denotes a class within a society and not a culture or sub-culture within a civilization. Hence I do not believe it is possible to study the high civilizations satisfactorily until we have succeeded in analyzing their different cultural components. In other words, the essential basis of the study of history must be, not just a comparative study of the higher civilizations, but a study of their constituent cultures, and here we must follow, not the grand synoptic method of the philosophers of history, but the more laborious and meticulous scientific technique of the social anthropologists.[2]

[1] See above, "Oswald Spengler and the Life of Civilizations," pp. 373, 374.

[2] See above, "Arnold Toynbee and the Study of History," p. 392.

While this continuity in Dawson's thought is most striking, as the above quotations indicate, there has at the same time taken place a process of development by which his earlier views have been deepened and broadened so as to give greater attention to matters previously passed over without much comment. The classification of cultures and the position of language within culture are two problems to which Mr. Dawson has recently given considerable study (we discuss his present view of language in a later part of this essay); but possibly the most impressive instance of development in Dawson's sociology is found in his attitude toward the importance of the intellectual element in a super-culture or civilization.

In the criticism of Toynbee's views which we have just quoted, it will be observed that Dawson sees the extension of the area of communication as the essential feature by which a civilization is distinguished from lower forms of culture. Now normally it is by the geographic expansion of a civilization's military power or political control that such extension in the area of communication takes place. How then shall we evaluate the face of geographic expansion—as a sign that a civilization is losing its cultural quality and degenerating into mere cosmopolitanism, or as an indication that it has been able to communicate its basic values and outlook on life to other peoples?

There is undoubtedly something to be said for both of these interpretations of the geographic expansion of a culture, and no doubt the particular explanation found valid will differ with the circumstances of each case. We should note, however, that in Dr. Toynbee's view, "The history of almost every civilization furnishes examples of geographical expansion coinciding with deterioration in quality." And again, "More often geographical expansion is a concomitant of real decline and coincides with a 'time of troubles' or a universal state—both of them stages of decline and disintegration." [3] And the reason for this is that geographic expansion is closely connected with militarism, which Toynbee sees as "the commonest cause of the breakdowns of civilizations." [4]

[3] Arnold Tonybee, *A Study of History* (Somervell abridgement, Oxford, 1946), pp. 191, 190.

[4] *Ibid.*, p. 190.

But what is significant in relation to the changes in Dawson's thought on this question is the fact that in his earlier essays in the 1920's, he tended to regard the geographic expansion of a culture as achieved mostly or primarily at the expense of cultural quality, while in his recent writings on culture in the 1950's he is inclined to emphasize the achievement by which a civilization has opened up new areas of communication and made its own values part of the cultural outlook of other peoples.

Thus, in the fifth essay in the present volume (first published in 1924), he refers to the Hellenistic superculture and its geographic expansion into Asia as "a mechanical and external creation, compared with the vital and internal impulse that created the Greek City-State." He sees it as combining superficial and abstract progress with a vital decline in the quality of the culture being imparted, so that "the vivid and highly differentiated life of the regional city-state" faded away "into a formless, cosmopolitan society, with no roots in the past and no contact with a particular region, a society which was common to the great cities everywhere from Mesopotamia to the Bay of Naples." [5]

In his observations of the last few years, while not rejecting his analysis of the causes of the decline of the Greek city-states, Mr. Dawson takes a somewhat different view of the character of Hellenistic civilization. Precisely because it was capable of being taught to other peoples not of Greek origin, the Hellenistic superculture possessed an inner life of its own which allowed it to transcend the particular fate of decline or breakdown which might come upon the regional city-states where Hellenism had its origin. As he remarks on this point in a letter to the present writer (written January 18, 1955):

With regard to the superculture and the organic culture, I have changed my views to some extent of late years and would qualify considerably what I wrote on the Hellenistic culture in *Progress and Religion* [parts of this fifth essay we have quoted from were later incorporated into this work]. It is quite true, as I say in *Progress and Religion*, that the Hellenic culture declined through the withering away of its organic substratum in the regional cultures.

[5] Cf. above, pp. 58, 60.

(The case of Hellenism is unique, because it is the only culture I know of in which the regional unit, the *polis,* also became the organ of the higher culture).

On the other hand, I entirely disagree with Toynbee about geographical expansion coinciding normally with cultural decline. The *normal* process is quite the opposite, e.g. the great age of medieval culture was also the age of the territorial expansion of the Franco-Norman culture, the great age of Spanish culture was the age of Spanish territorial expansion and the latter ceased before the former by a generation or two.

So too with Western European culture generally, the age of expansion was the age of cultural achievement. So again with Islam.

Speaking of the question of whether supercultures are subject to growth and decay—he seemed to imply that the Hellenistic superculture was, in his original criticism of it in the 1920's—Mr. Dawson defines his position as follows:

I would say that *Athens* experienced a breakdown then [i.e. the fourth century B.C.], but by no means Hellenism itself. But on the whole I do not believe that civilizations have life-cycles. Peoples have, and if a culture is bound up with a people, then it also must. But in so far as a civilization becomes a superculture and is transmitted to an indefinite number of peoples, its development may transcend this cycle.

And again, in the same letter as the above passage (January 1, 1955):

A superculture which is a world civilization, like Hellenism, Christendom and Islam, is potentially universal and eternal. It ends only when it is destroyed by atom bombs or when it is absorbed by another world civilization greater than itself.

At a further point in this letter of January 1, 1955 he specifically dissociates his views on the organic and intellectual elements in a civilization from the position on this matter held by Spengler:

I think Spengler quite realized the existence of these universal cultures which are civilizations, but he disliked them. He thought that when a culture is taught it becomes dead, whereas I should say that when a culture can be transmitted by teaching, it attains a higher level of existence.

It should be noted that Spengler's use of the term *civilization* differs from that of Dawson, since Spengler applies it to the last phase of a culture, which he identifies as a period of petrifaction and death, when the creative impulse of the people that has created the original culture has played itself out; while Dawson thinks of a civilization as transcending the limitations of the regional culture in which it had its origin and uniting many peoples in a new supercultural unity. For Dawson, this last phase of a culture, which Spengler holds in such low esteem, is a time of the greatest seminal importance for the future; for it is precisely then that a culture acquires "new contacts and opportunities for expression," and during this "decisive period of intercourse and fusion" sets an indelible character upon the daughter-cultures that are being formed within it.[6]

Finally, we should observe that Dawson's present view on the intellectual element in a civilization involves a high regard for education in intercultural contacts, since it is by the process of teaching its fundamental values to other peoples that a civilization achieves a relative universality, that is, transcends the boundaries of its region of origin.

Since the publication in 1948 of his last volume specifically devoted to analysis of culture (the first series of Gifford Lectures, *Religion and Culture*), Mr. Dawson's thought has been exploring new trails along a number of lines, including the problem of proper classification of cultures: how one is to distinguish, for example, subcultures from regional cultures, and these again from national cultures and civilizations. In his correspondence with the present writer, which may eventually be published, these and other matters have been given critical examination, and the result has been an extension in the area of Dawson's sociological thought and a more precise statement of the principles it involves.

Sociology and History

As we have noted above, Dawson's interest in the wider perspectives of world history is balanced by a regard for the

[6] See above, p. 377. For a more detailed statement of these differences, see the entire essay on "Oswald Spengler and the Life of Civilizations," pp. 366–80.

smaller and more local factors which enter into movements of historical change—the structure of the primary social unit, the relation of the regional group to its environment, the effect of the region upon a people's view of life, and the constituent contributions of several different regional peoples to the wider cultural unities called civilizations. His ultimate goal may be to show the relationship of these broader cultural unities to one another in the movement of world history, but he believes this relationship cannot be understood without an examination of these facts which are usually considered the province of sociology and anthropology—disciplines where social change is studied on a more limited level than that of the cultural historian.

His concern for the first of these factors—the primary social unit—is evidenced in certain themes which run as a connecting thread throughout most of his works of historical analysis. One of these is the influence exercised upon culture by peasant and by tribal societies, both in themselves and in their interaction with the higher culture of the city. For example, in Dawson's view the Archaic civilizations of Egypt and Mesopotamia result from and are conditioned by the ethos of the peasant society, which underlay their greatest achievements.[7] Nor can the classical civilizations of Greece and Rome be understood, he maintains, without seeing them as the union of the older city civilization of the East with the tribal structure of the barbarian war bands which invaded the Mediterranean area toward the end of the second millennium B.C.[8] And, as a final example, medieval culture is seen as the offspring of the union of the classical culture of the Mediterranean cities with the tribal cultures of Northern Europe, brought about through the agency of the Church.[9]

Mr. Dawson's continuing interest in the primary social unit and its influence upon cultural development is shown in a recent letter where he comments upon the studies of the peasant village in different parts of the world now being

[7] See Chapters V, VI and VII in *The Age of the Gods.*

[8] See above, "The Origins of Classical Civilization," pp. 151–57.

[9] See *The Making of Europe,* especially Chapters V and XI; also Chapter IV for Dawson's analysis of tribal society and culture.

made by contributors to *The American Anthropologist:*

These studies strengthen my conviction on the importance of the village as the primary unit of culture and they also show how the higher cultures rest on different types of village society, though it is not clear whether the difference between the higher cultures can be explained by the difference between the primary units or whether the opposite is the case.

These studies also appear to show certain general differences between the European or Northwest European village and those of Asia and Africa. In the latter the village seems to form part of a wider kinship group, that is to say, that there is a strong tribal element still surviving in Asiatic and African societies which has disappeared in Europe, save in a few exceptional regions. I wonder whether this disappearance of the wider kinship group in Europe is due to exceptional development of the monogamous family as the foundation of society. (Letter of September 7, 1955.)

The importance of physical environment in influencing the culture and social development of a people is another key principle which Dawson as a cultural historian holds in common with the anthropologists. One instance of his recognition of the influence of the region is found in his ascribing the diversity of the European cultural development to the nature of the European continent and its particular geographic construction—innumerable valleys and peninsulas shut off from one another by mountains but open to intercourse by sea. As a result, "The sea ways have been the high road of European civilization, for they alone have rendered possible the combination of regional independence with the stimulus of commercial intercourse and mutual influence to which Europe owes the richness and variety of its cultural life." [10]

On the other hand, when a people loses contact with the region it is occupying, this has usually seemed to Dawson a portent of cultural decline. For the particularism of a local society is at the same time a means of nourishing the culture by a contact with the realities of nature. One example of a society's loss of regional roots and their replacement by cosmopolitanism is provided by the decline of the Greek city-states on the mainland of Greece in the fourth and third

[10] *The Age of the Gods,* p. 170.

centuries B.C.; and another by the fate of Moslem Spain in the tenth and eleventh centuries of the Christian era. Of the latter development Dawson observes (and his analysis recalls his description of the decline of the Greek city-states which we discussed earlier in this Note):

> Unfortunately Moslem Spain, in spite of its high civilization, was based on insecure social foundations, and the very age which produced so brilliant a flowering of intellectual culture was also the age of its political decline and fall. The Moslem State in Spain no less than in Egypt and Mesopotamia was an artificial creation which had no organic relation to the life of the people and rested its power on mercenary troops and on the class of slaves and freedmen from which most of its servants and officials were drawn. . . .
>
> This premature blighting of the brilliant civilization of Moslem Spain is typical of the fate of this (Islamic) Mediterranean world as a whole. Everywhere we find the same wealth of material and intellectual culture and the same lack of social vitality or free political activity.[11]

The effects of occupation and geographic environment upon the world view or religious outlook of the less advanced peoples have often been recognized by anthropologists; and one of the chief tasks Dawson undertook in *The Age of the Gods* was to show how the difference between the way of life of the peasant and that of the pastoral nomad had corresponding effects upon their approach to the supernatural. However, in Dawson's view not even the world religions have wholly transcended the limits of the geographic region where they had their origin, and certain psychological orientations which they assume have to be related to the experience of the regional people among whom the religion had its beginnings.

Thus, speaking of the desert as one of the forces which influenced the development of Semitic religion in the direction of Prophecy more than of Priesthood (we may assume the primary reference here is to Islam and perhaps to Judaism), he points out:

[11] *Medieval Essays,* pp. 127, 130. For comparison with this passage, see above, "Progress and Decay in Ancient and Modern Civilization," Dawson's analysis of the decline of Greece, pp. 62 ff.

In contrast to the Greeks and to the peoples who created the archaic culture, the Semitic peoples in historic times were not deeply concerned with the problem of the order of nature. They saw the world in a more primitive fashion as a battlefield of contending forces—of superhuman powers which had to be placated and obeyed rather than controlled and understood. The Semitic background was not the world of the Mediterranean where the gods are the friends of man and crown his labour with the vine and the olive, but the world of the desert in which man exists only on sufferance and is always at the mercy of alien powers. In such a world there is little room for rational calculation, and life is ruled by fate and chance and personal luck and prowess. And the wise man does not trust too much to his own prowess but looks for help to supernatural guidance and warnings, to divination and to an implicit obedience to an incomprehensible divine will.[12]

However, despite the geographic influences which may be involved in its origin, every world religion possesses a vision which is potentially universal. Thus, although Islam originated in the world of the desert and carries with it attitudes and ideas engendered by such an environment, its appeal is not restricted simply to desert-dwelling peoples.

. . . in the case of Islam, we see a new attitude to life, which first arose in the arid plateau of Arabia, transforming the lives and social organization of the Slavonic mountaineers of Bosnia, the Malay pirate of the East Indies, the highly civilized city dwellers of Persia and Northern India, and the barbarous Negro tribes of Africa.[13]

As Dawson remarks elsewhere on the spread of Islam to regions so different from its original environment, "For a vision to be so universal in its effects, there must also be something universal in its causes, and we cannot suppose it to be a merely fortuitous product of local circumstances." [14]

The last of these factors of a sociological nature which

[12] *Religion and Culture,* p. 73. For a reference to the influence of geography on the formation of Indian religion, see above, pp. 62–3.

[13] *Progress and Religion* (1st ed., London, 1929), p. 76.

[14] See above, "Sociology and the Theory of Progress," p. 50.

Dawson finds so important in the dynamics of culture is the contribution which regional peoples make to the cultural unity which is a civilization. Dawson's own work has been greatly enriched by his awareness of the complexity of cultural elements which go to make up a civilization,[15] and, as we have noted above, it is one of his chief criticisms of Spengler and Toynbee that they fail to do justice to this complexity and tend to neglect the cultural traditions of the primitive and barbarian societies which have so greatly affected the formation and character of the higher cultures. In his assertion of a fundamental continuity between civilizations and more primitive societies, Dawson finds himself in basic disagreement with the philosophers of history, whose gaze is fixed too intently upon civilizations as such to allow them to perceive the true character of the unit they are studying. In reply to Toynbee's attempt to posit a radical difference between civilizations and peoples of lower culture, such as the human societies of prehistoric times or those of the non-civilized world today, Dawson observes:

All these belong to the same world of history as the higher civilizations. They possess language and culture and religion and art. And they differ from one another as much or more than they differ from the civilizations. There is no excuse for lumping them all together at the bottom of the scale and grouping the civilizations all together at the top.[16]

In this contrast between the conceptions of culture held by Dawson and Toynbee, it is significant that A. L. Kroeber, the dean of American anthropologists, tends rather to favor the view held by Dawson, that there is a basic similarity in character between the civilizations and the more primitive societies. In a communication to *The American Anthropologist* some years ago, Dr. Kroeber defined his position in the following terms:

Nor do I accede to the view of Spengler, Toynbee and

[15] See *The Making of Europe and Religion and the Rise of Western Culture,* especially Chapters 7, 9 and 13 in the former, and 5 and 6 in the latter.

[16] See above, "Arnold Toynbee and the Study of History," p. 391.

others that civilizations (or "culture") and history begin only at a certain level. It is historic *records* that begin at a certain level. Also, readiness of sophisticated and lettered people to consciously admit explicit cultural values usually begins only at a certain level not too remote from that of their own culture. And it is certainly simpler for them not to be bothered about the so varied primitives who yet look so much alike. Nevertheless, values exist in lowly cultures, definite styles occur in them, and patterns are there; and except as a matter now and then of pragmatic convenience, no anthropologist—or certainly very few of them—will admit the validity of splitting the continuum of human culture into two strata of which one totally or essentially lacks certain qualities that characterize the other.[17]

Although Dawson's own attention has been focused mainly on the higher civilizations and upon the cultural influence of the world religions, he believes that often it is only by studying the lower cultures that the sources and achievements of the advanced cultures can be understood and evaluated. In a letter of comment upon what is needed before an adequate schema of the various epochs of world history can be written, he particularly emphasized the importance of the cultures of barbarian peoples.

. . . We need much further study of the great historical cultures and especially of the relation between these cultures and the smaller regional units which the anthropologists are studying. There is also a great need for more study of the intermediate units—the more advanced barbarian cultures, for example, the cultures of the Yoruba and Bini in West Africa (as these existed within living memory), which are too barbarous for the historians and too civilized for the anthropologists. I think that it is only by the study of these cultures that we can understand the intermediate cultures of antiquity—the Hittites, the Kassites, the Assyrians, even the Persians.

The kind of thing we need is a complete survey of a single area, as for example West Africa, which would show the general pattern of primitive and intermediate cultures in con-

[17] Communication by A. L. Kroeber in *The American Anthropologist*, V. 53, No. 2, April–June 1951, pp. 279–83.

tact with and under pressure from the world cultures of Islam and Western Europe. (Letter of December 28, 1951.)

Thus for the proper development of a world history of culture the historian needs the work of the sociologist and the anthropologist as well as his own investigations. If this is the case, by what principle may each expect to mark out his respective role and function in the common task?

In the article "Sociology as a Science," included in this volume, Dawson points out that sociology and history are complementary parts of the single science of social life, that it is the task of sociology to provide "a general systematic analysis of the social process," while history aims to give "a genetic description of the same process in detail." Sociology deals with the structure of society, history with its evolution. On this distinction in function he bases an analogy to biological science: sociology is related to history "as general biology . . . to the study of organic evolution."

To illustrate how sociology and history might co-operate in the study of a specific society, so as to delineate more clearly its social structure and culture, Dawson takes as his model an historical community—the city-state of ancient Greece.

Thus a sociological study of Greek culture would concern itself primarily with the organic structure of Greek society—with the city-state and its organization, the Greek family and its economic foundation, the functional differentiation of Greek society, the place of slavery in the social order, and so forth; but all these elements must be studied genetically and in relation to the general development of Greek culture on the basis of the material provided by the historian; while the latter, on his side, requires the help of the social analysis of the sociologist in order to interpret the facts that he discovers and to relate them to the organic whole of Greek culture, which is the final object of his study.[18]

However, it is the anthropologists rather than the sociologists who have accomplished most in the direction of community studies. For sociology in the past has been so much concerned either with the attempted remedy of immediate social problems or with the development of mechanistic

[18] See above, "Sociology as a Science," p. 31.

theories to explain the working of the laws of society that it had but little time left for study of the community as such. As a result, it has been the anthropologists who have undertaken the pioneer and eminently successful analyses of modern social communities like Yankee City and Southern Town.[19]

A basic question raised by Dawson's sociological approach to history is the corresponding one of how much part historical evidence should be allowed to play in the validation of sociological principles. Until recently, the general practice in American sociology has been to concentrate upon particular contemporary problems as representing the only kind of evidence which is truly empirical; it seems likely that this attitude is itself a sort of provincialism and unduly restricts the area for testing of sociological concepts. It is significant, we believe, that Max Weber in Germany in the early part of the present century found that his sociological studies achieved a clearer focus when he concentrated his attention on a particular historical problem; and as a result of this study, he enlarged his field of investigation to include the historical development of several different societies as they related to this question.[20] More recently, Robert Redfield's turning to history to clarify the meaning of the folk society and to allow greater scope for its application, affords another convincing testimony of the need for historical perspective in developing sociological conceptions.[21]

Moreover, for the formulation of the principles of social interaction, sociology has come to rely in increasing measure upon the evidence contributed by the anthropologists' study of primitive societies. The value of historical evidence to

[19] Cf. W. L. Warner and Paul S. Lunt, *The Social Life of a Modern Community* (Yale University Press, 1941); *The Status System of a Modern Community* (1942); J. Dollard, *Caste and Class in a Southern Town* (Harper & Brothers, 1949).

[20] See Weber's three volumes of *Gesammelte Aufsaetze zur Religionssoziologie*, parts of which have been translated into English, including the well-known *Protestant Ethic and the Spirit of Capitalism*. For a brief view of Weber's thought on this subject, see Parts III and IV of *From Max Weber: Essays in Sociology*, translated by H. H. Gerth and C. W. Mills (New York, 1946).

[21] R. Redfield, *The Primitive World and its Transformations* (Cornell University Press, 1953).

sociology is of a similar kind to that provided by anthropology. The isolation of basic factors in a social problem which we find in anthropological field work is offered also by historical analyses of past epochs. The combination of sympathy with detachment which the anthropologist should bring to his study is likewise a prerequisite for sound historical investigation. Both the cultural historian and the anthropologist can help the sociologist to overcome what is possibly his major difficulty: that the very wealth of the material available blurs the outlines of the problem he wishes to study. Through the models of social and cultural situations which they provide, anthropology and history can give to sociology a clearer vision and a more precise understanding of its own subject-matter and methods of procedure.

In this connection, it is not without significance that E. E. Evans-Pritchard, former president of the Royal Anthropological Institute and one of Great Britain's leading social anthropologists, has recognized the kinship of his own discipline to history and its need to make greater use of methods of an historical nature. In his presidential address at Oxford in 1950 Dr. Evans-Pritchard made the following observations:

The value of each discipline to the other will, I believe, be recognized when anthropologists begin to devote themselves more to historical scholarship and show how knowledge of anthropology often illuminates historical problems.

The thesis I have put before you, that social anthropology is a kind of historiography, and therefore ultimately of philosophy or art, implies that it studies societies as moral systems and not as natural systems, that it is interested in design rather than in process, and that it therefore seeks patterns and not scientific laws, and interprets rather than explains. . . .

I expect that in the future there will be a turning toward humanistic disciplines, especially towards history, and particularly towards social history or the history of institutions, of cultures and of ideas. . . . I believe that during this second half of the century . . . it [i.e. social anthropology] will take as its province the cultures and societies, past as well as present, of the non-European peoples of the world.[22]

[22] "Social Anthropology: Past and Present," the Marett Lecture, delivered in Exeter College Hall, Oxford, on June 3, 1950, printed in *Man*, 1950, No. 198.

The Nature of Culture

From these preliminary observations, we may now pass to a more detailed consideration of Dawson's conception of culture. He has described a culture as "a common way of life—a particular adjustment of man to his natural surroundings and his economic needs." Observing that both the biological and intellectual elements co-operate in the formation of a culture, he points out that there are both similarities and a basic difference between this process and the development of the way of life of an animal species.

It is true that three of the main influences which form and modify human culture are the same as in the case of the formation of an animal species. They are (1) race, i.e. the genetic factor; (2) environment, i.e. the geographical factor; (3) function or occupation, i.e. the economic factor. But in addition to these there is a fourth element—thought or the psychological factor—which is peculiar to the human species and the existence of which frees man from the blind dependence on material environment which characterizes the lower forms of life.[23]

In his most recent definition of culture, Dawson finds that it is language which most prominently manifests the specific form of the intellectual element in culture. In a yet unpublished essay written in 1954, he remarks: "The linguistic factor is in a sense the most important of all, since language provides the psychological medium in which all the others operate and through which they attain consciousness and continuity." And in another part of the same essay:

Thus the language community is the most fundamental of all human groups and language is the most fundamental element in culture. As the use of language distinguishes man from the other animals, so it is the formation and use of a particular language which distinguishes one culture from another.

It is to be noted that this increased emphasis on the importance of language is closely related to Mr. Dawson's deeper appreciation of the intellectual elements in a super-

[23] See above, "The Sources of Culture Change," pp. 16, 17.

culture of which we have spoken above, by means of which a civilization is able to achieve a larger area of communication with societies with which it comes into contact. For even in the most primitive cultures, language opens up "wider possibilities of communication and understanding and social co-operation" which are the primitive analogue to the achievement of the higher civilization in extending its area of influence to embrace many different peoples.

The first three factors identified in Dawson's definition of culture are the same as Le Play's folk, place and work and correspond to the biological equivalents of organism, function and environment. Through this correspondence there exists the means to relate the social to the biological sciences; for the work of the historian and the sociologist requires an intimate understanding of those things which man has in common with other forms of animal life. Because of the importance of these elements in conditioning human life and culture, Dawson maintains that the approach of the natural sciences has a primary place when the sociologist is studying the relation of the human social group to its natural environment and its economic activities. He observes, "In a thousand ways human life is conditioned and determined by material factors, and there is a legitimate materialism which consists in the definition and analysis of these relations." [24]

However, a social science interested only in these factors and neglecting the specifically human element of thought or psychology would oversimplify the cultural picture and expose itself to the error of determinism. Indeed, despite their recognition of the autonomous character of the religious element in social life, this was an error to which Le Play and his school inclined, for with their emphasis on folk, work and place, they "tended to overestimate the importance of the economic and geographical factors and to neglect the contribution of history." This resulted from the fact that Le Play did not conceive religion (and, we may add, the intellectual factor in general) as a dynamic element within culture, but rather thought of it "as an invariable which governs social life from outside without entering into it." [25]

[24] See above, "Sociology as a Science," p. 32.
[25] *Ibid.*, p. 33.

Where Dawson goes beyond Le Play and makes his specific contribution to cultural theory is in his conception of culture as an organic unity of spiritual and biological elements, in which the intellectual factor is not something existing apart from a people's organized way of life, but is indissolubly united with it. In fact, for Dawson the intellectual element is "the soul and formative principle of a culture," and is "consubstantial with its material substratum." [26] Its position in culture may best be understood by seeing it as part of a psycho-physical unity comparable to man himself. Developing this analogy he asserts:

In reality a culture is neither a purely physical process nor an ideal construction. It is a living whole from its roots in the soil and in the simple instinctive life of the shepherd, the fisherman, and husbandman, up to its flowering in the highest achievements of the artist and the philosopher; just as the individual combines in the substantial unity of his personality the animal life of nutrition and reproduction with the higher activities of reason and intellect.[27]

This conception enables Dawson to consider every human culture from two different viewpoints: as a manifestation of the life of the spirit, though never, be it noted, as simply an "ideal construction"; and as the response of biological life to the conditions of the environment. The more primitive a culture, the more "earthbound and socially conditioned" will its religion appear to be (for it is through religion and its conceptions that the intellectual factor preeminently expresses itself in primitive life); but even under these conditions, where the material factors seem completely to dominate a people's way of life, there is always a certain margin of freedom by which new conceptions of reality may introduce a factor for change.[28]

In his earliest published essay (1921) which we present in this volume, it appears that Dawson's conception of culture is the result of a synthesis of the sociological views of Comte with those of Le Play. Dawson is indebted to Le Play for putting his sociology into touch with the con-

---

[26] *Progress and Religion* (1st ed.), p. 76.

[27] *Progress and Religion*, p. 45.

[28] See *Religion and Culture*, pp. 52–54.

crete bases of human life, through the latter's classic study of the family in relation to its natural environment. On the other hand, while criticizing Comte for embarking upon "grandiose schemes for the reconstitution of society" and for creating a theory of society which "was at the same time . . . a system of moral philosophy and a non-theological substitute for religion," Dawson is impressed with Comte's recognition that the "study of social institutions must go hand in hand with the study of the intellectual and spiritual forces which give unity to the particular age and society in question." And despite his distrust of Comte's philosophy of history and the manner in which it became a substitute for sociology, he praises Comte for stressing "the formation and growth of a living community" in the historical development of mankind, "which embraces every aspect of human life and thought, and in which every age has a living and internal connection with the past and the future." And thus he finds himself in full agreement with Comte's view that "the causes of progress must be sought . . . in man's psychical development rather than in the play of external circumstances." [29]

However, it would be misleading to assume that Dawson's conception of sociology is simply the result of a personal attempt to synthesize the thought of Comte with that of Le Play. While both of these thinkers exercised considerable influence upon his views of society, it was not so much directly as through the mediation of Victor Branford and Patrick Geddes, who founded *The Sociological Review* for the purpose of making Le Play's ideas better known in England and established the Le Play House in London for the same purpose. Moreover, Geddes and Branford had already provided their own synthesis of Comte with Le Play, although they dealt with the matter in a somewhat different fashion from Dawson. It was through their influence, as well as others in *The Sociological Review* group like Lewis Mumford (a disciple of Geddes and Branford), that the influence of Le Play's ideas impressed itself on Dawson.

Nor was Comte the chief source upon which Dawson drew in developing his ideas about a civilization as essentially a spiritual community; it was rather the earlier work of

[29] See above, "Sociology and the Theory of Progress," pp. 47, 48.

the St. Simonians which was the original influence directing his thought along these lines. Mr. Dawson has remarked in a letter to the present writer on the respective parts played by Geddes and Branford, Comte and the St. Simonians in the formation of his sociological thought:

One must remember that the Geddes-Branford sociology was purely French by origin and with rather an anti-German bias. It represents a synthesis of Comte-Leplay-Bergson, with a strong inclination to biological terms and explanations. (Geddes was a biologist and a close friend of Sir Arthur Thomson.)

I diverged from them, first by my sympathy with the German tradition, for example, Herder instead of Montesquieu, and in more recent times Troeltsch and Weber. Secondly, by going back from Comte to the St. Simonians and Catholic social thinkers from whom Comte himself had taken so much. In the case of the St. Simonians, I have always regarded Bazard's *Doctrine de St. Simon* (1824) as the real starting point of modern sociology (and I believed it owed more to Bazard than to St. Simon).

On the other hand, I agreed entirely with Geddes in the value he attached to Aristotle, and he owed this not to Comte but to his own biological studies. My own interest in Aristotle goes back to my Oxford days when I studied the *Politics* with Ernest Barker. Also in those early days I was influenced by Fustel de Coulanges, and his study of the city prepared me for Geddes' view of the city as the centre of sociological study.

Thus my study of sociology was conditioned by my earlier humanist studies, and the Geddes-Branford school had reached the same point from the opposite direction; that is, from biological and geographical science to a humanist sociology. (Letter of July 4, 1954.)

It is important to emphasize that, although many have considered Comte the founder of modern sociology, Dawson believes that the real founders were those earlier social thinkers upon whom Comte drew but whom he did not credit for their contributions to his thought.

What is particularly significant in this early essay of Dawson's which we were discussing above is that he is as firmly convinced as Comte was of the movement of progress in human history, but he sees it achieved in more complex fashion, because of the ambivalent relationship between material and spiritual elements in culture. To avoid the errors of Comte's idealism, Dawson would direct the attention of students of society to the study of supercultures and civilizations, which are the actual historical embodiment of the movement of human progress. By studying these unities in the spirit and with the methods of Le Play, it should be possible to secure a more accurate knowledge of the manner in which biological and social elements combine in the formation of a civilization, and thus provide a more intelligent direction of those forces which at present operate for the creation of a world-wide society.

Thus the investigation of the character of civilizations and the study of the laws by which they flourish and decline, which has been the work of Spengler, Toynbee, Danilevsky, and many others, including Dawson himself, is a legitimate task for the cultural historian; but it must be pursued with an awareness of the local societies which interact with each other and with the wider cultural unity; for it is these that contribute the vital energies by which alone the life of a civilization can develop and expand.

It is a realization of this fact which lies behind Dawson's emphasis upon the vital contact a culture must maintain with its region. Despite his concern with the intellectual elements in culture, he is profoundly aware of the material foundations in which these elements have their roots. Indeed, notwithstanding his trenchant criticism of Spengler's fundamental thesis that culture is biologically determined, Dawson has considerable sympathy with Spenglerian insights into the influence of biology and geographic environment upon the course of history. This attitude is especially evident in his description of the process of cultural degeneration which results from an unwholesome urbanization.

First comes the concentration of culture in the city, with a great resultant heightening of cultural activity. But this is followed by the lowering of the level of culture in the country and the widening of the gulf between townsman and peasant. In some cases, as in ancient Greece, this amounts to a gradual but thorough rebarbarization of the country, in others—as in Russia since Peter the Great, and in the Hellenistic East since Alexander—the peasants still cling to the traditions of a native culture, while the towns adopt a ready-made urban civilization from abroad. In the last stage the cities lose all economic and vital contact with the region in which they are placed. They have become parasitic; less dependent on nature and more dependent on the maintenance of an artificial political and economic system. . . .

No civilization, however advanced, can afford to neglect these ultimate foundations in the life of nature and the natural region on which its social welfare depends, for even the highest achievements of science and art and economic organization are powerless to avert decay, if the vital functions of the social organism become impaired.[30]

In his exposition of this process at work in the decline of Greek culture, Dawson implies the need for a local differentiation of culture in particular regional forms if social health is to be maintained. Otherwise the purely intellectual element, losing its roots in the life of a particular people, exposes society to the dangers of a sterile cosmopolitanism. Rather then regarding national and regional particularities as simply an obstacle to be overcome in the development of civilization, Dawson looks upon them as a necessary counterbalance and complement to the values sought after in an ecumenical organization of culture. Consequently he does not consider the particular and the universal elements in culture as barren negations of each other, but rather as fruitful opposites, the tension between which is necessary for attaining a high level of cultural creativeness.

And while recognizing that national and regional cultures are the product of the influence of material factors like race and geography upon human achievement, he would maintain that such factors are capable of being moulded into high culture forms by man's creative spirit. Nor would he regard the gradual abolition of cultural particularism as a desirable objective to be sought after: in a striking passage in *The Judgment of the Nations*, he contrasts the "immense richness and vitality of European culture in its manifold development in the different nations through the ages" with the eighteenth-century "philosophic ideal of a society founded on abstract rational principals [that] seemed lifeless and empty." [31] For Dawson, the insights of Edmund Burke and the German Romantics concerning the organic nature of any living culture are factors of primary importance in any proposed world order.

Nevertheless he would certainly agree—indeed it is one of the chief bases of his criticism of the modern European development—that national particularism always presents the danger that it will exaggerate its own importance and ignore the broader cultural unity of which it is merely a part. By so doing it destroys the wider vision of reality which is the natural complement to regional values, and which must form the necessary framework for any people's development of a high civilization.

It is because of his consciousness of the organic element in culture that Dawson is opposed to the abstract intellectualism of Hegel's conception of history. To the Hegelians "two successive cultures are not independent organisms, they are merely the embodiment of a pair of complementary propositions in the process of Neo-Hegelian dialectic." Hence, for the Hegelians, the fall of Greek culture does not require any historical explanation, it was a natural result of the passing of the Hellenic idea, and called forth by its own inner logic the Magian idea which succeeded it. [32]

Dawson's objection to Hegel and his disciples is that, by an opposite road, they reach substantially the same goal as Spengler: that is, they eliminate any contribution which science and the individual human mind may make to an understanding of history. For Spengler, this results from a denial of man's ability to transcend the biological factors by which his thinking is necessarily determined; for Hegel, it flows from the refusal to admit the influence of non-intellectual factors on the movement of history. For if the development of history is simply the working out of the Idea, those fields which deal with the particular and the contingent have nothing to contribute to its understanding. Thus the significance of the unique event for man's historical development, and the conditioning of that development by material factors are equally ignored by the Hegelian con-

[31] See above, "Vitality or Standardization in Culture," pp. 82–83.

[32] See above, "Oswald Spengler and the Life of Civilizations," p. 378.

ception of history, which sees the end already predetermined by its beginnings.

As against such a view of history determined in its movement by an inevitable necessity, Dawson cites a few of the numerous instances of historical accidents which emphasize the intrusion of brutal reality into the historical process and its upsetting effect upon the neat categories of a purely logical explanation of history.

It is even possible for one culture to kill another, as we see in the case of the destruction of the Peruvian civilization by the Spaniards, and in the countless instances in which primitive cultures have withered away in contact with modern European civilization. Nor is it only the lower cultures that are destroyed in this way. There are also instances of highly developed urban civilizations falling victim to barbarian invaders, as when the flourishing culture of the Danube provinces was wiped out in the fifth century A.D., or when the cities of Eastern Iran were destroyed by the Mongols.[33]

Dawson's final remarks on this point show his conception of the duality of the cultural process as reflected in the movement of world history. The intellectual elements in a culture like religion and science "do not die with the culture of which they formed part. They are handed on from people to people, and assist as a creative force in the formation of new cultural organisms." [34] But in order to do this, they must take form in the individual cultures of particular peoples; they must descend into the world of matter and time and suffer the hazards and misadventures to which human societies are subjected. While not restricted to the culture or society where they had their origin, their development and spread is contingent upon their being accepted by other societies and made a part of a new cultural growth. Where they fail to achieve this embodiment, ideas no longer have historical reality. Thus the movement of "intellectual and religious synthesis" which constitutes the progress of humanity is not something detached from the accidents of

[33] See above, "Oswald Spengler and the Life of Civilizations," p. 379.

[34] *Ibid.*, p. 380.

history, but something which depends upon historical events for whatever realization it is to achieve. Only by recognizing both the spiritual element in culture and the material factors by which its development is conditioned is it possible to comprehend

. . . that real element of integration and progress, which causes different civilizations to be, not closed worlds without meaning for one another, but progressive stages in the life of humanity.[35]

If such are the historical orientations of Christopher Dawson's thought, a closer examination of its sociological foundations is essential. History, according to Dawson, is necessarily secondary in the study of culture, since it can explain only the changes in a culture that occur after its original formation. The basic character of a culture is determined by the life of a human group in its primary relation to its environment and functions, and it is essentially these which the anthropologist and the sociologist must investigate.[36]

Following Le Play, Dawson finds the link between the genetic and the geographic factors in culture in the so-called primary nature occupations, which are the response of a people to the opportunities presented by the region they inhabit. These occupations are six in number and form the foundation for all material culture. Le Play identifies the types formed by these occupations as: (1) the hunters and food-gatherers; (2) the pastoral peoples; (3) the fishermen of the sea coasts; (4) the agriculturalists; (5) the foresters; and (6) the miners. These occupations are primary in so far as they require some sort of direct contact with nature to bring forth their product.[37]

Moreover, in these primary occupations agriculture holds a unique position, for it requires a much closer relation to the special features of a particular region than do the other primary forms of exploiting nature and her resources. A hunting culture, as Dawson observes, may be uniform throughout half a continent, "while a sedentary agricultural

[35] *Ibid.*, p. 380.
[36] See above, "Sociology as a Science," p. 32.
[37] *Progress and Religion*, p. 54.

one will develop new regional types according to every variation of climate and vegetation." [38] A farming people thus
marries a particular region in order to make it bear more
abundant fruit; this involves the disadvantage of restriction to a specific area but the advantage of a much fuller
development of its resources.

Citing specific examples of human cultures which have
grown out of a particular environment and are based upon
products of that region—"the wine and olive of the Mediterranean, the rice and mulberry of China, the coco-nut and
taro of the Pacific Islands, the maize and tobacco of Central
America"—Dawson points out the tremendous influence
which the material foundation exerts upon the character of
a culture.

This intimate communion of human culture with the soil
in which it is rooted shows itself in every aspect of material
civilization—in food and clothing, in weapons and tools,
in dwellings and settlements, in roads and methods of communication. In every direction, the natural character of the
region determines the modes in which a culture will express
itself, and these in turn react upon the character of the culture itself. [39]

Yet the development of a culture is not simply passive
response to an environment, but is an act of creative co-
operation with its potentialities. Here also the metaphor of
marriage is an appropriate one, for it is by some degree of
union with and mastery over its environment that every
society, even the most primitive one, achieves its organized
way of life. Moreover, when pursued for a long enough
period of time, the primary nature occupation by which a
people asserts its mastery affects not only the environment
but the physical character of the group itself. There is thus
an intimate interaction between the racial and geographic
factors in culture, which not only brings forth social and
economic organization but transforms the two parents in
the process.

If this communion endures without change for a suf-

[38] *Ibid.*, p. 57.
[39] *Ibid.*, p. 58.

ficiently long period, it will produce not merely a new way of life, but a new type of man—a race as well as a culture. Thus in the Eastern Hemisphere each climatic zone possesses its specific racial type: the Negroids of the tropical forest, the Mediterranean race in the warm temperate zone, the Nordic race in the cooler latitudes, and the Lapps of the Arctic regions.

And each of these races formerly possessed, broadly speaking, its own cultural type, so that we may speak interchangeably of Negroid race and Negroid culture, Nordic race and Nordic culture, Arctic race and Arctic culture.

Such a condition is, of course, only possible where conditions of segregation have endured unchanged for vast ages.[40]

Elsewhere Dawson speaks of the tendency of a culture to stabilize itself and persist substantially unchanged for centuries, once it has achieved some sort of equilibrium with its environment. He compares this with the process by which particular biological species arise in response to the conditions of a particular environment, even though in the formation of a culture the human element exercises a power of active choice which is not present in the formation of a species.[41]

This conception of the persistence of a culture's pattern under conditions of marked isolation seems to connect Dawson with the diffusionist schools in anthropology, both English and German. Although aware of and apparently concurring in the criticisms made of these schools by other anthropologists, Dawson ascribes to Graebner and Schmidt, the founders of the German *Kulturkreislehre,* the inauguration of a new approach to cultural study—the conception of a culture-complex as an interrelated group of social phenomena—which has exercised great influence on leading American anthropologists: Kroeber, Lowie, Goldenweiser, and Wissler were specifically mentioned at the time Dawson made this point back in 1929 (in *Progress and Religion*). He also quotes approvingly as a basis for his own viewpoint the remark of W. H. R. Rivers, possibly the greatest member of the English diffusionist school, that "The evidence from Melanesia suggests that an isolated people does

---

[40] *Ibid.,* p. 55.
[41] See above, "The Sources of Culture Change," pp. 17, 18.

not change or advance, but that the introduction of new ideas, new instruments and new techniques leads to a definite process of evolution, the products of which may differ greatly from either the indigenous or the immigrant constituents, the result of the interaction thus resembling a chemical compound rather than a physical mixture." [42]

What seems interesting here is the fact that the diffusionist historical schools were originally formed in protest against the domination of anthropology by methods of natural science. Yet in his idea of the stability of primitive culture, Dawson seems to consider one basic cause for it to lie in the fact that in conditions of isolation the material factors in culture are the governing influences and hence the life of the social group bears a marked similarity to the life of the biological species which has attained adjustment to its environment. As Dawson expresses this point elsewhere, "Here sociology approaches the standpoint of the natural sciences and comes closer to the biologist than to the historian." [43]

Also significant of the weight which Dawson accords to material factors in culture is the view, which we have cited above, that racial characteristics themselves are the product of a social group's interaction with its geographic environment.

. . . In these cases [of primitive isolation] . . . culture becomes inseparable from race.

But this does not mean, as the racialists believe, that culture is the result of predetermined racial inheritance. On the contrary, it would be more true to say that race is the product of culture, and that the differentiation of racial types represents the culmination of an age-long process of cultural segregation and specialization at a very primitive level. . . . [44]

But not only in the case of the primitive "race-forming precultures" is this factor operative, but even in such recent

---

[42] *Psychology and Politics,* p. 118, quoted in *Progress and Religion,* pp. 59–60. For the reference to the influence of Graebner and Schmidt on American anthropology, see p. 52.

[43] See above, "Sociology as a Science," p. 32.

[44] *Religion and Culture,* pp. 47–48.

instances as the immigration of European peoples to new lands. As an example of this on a limited scale, Dawson cites the physical and psychological transformation which a century of living in a new environment has brought about in the original English and Irish immigrants to Australia.[45]

However, in the final analysis it is the intellectual element in social life which is predominant and which gives a culture its specific form. To this element Dawson assigns quite an inclusive content—since he classes under it such aspects of culture as religion, art, philosophy, science and language. (We have noted earlier Dawson's recent emphasis on the importance of language in the study of culture.) Essentially the intellectual element consists in a common set of values which serve to unify the various activities of the group. Such values find expression pre-eminently, Dawson believes, in a society's religious beliefs, since it is here that they acquire a sacredness which enables them to resist the disintegrating forces at work within a society.[46]

The maintenance of a society involves both a community of belief—certain agreed-upon values, whether explicit or implicit—and a continuous and conscious social discipline. To secure these objectives, there must be some factor in culture which can command the allegiance of the society's members against the temptations of an antisocial individualism. In primitive society, and even in most higher civilizations, this factor is found in the existence of transcendent powers who are believed to control the life of nature and of man. Dawson observes that to the vast majority of peoples throughout history, "For a community to conduct its affairs without reference to these powers, seems as irrational as for a community to cultivate the earth without paying any attention to the courses of the seasons." [47]

It is precisely here, in the conscious discipline exerted by religious beliefs over its members, that the adaptation of a

[45] *Ibid.*, p. 48. This observation agrees with that made by Boas and others on the changes in physical type which distinguish the offspring of immigrants to America from their foreign-born parents.

[46] *Ibid.*, pp. 48–50. For a similar view of the social function of religion, see *African Political Systems,* ed. by M. Fortes and E. E. Evans-Pritchard (London, 1940).

[47] *Ibid.*, p. 49.

social group to its environment differs from that of an animal species. However much a human group may seem to approach the biological level in conforming to the character of its environment, this conformity is only achieved by an act of choice: the deliberate adherence of the group to the common set of values which enables it to organize its activities. Thus, even at its lowest level, culture implies the existence of the distinctively human element which makes use of the environment for the attainment of particular social ends.

We have mentioned above that, in Dawson's view, there are several different areas which make up the intellectual element in culture. In one of the articles included in the present volume he suggests the relationship which these various provinces in intellectual culture bear to one another, as also their organic interrelation in the unity of the culture and the sequence of their respective appearance. In this passage one notes particularly the emphasis given to the intuitive aspects of intellectual culture.

. . . it seems to be the fact that a new way of life or a new view of Reality is felt intuitively before it is comprehended intellectually, that a philosophy is the last product of a mature culture, the crown of a long process of social development, not its foundation. It is in Religion and Art that we can best see the vital intention of the living culture. . . .
[For] the same purposeful fashioning of plastic material which is the very essence of a culture, expresses itself also in art. The Greek statue must be first conceived, then lived, then made, and last of all thought. There you have the whole cycle of creative Hellenic culture. First, Religion, then Society, then Art, and finally Philosophy.[48]

This analogy between social effort and the artist forming his material so as to embody within it his artistic vision is a favorite one with Dawson to express the dynamic and creative aspects of culture. He uses it most incisively in the following passage, in which he shows the creativeness involved in the adaptation which a culture makes to its environment.

[48] See above, "Civilization and Morals," pp. 57–58.

We do not regard the dependence of an artist on his material as a sign of weakness and lack of skill. On the contrary, the greater the artist, the more fully does he enter into his material, and the more completely does his work conform itself to the qualities of the medium in which it is embodied. In the same way the conformity of a culture to its natural environment is no sign of barbarism. The more a culture advances, the more fully does it express itself in and through its material conditions, and the more intimate is the co-operation between man and nature.[49]

Nor is this comparison between art and culture merely an accidental one, for Dawson believes there is a fundamental affinity between them. Art indeed is a flowering of culture and represents a society's fundamental aspirations in their most concentrated expression. It is thus a key to the inner character of a culture. Far more than statistical facts, art enables the student of culture to penetrate to the peculiar spirit of the society he is studying, to perceive its specific form and appreciate its particular outlook upon life.

To understand the art of a society is to understand the vital activity of that society in its most intimate and creative moments. . . . Hence an appreciation of art is of the first importance to the historian and the sociologist, and it is only by viewing social life itself as an artistic activity that we can understand its full meaning.

No amount of detailed and accurate external knowledge will compensate for the lack of that immediate vision which springs from the comprehension of a social tradition as a living unity.[50]

A. L. Kroeber has pointed out that it requires something of the faculties of the artist to seize upon the specific character of a culture.[51] For this reason, he asserts, some of the best delineations of culture patterns have come from non-anthropologists who have had the intuition needed to grasp the underlying spirit of the culture they were describing. It will be recalled that Oswald Spengler's *The Decline of the*

[49] *Progress and Religion*, p. 57.
[50] See above, "Art and Society," pp. 76, 75.
[51] *Anthropology* (Harcourt, Brace, New York, 1948), p. 317.

West contains very perceptive descriptions of the particular character of several of the civilizations he compares with one another in his view of world history, although he makes this character so all-pervasive that no aspect of the culture can escape its influence. In the light of his intuitive perception of cultural patterns, it is significant that Spengler was neither a professional historian nor an anthropologist; but he *was* an individual of extremely wide cultural background.

Kroeber, in his volume of *Configurations of Culture Growth,* specifically commends Spengler for his ability to grasp the peculiar character of various civilizations and considers this one of Spengler's outstanding contributions to cultural study. And Ruth Benedict, in her delineation of the contrasting attitudes toward life she finds in certain primitive cultures, made use of particular Spenglerian themes as a conceptual basis for her work.[52] It is possibly as a result of this fact (as well as of her own humanistic studies) that she makes a strong plea for more students trained in the humanities to enter the field of anthropology. Only in this way, she believes, can anthropology make full use of the cultural materials with which it deals.[53]

So far as history is concerned, it is Dawson's belief that a training in the humanities and an appreciation of aesthetic values have formed the basis for much of the most important historical writing of the last two centuries. In fact, the very attitudes which determined the writing of history in a particular way and, at different periods, gave it new motivations and new goals, have been derived from an aesthetic approach to history. In a letter of March 6, 1954 to the present writer, Mr. Dawson suggests his views on this matter:

. . . the whole principle of liberal education is aesthetic, and up to the present, history itself has depended on a pre-existing aesthetic attitude.

Thus eighteenth-century historiography is based on the aesthetic and criticism of French classical culture, nineteenth-century historiography got its new impetus (as in Ranke) from

[52] See *Patterns of Culture* (Mentor, 1948), pp. 48–51.

[53] See her article "Anthropology and the Humanities," in *The American Anthropologist,* V. 50, October 1948, p. 589.

the Romantic aesthetic, and in my own experience and that of other historians I have known, one starts with an aesthetic intuitive vision of a culture in its literary and artistic products and then proceeds to study and criticize and compare and analyze.

But the study of culture is not merely the contemplation of a static object; it is rather like tracing the development of an organic process and essentially implies movement in time. Just as the modern sciences are increasingly concerned with aspects of development in their subject matter and have become profoundly historical in spirit, surveying "the whole world of nature as it lives and moves," [54] so history's interest in the organic cultural evolution of society leads it in the direction of science and scientific methods. Empirical methods are as necessary as intuitive vision for the study of a society and its culture and history; they are needed to investigate, to compare, and to test one's conclusions; their use, however, is not primary, but secondary; they are not so much creative as critical; they may serve to modify or to reject one's original view, but of themselves they will not establish a new theory. It is the idea or conception which forms the basis for empirical work; and this is not arrived at by means of accumulation of facts, but rather by a certain intuitive faculty which is as necessary to significant scientific thinking as it is to aesthetic creation. Certain remarks of Dawson in an article replying to an academic historian who criticized broader interpretations in history make this point clear.

The academic historian is perfectly right in insisting on the importance of the techniques of historical criticism and research. But the mastery of these techniques will not produce great history, any more than a mastery of metrical technique will produce great poetry. For this something more is necessary—intuitive understanding, creative imagination, and finally a universal vision transcending the relative limitations of the particular field of historical study. The experience of the great historians such as Tocqueville and Ranke leads me to believe that a universal metahistorical vision of this kind, partaking more of the nature of religious con-

[54] See above, "Sociology as a Science," p. 29.

templation than of scientific generalization, lies very close to the sources of their creative power.[55]

Related to his conception of social life as an artistic activity, a creative interaction between a human society and its environment, is one of Dawson's most significant insights about culture. This is the principle that all cultural creativeness depends upon a certain polarity or diversity between the component elements in a culture, and that the greater the creativeness of a culture or a period, the more likely is this tension between opposite poles to be manifested.

This creative tension is not without its dangers, however, since an increase in its intensity may lead to a society's being torn asunder. This is what Dawson believes to have happened at the time of the Reformation between the opposite cultural poles of Northern and Southern Europe; and at an earlier period in Greece, when the Peloponnesian War marked the split between the Ionian and Dorian strains in Greek civilization, as represented respectively by Athens and Sparta.[56]

The Dynamics of Culture Change

Based upon his conception of the organic nature of culture, Dawson identifies five main types of culture change: (1) that of a people developing its way of life in its original environment without the intrusion of human factors from outside; (2) the case of a people coming into a new geographical environment and readapting its culture in consequence; (3) the mixture of two different peoples, each with its own way of life and social organization, usually as a result of conquest but occasionally as a result of peaceful contact (this, which Dawson considers the most typical of all kinds of culture change, also involves a change of the second type for at least one of the peoples); (4) the adoption by a people of some element of material culture from elsewhere; and (5) the modification of a people's way of life owing to the adoption of new knowledge or beliefs, or to some change in its conception of reality.[57]

[55] See above, "The Problem of Metahistory," p. 287.

[56] See above, "Cultural Polarity and Religious Schism," pp. 90–91.

[57] See above, "The Sources of Culture Change," pp. 19–21.

The principle of dynamic tension underlies most of these five causes of change in a people's culture. The two most important causes—the third and fifth which Dawson cites —are those in which the creative tension is at its greatest degree of intensity. One of these is the cultural situation presented by two different peoples who are gradually interfused with each other over a long period of time, as a result of an original act of conquest or migration. Such a cause is to be found at work in the genesis both of Greek culture and of Western civilization, in each of which, as mentioned above, the tension became too great for the culture to sustain without internecine conflict and division.

The other cause of greatest importance for cultural change is that which occurs when a people secures new knowledge or adopts a new view of reality. It is this type which Dawson believes to exercise the greatest and most lasting influence of all. He finds the paramount example of such change in the coming of a new religion which, even though it has roots in a people's past experience, transforms their way of life and turns their social development into new and unexpected channels.

Not only is the change wrought by a new view of reality most sweeping, but to the degree that the spiritual tradition which it establishes is a powerful one, it will mould the outlook of peoples living in that cultural area for many centuries to come. Thus the view of reality which acts as a ferment of change in its beginnings, operates to maintain the stability of a culture or civilization once it has become accepted.

The ultimate barriers between peoples are not those of race or language or region, but those differences of spiritual outlook and tradition which are seen in the contrast of Hellene and Barbarian, Jew and Gentile, Moslem and Hindu, Christian and Pagan. In all such cases there is a different conception of reality, different moral and aesthetic standards, in a word, a different inner world.[58]

[58] *Progress and Religion,* p. 76. It should be noted that while Dawson considers language "the most fundamental element in culture," so that the "use of a particular language distinguishes one culture from another" (see above, p. 429), the civilizations and the world religions are *supercultures,* embracing many different regional cultures and linguistic groups within their area of communication.

There is one exception which Dawson finds to this general law that the persistence of a world religion in a particular area leads to conservatism and cultural stability. That is in the effect of Christianity on Western civilization. Although Christianity created the unity that is Europe, it has not been content merely to stabilize and conserve that unity. Instead it has been a continuing influence for change throughout each of the different periods in Western cultural history. Not only has it inspired the religious development of the West and served as a means for the transmission of the Western cultural heritage to peoples of the most diverse social backgrounds, but it has also had a powerful though indirect influence on the successive movements of reform and revolution by which Western society has been distinguished from the other world cultures.

In fact, no civilization, not even that of ancient Greece, has ever undergone such a continuous and profound process of change as Western Europe has done during the last nine hundred years. It is impossible to explain this fact in purely economic terms by a materialistic interpretation of history. The principle of change has been a spiritual one and the progress of Western civilization is intimately related to the dynamic ethos of Christianity, which has gradually made Western man conscious of his moral responsibility and his duty to change the world.[59]

In considering the five basic types of cultural change which Dawson enumerates, we find that the conception of cultural stability underlies each and defines it by contrast. It is only when a tension is set up between the otherwise stable culture and new influences from outside that major change may be expected to occur. Moreover, precisely because change is something out of the ordinary and interferes with the previous mode of a culture's functioning, there is a limit to the amount of change of which a society is capable without breakdown. This limitation is a result of the organic nature of culture, which implies that culture is not simply an intellectual development or the result of a movement of ideas, but has its roots firmly planted in the soil of its geographic environment.

[59] *The Judgment of the Nations*, p. 23.

When change within a culture is too abrupt or when the environment or conflict with other social groups demands too great a degree of adjustment to new conditions, the effort required of a society may be beyond the optimum of which it is capable and the culture will go under rather then maintain itself. Abruptness of change developed from within the culture itself is only likely to occur in the case of high civilizations, since these already contain such a complexity of elements that the interaction of the latter with one another may set off rapid change; but abrupt change in less advanced cultures is almost always a result of the intrusion of some external force impinging upon the adaptation they have achieved; the most common of such external forces are extensive changes in the regional environment or the impact of other societies.

Life necessarily implies change, but this does not mean that change always implies life. There is always a limit to the amount of change of which an organism is capable, and this is no less true of the social than of the physical organism. A species may adapt itself to a slight change in climate and may flourish the more for it, but if the change is very great a whole series of species may become extinct and new ones may take their place. And, as a rule, the more specialized and elaborate is the type the more easily does it succumb to change, while the more plastic and adaptable forms of life survive. . . .

In the same way human cultures or forms of social life develop and enrich themselves by cultural change, but if the change is too great or too sudden or the culture too stereotyped and fixed, change brings death instead of progress.

It is not a question of racial deterioration but one of social failure. The Red Indians were probably as fit and fine a type of man as has ever existed, but their culture could not compete with the more highly organized form of civilization of the European colonists. And so they vanished with the buffalo and the open prairie before the plough and the rifle and the railway.[60]

In this passage, written by Dawson in 1931, there seems to be an anticipation of Toynbee's concept of environmental

[60] *The Modern Dilemma*, pp. 35–36.

challenges which are too severe for a society to meet successfully. However, where Toynbee thinks of the over-severe challenge as inhibiting the progress of a less advanced society toward civilization, or as a cause of breakdown once the level of civilization has been achieved, Dawson considers that the destruction of the culture itself is involved. This is related to a basic difference in viewpoint between Dawson and Toynbee on the nature of culture: Dawson holding that all culture, including the level of the primitive, is only achieved by an effort of social discipline and mastery of the environment, Toynbee tending to think of civilization alone as requiring that expenditure of social energy which he designates a response.

For Toynbee, therefore, there is a sharp distinction between the dynamic equilibrium which characterizes a civilization, in which the dialectic of challenge and response is continually in operation to push the society forward toward new goals, and the state of primitive society, in which the cake of custom is unbroken and fixation on cultural routine results from mere inertia. In Toynbee's view there is apparently no period in which an advanced society like a civilization has met its challenges successfully and has achieved harmony among its constituent elements and with its environment; if a civilization is not moving forward, in Toynbee's view, it is either in a state of breakdown or cultural stagnation, in the latter instance resembling, on a higher level, the immobility of primitive culture.[61]

Thus, whereas for Toynbee primitive societies as we know them at present are essentially static, and this is what distinguishes them from civilizations (or at least civilizations in the process of growth), for Dawson both primitive and advanced cultures can only be maintained by dynamic effort: when this fails, the culture itself goes out of existence. Toynbee will admit the previous dynamism of primitive societies in having reached the particular level of culture they now enjoy; but he fails to see that even keeping a culture going is not possible without social co-operation and hard work.

[61] See *A Study of History* (Somervell abridgment), sections on the genesis and growth of civilizations, but especially pp. 48–51 and 209–216.

Dawson observes in this connection:

> To the outside observer the most striking feature of primitive culture is its extreme conservatism. Society follows the same path of custom and convention with the irrational persistence of animal life.
>
> But in reality all living culture is intensely dynamic. It is dominated by the necessity of maintaining the common life, and it is possible to ward off the forces of evil and death and gain life and good fortune only by a continuous effort of individual and social discipline.[62]

In addition to the organic basis for limited change which we have discussed above, there is also the psychological basis, the fact that an individual and a society both require a feeling of security, of connection with social roots in the past, if change is not to be merely destructive. (It is interesting to speculate to what extent this psychological need, with the limits it imposes upon the amount of change which an individual or a society is capable of absorbing, is a result of man's physical nature and the biological foundations of human culture.)[63]

Dawson recognizes this psychic aspect which conditions acceptance of social change when he speaks of the need for a new invention, whether social or material in nature, to be related to the vital spirit of the culture if it is to be a cause of progress rather than decline.[64] Somehow or other the new invention must be incorporated into the fabric of the existing culture and made consonant with the society's needs and previous experience. This happened, as Dawson notes, with the introduction of the horse to the culture of the Plains Indians; but much more often is it likely that the new element cannot be incorporated successfully without such radical social change taking place as to destroy the basis for the culture's continued existence. As an example of this outcome, "Today the Esquimaux are learning a new

[62] *Religion and Culture*, p. 56.

[63] *Progress and Religion*, pp. 211–213, discusses this matter in relation to the effects upon social vitality of urban-industrial life.

[64] *Ibid.*, pp. 77–78.

manner of life, they are becoming civilized, but at the same time and for the same reason they are a dying race." [65]

If a culture proves strong enough, it will eventually throw off, sometimes sooner, sometimes later, changes that have been introduced into it from outside and for which there is no sufficient basis in its own past experience. If the change comes attended by a superior technology, it will usually destroy the culture it has conquered. The most common instances of this are the reactions of primitive peoples to contact with modern Western civilization, but it is not only more primitive societies that are endangered by rapid social change brought on by agencies external to their society.

The most civilized people of antiquity, the Greeks, failed, not because their civilization became unprogressive, but because it was too complex and refined. Their standards of life, their ideals of civic and individual liberty and enjoyment, were too high to stand the strain of political competition, and they went down before ruder and harder peoples like the Macedonians and the Romans, who asked less of life and got more.[66]

Although the Greeks lost their political independence, the forms of their culture were retained and transmitted by their conquerors to new peoples, even though on a lower level of cultural quality. For Western civilization, ruled by the same desire for a high standard of living—both economically and politically—which was the downfall of the Greeks, the prospects for a continuance of the traditional forms of their culture should conquest occur are considerably less hopeful. For the new barbarians possess no sympathy for the way of life of the peoples of the West and are bent upon destroying not only Western social structure and political institutions, but the traditional system of values as well.

Nor is this external danger the only one which a highly developed culture like the modern West faces. The changes

[65] See above, "The Sources of Culture Change," p. 18.
[66] *The Modern Dilemma*, p. 37.

introduced into its way of life over the past century by the scientific revolution raise the question whether it is possible for the cultural tradition of the West to assimilate these changes, or whether they are so great that a new type of technological civilization must succeed to the humanist and religious forms of the past. While recognizing the latter possibility, Dawson believes that the coming of such a civilization would be self-destructive, for it could not long maintain itself against man's deeper spiritual needs. In a letter to the present writer Mr. Dawson remarks:

> I think an entirely technological culture would be an entirely barbarous culture. No one believes that civilization can carry on without some element of higher spiritual culture. . . .
> The coming of age of technology only makes the need for Christian culture (or some alternative religious or humanist culture) more imperative. Even if, *per impossibile,* all the spiritual traditions of culture could be temporarily suppressed, it could only lead to a nihilist revolution which would destroy the technological order itself, as I have pointed out many times in my writings. Orwell's *1984* is a good picture of a pure technological order and the only fault I find with it is that he seems to believe it is a possibility. (Letter of January 29, 1955.)

In connection with the destruction of cultural values and traditions brought about in a society by tremendous social changes, whether as a result of foreign impact or of internal causes, Dawson finds himself in some measure of agreement with Kroeber's observations on the death of a culture.

> What seems to be actually involved in such cases [Kroeber writes] is the dissolution of a particular assemblage of cultural content, configurated in a more or less unique set of patterns belonging to a nation or a group of nations. Such particular assemblages and constellations do unquestionably "die out"; that is, they dissolve away, disappear, and are replaced by new ones. . . .
> The corresponding societies, the culture-carrying groups, have a way of going on; much of the cultural content continues to exist and function somewhere, and may amplify;

it is the particular set of patterned interweavings of content characterizing a civilization that breaks down.[67]

Thus the people themselves that possessed the culture continue their existence, but under different cultural patterns, and no longer taking so active a part, it may be, in the new patterns, especially if these have been brought in from outside. And in some cases, if Spengler is correct, there occurs a marked deterioration in the quality of the culture, sometimes descending to the level of what Spengler terms "fellahin peoples."

Dawson believes, however, that Kroeber is possibly too optimistic concerning the fate of the culture-carrying group and that he does not distinguish sufficiently between the mass of the people who accept a culture and the ruling group who have been responsible for introducing and preserving it. In a note on Kroeber's passage on the death of a culture he remarks:

Actually I think Kroeber overstates the case for survival. I believe in many cases the change is accompanied by the physical destruction of the minority that is the bearer of the cultural tradition. This seems to have happened in the destruction of the French Creole element in Haiti, and the destruction or disappearance of the Latin-speaking ruling element in Roman Britain and Germany in the fifth century A.D.

The mass deportations that accompanied and followed the first and second world wars opened our eyes to this factor in culture change: for example, the destruction of the Greek population in Anatolia after the first world war, and (I believe) the destruction of the Tartars of the Crimea after the second.

If this observation is correct, it would appear to lend some support to Spengler's view about the lower quality of the culture of "fellahin peoples" after the passing of a high civilization.

However, the apparent destruction of a culture does not always mean the permanent loss of its cultural influence. Indeed, the most challenging problem arising from contacts

[67] A. L. Kroeber, *Anthropology*, pp. 382–84.

between cultures is how the traditions of a conquered or subordinate people reassert themselves centuries after the original encounter with their conqueror has taken place. The most common example of this reassertion of the culture tradition of a subordinate people has occurred in the conquest of a peasant society by a nomad warrior aristocracy; and most of the classic civilizations in which the world religions appeared were creations of this type. In these cases the conquest was the starting point of a process of fusion and growth by which the two peoples and their cultural traditions were gradually united to produce a new cultural entity. As one example of this process, Dawson suggests that, if his hypothesis on the origins of Indian culture is correct, "We should interpret the rise of the classical Indian systems of thought and social organization as due to the reassertion of the submerged archaic Indian culture against the warrior culture of the Aryan invaders." [68]

Dawson believes that such an organic fusion of different cultural growths, where it occurs, is distinguished by three identifiable stages. First, there is the period of fertilization and growth, second, the period of progress or flowering of the hybrid creation, and finally there is the period of maturity, in which the new cultural entity is stabilized in patterns which endure as long as that culture lasts.[69]

There is nothing absolute or determined about these stages: first, because they do not occur in all encounters of different cultural traditions, even where conquest has brought two societies into close intimacy with each other; and secondly, because there is no means of predicting with assurance how much or what elements each people taking part in the process will contribute to the final product which is the stabilized form of the new culture.

Although this pattern of three stages is most readily identifiable in the mixing of two different peoples to form a regional culture, it is possible that it may also underlie the development of civilizations or supercultures. Here, however, the complexity of the cultural pattern and the number of peoples being brought into fertilizing contact with one an-

[68] *Religion and Culture*, p. 199.

[69] *Progress and Religion*, p. 62; cf. also *Enquiries*, pp. 67–68, 72–73.

other make it most difficult to disentangle the threads and identify clearly the course of its development.[70]

View of World History

Although Dawson has explicitly disclaimed the possibility of writing at present a history truly world-wide in scope, so as to do proper justice to each cultural tradition,[71] there is implicit throughout his work a conception of the development of world history which we believe should be presented here, as a conclusion to the present essay.

Dawson's view of the movement of world history turns upon the major changes which have taken place in man's view of reality as these have found expression in the life of particular societies and cultures.

According to Dawson, there are four great world ages in the development of mankind, each distinguished by a different conception of the universe. The first stage is that of primitive culture; the second is characterized by the rise of the archaic civilizations in Egypt and Mesopotamia and Asia Minor; the third is marked by the rise and spread of the world religions; and the fourth stage is that which has been inaugurated by the scientific developments arising in Western civilization. This fourth stage, in Dawson's view, is closely related to the Christian conception of man and the universe.

The difference between the first and second ages in world history is the difference between the unreflective vision of reality held by primitive food-gatherers and hunters and the ordered understanding of natural laws which formed the foundation of the archaic culture. Of this conception of man's co-operation with nature's laws, from which flowed

[70] In the article in *Enquiries* which we have cited immediately above, Dawson seems to apply these three stages to supercultures like Christendom, Islam, China, etc., and not simply to regional cultures. His latest views on this subject, however, are expressed in his letter of January 1, 1955 to the present writer, from which we have already quoted: "But on the whole I do not believe that civilizations have life-cycles. Peoples have, and if a culture is bound up with a people, then it also must. But in so far as a civilization becomes a superculture and is transmitted to an indefinite number of peoples, its development may transcend this cycle."

[71] See above, "Europe in Eclipse," pp. 395 ff.

the discovery of the higher agriculture, the working of metals and the invention of writing and the calendar, Dawson observes:

It governed the progress of civilization for thousands of years and only passed away with the coming of the new vision of Reality which began to transform the ancient world in the fifth and sixth centuries B.C.—the age of the Hebrew Prophets and the Greek Philosophers, of Buddha and Confucius, an age which marks the dawn of a new world.[72]

What causes led to the change in the view of reality which marked the transition between the second and third great ages of world history? One reason lay in the limitations of the archaic civilization itself. In its co-operation with the processes of nature it had realized an enormous material progress—"relatively the greatest perhaps the world has ever seen," says Dawson. However, "Each culture was bound up with an absolutely fixed form from which it could not be separated. When once it had realized its potentialities, it became stationary and unprogressive."[73] This resulted in so complete an identification of religion with the social order that both religion and culture were stifled, the former losing its spiritual character and the latter so restricted by the bonds of religious tradition "that the social organism became as rigid and lifeless as a mummy."[74] It was against this idolatry of the archaic religion cultures and the denial of the transcendent character of spiritual reality that the great world religions rose in revolt.

However, in their desire to emphasize the independence of the spirit from the material order, the world religions often erred in the opposite direction by teachings that were equally injurious to religion as a social force. Through their condemnation of matter and the body as evil, their flight from nature and the world of sense, their denial of the reality of the world and the value of the social order, the new world religions tended to weaken, if not destroy, the bridge which the archaic civilization had built between religion and culture. In fact, it was largely through the continued survival of the traditions of the archaic nature religions that the

[72] See above, "The Sources of Culture Change," p. 22.
[73] *Progress and Religion*, pp. 117–18.
[74] *Religion and Culture*, p. 206.

material civilization of the Orient was preserved. As Dawson remarks upon the effects of the new world religions on material progress:

The great achievements of the new culture lie in the domain of literature and art. But, from the material point of view, there is expansion rather than progress. The new culture simply gave a new form and a new spirit to the materials that it had received from the archaic civilization. In all essentials Babylonia, in the time of Hammurabi, and even earlier, had reached a pitch of material civilization which has never since been surpassed in Asia. After the artistic flowering of the early Middle Ages the great religion-cultures became stationary and even decadent.[75]

The changes that created the fourth great age in world history had their origins in Western Europe and cannot be understood without a study of the new Christian culture that had arisen in that area. In contrast to the cleavage between religion and culture which occurred to a greater or less degree in the Oriental religions, Christianity, through its doctrine of the Incarnation, was better able to reconcile the conflicting demands of the spiritual and material orders. The spiritual world could maintain its transcendent character and at the same time interpenetrate the world of man with its dynamic force. Dawson notes the effects of this upon the social and cultural development of Western civilization.

Its religious ideal has not been the worship of timeless and changeless perfection, but a spirit that strives to incorporate itself in humanity and to change the world. In the West the spiritual power has not been immobilized in a sacred social order like the Confucian State in China or the Indian caste system. It has acquired social freedom and autonomy, and consequently its activity has not been limited to the religious sphere but has had far-reaching effects on every aspect of social and intellectual life.[76]

[75] See above, "Religion and the Life of Civilization," pp. 125–26.
[76] "Christianity and the New Age," in *Essays in Order,* by Maritain, Wust and Dawson (New York, 1931), pp. 228–29.

Dawson recognizes that the goal of reconciliation between the power of the spirit and the resisting institutions of the temporal order has never been adequately realized in any epoch in Western history. Nevertheless it has been the driving force behind the unique achievements of Western culture and has made that culture a power for change in the rest of the world as well as among its own peoples.

In one of his more recent essays Dawson suggests a psychological basis for the social and material changes which Western civilization has inaugurated and ultimately spread to other parts of the world. It was through the influence of the Christian ethos upon the psyche of the individual person that there developed the new attitude toward life which became the source for the new culture and the tremendous social transformation that it wrought.

Even today very little thought is given to the profound revolution in the psychological basis of culture by which the new society of Western Christendom came into existence. Stated in terms of Freudian psychology, what occurred was the translation of religion from the sphere of the Id to that of the Super-Ego. . . .

With the reception of Christianity, the old gods and their rites were rejected as manifestations of the power of evil. Religion was no longer an instinctive homage to the dark underworld of the Id. It became a conscious and continual effort to conform human behavior to the requirements of an objective moral law and an act of faith in a new life and in sublimated patterns of spiritual perfection.[77]

But since all civilizations are essentially distinguished from barbarism by the greater prominence given to the Super-Ego and by the rational control of instinctive impulses through an ordered understanding of their significance, in what way does Christianity differ from the religions that form the basis of the other world cultures? Is not its psychological basis identical with theirs in asserting the superior claims of the Super-Ego against the Id? No, Dawson would reply, one may distinguish definite differences in the relationship established between these two forces in the moral universes of the different world religions. For example,

In some cases, as in Hinduism, the sharp breach with the

forces of the Id which was characteristic of the conversion of the West has never taken place, and life is not conceived as a process of moral effort and discipline but as an expression of cosmic libido, as in the Dance of Siva.

On the other hand, in Buddhism we see a very highly developed Super-Ego. But here the Super-Ego is allied with the death-impulse so that the moralization of life is at the same time a regressive process that culminates in Nirvana.[78]

While Western culture has witnessed religious movements that show a similar tendency, as in Manicheanism and Albigensianism, these were but eccentric developments and not typical of the central Western religious tradition. The effect of this tradition has been to produce a different kind of personality from those which are representative of the other world cultures.

But the characteristic feature of Western civilization has always been a spirit of moral activism by which the individual Super-Ego has become a dynamic social force. In other words, the Christian tradition has made the conscience of the individual person an independent power which tends to weaken the omnipotence of social custom and to open the social process to new individual initiatives.[79]

But although this social dynamism was implicit in Christianity from the beginning and provided the impetus for the conversion of the ancient world and the transmission of Christian culture to new peoples through the dark ages of barbarian and Islamic invasion, it was not until the thirteenth century that its significance was fully understood. In the spirituality of St. Francis, in which the spirit of Christian humanism received its most profound expression, in the philosophic synthesis of St. Thomas, who reconciled reason with faith and laid the foundations for a scientific approach to reality, and in the vision of Roger Bacon, who saw in scientific invention a creative social force of incalculable power, the new conception of reality finally reached maturity.[80]

From this point of view the importance of the twelfth

[78] *Ibid.*, p. 15.

[79] *Ibid.*, p. 16.

[80] See *Progress and Religion*, pp. 170–76; also *Medieval Essays*, pp. 109–11 and 142–51.

and thirteenth centuries is due to their first embodiment of Christian culture in new dynamic social forms. For the first Christian culture—that of the Byzantine-patristic age—was the outcome of the application of Christian ideas to an already mature and static culture. And it was for this reason that the social dynamism of Christianity could find no adequate expression in the society and culture of the Byzantine Empire.

The subsequent development of Western culture from the Renaissance onwards is the result of the growth of this new dynamic Western Christian society and culture. For with the Renaissance there began that movement of vast expansion of Western civilization, not only geographically but also in the fields of science and technology, which has been the outstanding feature of the last four centuries of world history. By this movement the fourth world age reaches out to its material realization. The uniqueness of this epoch created by Western man is directly related to the missionary goals implanted in the soul of the West by more than a thousand years of Christian teaching; the new culture introduced by the Renaissance had its roots especially in the socio-religious ideals of the medieval period. Western humanism and Western science, as well as Western exploration and colonization, were not the quick-ripening fruits of a hothouse growth; they were, rather, the fruits of a millennium of cultivation, "the results of centuries which had ploughed the virgin soil of the West and scattered the new seed broadcast over the face of the earth." [81]

Despite the interpretation which sees the Renaissance as primarily a revolt against the Christian past (a view now largely abandoned by scholars,[82] but still a strong influence on the thought of many non-historians), Dawson points out that the whole era of culture inaugurated by the Renaissance and continuing through the nineteenth century would be impossible to understand if one were to sever it from its Christian origins.

"The great men of the Renaissance were spiritual men even when they were most deeply immersed in the temporal order.

[81] *The Judgment of the Nations*, p. 24.

[82] See Wallace Ferguson, *The Renaissance in Historical Thought* (Cambridge, 1948).

It was from the accumulated resources of their Christian past that they acquired the energy to conquer the material world and to create the new spiritual culture."

Now what I said here [in this passage written eighteen years ago] about the origins of the Humanist culture seems to me to be equally true of the age of the Enlightenment and the nineteenth century, when Western culture conquered and transformed the world. . . .

The activity of the Western mind, which manifested itself alike in scientific and technical invention as well as in geographical discovery, was not the natural inheritance of a particular biological type; it was the result of a long process of education which gradually changed the orientation of human thought and enlarged the possibilities of social action.[83]

Thus in Dawson's view the Western cultural development lies at the center of world history, and it has been the dynamic influence of Europe and her offspring in the New World which has made possible the present opportunity for a world society. Where many contemporary philosophers of history either despair of the West or so berate it for its sins and shortcomings as to set it below the Orient in an order of moral or spiritual values (consider Muller's *Uses of the Past* or Toynbee's *The World and the West* for representative examples of this trend), Dawson maintains that, despite its secularism and self-seeking, Western culture is distinguished by a moral energy and spiritual dynamism which it has inherited from its Christian past, and that it is this energy which has caused the spread of Western institutions to the rest of the globe and has made the other cultures part of one world of cultural communication. Thus it is through an understanding of Europe that we can comprehend the forces that are shaping the destinies of the modern world, for even those movements that are in revolt against the West owe their origins to Western inspiration and would not have developed in the way they did without European influence. Dawson has remarked on this fact in an article written some years ago:

The movement of Oriental revolt against the European he-

[83] *Religion and the Rise of Western Culture*, pp. 9–10.

gemony is itself largely of Western inspiration. Its ideology is purely European and owes nothing to the cultural traditions of the peoples whom it is seeking to free. Even in the literary sphere the leaders of Oriental thought, as conceived in Europe, are themselves men of Western culture and education. The central fact of the whole situation of East-West relations is not the relatively weak and superficial cult of Oriental ideas in the West, but the incomparably more powerful and far-reaching movement of Occidental ideas in the East, where the traditional cultures have been shaken to their foundations.[84]

However, the influence of the West upon the East has not been merely a subversive one. It has been through the efforts of European archaeologists and linguists that the civilizations of the Orient have come to recognize the greatness of their own history and culture and have been afforded a clearer perception of their own specific character. As Dawson assesses the results of this work of European scholarship in the last essay of the present volume:

Not only did it immeasurably widen the frontiers of Western civilization and lay the foundations of a new understanding between East and West, it also gave the non-European peoples a new understanding of their own past. Without it, the East would be unconscious of the greatness of its own heritage, and the memory of the earliest Asiatic civilizations would still be buried in the dust.

This is an enduring inheritance for the whole world, East and West, which will outlast political ideologies and economic empires.[85]

Nevertheless, one cannot ignore or minimize the extent to which Western secular culture threatens the traditional cultures of the East. Despite the optimistic views concerning their future advanced by such writers as Muller and Northrop, and the belief of some that the Oriental religions are better suited for survival than Christianity in the intermingling of cultures and religions which the present epoch

[84] "The Revolt of the East and the Catholic Tradition," in *The Dublin Review*, V. 183, July 1928, pp. 1–14.

[85] See above, "Europe in Eclipse," p. 401.

is witnessing, there are signs that the Oriental religion-cultures have entered upon a stage of decline and retreat before secularized civilization from which they can recover only with difficulty.

As a result, the Oriental religions today are in danger of being overwhelmed by secular movements which have originated in Western culture. The reason for this weakness of the Oriental religions lies in their loss of an organic contact with the lives of the people. As Dawson observes in a recent article, commenting upon the spread of Communism in Asia, "If Communism is viewed in this light [i.e., as a religion], why should it prove so attractive to Asians who are already well provided with real theological religions? The answer, I think, is that the great Oriental religions are no longer culturally active and that they have become divorced from social life and from contemporary culture." [86]

The precarious nature of their situation is intimated by Dawson in the following passage depicting the significance of the present world crisis:

As Hellenism gradually expanded during the Hellenistic and Roman periods, until it embraced the whole of the ancient world, so too Western culture has expanded during the last five hundred years to embrace the whole of the modern world. And as the unity of the ancient world was finally broken in two by the rise of Islam, so the modern world is being broken in two by the rise of Communism.

Consequently I think that the great Oriental world religions today occupy a similar position to that of the religions of the ancient East—Egypt, Babylonia and Asia Minor in the Roman World. If so, the most serious rivals to Christianity at the present day are not the old religions of the East, but the new political substitute-religions, like Communism, Nationalism and so forth. One cannot escape the urgency of this question, on which the whole future of the world depends. [87]

It is from the viewpoint of world history, comparing the present situation of the Oriental religions with the revolu-

[86] "Civilization in Crisis," *The Catholic World*, January 1956.

[87] Letter of March 5, 1952 to the present writer, reprinted in *Four Quarters* (La Salle College quarterly, June 1954).

tionary developments which attended the rise of Islam in the seventh century A.D., that Dawson foresees such acute danger for the traditional religious cultures of the East, and not for them alone, but for Christianity as well.

One difference, however, that may suggest a more hopeful outcome on this occasion is the fact that Islam derived its dynamic drive from a fervently held religious belief, with sanctions in a supernatural order of reality, while Communism, for all its quasi-religious motivation, is essentially earthbound and can appeal to nothing higher than man's hope for a materialistic Utopia. Thus the power of the Oriental religions to resist the onrush of secular ideologies will be proportionate to their ability to maintain their religious character and at the same time re-establish contact with the daily lives of the people; whether this is possible, in the light of the "detachment" which Oriental religion has prominently displayed in the past, only the future can tell.

For Dawson the significance of the present moment in world history lies in the fact that Western civilization, both by its technical inventions and its ideological impact, has been able to break down the barriers which previously isolated the closed cultures of the great world religions from one another and has united them in a new and wider intercultural society. But in this process of development and expansion, Western civilization has increasingly lost contact with the spiritual sources of its creative power. As a result, the moment of its greatest material triumph is also the time of its greatest spiritual crisis.

The events of the last few years portend either the end of human history or a turning point in it. They have warned us in letters of fire that our civilization has been tried in the balance and found wanting—that there is an absolute limit to the progress that can be achieved by the perfectionment of scientific techniques detached from spiritual aims and moral values.[88]

And yet this crisis of culture is a time in which Europe can fulfill the opportunity that has been granted her, in which she can give form and direction to the new world society now in the process of being born. The science and

[88] *Religion and Culture*, p. 215.

technology of which Western civilization is the creator need not become the instruments for the destruction of humanity, but can be employed to subserve the higher purpose of uniting mankind in a supranational spiritual community.

The great Revolution of the eighteenth century which ushered in the modern era and overthrew the political and social structure Europe had possessed for more than a thousand years was in many ways similar to the contemporary period. The armies of the French Revolution and later those of Napoleon undermined or overthrew the monarchies of the *ancien régime,* abolished serfdom, and stirred nationalism in the hearts of almost all the peoples of Europe. In our own day the impact of European nationalism and Western ideologies and the spread of the European revolutionary tradition has had similar effects in Asia and Africa to that which the French Revolution had on Europe and the Americas in the past century and a half. The ideals of political liberty, national self-determination and social equality have spread to the most remote peoples of the world, until now they have become practically universal in their acceptance.

It is not inappropriate, therefore, that Christopher Dawson should look back to the age of the French Revolution to perceive the momentous nature of the contemporary period and its meaning for world history. The reaction of one of the most profound of the Conservative thinkers of that age to the revolutions that had broken into his way of life suggests the attitude which Dawson would commend to the peoples of the West at the present day.

More than a century ago Joseph de Maistre, the last representative of the old pre-nationalist Europe, an exile in the city of Peter the Great and Lenin, discerned with almost prophetic insight the meaning of the revolutions that had destroyed his own happiness and broken down the traditional order of European life which he valued so highly. France and England, he writes, in spite of their mutual hostility, have been led to co-operate in the same work. While the French Revolution sowed the seeds of French culture throughout Europe, England has carried European culture into Asia and has caused the works of Newton to be read in the language of Mahomet. The whole of the East is yielding to the ascendancy of Europe, and events have given England 15,000 leagues of common frontiers with China and Thibet.

"Man in his ignorance often deceives himself as to ends and means, as to forces and resistance, as to instruments and obstacles. Sometimes he tries to cut down an oak with a pocket-knife and sometimes he throws a bomb to break a reed. But Providence never wavers and it is not in vain that it shakes the world. Everything proclaims that we are moving towards a great unity which, to use a religious expression, we must hail from afar. We have been grievously and justly broken, but if such eyes as mine are worthy to foresee the divine purpose, we have been broken only to be made one." [89]

[89] *The Modern Dilemma,* pp. 33–34.

SOURCES

Part One: Towards a Sociology of History

SECTION I: THE SOCIOLOGICAL FOUNDATIONS OF HISTORY

1. The Sources of Culture Change

The Introduction to Mr. Dawson's first published volume, *The Age of the Gods* (1928).

2. Sociology as a Science

Published in the symposium *Science for a New World* (1934), edited by Sir Arthur Thomson and J. G. Crowther (Eyre & Spottiswoode, London; Harper & Brothers, New York).

3. Sociology and the Theory of Progress

Published in *The Sociological Review* (Vol. XIII, April 1921) under the title "On the Development of Sociology in Relation to the Theory of Progress."

4. Civilization and Morals

Published in *The Sociological Review* (Vol. XVII, July 1925); reprinted in Dawson's *Enquiries* (1933).

5. Progress and Decay in Ancient and Modern Civilization

Published in *The Sociological Review* (Vol. XVI, January 1924). A part of this article was incorporated in Dawson's *Progress and Religion* (1929).

SECTION II: THE MOVEMENT OF WORLD HISTORY

SECTION III: URBANISM AND THE ORGANIC NATURE OF CULTURE

1. The Evolution of the Modern City

Published in *The Town Planning Review* (Vol. X, 1923).

2. Catholicism and the Bourgeois Mind

Published in *The Colosseum* (London, December 1935).

3. The World Crisis and the English Tradition

Published in *The English Review* (Vol. 56, March 1933); reprinted in *Enquiries* (1933).

4. Bolshevism and the Bourgeoisie

From "The Significance of Bolshevism," published in *The English Review* (Vol. 55, September 1932); reprinted in *Enquiries* (1933).

Part Two: Conceptions of World History

SECTION I: CHRISTIANITY AND THE MEANING OF HISTORY

1. The Christian View of History

Published in *Blackfriars* (Vol. XXXII, July-August 1951).

2. History and the Christian Revelation

Adapted from the first half of Chapter V of *Religion and the Modern State* (1935) and combined with portions of Chapter VII from the same volume.

3. Christianity and Contradiction in History

Condensed version of Chapter V of *Beyond Politics* (1939), "Christianity and Politics."

4. The Kingdom of God and History

From the symposium *The Kingdom of God and History*, edited by H. G. Woods *et al.*; Vol. 3 of Official Oxford Conference Books, published in England by Allen & Unwin (1938) and in the United States by Willette, Clark & Co.

SECTION II: THE VISION OF THE HISTORIAN

1. The Problem of Metahistory

Published in *History Today* (Vol. I, June 1951).

2. St. Augustine and the City of God

From the article "St. Augustine and His Age," in the symposium *A Monument to St. Augustine* (1930); reprinted in *Enquiries* (1933).

3. Edward Gibbon and the Fall of Rome

A combination of Dawson's lecture to the British Academy (1934), published under the title *Edward Gibbon* in the *Proceedings of the British Academy* (Vol. XX, 1934) and printed as a pamphlet by Oxford University Press, with the preface Dawson contributed to the Everyman edition of Gibbon's *Decline and Fall of the Roman Empire* (J. M. Dent & Sons Ltd., London; E. P. Dutton Co., New York). Most of the excerpt from the Everyman preface is in Section III of the present version.

4. Karl Marx and the Dialectic of History

From Chapter V of *Religion and the Modern State* (1935).

5. H. G. Wells and the Outline of History

Published in *History Today* (Vol. I, October 1951).

6. Oswald Spengler and the Life of Civilizations

A combination of the article of this title published in *The Sociological Review* (Vol. XIV, July 1922) with material on Spengler in Dawson's *Progress and Religion* (1929).

7. Arnold Toynbee and the Study of History

Published in *International Affairs* (Vol. XXXI, April 1955) under the title "Toynbee's Study of History: The Place of Civilizations in History."

8. Europe in Eclipse

Published in *Criterio* (Buenos Aires, Argentina, December 1954).

INDEX

I: General [1]

Acton, 28, 282, 385
Aegean civilization, 154–155, 156–157
African Christianity, 296–302
Alexander, 254, 370, 376
Anabaptists, 128, 277, 299
Anarchists, 128, 129
Apocalypse, 251, 252, 291, 309
Arabia, 22, 136, 375
Arabian culture, 369, 374, 375
Archaic civilizations, 101–102, 133–134, 146, 150
Aristotle, 241, 374, 377, 399
Arjuna, 183
Aryans, 69, 101, 138, 147–150
Asia Minor, 117, 118, 125, 150, 154, 155, 157, 363
Asian religion cultures, 105–106, 125
Assyria, 58, 157, 249
Atman, 122, 182
Augustus, 72, 131
Australian food-gatherers, 102, 135, 391–392
Autobiography of an Unknown Indian, 390

Babylon, 251, 276, 293, 303, 347
Babylonia, 22, 50, 118, 121, 126, 144, 146, 148, 157, 363, 369
Bakunin, 224
Barbarian invasions, 153, 155, 376, 398
Baroque culture, 65, 106, 205–207
Bayle, 321, 322–323
Bede, Saint, 239–240
Bergson, H., 204
Bhagavad-Gita, 183, 233
Biblical criticism, 275
Bloch, Marc, 285
Bollandists, 331
Bolshevism, 223, 224, 226, 228
Bossuet, 207, 283, 288, 346

Brahmanism, 177, 178
Breasted, J., 134, 143
Buckle, 32, 45, 115
Buddha, 22, 70, 98, 180, 269, 388
Bukharin, 353–354
Burke, Edmund, 45, 82, 111, 259–260
Bury, J. B., 29, 327
Byzantine Church, 88, 130, 186
Byzantine culture, 76, 106, 377, 398

Calvin, John, 275, 276
Catholic Church; 274–275, 328, 330, 402
Catholic historiography, 330–332, 346–348
China, 34, 52, 59, 60, 101, 106, 121, 137, 163, 168, 369, 374, 398
Chinese culture, 69, 70, 138, 162–163, 385, 401
Christ, 95, 233, 234–235, 252, 256, 263, 264, 280, 290, 291, 308–309, 311
Christendom, 49, 52, 59, 60, 92, 102, 156, 241, 256, 273–274, 344, 362, 396, 398
Christian tradition, 274–275, 276–279
Church, conceptions of, 261–264, 292–293, 294, 313–318
Cicero, 305, 307, 329
City of God, 251, 271, 276, 294, 308–310, 313–317, 362
class, 110–111
Collingwood, 232, 283, 284, 378–379
Communism, 209, 244–246, 389, 398; *see also* Bolshevism
communities of obedience, 361–362
communities of will, 361–362

[1] *See also* II Topics.

465

II: Topics

MENTOR Books on History and Politics

THE USES OF THE PAST   by Herbert J. Muller

The civilizations of the past, how they flourished, why they fell, and their meaning for the present crisis of civilization.   (#MD112—50¢)

THE LOOM OF HISTORY   by Herbert J. Muller

A richly panoramic history of the fabled cities of Asia Minor and its role as the crossroads of East and West, through the centuries.   (#MQ341—95¢)

HISTORY OF THE WORLD IN 240 PAGES
     by René Sédillot

World history from prehistoric times to the present in one volume. Ideal for rapid reference. (#MP411—60¢)

A HISTORY OF THE WESTERN WORLD by L. J. Cheney

A concise picture of the men and nations who shaped Western civilization from the Stone Age to the 20th Century.   (#MD274—50¢)

THE WORLD OF ROME   by Michael Grant

A brilliant survey of the conquests and culture of the Romans from 133 B.C. to A.D. 217. Profusely illustrated with photographs, line drawings and maps.
     (#MT351—75¢)

THE GREEK EXPERIENCE   by C. M. Bowra

An extraordinary study of Greek culture, its achievements and philosophy. 48 pages of photos.
     (#MP349—60¢)

GREEK HISTORICAL THOUGHT edited
     by Arnold J. Toynbee

The eminent historian's brilliant translations of Greek historical experience from Homer to the age of Heraclius —a stimulating guide for our own times.
     (#MD164—50¢)

THE NATURE OF THE NON-WESTERN WORLD
     by Vera Micheles Dean

A noted expert on foreign affairs throws new light on the conflict between East and West as she probes the beliefs, traditions and emotions that motivate the people of the non-Western nations.   (#MD190—50¢)

ISLAM IN MODERN HISTORY by Wilfred Cantwell Smith

A noted scholar discusses the impact of Mohammedanism on Middle Eastern political life today.
     (#MD268—50¢

THE HEDGEHOG AND THE FOX   by Isaiah Berlin
A distinguished British scholar analyzes Tolstoy's view of history as revealed in his great novel, *War and Peace*. By the editor of *The Age of Enlightenment: The 18th Century Philosophers*.   (#MD198—50¢)

MAINSPRINGS OF CIVILIZATION
by Ellsworth Huntington
A penetrating analysis of how climate, weather, geography, and heredity determine a nation's character and history. Diagrams, maps, tables, bibliography.
(#MQ248—95¢)

THE PUBLIC PHILOSOPHY   by Walter Lippmann
A penetrating and challenging analysis of the changing state of Western democracies, by one of America's most influential political commentators.   (#MP393—60¢)

THE PRINCE   by Niccolo Machiavelli
The classic work on statesmanship and power, the techniques and strategy of gaining and keeping political control.   (#MP417—60¢)

RUSSIA AND AMERICA: DANGERS AND PROSPECTS
by Henry L. Roberts
A penetrating analysis of our relations with Russia, in view of the sinister global tensions created by atomic discoveries.   (#MD182—50¢)

GANDHI: HIS LIFE AND MESSAGE FOR THE WORLD
by Louis Fischer
The life story of one of the greatest inspirational and political leaders of our time gives insight into India's pivotal place in world affairs.   (#MP390—60¢)

THE CHANGING SOCIETY OF CHINA
by Ch'u and Winberg Chai
The nature of Chinese civilization as revealed in its social institutions, philosophy and religion, art and literature, and the impending threat of Communist totalitarianism.
(#MT365—75¢)

AMERICAN DIPLOMACY: 1900-1950
by George F. Kennan
A trenchant appraisal of U. S. foreign relations by a distinguished diplomat.   (#MP360—60¢)

THE DYNAMICS OF SOVIET SOCIETY
by W. W. Rostow and others
An authoritative synthesis and interpretation of the political, economic, and social structure of Soviet Russia.
(#MP406—60¢)

Books of Special Catholic Interest

THE PAPAL ENCYCLICALS IN THEIR HISTORICAL CONTEXT   **edited by Anne Fremantle**

For the first time in one volume, the teachings of the Catholic Church as expressed by the Popes in their official letters.   (#MT256—75¢)

THE AGE OF BELIEF: THE MEDIEVAL PHILOSOPHERS   **selected and edited by Anne Fremantle**

Basic writings of the most important philosophers from the 5th to the 15th century.   (#MD126—50¢)

HUMAN DESTINY   **by Lecomte du Nouy**

In this best-selling book, a world-famous scientist proves that science and religion may walk hand in hand and presents a reassuring view of man's dignity and true place in the universe.   (#MP410—60¢)

OF THE IMITATION OF CHRIST   **by Thomas à Kempis**

The great 15th century classic of devotional literature in a widely acclaimed modern translation by Abbot Justin McCann.   (#MD193—50¢)

A TREASURY OF EARLY CHRISTIANITY   **edited by Anne Fremantle**

A unique one-volume collection of the letters, essays, poetry, meditations, creeds, and councils of the early Church Fathers.   (#MT285—75¢)

THE SEVEN STOREY MOUNTAIN   **by Thomas Merton**

The spiritual autobiography of a young man who withdrew from a full, worldly life to the seclusion of a Trappist monastery.   (#T929—75¢)

DELIVER US FROM EVIL   **by Thomas A. Dooley, M.D.**

Dr. Dooley's first book tells of his experience as a Navy doctor in Indo-China where he and his shipmates fed, clothed, and treated thousands of refugees, and helped them escape to freedom.   (#D1992—50¢)

To Our Readers: We welcome your request for our free catalog of SIGNET and MENTOR books. If your dealer does not have the books you want, you may order them by mail, enclosing the list price plus 5¢ a copy to cover mailing. The New American Library of World Literature, Inc., P.O. Box 2310, Grand Central Station, New York 17, N. Y.